DATE DUE

DE 19 '01			
FE 1 '10			

DEMCO 38-296

Aaron Copland

Aaron Copland. *Photo by John Ardoin, courtesy of Aaron Copland.*

Aaron Copland

A Bio-Bibliography

JOANN SKOWRONSKI
Donald L. Hixon, *Series Adviser*

Bio-Bibliographies in Music, Number 2

Greenwood Press
Westport, Connecticut • London, England

Library of Congress Cataloging in Publication Data

Skowronski, JoAnn.
  Aaron Copland : a bio-bibliography.

  (Bio-bibliographies in music, ISSN 0741-6968 ; no. 2)
  Includes index.
  1. Copland, Aaron, 1900-   —Bibliography.
2. Copland, Aaron, 1900-   —Discography. I. Title.
II. Series.
ML134.C66S55 1985   016.78'092'4   84-22417
ISBN 0-313-24091-4 (lib. bdg.)

Library of Congress Catalog Card Number: 84-22417
ISBN: 0-313-24091-4
ISSN: 0741-6968

First published in 1985

Greenwood Press
A division of Congressional Information Service, Inc.
88 Post Road West, Westport, Connecticut 06881

Printed in the United States of America

10 9 8 7 6 5 4 3 2 1

To my husband, Ray,
for his assistance in the
preparation of this book

CONTENTS

Preface   ix

Biography   3

Works and Performances   8

Discography   29

Bibliography by Copland   70

Bibliography about Copland   89

Appendix I: Alphabetical List of Compositions   234

Appendix II: Classified List of Compositions   237

Index   241

PREFACE

Copland has composed over one hundred works and his style has influenced the course of American music. This bio-bibliography is a
compilation of the extensive writings by and about Copland as well as
a detailed catalog of his works and recordings. The book is divided
into four major sections: <u>Biography</u>, <u>Works and Performances</u>,
<u>Discography</u>, and <u>Bibliography</u>. In addition, there are two appendixes
and one index.

The first section gives an overview of Copland's life. Stylistic
characteristics during various periods of the composer's career are
noted along with principal compositions written during these periods.

<u>Works and Performances</u> is a chronological listing of over one
hundred compositions, including dates of composition, commissions,
dedications, premiere performances, publishers, and related data. If
more than one composition was completed in the same year, the compositions are arranged alphabetically under that year. Works that were
revised later but retain the same composition name and basically the
same form are found under the original completion date. Juvenilia and
other unpublished works are included. Appendixes provide an alphabetical listing of works as well as a classified listing, both of
which refer back to the detailed entry in the chronological section.

An extensive discography lists 376 entries of commercially-produced
discs containing the composer's works, some of which were performed or
conducted by him. Information provided in each entry includes the
recording company and disc number, year that it was pressed, speed,
performers, conductors, and album titles as well as other compositions
and their composers on the disc. This section is arranged alphabetically by composition title. Discography entries are listed alphabetically by the recording company under each composition title.

The annotated bibliography lists 1192 references both by and about
Copland. Over one hundred of Copland's writings are listed first,
followed by the extensive general bibliography. The numbering is con-
secutive throughout. Books, journals, newspapers, and dissertations
are included. Entries are listed alphabetically by author, or by
title if there is no author. All names spelled with Mc are filed as
if they were spelled Mac. Initials are filed before words; therefore,
BBC is found at the beginning of the B's. Books designed for young

people are included but are designated as juvenile literature for the
researcher's information. Entries in foreign languages are included.
However, if a book is in English and has been translated into other
languages, as in the case of many of Copland's books, only the English
version is listed. Reprinted books list the date of the original
publication.

The index includes personal and corporate names, recording album
titles, events, concert sites, and book and composition titles appearing
in the entries and in the annotations. References to the bibliography
are indicated by page numbers. Otherwise, the letters and numbers in
the index refer to the sections in the book and the item numbers in
these sections. Item numbers preceded by "B" are to be found in the
Bibliography section, those with "D" in the Discography, and with "W"
in Works and Performances. Cross references are provided in the index
from various forms of names and titles. Within the body of the work
itself, cross references are made from one section to the other by use
of the alphanumerical entry codes.

Many bibliographic sources were used in the compilation of this book.
Among them were the National Union Catalog, Music Index, Readers' Guide
to Periodical Literature, RILM Abstracts of Music Literature, Bibliography Index, Biography Index, British Humanities Index, Essay and
General Literature Index, and indexes to numerous newspapers, to name
only a few. Several large university and public libraries in the Los
Angeles area were used in this research.

Aaron Copland

BIOGRAPHY

Born in Brooklyn, New York, on November 4, 1900, Aaron Copland was the youngest of five children of Russian-Jewish immigrants. His first composition, at age eight, was a song for his sister-in-law, who had brought him cherries when he was ill. Piano lessons were given to him by his sister Laurine when he was eleven. He arranged to begin formal piano lessons with Leopold Wolfsohn when he was thirteen. Later Copland studied piano with Clarence Adler and subsequently with Victor Wittgenstein. Copland describes his early musical background in detail in an autobiographical chapter in Our New Music (1941).

Copland surprised his family by his interest in becoming a composer because no one else in the family was keenly interested in music. He began studying composition through a correspondence course. At sixteen he began his theory lessons with Rubin Goldmark. Some conflict arose between them as Copland's emerging modern style was not understood or encouraged by Goldmark. Copland's piano solo, The Cat and the Mouse (1920), was an early composition that offended Goldmark by its tonalities, but it seems conservative by current standards of modern music. Copland's second significant work, Old Poem (1920), also was composed while he was studying with Goldmark.

After graduating from Boy's High School in Brooklyn in 1918, Copland read of a new school for American musicians in France. He was the first student to apply and be accepted at that school. In June 1921 he began composition studies at the Fontainebleau School of Music with Paul Vidal, who turned out to be as musically conservative as his former teacher, Rubin Goldmark. After visiting one of Nadia Boulanger's harmony classes, Copland realized that she was an instructor who had progressive ideas. Soon he began studying with her. Boulanger's influence on Copland and several other important American composers was significant.

While in Europe during the early 1920's, Copland attended numerous concerts featuring the works of modern composers such as Stravinsky, Schoenberg, and Hindemith. The song As It Fell upon a Day (1923) and the ballet Grohg (1922-1925) were among Copland's major works composed abroad. Also, while at the Fontainebleau, Copland played The Cat and the Mouse at a student concert and was approached by a publisher afterwards. As a result, this piano solo became his first published work. It is still widely performed.

When Copland was preparing to end his studies in France and return
to the United States in 1924, Boulanger asked him to compose a work for
her. She had been invited to perform as organ soloist with the New
York Symphony, and she offered Copland the opportunity to compose a
work for this event. He accepted this challenge even though none of
his orchestral works had been performed before. Boulanger was the
soloist in the performance of the Symphony for Organ and Orchestra
(1924) on January 11, 1925, with Walter Damrosch conducting the New
York Symphony. Copland revised this work in 1928 as his First
Symphony (without organ).

After his return to the United States, Copland planned to support
himself by teaching. However, no students responded to his advertise-
ment, and he took a job playing piano in a hotel trio. As he was
interested in associating with other composers and hearing their ideas
and their music, when Marion Bauer told him about the League of Composers, he joined and soon became an important force in the organization.
The group sponsored the performance of Copland's two piano pieces, The
Cat and the Mouse and Passacaglia (1922) in New York during the fall of
1924. These became his first works to be performed in the United
States. Copland also wrote numerous articles for the League's publication Modern Music.

Copland's economic situation improved when he received a Guggenheim
Fellowship in 1925. He was the first composer to receive this award,
and it was renewed the following year. By this time several of his
compositions had been performed, and he had become good friends with
Serge Koussevitzky, conductor of the Boston Symphony, and Paul
Rosenfeld, a notable music critic. Koussevitzky urged the League of
Composers to commission Copland for a new work to be presented at one
of the League's concerts, and Rosenfeld found a patron, Alma Morgenthau
Wertheim, to help support him.

Copland spent the summer of 1925 at the MacDowell Colony in Peter-
borough, New Hampshire, working on Music for the Theatre, which was the
result of his League commission. In this five-movement work he consciously incorporated many jazz techniques in an attempt to give it an
American sound. Another work that emphasized these techniques,
especially in the second movement, was his Concerto for Piano and
Orchestra (1926). This was his last symphonic effort using jazz, but
he later utilized these elements in his Four Piano Blues (1926-1948).

In 1927, Copland became a lecturer at the New School for Social
Research in New York City where he taught modern music for ten years.
Later he helped organize the Festivals of Contemporary American Music
at Yaddo in Saratoga Springs, New York. He was also a founder of
Arrow Music Press. He helped organize the American Composers Alliance
of which he was the president for many years. The Alliance resembled
a union in that it attempted to unify the composers so they would
receive better remuneration for their compositions.

With Roger Sessions, Copland founded the Copland-Sessions Concerts,
which were designed to present the works of relatively unknown composers. A total of eight concerts were presented during the years 1928
to 1931. Over half of the compositions were by Americans, including
Roy Harris, Virgil Thomson, Walter Piston, and Copland.

When a prize of $25,000 was offered in a composition contest by the
RCA Victor Company in 1929, Copland eagerly began working on his
Symphonic Ode. He turned away from using jazz idioms in this work,

instead utilizing sparse sonorities and much dissonance. As the dead-
line neared, Copland realized that he would be unable to complete it in
time. So instead, he extracted three dances from his ballet Grohg and
entered these as Dance Symphony (1925). Five compositions were
selected to share the prize and Copland received $5,000 as one of the
winners.

The Symphonic Ode was completed in 1929. It is written in an
abstract, dissonant style. Other works with these characteristics include Piano Variations (1930), Short Symphony (1932-1933), and Statements (1934). All four complex works contain lean textures and difficult
rhythms.

In Our New Music, Copland wrote that he became increasingly dis-
satisfied with writing modern music that was not being understood nor
enjoyed by the public. As a result, he adopted simpler techniques
which resulted in a dramatic change in his style. He began writing in
this simpler style with El Salón México in 1936 after a visit to Mexico
in which he was inspired by the surroundings, especially a popular
dance hall. Folk tunes and elements are evident in El Salón México as
well as in subsequent works such as the ballet Billy the Kid (1938) in
which the melody of the cowboy song, Bury Me Not on the Lone Prairie,
figures prominently. Seven episodes were extracted from this ballet to
form a concert suite.

The Columbia Broadcasting System (CBS) commissioned Copland to write
Music for Radio in 1937. This also is written in a simplified style
and is characterized as having an American sound. After it was
performed on the radio, listeners were asked for suggestions for a
title. Saga of the Prairie was selected from the replies. Quiet City
(1939, revised 1940) was adapted from his film music for The City
(1939) and is also written in this popular melodic style.

Music written for young people includes his play-opera The Second
Hurricane (1937) for high school students. Edwin Denby's libretto
concerns the dilemma of a group of teen-agers who assist in coping with
the disaster of a hurricane. Other simple music for students includes
Two Children's pieces (1936), which consists of the piano pieces Sunday
Afternoon Music and The Young Pioneers. The chorus What Do We Plant?
(1935) was written for a high school women's chorus, while An Outdoor
Overture (1938) was composed for the orchestra of the High School of
Music and Art in New York.

In 1940, Copland began a twenty-five year association with the
Berkshire Music Center at Tanglewood in Lenox, Massachusetts. He
became head of the composition department, assistant director, and
faculty chairman.

Copland toured South America twice as a musical ambassador by performing, lecturing, and conducting. In 1941 a subcommittee of the
Federal Coordinator of Inter-American Relations sponsored him and in
1947 the State Department sent him. During his first cultural tour he
completed his Piano Sonata (1941), which is similar in style to his
early sparse works of the 1920's. However, Lincoln Portrait, which
was completed the following year, uses portions of the ballad Springfield
Mountain and Stephen Foster's De Camptown Races. The narration is
drawn from Abraham Lincoln's speeches and writings. Another patriotic
work written during World War II was Fanfare for the Common Man (1942),
one of a group of ten fanfares written by ten composers which originally
were published together.

Two ballets soon followed in the simple, melodic style geared to general audiences. Rodeo (1942), which was composed for Agnes de Mille, is the story of a cowgirl who gets her man. Four dance episodes were extracted to form a concert suite. Appalachian Spring (1944) was commissioned by the Elizabeth Sprague Coolidge Foundation for Martha Graham and her dance company. Variations on the Shaker song Simple Gifts are heard in this work. The ballet centers around a couple who rejoice in the coming of spring and the construction of their home. The music received the 1944-1945 New York Music Critics' Circle Award and the 1944 Pulitzer Prize in Music.

The Sonata for Violin and Piano (1943) and the Third Symphony (1946) do not quote folk songs directly, but they show Copland's continued interest in folk music characteristics. The Third Symphony received the Boston Symphony Merit Award and was also voted the outstanding orchestral work of 1946-1947 by the New York Music Critics Circle.

The Concerto for Clarinet and String Orchestra (1948), which was commissioned by Benny Goodman, contains elements of a Brazilian melody. The Twelve Poems of Emily Dickinson (1949-1950) and Old American Songs, Sets I and II (1950-1952) are two song cycles for voice and piano which display Copland's ability to reflect the emotions of the text in his music. The Third Symphony and the Old American Songs share some of the same thematic material. On numerous occasions Copland has borrowed ideas from his previous works as well as popular and folk music.

The Tender Land, an opera produced in 1954 does not use popular sources directly but is generally considered to have an American sound typical of certain of Copland's music. Richard Rodgers and Oscar Hammerstein II commissioned this work through the auspices of the League of Composers to celebrate the League's thirtieth anniversary.

Copland was named Harvard University's Charles Eliot Norton Professor of Poetry for 1951-1952, becoming the first composer to receive this honor. The six lectures he gave were published as Music and Imagination (1952). He had previously lectured at Harvard in 1935 and 1944.

He composed functional music for the theater, such as The Five Kings (1930), for television, such as The World of Nick Adams (1957), and even for a puppet show at the New York World's Fair, a piece entitled From Sorcery to Science (1939). His scores for films include Our Town (1940), The Red Pony (1948), and The Heiress (1949). The score for the latter movie received an Oscar from the Academy of Motion Picture Arts and Sciences for the best dramatic film score in 1950.

In the 1950s Copland's compositions became even more austere as he utilized twelve-tone techniques in works such as the Quartet for Piano and Strings (1950) and Piano Fantasy (1957). The Quartet was his first major attempt at dodecaphony. The twelve-tone row is introduced in the first movement and appears in retrograde in the second. The Quartet was commissioned by the Elizabeth Sprague Coolidge Foundation, and the Fantasy, by the Juilliard School of Music.

The Nonet (1960) continues the use of serial techniques but is more diatonic. This chamber work employs elements of the Baroque contrapuntal style also. Connotations (1962) and Inscape (1967) both are dissonant and use twelve-tone idioms. The tone row in Connotations begins with three four-voice chords which expand into variations. This work received much interest because it was commissioned for the opening of Philharmonic Hall at New York's Lincoln Center for the Performing Arts on September 23, 1962. Inscape, which is based on two tone rows, was also commissioned by the New York Philharmonic, for its 125th anniversary season.

During the past few decades Copland has been conducting orchestras more and composing less. Among his more recent compositions is the Duo for Flute and Piano (1971), which is written in a lyrical, tonal style. Other chamber works include Threnody I: Igor Stravinsky in Memoriam (1971) and Threnody II: Beatrice Cunningham in Memoriam (1972). Night Thoughts (1972) is a piano solo composed for the 1972 Van Cliburn International Piano Competition in Fort Worth, Texas.

The American Academy of Arts and Letters elected Copland to membership in 1954, and Copland has been active as chairman of the League of Composers board of directors. Among the many honors the composer has received are the Presidential Medal of Freedom for Peacetime Service awarded by President Lyndon B. Johnson (1964), the German Republic Commander's Cross of the Order of Merit (1970), Yale University's Henry Howland Memorial Prize (1970), the American Symphony Orchestra League's Gold Baton (1978), and the Kennedy Center Honors in Washington, D.C. (1979). In addition, he has received honorary doctorates from numerous universities, including Princeton University (1956), Harvard University (1961), Rutgers University (1967), and the University of Leeds in England (1976).

Most of Copland's compositions are available on commercially-produced discs and many were recorded under his direction. Boosey & Hawkes Music Publishers carries most of his published scores. His books are: What to Listen For in Music (1939), Our New Music (1941), Music and Imagination (1952), Copland on Music (1963), and The New Music, 1900-1960 (1968, a revision of Our New Music). Major books about the composer include Arthur Berger's Aaron Copland (1953), Arnold Dobrin's Aaron Copland, His Life and Times (1967), Julia Smith's Aaron Copland, His Work and Contribution to American Music (1955), and Aaron Copland, a Complete Catalogue of His Works, compiled by his publisher, Boosey & Hawkes (1960). (See Bibliography for annotated and extensive additional listings.)

Copland has written in various musical contexts and his styles have been diverse. The music most people know as Copland's consists of works produced during the 1930's and 1940's. These popular compositions include music written for the ballets Billy the Kid, Rodeo, and Appalachian Spring, as well as rousing patriotic works, such as Lincoln Portrait and Fanfare for the Common Man.

In contrast, there are his early sparse, dissonant works written in the 1920's before he consciously decided to write popular music, and his music of the 1960's based on twelve-tone idioms. Most listeners enjoy the popular simplified lyrical works which have an American sound and have never heard his more complex music.

Copland was the first serious composer to establish tonalities that are identified as distinctly American. The Pulitzer Prize, Oscar, and Guggenheim Fellowship are clear evidence of his stature as a composer. The universal appeal of his music is demonstrated by the fact that it has been performed throughout the world. Copland's impact on contemporary music has been significant. Aaron Copland is undoubtedly a key architect of twentieth century American music.

WORKS AND PERFORMANCES

191-?

W1. String Quartet (Unfinished)
     Manuscript.

1916?

W2. Capriccio
     Violin and piano.
     Manuscript.

1917

W3. Melancholy; a Song à la Debussy (Unfinished)
     Words by Jeffery Farnol.
     Manuscript.

W4. Moment Musicale; a Tone Poem
     Piano.
     Manuscript.

1917 or 1918

W5. Danse Characteristique (Unfinished)
     Piano duet: one piano, four hands.
     Arranged for orchestra, 1919.
     Manuscript.

1918

W6. Night
     Song for high voice with piano accompaniment.
     Words by Aaron Schaffer.
     Manuscript.

1911?-1918

W7.   Notebook with Original Songs
      Partial contents: A Summer Vacation (words by Aaron Schaffer);
        After Antwerp (E. Cammaerts); Spurned Love (T. B. Aldrich); My
        Heart Is in the East (Aaron Schaffer); harmony exercises.
      Manuscript.

1918

W8.   Poem
      Cello with piano accompaniment.
      Manuscript.

1918 or 1919

W9.   Waltz Caprice
      Piano.
      Manuscript.

1919

W10. Lament
      Cello and piano.
      Accompanied by an incomplete sketch of an arrangement for piano
        and violin.
      Manuscript.

W11. Prelude for Violin and Piano
      Manuscript.

W12. Simone
      Song for soprano and piano.
      Words by Remy de Gourmont.
      Manuscript.

192-?

W13. Fragment, for Trio
      Violin, cello, and piano.
      Unfinished.
      Manuscript.

1920

W14. The Cat and the Mouse (Scherzo Humoristique; Le Chat et la
        Souris; Humoristic Scherzo)
      Piano solo; $3\frac{1}{2}$ min.
      Premiere: the composer at a student performance, September 23, 1921,
        at the Fontainebleau School at Salle Gaveau, Paris.
      New York: Boosey & Hawkes - United States; Paris: Durand (outside
        the United States).

W15. Music I Heard
      Song for soprano with piano accompaniment.
      Words by Conrad Aiken.
      Manuscript.

W16. Old Poem (Vieux Poème)
      Song for high voice and piano; 2½ min.
      Text translated from the Chinese by Arthur Waley; translation
        into French by Jules Casadesus.
      Premiere: Charles Hubbard accompanied by the composer at the Salle
        des Agriculteurs, Paris, January 10, 1922, along with the premiere
        of Pastorale (1921).
      Paris: Salabert.

1918-1920

W17. Three Sonnets for Piano
      Manuscript.

1921

W18. Four Motets
      Mixed chorus (SATB), a capella; 11 min.
      Texts drawn from Biblical sources.
        1. Have Mercy on Us, O My Lord.
        2. Help Us, O Lord.
        3. Sing Ye Praises to Our King.
        4. Thou, O Jehovah, Abideth Forever.
      Premiere: the Paris-American-Gargenville Chorus, conducted by
        Melville Smith at the Fontainebleau School, autumn 1924.
      New York: Boosey & Hawkes.

W19. Pastorale
      High voice and piano; 3 min.
      Translated from the Kafiristan by Edward Powys Mathers.
      Premiere: Charles Hubbard accompanied by the composer at the Salle
        des Agriculteurs, Paris, January 10, 1922.
      Manuscript.

W20. Prelude (Second) for Violin and Piano
      Manuscript.

1920-1921

W21. Sonata for Piano, G Major
      Manuscript.

W22. Three Moods for Piano Solo (Trois Esquisses pour Piano Seul)
      The sections are entitled:
        1. Embittered.
        2. Wistful.
        3. Jazzy.
        4. Petit Portrait (Supplement).
      New York: Boosey & Hawkes.

1922

W23. Passacaglia
      Piano solo; 5 min.
      Premiere: Daniel Ericourt at the Société Musicale Indépendante,
        Paris, January 1923.

Dedicated to Nadia Boulanger.
Paris: Salabert.

1923

W24. **As It Fell upon a Day**
Soprano accompanied by flute and clarinet; $5\frac{1}{2}$ min.
Words by Richard Barnefield.
Premiere: Ada MacLeish at the Société Musicale Indépendante,
Paris, February 6, 1924.
New York: Boosey & Hawkes.

W25. **Cortège Macabre**
Orchestra; 8 min.
Taken from the composer's ballet Grohg.
Premiere: Rochester Philharmonic Orchestra, conducted by Howard
Hanson, May 1, 1925.
Dedicated to Harold Clurman who wrote the script for Grohg.
Also arranged for two pianos.
New York: Boosey & Hawkes. **See also:** W28

1924

W26. **Symphony for Organ and Orchestra**
25 min.
Premiere: Nadia Boulanger, organist, with the New York Symphony
Orchestra conducted by Walter Damrosch, January 11, 1925.
Dedicated to Nadia Boulanger.
Revised 1928 for orchestra only as First Symphony.
New York: Boosey & Hawkes. **See also:** W35

1925

W27. **Dance Symphony**
Orchestra; 14 min.
Taken from the composer's ballet Grohg. **Dance of the Adolescent**
is the opening movement. There are three movements.
Received $5,000 prize in the RCA Victor Company Contest.
Premiere: Philadelphia Orchestra conducted by Leopold Stokowski at
the Philadelphia Academy of Music, April 15, 1931.
Also arranged for two pianos.
New York: Arrow Press. **See also:** B404, W28

1922-1925

W28. **Grohg**
Ballet in one act for orchestra; 38 min.
Script by Harold Clurman.
Manuscript. **See also:** W25, W27

1925

W29. **Music for the Theatre**
Chamber orchestra; 22 min.
Composed at the MacDowell Colony in New Hampshire while working
under a Guggenheim Fellowship during the summer of 1925.

Suite in five parts:
1. Prologue.
2. Dance.
3. Interlude.
4. Burlesque.
5. Epilogue.
Premiere: Boston Symphony Orhcestra with Serge Koussevitzky conducting, November 20, 1925, Boston.
Dedicated to Serge Koussevitzky.
New York: Arrow Press.

W30. Two Compositions for Chorus of Women's Voices
9 min.
The two compositions are:
1. The House on the Hill (words from Children of the Night by
Edwin Arlington Robinson) SSAA, a capella.
2. An Immorality (words from Lustra by Ezra Pound) SSA, soprano
solo, with piano accompaniment.
Premiere: Women's University Glee Club with Gerald Reynolds conducting, New York, April 24, 1925.
Dedicated to Thomas Whitney Surette and Gerald Reynolds.
Boston: E. C. Schirmer.

1926

W31. Concerto for Piano and Orchestra (Jazz Concerto)
16 min.
In one movement with two contrasting parts.
Premiere: the composer, pianist, with the Boston Symphony con-
ducted by Serge Koussevitzky
Dedicated to Alma Morgenthau Wertheim
Also arranged for two pianos.
New York: Arrow Press.

W32. Sentimental Melody
Piano solo; 1 min.
Premiere: the composer first performed it in 1927 for the Ampico
Recording Company.
Mainz: Schott Söhne.

1927

W33. Two Pieces for Violin and Piano (Deux Pièces pour Violon et Piano)
7 min.
The two pieces are entitled:
1. Nocturne.
2. Ukulele Serenade.
Premiere: Samuel Dushkin, violin, and the composer at the piano
at the Société Musicale Indépendante, Paris, May 5, 1926.
Mainz: Schott Söhne.

W34. Song (E. E. Cummings)
Medium voice and piano; 2 min.
Words from a poem by E. E. Cummings.
Premiere: Ethel Luening accompanied by the composer at the New
School for Social Research, New York.
New York: Arrow Press.

1928

W35.   First Symphony
        Large orchestra; 25 min.
        Orchestral version of Symphony for Organ and Orchestra (1924).
        Premiere: Ernest Ansermet conducted the Berlin Symphony Orchestra,
            December 1931.
        Prelude is also arranged for chamber orchestra (1934).
        New York: Arrow Press. See also: W26

1923-1928

W36.   Two Pieces for String Quartet
        11 min.
        The two pieces are entitled:
            1. Lento Molto (1928).
            2. Rondino (1923).
        Premiere: Lenox String Quartet, May 6, 1928, at the Edyth Totten
            Theater, New York in the second of the Copland-Sessions Concerts.
            The Rondino was performed alone at the Fontainebleau School
            September 1924.
        Also arranged for string orchestra while the composer was at the
            MacDowell Colony during the summer of 1928. The arrangement's
            premiere occurred December 14, 1928 at Symphony Hall, Boston by
            Serge Koussevitzky conducting the Boston Symphony Orchestra.
        New York: Arrow Press.

1928

W37.   Vocalise
        High voice and piano; 4 min.
        Commissioned by Leduc et Cie., Paris as part of a group of vocalises.
        Premiere: Ethel Luening with the composer at the piano at the New
            School for Social Research, October 11, 1935.
        New York: Boosey & Hawkes.

1928-1929; revised 1955

W38.   Symphonic Ode
        Orchestra; 19 min.
        This one-movement work was to be entered in a competition by the
            RCA Victor Company for a $25,000 prize. Copland was unable to
            complete it in time, so he entered the Dance Symphony instead.
        Premiere: Serge Koussevitzky conducting the Boston Symphony
            Orchestra, February 19, 1932.
        Written for the Boston Symphony Orchestra's fiftieth anniversary
            season. Revised in 1955 for the group's seventy-fifth anniver-
            sary and was presented February 8, 1960 by Charles Munch con-
            ducting the Boston Symphony. This revision was dedicated to the
            memory of Serge and Natalie Koussevitzky.
        New York: Boosey & Hawkes. See also: B247, B451, B801, B957,
            B1084, B1183.

1929

W39. Vitebsk (Study on a Jewish Theme)
      Trio for violin, cello, and piano; 11 min.
      Premiere: Alphonse Onŋou, violin, Robert Maas, cello, and Walter
          Gieseking, Piano at a League of Composers' concert, February 16,
          1929, New York.
      Dedicated to Roy Harris.
      New York: Arrow Press.

1930

W40. Piano Variations
      Piano solo; 11 min.
      Later revised as Orchestral Variations (1957).
      Premiere: the composer at a League of Composers' concert, January
          4, 1931, New York.
      Dedicated to Gerald Sykes.
      New York: Arrow Press. See also: W92

1931

W41. Miracle at Verdun
      Small orchestra.
      Incidental music for a play by Hans Chlumberg.
      Premiere: Theatre Guild at the Martin Beck Theatre, New York,
          March 16, 1931.
      Manuscript.

1932

W42. Elegies
      Violin and viola.
      Premiere: Ivor Karman, violin, and Charlotte Karman, viola, at a
          League of Composers' concert, New York, April 2, 1933.
      Manuscript.

1932-1933

W43. Short Symphony (Symphony No.2)
      Orchestra; 15 min.
      Premiere: Carlos Chávez conducting the Orquésta Sinfónica de
          México in México, D.F. The United States premiere was by Leopold
          Stokowski conducting the NBC Symphony Orchestra in a radio per-
          formance in 1944.
      Dedicated to Carlos Chávez.
      Also arranged for string quartet, clarinet and piano as the Sextet
          (1937).
      New York: Boosey & Hawkes. See also: W52

1934

W44. Hear Ye! Hear Ye!
      Ballet; 35 min.
      Script by Ruth Page.
      Premiere: Ruth Page & Company, November 30, 1934, with Rudolf Ganz

conducting at the Chicago Opera House.
Manuscript.

W45. Statements
Orchestra; 19 min.
The sections are entitled:
  1. Militant.
  2. Cryptic.
  3. Dogmatic.
  4. Subjective.
  5. Jingo.
  6. Prophetic.
Premiere: the last two movements only were commissioned by the
  League of Composers and performed by the Minneapolis Symphony
  Orchestra conducted by Eugene Ormandy, January 9, 1936. The
  complete work was first performed January 7, 1942 by the New York
  Philharmonic conducted by Dimitri Mitropoulos.
Dedicated to Mary Senior Churchill.
New York: Boosey & Hawkes.

1935

W46. What Do We Plant?
Chorus for women's voices (SA) and piano; 2½ min.
Words by Henry Abbey.
Written for the Girl's Glee Club of the Henry Street Settlement
  Music School, New York.
New York: Boosey & Hawkes.

1936

W47. Fantasia Mexicana (Mexican Fantasy)
Orchestra; 3 min.
Adapted from El Salón México for the film Fiesta by Johnny Green.
Arranged for orchestra by Don Bowden.
Also arranged for piano solo by Johnny Green.
New York: Boosey & Hawkes. See also: W48

W48. El Salón México
Orchestra; 11½ min.
Draws upon melodies in Frances Toor's Cancionero Mexicano and
  Ruben M. Campos' El Folklore y la Musica Mexicana and a popular
  dance hall in Mexico City.
Premiere: Carlos Chávez conducting the Orquésta Sinfónica de
  México, August 27, 1937.
Dedicated to Victor Kraft.
Also arranged for piano solo and for two pianos by Leonard Bern-
  stein; also arranged for concert band by Mark H. Hindsley.
New York: Boosey & Hawkes. See also: W47

W49. Two Children's Pieces
Piano solo; 2½ min.
The two pieces are entitled:
  1. Sunday Afternoon Music.
  2. The Young Pioneers.

Lazar Saminsky and Isadore Freed invited the composer to submit piano works for young students for their collection by contemporary composers.
Premiere: the composer, February 24, 1936, New York.
New York: C. Fischer.

1937

W50. **Music for Radio** (Saga of the Prairie; Prairie Journal)
Orchestra.
Commissioned by the Columbia Broadcasting System.
Premiere: CBS Symphony Orchestra with Howard Barlow conducting, July 25, 1937, for a live broadcast. The subtitle was added after listeners wrote in their suggestions.
New York: Boosey & Hawkes.

W51. **The Second Hurricane**
Play-opera for high school performance; 90 min.
Libretto by Edwin Denby.
Premiere: Henry Street Settlement Music School, New York, April 21, 1937, conducted by Lehman Engel. Orson Wells was the stage director at the Playhouse in New York. Grace Spofford, director of the school suggested the idea to the composer.
Dedicated to Victor, Rudi, Germaine, Ruth, Paul, and Virgil.
New York: Boosey & Hawkes. **See also:** B188, B288, B736, B856, B1008, B1088

W52. **Sextet**
String quartet, clarinet, and piano; 15 min.
Arrangement of Short Symphony (Symphony No.2) (1933).
Premiere: P. Winter, H. Rosoff, E. Vardi, and B. Greenhouse, strings, A. Christman, clarinet, and Judith Sidorsky, piano, at Town Hall, New York, February 26, 1939.
Dedicated to Carlos Chávez.
New York: Boosey & Hawkes. See also: W43

1938

W53. **Billy the Kid**
Ballet in one act.
Suggested by Lincoln Kirstein and written for the Ballet Caravan.
Premiere: October 1938 with Eugene Loring and the Ballet Caravan.
Manuscript.

Also arranged as a symphonic suite for orchestra; 22 min.
The sections are entitled:
1. The Open Prairie.
2. Street in a Frontier Town.
3. Card Game at Night (Prairie Night).
4. Gun Battle.
5. Celebration Dance (after Billy's Capture).
6. Billy's Death.
7. The Open Prairie Again.
Premiere: William Steinberg conducting the National Broadcasting Company Symphony Orchestra at Radio City, New York, November 9, 1940.

Various arrangements for one and two pianos, band, chamber
orchestra, violin and piano, and cello by Copland and others.
New York: Boosey & Hawkes.

W54. Lark
Baritone and mixed chorus (SATB), a capella; 5 min.
Words by Genvieve Taggard.
Premiere: Collegiate Chorale conducted by Robert Shaw, April 13,
1943, Museum of Modern Art, New York.
Boston: E. C. Schirmer.

W55. An Outdoor Overture
Orchestra; $9\frac{1}{2}$ min.
Premiere: Alexander Richter directing the orchestra of the High
School of Music and Art, New York, December 16, 1938.
Also arranged for band. First performance of this arrangement
was June 1942 by the Goldman Band conducted by the composer in
New York.
New York: Boosey & Hawkes. See also: B316

1939

W56. The City
Chamber orchestra.
Incidental music for a documentary film.
Premiere: film was shown at the New York World's Fair, 1939.
Manuscript.

W57. The Five Kings
Five instruments.
Incidental music for Shakespeare's Historical Chronicle Plays.
Premiere: Mercury Theatre, Boston, February 27, 1939.
Manuscript.

W58. From Sorcery to Science
Orchestra.
Incidental music for a puppet show.
Premiere: New York World's Fair, Hall of Pharmacy, May 12, 1939.
Manuscript.

W59. Of Mice and Men
Orchestra.
Film music for Hal Roach's movie based on John Steinbeck's novel.
Premiere: Roxy Theatre, New York, February 16, 1940.
Manuscript.

1939; revised 1940

W60. Quiet City
Clarinet, saxophone, trumpet, and piano; 9 min.
Incidental music for the play by Irwin Shaw.
Premiere: by the Group Theatre Production, Boston, February 27,
1939.
Revised in 1940 for trumpet, English horn, and string orchestra.
Dedicated to Ralph Hawkes of Boosey & Hawkes.

Premiere: revised version presented by Daniel Saidenberg conducting
the Saidenberg Little Symphony Orchestra.
New York: Boosey & Hawkes.

1940; revised 1952

W61. John Henry (Railroad Ballad)
Small orchestra; 3½ min.
Adapted from the folk-tune John Henry.
Commissioned by the Columbia Broadcasting System.
Premiere: CBS Symphony Orchestra, March 5, 1940.

Revised in 1952 and scored for a larger orchestra.
Premiere: revised version first presented at the National Music
Camp, Interlochen, Michigan, 1953.
New York: Boosey & Hawkes.

1940

W62. Our Town
Orchestra; 9 min.
Music from the film based on the play by Thornton Wilder.
Some of the film music arranged as a concert piece.
Premiere: concert music was presented June 9, 1940 by Howard
Barlow conducting the Columbia Broadcasting Symphony Orchestra.
Later revised for a Boston Pops Concert and dedicated to Leonard
Bernstein.
Also, three excerpts arranged for piano solo:
1. Story of Our Town.
2. Conversation at the Soda Fountain.
3. The Resting-Place on the Hill.
New York: Boosey & Hawkes.

1941

W63. Episode
Organ solo; 4 min.
The H. W. Gray Company asked Copland to contribute a piece for
organ in a series by contemporary composers.
Premiere: William Strickland, New York, March 9, 1941.
New York: Boosey & Hawkes.

W64. Piano Sonata
Piano solo; 23 min.
Commissioned by Clifford Odets and dedicated to him.
Premiere: the composer at La Nueva Musica, Buenos Aires, October
21, 1941.
New York: Boosey & Hawkes.

1942

W65. Las Agachadas (The Shakedown Song)
Solo group and eight-part mixed chorus; 6 min.
Based on Kurt Schindler's Folk Music and Poetry of Spain and
Portugal (No.202 in the collection).
Commissioned by the Schola Cantorum to honor its first conductor
Kurt Schindler.

Premiere: Schola Cantorum at Town Hall, New York, March 25, 1942.
New York: Boosey & Hawkes.

W66. Danzón Cubano
Two pianos, four hands; 6 min.
Written to commemorate the twentieth anniversary of the League of
   Composers of which the composer was an active member.
Premiere: Leonard Bernstein and the composer, December 17, 1942,
   Town Hall, New York.
Also arranged for orchestra by the composer; arranged for piano
   solo by Leo Smit.
New York: Boosey & Hawkes.

W67. Fanfare for the Common Man
Four horns, three trumpets, three trombones, tuba, and percussion;
   2½ min.
Published as part of ten fanfares by ten composers originally.
Premiere: Eugene Goossens **conducted** the Cincinnati Symphony Orches-
   tra March 14, 1943.
New York: Boosey & Hawkes.

W68. Lincoln Portrait
Speaker and orchestra; 14 min.
Text drawn from Abraham Lincoln's speeches and writings.
Commissioned by Andre Kostelanetz and the Cincinnati Symphony
   Orchestra. Dedicated to Andre Kostelanetz.
Premiere: William Adams, narrator with the Cincinnati Symphony
   Orchestra conducted by Andre Kostelanetz on radio, May 14, 1942.
Also arranged for speaker and band.
New York: Boosey & Hawkes. See also: B227

W69. Music for Movies
Chamber orchestra; 16 min.
Suite consists of five sections:
   1. New England Countryside.
   2. Barley Wagons.
   3. Sunday Traffic.
   4. Grovers Corners.
   5. Threshing Machines.
Material is taken from his film music for The City (no.1 and 3),
   Of Mice and Men (no.2 and 5), and Our Town (no.4).
Premiere: Saidenberg Little Symphony Orchestra, February 17, 1943,
   Town Hall, New York.
Dedicated to Darius Milhaud.
New York: Boosey & Hawkes. See also: W56, W59, W62

W70. Rodeo
Ballet for orchestra.
Commissioned by the Ballet Russe de Monte Carlo.
Ballet suggested by Agnes de Mille.
Premiere: October 16, 1942 in New York's Metropolitan Opera House.

Orchestral suite consists of four dance episodes from the ballet:
   1. Buckaroo Holiday.
   2. Corral Nocturne.
   3. Saturday Night Waltz.
   4. Hoe-Down.

Premiere: suite performed by Arthur Fiedler conducting the Boston
  Pops Orchestra, May 28, 1943.
Also, no.1-4 arranged for piano solo; no.4 arranged for string
  orchestra; no. 4 arranged for violin and piano; no.3 and 4
  arranged for two pianos by Arthur Gold and Robert Fizdale.
New York: Boosey & Hawkes.

1943

W71. North Star
  Orchestra.
  Film music for the Samuel Goldwyn production directed by Lewis
    Milestone.
  Premiere: film opened in 1943.
  Includes two choruses (texts by Ira Gershwin):
    1. Song of the Guerrillas, for baritone solo, male chorus, and
       piano or orchestra.
    2. The Younger Generation, for treble voices or mixed chorus
       and piano.
  New York: Boosey & Hawkes.

W72. Sonata for Violin and Piano
  17 min.
  Premiere: Ruth Posselt, violin, accompanied by the composer at
    Town Hall, New York, January 17, 1944.
  Dedicated to Harry H. Dunham.
  New York: Boosey & Hawkes.

1944

W73. Appalachian Spring (Ballet for Martha)
  Ballet for thirteen instruments; 34 min.
  Commissioned by the Elizabeth Sprague Coolidge Foundation.
  Premiere: Martha Graham and her dance company at the Library of
    Congress, Washington, D.C., October 30, 1944, conducted by Louis
    Horst.
  Also arranged as an orchestral suite for symphony orchestra; 23
    min.
  Premiere: orchestral suite first performed by Artur Rodzinski con-
    ducting the New York Philharmonic, October 4, 1945.
  Title is taken from a poem by Hart Crane.
  Dedicated to Elizabeth Sprague Coolidge.
  Also, the excerpt Variations on a Shaker Melody was arranged for
    band in 1956.
  New York: Boosey & Hawkes.   See also: B112

1944; revised 1962

W74. Letter from Home
  Orchestra; 7 min.
  Commissioned by the American Broadcasting Company and Paul
    Whiteman.
  Premiere: Philco Radio Orchestra conducted by Paul Whiteman on the
    Philco Radio Hour, October 17, 1944.
  New York: Boosey & Hawkes.

1945

W75. The Cummington Story
      Orchestra.
      Music for a documentary film of the Overseas Unit of the United
        States Office of War Information.
      Manuscript.

W76. Jubilee Variation
      Orchestra; 3 min.
      Consists of a single variation on a theme by Eugene Goossens.
        Goossens developed a theme and ten composers each contributed
        one variation on this theme.
      Premiere: Eugene Grossens conducting the Cincinnati Symphony
        Orchestra, October 18, 1946.
      Manuscript.

1946

W77. Third Symphony (Symphony No.3)
      Orchestra; 38 min.
      Commissioned by the Koussevitzky Music Foundation.
      Dedicated to the late Natalie Koussevitzky.
      Premiere: Serge Koussevitzky conducting the Boston Symphony
        Orchestra
      New York: Boosey & Hawkes. See also: B390

1947

W78. In the Beginning
      Mezzo-soprano solo and mixed chorus, a cappella; 17 min.
      Text from Genesis.
      Commissioned by the Harvard University Symposium on Music Criticism.
      Premiere: Robert Shaw conducting the Harvard University Collegiate
        Chorale at the Harvard University Memorial Church, Cambridge,
        Massachusetts, May 2, 1947.
      New York: Boosey & Hawkes.

1948

W79. Concerto for Clarinet and String Orchestra, with Harp and Piano
      $17\frac{1}{2}$ min.
      Commissioned by Benny Goodman.
      Premiere: Benny Goodman and the NBC Symphony Orchestra, November 6,
        1950, conducted by Fritz Reiner on radio. Concert premiere by Ralph
        McLane, soloist, with Eugene Ormandy conducting the Phila-
        delphia Orchestra.
      New York: Boosey & Hawkes. See also: B545, B692, B1166

1926-1948

W80. Four Piano Blues
      Piano solo; 8 min.
      The four sections are:
        1. Freely Poetic.
        2. Soft and Languid.

3. Muted and Sensuous.
4. With Bounce.
Dedicated to Leo Smit, Andor Foldes, William Kapell, and John
    Kirkpatrick.
Premiere: Leo Smith at a League of Composers Concert, March 13,
    1950, Carl Fischer Hall, New York. No.4 was first performed
    alone by Hugo Balzo, May 7, 1942, Montevideo.
New York: Boosey & Hawkes. See also: B715

1948; revised 1977

W81. Midsummer Nocturne
      Piano solo.
      New York: Boosey & Hawkes.

1948

W82. The Red Pony
      Orchestra.
      Film music for the story by John Steinbeck.
      Premiere: film was first shown at the Mayfair Theater, New York,
          March 8, 1949.

      Also arranged as an orchestral suite; 23 min.
          1. Morning on the Ranch.
          2. The Gift.
          3. Dream March and Circus Music.
          4. Walk to the Bunkhouse.
          5. Grandfather's Story.
          6. Happy Ending.
      Orchestral suite commissioned by Efrem Kurtz.
      Premiere: Efrem Kurtz conducting the Houston Symphony Orchestra,
          October 30, 1948.
      Also, no.3-6 arranged for band.
      New York: Boosey & Hawkes.

1949

W83. The Heiress
      Orchestra.
      Film music for the drama based on Washington Square by Henry James.
      Premiere: Radio City Music Hall, New York, October 6, 1949.
      Received an Oscar from the Academy of Motion Picture Arts and
          Sciences for the year's best film score.
      Manuscript.

W84. Preamble for a Solemn Occasion
      Speaker (optional) and orchestra; 6 min.
      Commissioned by the National Broadcasting Company for the United
          Nations to celebrate the Declaration of Human Rights.
      Premiere: Sir Laurence Olivier, narrator, with Leonard Bernstein
          conducting the Boston Symphony Orchestra, December 10, 1949.
      Also arranged for organ solo and for band.
      New York: Boosey & Hawkes. See also: B248

1950

W85. Old American Songs Set I
Medium voice and piano; 13 min.
The songs are:
1. The Boatmen's Dance.
2. The Dodger.
3. Long Time Ago.
4. Simple Gifts.
5. I Bought Me a Cat.
Premiere: Peter Pears and Benjamin Britten, June 17, 1950.
Also arranged for medium voice and orchestra, and for chorus.
New York: Boosey & Hawkes.

W86. Quartet for Piano and Strings
21 min.
Commissioned by the Elizabeth Sprague Coolidge Foundation for its
    twenty-fifth anniversary celebration.
Premiere: October 29, 1950, Library of Congress, Washington,
    D.C., by the New York Quartet, consisting of M. Horzowski, A.
    Schneider, M. Katims, and F. Miller.
New York: Boosey & Hawkes. **See also:** B416, B489, B715

1949-1950

W87. Twelve Poems of Emily Dickinson
High voice and piano; 28 min.
The songs are:
1. Nature, the Gentlest Mother.
2. There Came a Wind like a Bugle.
3. Why Do They Shut Me Out of Heaven?
4. The World Feels Dusty.
5. Heart, We Will Forget Him.
6. Dear March, Come In!
7. Sleep Is Supposed to Be.
8. When They Come Back.
9. I Felt a Funeral in My Brain.
10. I've Heard an Organ Talk Sometimes.
11. Going to Heaven.
12. The Chariot.
Premiere: at the Sixth Annual Festival of Contemporary American
    Music, Columbia University's McMillan Memorial Theatre, May 18,
    1950, by Alice Howland with the composer at the piano.
No.1-2, 4-7, 11-12 also arranged for voice and chamber orchestra
New York: Boosey & Hawkes. **See also:** B715, B1132

1952

W88. Old American Songs Set II
Medium voice and piano; 12 min.
The songs are:
1. The Little Horses.
2. Zion's Walls.
3. The Golden Willow Tree.
4. At the River.
5. Ching-a-Ring Chaw.

Also arranged for medium voice and orchestra and for chorus.
Premiere: Grace Bumbry with the composer conducting the Ojai
  Festival Orchestra, Ojai, California, May 25, 1953.
New York: Boosey & Hawkes.

1954

W89. Dirge in Woods
      High voice and piano; $3\frac{1}{2}$ min.
      Words by George Meredith.
      Written to commemorate Natalie Boulanger's fiftieth year of
        teaching.
      Premiere: at the Fontainebleau School of Music, for Boulanger,
        1954. First performance to which the public was invited was by
        Adele Addison in Carnegie Hall, New York, March 28, 1955.
      New York: Boosey & Hawkes. See also: B808

W90. The Tender Land
      Opera for nine soloists, chorus, and orchestra; 100 min.
      Text by Horace Everett.
      Commissioned by Richard Rodgers and Oscar Hammerstein II for the
        League of Composers' thirtieth anniversary.
      Premiere: Thomas Schippers conducting the New York City Opera
        Company, New York City Center, April 1, 1954.
      The work was revised soon after its premiere.
      Also arranged as an orchestral suite; 19 min.
        1. Introduction and Love Music.
        2. Party Scene.
        3. Finale: The Promise of Living.
      Also excerpts arranged for solo voice and for chorus.
      New York: Boosey & Hawkes. See also: B120, B444, B477, B700,
        B742, B833, B977, B989, B1024, B1081, B1091, B1151, B1168, B1192

1955; revised 1965

W91. Canticle of Freedom
      Chorus and orchestra; 13 min.
      Words by John Barbour from his poem The Bruce.
      Commissioned by the Massachusetts Institute of Technology for
        the dedication of the M.I.T. Kresge Auditorium and M.I.T. Chapel
      Premiere: May 8, 1955, by Klaus Liepmann conducting the M.I.T.
        Chorus and Orchestra.
      New York: Boosey & Hawkes. See also: B208, B452

1957

W92. Orchestral Variations
      12 min.
      Based on the composer's Piano Variations (1930).
      Commissioned by the Louisville Philharmonic Orchestra.
      Premiere: Robert Whitney conducting the Louisville Philharmonic
        Orchestra in Louisville, Kentucky, March 5, 1958.
      New York: Boosey & Hawkes. See also: W40, B714

W93. Piano Fantasy
      Piano solo; 30 min.
      Commissioned by the Juilliard School of Music to commemorate its
          fiftieth anniversary.
      Premiere: William Masselos at the Juilliard Concert Hall, New
          York, October 25, 1957.
      Dedicated to the memory of William Kapell.
      New York: Boosey & Hawkes. See also: B202, B373, B384, B904,
          B972, B1079, B1127

W94. The World of Nick Adams
      Orchestra.
      Incidental music for a television show adapted from Ernest
          Hemingway's writings.
      Premiere: November 10, 1957, Columbia Television Network
          with Alfredo Antonini conducting.
      Manuscript.

1959; revised 1962

W95. Dance Panels
      Ballet in seven sections; 26 min.
      Commissioned for Jerome Williams.
      Premiere: Bavarian State Opera with the composer conducting,
          Munich Opera House, Munich, Germany, December 3, 1963.
      Also arranged for piano solo.
      New York: Boosey & Hawkes. See also: B428, B720

1960

W96. Nonet
      3 violins, 3 violas, 3 violoncellos; 15 min.
      Commissioned by the Dumbarton Oaks Research Library to honor the
          fiftieth wedding anniversary of Mr. and Mrs. Robert Woods Bliss.
      Premiere: April 25, 1961, during the Second Inter-American Music
          Festival in Washington, D.C., Cramton Auditorium, Howard Uni-
          versity, conducted by the composer.
      Dedicated to Nadia Boulanger.
      New York: Boosey & Hawkes. See also: B398, B718, B1011

1961

W97. Something Wild
      Orchestra.
      Film music for the movie based on Alex Karmel's novel Mary-Ann.
      Premiere: movie released December 1961.
      Some of this music was used later in the composer's Music for a
          Great City (1964).
      Manuscript. See also: B718, W101

1962

W98. Connotations
      Orchestra; 19½ min.
      Commissioned by the New York Philharmonic to celebrate the opening
          of Lincoln Center for the Performing Arts Philharmonic Hall.

Premiere: Leonard Bernstein conducting the New York Philharmonic
  September 23, 1962, Lincoln Center.
Dedicated to Leonard Bernstein and the New York Philharmonic.
New York: Boosey & Hawkes. See also: B157, B246, B327, B424,
  B468, B551, B585, B592, B593, B598, B719, B772, B948, B1000,
  B1066, B1094

W99. Down a Country Lane
      Piano solo.
      Commissioned by Life Magazine.
      Also arranged for school orchestra.
      New York: Boosey & Hawkes.

1964

W100. Emblems
      Symphonic band; 11 min.
      Commissioned by the College Band Directors National Association.
      Premiere: University of Southern California Trojan Band at a
        convention of the association, December 18, 1964.
      New York: Boosey & Hawkes.

W101. Music for a Great City
      Orchestra.
      The sections of the suite are entitled:
        1. Skyline.
        2. Night Thoughts.
        3. Subway Jam.
        4. Toward the Bridge.
      Commissioned by the London Symphony Orchestra.
      Premiere: the composer conducting the London Symphony Orchestra,
        Festival Hall, London.
      Incorporates some of the music written for the motion picture
        Something Wild (1960).
      New York: Boosey & Hawkes. See also: B159, B287, B387, B721,
        B810, B867, W97

1966

W102. In Evening Air
      Piano solo.
      Excerpt from the composer's film music for The Cummington Story
        (1945).
      New York: Boosey & Hawkes. See also: W75

1967

W103. Inscape
      Orchestra; 12½ min.
      Commissioned for the New York Philharmonic Orchestra's 125th
        anniversary season.
      Idea and title drawn from the nineteenth century Jesuit poet
        Gerald Manley Hopkins.
      Premiere: Leonard Bernstein conducting at the University of Michi-
        gan, Ann Arbor
      New York: Boosey & Hawkes. See also: B598, B621, B643, B724, B906

1969

W104. Ceremonial Fanfare
Brass ensemble: 4 horns, 3 trumpets, 3 trombones, and tuba.
New York: Boosey & Hawkes.

W105. Happy Anniversary
Orchestra; 1 min.
Adapted from the well-known tune Happy Birthday.
Arranged for a celebration of Eugene Ormandy's seventieth birth-
day.
New York: Boosey & Hawkes.

1969; revised 1975

W106. Inaugural Fanfare
Wind ensemble: winds, brass, and percussion.
New York: Boosey & Hawkes.

1971

W107. Duo for Flute and Piano
Premiere: Elaine Shaffer, violin, and Hephziban Menuhin, piano,
October 2, 1971 in Philadelphia.
Dedicated to the memory of William Kincaid who was the Philadelphia
Symphony Orchestra's principal flutist for many years.
Commissioned by the Philadelphia Symphony Orchestra.
Also arranged for violin and piano (1978).
New York: Boosey & Hawkes.

W108. Larghetto Pomposo, Marcatissimo
Melody, 1 page.
Written for the Music Library Association's fortieth anniversary.
Premiere: performed during the week of January 27-30, 1971, at
meetings of the Music Library Association, Washington, D.C.
Manuscript.

W109. Three Latin American Sketches
Chamber orchestra; 10 min.
The three sections are entitled:
1. Estribillo.
2. Paisaje Mexicano.
3. Danza de Jalisco.
The first and third sketches were originally written in 1959
and were called Two Mexican Pieces. They were commissioned for
the Festival of Two Worlds at Spoleto, Italy.
Premiere: Andre Kostelanetz conducting the New York Philharmonic
at the New York Philharmonic Promenade Concert June 7, 1972.
No.3 also arranged for two pianos.
New York: Boosey & Hawkes. See also: B490, B558, B907

W110. Threnody I: Igor Stravinsky in Memoriam
Flute, violin, viola, and cello.
Premiere: June 2, 1973, by the Ojai Festival Orchestra, Ojai,
California.
New York: Boosey & Hawkes.

1972

W111. <u>Night Thoughts</u> (Homage to Ives)
    Piano solo; 6 min.
    Commissioned for the Fourth Van Cliburn International Quadrennial
      Piano Competition September 17-30, 1973 at Fort Worth, Texas.
    Premiere: performed during this competition, September 17-30, 1973.
      Vladimir Vladimirovich Viardo, winner, was the principal performer.
    New York: Boosey & Hawkes. <u>See also</u>: B297, B728, B1026

W112. <u>Threnody II: Beatrice Cunningham in Memoriam</u>
    Alto flute, violin, violin, viola, and cello.
    Premiere: June 2, 1973, by the Ojai Festival Orchestra, Ojai,
      California.
    New York: Boosey & Hawkes. <u>See also</u>: B728

DISCOGRAPHY

This list includes all commercially-produced discs, whether or not currently available. All are 33 1/3 rpm unless otherwise noted.

Las Agachadas

D1. CBS Masterworks 32 11 0017 mono 1967; 32 11 0018 stereo 1967; Columbia M 30375 stereo 1970.
New England Conservatory Chorus; the composer conducting.
With: Twelve Poems of Emily Dickinson; In the Beginning; Lark.

Appalachian Spring (Orchestral Suite, unless otherwise noted)

D2. Allegro-Royale 4056 mono 195-?
Hastings Symphony Orchestra; John Bath, conductor.

D3. American Recording Society ARS-26 mono 1953.
American Recording Society Orchestra; Walter Hendl, conductor.
With: Barber, Samuel. Overture to the School for Scandal.

D4. Canadian Broadcasting Corp./Société Radio-Canada SM 5000 stereo 1980.
Stratford Ensemble; Raffi Armenian, conductor.
With: Britten, Benjamin. Sinfonietta, Op.1; Varèse, Edgar. Octandre.

D5. Capitol SP 8702 stereo 1969.
Concert Arts Orchestra; Robert Irving, conductor.
With: Bernstein, Leonard. Fancy Free. Facsimile; Rodeo.
In: Great American Ballets.

D6. Colombo BP 120 stereo 1969 (Variations on a Shaker Melody, arranged for band).
North Texas State University Concert Band; Maurice McAdow, conductor.
With: Washburn, Robert. Symphony for Band; Rhodes, Phillip.

Pieces; Nelhybel, Vaclar. Adagio and Allegro.

D7. Columbia D3M 33720 stereo 1975 (previously released).
     London Symphony Orchestra; the composer conducting.
     With: Fanfare for the Common Man; Lincoln Portrait; Billy the Kid;
        Rodeo; Our Town; El Salón México; Dance Panels.
     In: A 75th Birthday Celebration.
     See also: B691

D8. Columbia M 30649 stereo 1971.
     London Symphony Orchestra; the composer conducting.
     With: Fanfare for the Common Man; Lincoln Portrait.
     In: Copland Conducts Copland.

D9. Columbia M 32736 stereo 1974 (complete ballet).
     Columbia Chamber Orchestra; the composer conducting.
     Discs issued with: Copland Rehearses Appalachian Spring, Columbia
        BTS 34 stereo 1974.
     See also: B518, B629, B983

D10. Columbia MG 30071 stereo 1970.
     New York Philharmonic; Leonard Bernstein, conductor.
     With: Rodeo; Billy the Kid; El Salón México; Music for the
        Theatre.
     In: The Copland Album.

D11. Columbia MG 31155 stereo 1972.
     New York Philharmonic; Leonard Bernstein, conductor.
     With: works by Samuel Barber, George Gershwin, Charles Ives, and
        Walter Piston.

D12. Columbia ML 5157 mono 1958 (complete ballet).
     Philadelphia Orchestra; Eugene Ormandy, conductor.
     With: Billy the Kid.

D13. Columbia ML 5755 mono 1962; MS 6355 stereo 1962.
     New York Philharmonic; Leonard Bernstein, conductor.
     With: El Salón México; Music for the Theatre (Dance).

D14. Columbia MS 7521 stereo 1970.
     New York Philharmonic; Leonard Bernstein, conductor.
     With: Fanfare for the Common Man; El Salón México; Billy the Kid
        (Celebration); Rodeo (Hoe-Down).
     In: Copland's Greatest Hits.

D15. Command CC 11038 SD stereo 1968.
     Pittsburgh Symphony Orchestra; William Steinberg, conductor.
     With: Billy the Kid.

D16. Cornell University 6 stereo 197-? (Variations on a Shaker Melody).
     Cornell University Wind Ensemble; Maurice Stith, conductor.

D17. Desto DST 6403 stereo 1964.
     Vienna Symphony Orchestra; Walter Hendl, conductor.
     With: Ives, Charles Edward. Three Places in New England.

D18. Everest LPBR 6002 mono 1958; SDBR 3002 stereo 1958.
London Symphony Orchestra; Walter Susskind, conductor.
With: Gould, Morton. Spirituals, orchestra.

D19. London CS 7031 stereo 1976.
Los Angeles Philharmonic; Zubin Mehta, conductor.
With: Bernstein, Leonard. Candide; Gershwin, George. An American
in Paris.

D20. London CSA 2246 stereo 1976.
Los Angeles Philharmonic; Zubin Mehta, conductor.
With: Ives, Charles Edward. Symphony No. 2. Holidays: Decoration
Day. Variations on America, organ; Bernstein, Leonard. Overture
to Candide; Gershwin, George. An American in Paris.
In: The Fourth of July.

D21. Mercury MG 50246 mono 195-?; SR 90246 stereo 1962.
London Symphony Orchestra; Antal Dorati, conductor.
With: Billy the Kid.

D22. National Geographic Society 07819 stereo 1979.
National Geographic Society Orchestra; Dennis Burnside, conductor.
With: Rodeo.

D23. RCA Red Seal ARL1-0109 stereo 1973.
Boston Pops Orchestra; Arthur Fiedler, conductor.
With: Fanfare for the Common Man; Billy the Kid (Street in a
Frontier Town, Celebration); El Salón México; Rodeo (Hoe-Down).
In: Copland's Greatest Hits.

D24. RCA Red Seal ARL!-2862 stereo 1978.
Dallas Symphony Orchestra; Eduardo Mata, conductor.
With: El Salón México; Rodeo.

D25. RCA Red Seal CRL3-3270 stereo 1979 (previously recorded).
[Various orchestras and conductors].
With: Rodeo; Kay, Hershy. Stars and Stripes (Suite); Gould,
Morton. Fall River Legend; Rodgers, Richard. Slaughter on Tenth
Avenue; Bernstein, Leonard. Fancy Free. 3 Dances; Gould, Morton.
Interplay; Ives, Charles Edward. Variations on America (arranged
by William Schuman); Gottschalk, Louis Moreau. Cakewalk (Suite,
arranged by Hershy Kay).
In: The Ballet Box; Favorite American Ballets.

D26. RCA Red Seal LSC 3184 stereo 1970.
Philadelphia Orchestra; Eugene Ormandy, conductor.
With: Billy the Kid.

D27. RCA Victor DM-1946 78 rpm mono 1946.
Boston Symphony Orchestra; Serge Koussevitzky, conductor.

D28. RCA Victor LM 2401 mono 1960; LSC 2401 stereo 1960.
Boston Symphony Orchestra; the composer conducting.
With: The Tender Land (Orchestral Suite).

D29. RCA Victrola AVM1-1739 mono 1976 (previously recorded 1945).
     Boston Symphony Orchestra; Serge Koussevitzky, conductor.
     With: Lincoln Portrait; El Salón México.

D30. Seraphim S-60198 stereo 197-?
     Concert Arts Orchestra; Robert Irving, conductor.
     With: Rodeo.

D31. Sine Qua Non SQN 7747 stereo 1975.
     Pittsburgh Symphony Orchestra; William Steinberg, conductor.
     With: Billy the Kid.

D32. Sound 80 S80-DLR-101 stereo 1979 (original scoring for thirteen
     instruments).
     St. Paul Chamber Orchestra; Dennis Russell Davies, conductor.
     With: Ives, Charles Edward. Three Places in New England.
     See also: B167, B576, B916

D33. State Prima PRIM 3 stereo 1978?
     Wren Symphony Orchestra; Howard Snell, conductor.
     With: Gershwin, George. An American in Paris.

D34. Telarc DG-10078 stereo 1982.
     Atlanta Symphony Orchestra; Louis Lane, conductor.
     With: Fanfare for the Common Man; Rodeo.

D35. Time-Life Records STL 470 stereo 1979 (previously recorded).
     [Various ensembles and conductors].
     With: Fanfare for the Common Man; Dance Symphony; Vitebsk; Piano
       Variations; The Tender Land (Suite); Billy the Kid; Rodeo; El
       Salón México; Quiet City; Symphony No. 3.
     In: Copland.

D36. Urania URLP 7092 mono 1953.
     Symphony Orchestra of Radio Berlin; Arthur Rother, conductor.
     With: Piston, Walter. The Incredible Flutist.

D37. Vanguard VRS-439 mono 1953.
     Vienna State Opera Orchestra; Franz Litschauer, conductor.
     With: El Salón México.

D38. Westminster MCA 1406 stereo 197-?
     Pittsburgh Symphony Orchestra; William Steinberg, conductor.
     With: Billy the Kid.

D39. Westminster WL 5286 mono 1954; 18284 mono 1956; WST 14284 stereo
       1968.
     National Symphony Orchestra of Washington, D.C.; Howard Mitchell,
       conductor.
     With: Fanfare for the Common Man; Billy the Kid; El Salón México.

As It Fell upon a Day

D40. Musical Heritage Society MHS 3578 stereo 1977.
Mary Beth Pell, soprano, with flute and clarinet provided by the
New York Flute Club.
With: Carr, Benjamin. Federal Overture; Gualdo da Vandero,
Giovanni. Trio-Sonatas; Shaw, Oliver. For the Gentlemen Suite;
Heinrich, Anton Philipp. The Dawning of Music in Kentucky;
Lanier, Sidney. Danse des Moucherons; Beach, Amy Marcy Cheney.
Pastorale; Thomson, Virgil. Sonata, Flute; Cowell, Henry.
Ballad, Woodwinds and Horn; Bennett, Robert Russell. Rondo
Capriccioso.
In: The Flute in American Music.

Billy the Kid (Ballet Suite, unless otherwise noted)

D41. CBS Records MY 36727 stereo 1981 (previously released, Columbia
M31823).
New York Philharmonic Orchestra; Leonard Bernstein, conductor.
With: Rodeo.

D42. Capitol P-8238 mono 195-?; HDR 21004 mono 195-?
Ballet Theatre Orchestra; Joseph Levine, conductor.
With: Schuman, William H. Undertow. See also: B483

D43. Columbia 19011-D 78 rpm mono 1949 (Prairie Night and Celebration
Dance).
New York Philharmonic Symphony Orchestra; Leopold Stokowski,
conductor.

D44. Columbia D3M 33720 stereo 1975 (previously released).
London Symphony Orchestra; the composer conducting.
With: Fanfare for the Common Man; Lincoln Portrait; Appalachian
Spring; Rodeo; Our Town; El Salón México; Dance Panels.
In: A 75th Birthday Celebration.
See also: B691

D45. Columbia M 30114 stereo 1971.
London Symphony Orchestra; the composer conducting.
With: Rodeo.

D46. Columbia M 31823 stereo 1973; MG 30071 stereo 1970; ML 5575 mono
1960; MS 6175 stereo 1960.
New York Philharmonic; Leonard Bernstein, conductor.
With: Rodeo.

D47. Columbia ML-2167 mono 195-?
New York Philharmonic Orchestra; Leopold Stokowski, conductor.
With: Works by Morton Gould and Charles Tomlinson Griffes.

D48. Columbia ML 5157 mono 1958.
Philadelphia Orchestra; Eugene Ormandy, conductor.
With: Appalachian Spring.

D49. Columbia MM–251 78 rpm mono 1949 (<u>The Open Prairie</u>, arranged for
      piano solo by Lukas Foss).
      Oscar Levant, piano.
      With: Gershwin, George. Second Rhapsody. <u>I Got Rhythm</u>.

D50. Columbia MS 7521 stereo 1970 (<u>Celebration</u>).
      Philadelphia Orchestra; Eugene Ormandy, conductor.
      With: <u>Fanfare for the Common Man</u>, El Salón México; <u>Rodeo</u> (Hoe-Down);
        <u>Appalachian Spring</u>.
      In: Copland's Greatest Hits.

D51. Command CC 11038 SD stereo 1968.
      Pittsburgh Symphony Orchestra; William Steinberg, conductor.
      With: <u>Appalachian Spring</u>.

D52. Everest LPBR 6015 mono 1955; SDBR 3015 stereo 197–?
      London Symphony Orchestra; the composer conducting.
      With: <u>Statements</u>.

D53. Mercury MG 50246 mono 195–?; SR 90246 stereo 1962.
      London Symphony Orchestra; Antal Dorati, conductor.
      With: <u>Appalachian Spring</u>.

D54. Music Guild MS 164 stereo 1970.
      Utah Symphony Orchestra; Maurice Abravanel, conductor.
      With: <u>Rodeo</u>.

D55. RCA Camden CAL 439 mono 1958.
      RCA Victor Symphony Orchestra; Leonard Bernstein, conductor.
      With: Gershwin, George. <u>An American in Paris</u>.

D56. RCA Red Seal ARL1–0109 stereo 1973 (<u>Street in a Frontier Town</u>;
        Celebration).
      Philadelphia Orchestra; Eugene Ormandy, conductor.
      With: <u>Fanfare for the Common Man</u>; El Salón México; <u>Rodeo</u> (Hoe-Down);
        <u>Appalachian Spring</u>.
      In: Copland's Greatest Hits.

D57. RCA Red Seal LSC 3184 stereo 1970.
      Philadelphia Orchestra; Eugene Ormandy, conductor.
      With: <u>Appalachian Spring</u>.

D58. RCA Victor DM–1214 78 rpm mono 1948 (Waltz).
      Dallas Symphony Orchestra; Antal Dorati, conductor.
      With: <u>Rodeo</u>.

D59. RCA Victor DM–1333 78 rpm mono 1950.
      RCA Victor Symphony Orchestra; Leonard Bernstein, conductor.
      With: <u>Statements: No.5 (Jingo)</u>.

D60. RCA Victor LM–1031 mono 1950.
      RCA Victor Symphony Orchestra; Leonard Bernstein, conductor.
      With: Gershwin, George. <u>An American in Paris</u>.
      See also: B483

D61. RCA Victor LM-1705 mono 1952 (Celebration Dance, Billy's Demise,
     The Open Prairie Again, arranged for two pianos).
     Arthur Austin Whittemore and Jack Lowe, pianos.
     In: 20th Century Music for Two Pianos.

D62. RCA Victor LM 2195 mono 1958; LSC 2195 stereo 1958.
     Morton Gould Orchestra; Morton Gould, conductor.
     With: Rodeo.

D63. RCA Victor WDM-1333 78 rpm mono 1950.
     RCA Victor Symphony Orchestra; Leonard Bernstein, conductor.
     With: Statements: No.5 (Jingo).

D64. Sine Qua Non SQN 7747 stereo 1975.
     Pittsburgh Symphony Orchestra; William Steinberg, conductor.
     With: Appalachian Spring.

D65. Time-Life Records STL 570 stereo 1979 (previously recorded).
     [Various ensembles and conductors].
     With: Fanfare for the Common Man; Appalachian Spring; Dance Sym-
     phony; Vitebsk; Piano Variations; The Tender Land (Suite);
     Rodeo; El Salón México; Quiet City; Symphony No.3.
     In: Copland.

D66. Turnabout TV 34169 stereo 1967.
     Dallas Symphony Orchestra; Donald Johanos, conductor.
     With: Fanfare for the Common Man; Rodeo.

D67. Westminster 8170 mono 197-?
     Utah Symphony Orchestra; Maurice Abravanel, conductor.
     With: Rodeo.

D68. Westminster MCA 1406 stereo 1970.
     Pittsburgh Symphony Orchestra; William Steinberg, conductor.
     With: Appalachian Spring.

D69. Westminster WL 5286 mono 1954; WL 18284 mono 1956; WST 14284
     stereo 1968.
     National Symphony Orchestra of Washington, D.C.; Howard Mitchell,
     conductor.
     With: Appalachian Spring; Fanfare for the Common Man; El Salón
     México.

D70. Westminster WST 14058 stereo 196-?
     Utah Symphony Orchestra; Maurice Abravanel, conductor.
     With: Rodeo.

D71. Westminster XWN 18840 mono 1958.
     Utah Symphony Orchestra; Maurice Abravanel, conductor.
     With: El Salón México; Rodeo.

Canticle of Freedom

D72. Vogt CSRV 2600 stereo 1978.
    Crane Chorus; Crane Symphony Orchestra (New York State University
      College, Potsdam); the composer conducting.
    With: Fanfare for the Common Man; Letter from Home; Old American
      Songs (Sets I and II); Symphonic Ode; The Tender Land (Suite).

The Cat and the Mouse

D73. Columbia M2 35901 stereo 1979.
    Leo Smit, piano.
    With: Piano Variations; In Evening Air; Passacaglia; Piano Sonata;
      Piano Fantasy; Four Piano Blues; Midsummer Nocturne; The Young
      Pioneers; Sunday Afternoon Music; Down a Country Lane; Night
      Thoughts.
    In: The Complete Music for Solo Piano.
    See also: B982, B1157

D74. Golden Age Recording GAR 1008-1009 stereo 1977?
    Joan Singer, piano.
    With: Passacaglia; Down a Country Lane; In Evening Air; Four Piano
      Blues; Piano Sonata; Sentimental Melody; Two Children's Pieces;
      Piano Variations; Night Thoughts; Piano Fantasy.
    In: All the Piano Music.

D75. Orion ORS 7280 stereo 1972.
    Robert Silverman, piano.
    With: Piano Sonata; Passacaglia; Four Piano Blues.
    In: Piano Sonata and Other Works.

D76. RCA Victor 15861 78 rpm mono 1940.
    Jesús María Sanroma, piano.
    With: Respighi, Ottorino. Notturno.

D77. RCA Victor M-646 78 rpm mono 1940?
    Jesús María Sanroma, piano.
    In: Piano Music of the Twentieth Century.

Concerto for Clarinet and String Orchestra, with Harp and Piano

D78. Columbia ML 4421 mono 1952; MS 4221 stereo 196-?
    Benny Goodman, clarinet; Columbia String Orchestra; the composer
      conducting.
    With: Quartet for Piano and Strings. See also: B209

D79. Columbia ML 5897 mono 1963; MS 6497 stereo 1963.
    Benny Goodman, clarinet; Columbia String Orchestra; the composer
      conducting.
    With: Old American Songs (Sets I and II).

D80. Columbia ML 6205 mono 1966; MS 6805 stereo 1966.
      Benny Goodman, clarinet; Columbia Symphony Orchestra; the composer
        conducting.
      With: Bernstein, Leonard. Prelude, Fugue, and Riffs; Stravinsky,
        Igor. Ebony Concerto; Gould, Morton. Derivations for Clarinet and
        Band.
      In: Meeting at the Summit.

D81. Mark MC 3344 stereo 1973?
      Paul Drushler, clarinet; Gordon Gibson, piano.
      With: Debussy, Claude. Première Rhapsodie for Clarinet; Poulenc,
        Francis. Sonata for Clarinet and Piano.

D82. Unicorn RHS 314 stereo 1976; UN1-75002 stereo 1977.
      Gervaise Alan de Peyer, clarinet; London Mozart Players; Bernard
        Jacob, conductor.
      With: Crusell, Bernard Henrik. Grand Concerto, Op.5, F Minor.
      See also: B691

Concerto for Piano and Orchestra

D83. Columbia ML 6098 mono 1965; MS 6698 stereo 1965.
      The composer, piano; New York Philharmonic; Leonard Bernstein,
        conductor.
      With: Music for the Theatre (Suite).

D84. Concert Hall F-4 mono 1952; 1238 mono 195-?; 1638 mono 1958.
      Leo Smit, piano; Rome Radio Orchestra; the composer conducting.
      With: Bloch, Ernest. Episodes. See also: B542

D85. Musical Masterpiece Society MMS 105 mono 196-?
      Leo Smit, piano; Rome Radio Orchestra; the composer conducting.

D86. Turnabout QTV 34683 quad 1976.
      Abbott Ruskin, piano; Massachusetts Institute of Technology Sym-
        phony Orchestra; David Epstein, conductor.
      With: Barber, Samuel. Piano Concerto, Op.38.

D87. Vanguard VRS 1070 mono 1961.
      Earl Wild, piano; Symphony of the Air; the composer conducting.
      With: Menotti, Gian Carlo. Concerto, Piano, F Major.

D88. Vanguard VSD 2094 stereo 1961.
      Earl Wild, piano; Symphony of the Air; Jorge Mester, conductor.
      With: Menotti, Gian Carlo. Concerto, Piano, F Major.

D89. Varèse Sarabande VC 81098 mono 1980 (previously released 1951).
      Rome Radio Orchestra; the composer conducting.
      With: Danzón Cubano; Our Town; Four Piano Blues; Ukelele Serenade;
        Rodeo (Hoe-Down); Nocturne.
      In: Copland Conducts and Plays Copland.

Connotations

D90. Columbia L2L 1007 mono 1962; L2S 1008 stereo 1962.
      New York Philharmonic; Leonard Bernstein, conductor.
      With: Beethoven, Ludwig van. Mass, Op.123, D Major. Gloria; Vaughan
        Williams, Ralph. Serenade to Music; Mahler, Gustav. Symphony, No.
        8, E Flat Major. Pt.1.
      See also: B424, B772

D91. Columbia MS 7431 stereo 1970.
      New York Philharmonic; Leonard Bernstein, conductor.
      With: Inscape.

Dance Panels

D92. Columbia D3M 33720 stereo 1975 (previously released).
      London Symphony Orchestra; the composer conducting.
      With: Fanfare for the Common Man; Lincoln Portrait; Appalachian
        Spring; Billy the Kid; Rodeo; Our Town; El Salón México.
      In: A 75th Birthday Celebration.
      See also: B691

D93. Columbia M 33269 stereo 1975.
      London Symphony Orchestra; the composer conducting.
      With: Danzón Cubano; Three Latin American Sketches; El Salón México.
      See also: D624

Dance Symphony

D94. Columbia MS 7223 stereo 1969.
      London Symphony Orchestra; the composer conducting.
      With: Short Symphony. See also: B496

D95. Composers Recordings CRI SD 129 mono 1959.
      Japan Philharmonic Symphony Orchestra; Akeo Watanabe, conductor.
      With: Stevens, Halsey. Symphony No.1.

D96. Orion ORS 79343 stereo 1979 (arranged for two pianos).
      Evelinde Trenkner, Vladimir Pleshakov, pianos.
      With: Vaughan Williams, Ralph. Introduction and Fugue, 2 Pianos;
        Mendelssohn-Bartholdy, Felix. Variations Brillantes.

D97. RCA Victor LM 2850 mono 1965; LSC 2850 stereo 1965; AGL1-1965
        stereo 197-?
      Chicago Symphony Orchestra; Morton Gould, conductor.
      With: Gould, Morton. Spirituals.

D98. Time-Life Records STL 570 stereo 1979 (previously recorded).
      [Various ensembles and conductors].
      With: Fanfare for the Common Man; Appalachian Spring; Vitebsk;
        Piano Variations, The Tender Land (Suite); Billy the Kid; Rodeo;
        El Salón México; Quiet City; Symphony No.3.
      In: Copland.

D99. Turnabout QTV-S 34670 quad 1976.
      Massachusetts Institute of Technology Symphony Orchestra; David
         Epstein, conductor.
      With: Piston, Walter. The Incredible Flutist.

Danzón Cubano

D100. Columbia M 33269 stereo 1975 (arranged for orchestra).
      London Symphony Orchestra; the composer conducting.
      With: Three Latin American Sketches; El Salón México; Dance Panels.

D101. Columbia ML 5914 mono 1963; MS 6514 stereo 1963 (arranged for
         orchestra).
      New York Philharmonic; Leonard Bernstein, conductor.
      With: Villa-Lobos, Heitor. Bachianas Brasileiras No.5; Guarnieri,
         Camargo. Brazilian Dance; Revueltas, Silvestre. Sensemaya;
         Fernández, Oscar Lorenzo. Batuque; Chávez, Carlos. Sinfonía
         India.
      In: Latin-American Fiesta.

D102. Columbia ML 2671 mono 196-?; MS 6871 stereo 196-? (arranged for
         orchestra).
      New York Philharmonic; Leonard Bernstein, conductor.

D103. Concert Hall CHC-51 mono 1947?
      Leo Smit and the composer, pianos.
      With: Three Blues; Our Town (Suite) arranged for piano.

D104. Mercury 50326 mono 196-?; 90326 stereo 196-? (arranged for
         orchestra).
      Minneapolis Symphony Orchestra; Antal Dorati, conductor.

D105. Mercury MG 50172 mono 1958; SR 90172 stereo 1958 (arranged for
         orchestra).
      Minneapolis Symphony Orchestra; Antal Dorati, conductor.
      With: El Salón México; Rodeo.

D106. New World Records NW 277 mono 1976 (previously recorded, arranged
         for solo piano).
      Leo Smit, piano.
      With: Piano Sonata; Piano Variations; Four Piano Blues.
      In: Works for Piano, 1926-1948.

D107. RCA Victor LM 2417 mono 1960.
      Vitya Vronsky, Victor Babin, pianos.
      With: Tchaikovsky, Peter Ilich. Swan Lake (Waltz). Serenade for
         Strings in C, Op.48 (Waltz). The Nutcracker (Waltz of the Flow-
         ers). Eugene Onégin (Waltz); Arensky, Antonii Stepanovich.
         Suite, Op.15, No.2 (Waltz); Rimsky-Korsakoff, Nicolai
         Andreevich. Dance of the Tumblers; Benjamin, Arthur. Jamaicalyp-
         so; Stravinsky, Igor. Circus Polka; Strauss, Richard. Der
         Rosenkavalier (Concert Waltz).
      In: 176 Keys; Music for Two Pianos.

D108. Varèse Sarabande VC 81098 mono 1980 (previously released 1947).
    Leo Smit and the composer, pianos.
    With: Concerto for Piano and Orchestra; Our Town; Four Piano
       Blues; Ukelele Serenade; Rodeo (Hoe-Down); Nocturne.
    In: Copland Concucts and Plays Copland.

Down a Country Lane

D109. Columbia M 33586 stereo 1975 (arranged for orchestra).
    London Symphony Orchestra; the composer conducting.
    With: The Red Pony; Music for Movies; John Henry; Letter from Home.
    In: Copland Conducts Copland.

D110. Columbia M2 35901 stereo 1979.
    Leo Smit, piano.
    With: Piano Variations; In Evening Air; Passacaglia; Piano Sonata;
      Piano Fantasy; Four Piano Blues; Midsummer Nocturne; The Young
      Pioneers; Sunday Afternoon Music; Night Thoughts.
    In: The Complete Music for Solo Piano.
    See also: B982, B1157

D111. Golden Age Recording GAR 1008-1009 stereo 1977?
    Joan Singer, piano.
    With: Passacaglia; In Evening Air; The Cat and the Mouse; Four
      Piano Blues; Piano Sonata; Sentimental Melody; Two Children's
      Pieces; Piano Variations; Night Thoughts; Piano Fantasy.
    In: All the Piano Music.

Duo for Flute and Piano

D112. Columbia M 32737 stereo 1974.
    Elaine Shaffer, flute; the composer, piano.
    With: Sonata for Violin and Piano; Nonet for Strings.
    In: Copland Performs and Conducts Copland.
    See also: B629, B983

D113. Laurel Protone LP-14 stereo 1976.
    Laila Padorr, flute; Anita Swearengin, piano.
    With: Vocalise for Flute and Piano; Dello Joio, Norman. The De-
      veloping Flutist (Suite); Piston, Walter. Sonata for Flute and
      Piano; Muczynski, Robert. Three Preludes for Unaccompanied
      Flute, Op.18.
    In: Music for Flute & Piano by Four Americans.

D114. Orion ORS 76242 stereo 1976.
    Keith Bryan, flute; Karen Keys, piano.
    With: Burton, E. Sonatina, Flute & Piano; Piston, Walter. Sonata,
      Flute and Piano; Van Vactor, David. Sonatina, Flute and Piano.
    In: American Music for Flute & Piano.

Emblems

D115. Century Records CUWE 1 stereo 1969.
      Cornell University Wind Ensemble; Maurice Stith, conductor.
      With: Schönberg, Arnold. Theme and Variations, Op.43a; Bielawa,
         Herbert. Spectrum; Rimsky-Korsakoff, Nicolai Andreevich. Mlada.
         Procession of the Nobles.

D116. Golden Imports SRI 75132 stereo 1978?
      Eastman Wind Ensemble; Donald Hunsberger, conductor.
      With: Schwantner, Joseph C. And the Mountains Rising Nowhere;
         Hanson, Howard. Young Composer's Guide to the Six-Tone Scale.

Episode

D117. Vista VPS 1038 stereo 1976.
      Walter Hillsman, organ.
      With: Ives, Charles. Variations on America. Adeste Fidelis in an
         Organ Prelude; Sessions, Roger. Chorale No.1 in G; Buck, Dudley.
         Concert Variations on The Star-Spangled Banner, Op.23; Barber,
         Samuel. Wondrous Love; Bremner, James. Trumpet Air; Barber,
         Samuel. Chorale Prelude on Silent Night.
      In: American Organ Music from Southwark Cathedral.

Fanfare for the Common Man

D118. Columbia D3M 33720 stereo 1975 (previously recorded on Columbia
         M 30649).
      London Symphony Orchestra; the composer conducting.
      With: Lincoln Portrait; Appalachian Spring; Billy the Kid; Rodeo;
         Our Town; El Salón México; Dance Panels.
      In: A 75th Birthday Celebration.
      See also: B691

D119. Columbia M 30649 stereo 1971.
      London Symphony Orchestra; the composer conducting.
      With: Lincoln Portrait; Appalachian Spring.
      In: Copland Conducts Copland.

D120. Columbia ML 6084 mono 1965; MS 6684 stereo 1965.
      Philadelphia Orchestra; Eugene Ormandy, conductor.
      With: Ives, Charles. Three Places in New England.

D121. Columbia MS 7289 stereo 197-?; MG 31190 stereo 197-?
      Philadelphia Orchestra; Eugene Ormandy, conductor.

D122. Columbia MS 7521 stereo 1970.
      Philadelphia Orchestra; Eugene Ormandy, conductor.
      With: El Salón México; Billy the Kid (Celebration); Rodeo (Hoe-
         Down); Appalachian Spring.
      In: Copland's Greatest Hits.

D123. RCA Red Seal ARL1-0109 stereo 1973.
      Philadelphia Orchestra; Eugene Ormandy, conductor.

With: <u>Billy the Kid</u> (<u>Street in a Frontier Town</u>; <u>Celebration</u>); <u>El Salón México</u>; <u>Rodeo</u> (<u>Hoe-Down</u>); <u>Appalachian Spring</u>.
In: Copland's Greatest Hits.

D124. RCA Red Seal **LSC** 3349 stereo 1973.
Philadelphia Orchestra; Eugene Ormandy, conductor.
With: Tchaikovsky, Peter Ilich. <u>1812 Overture</u>; Grieg, Edvard Hagerup. Piano Concerto in A Minor.
In: Music Featured at the 1973 Inaugural Symphonic Concert.

D125. Telarc **DG**-10078 stereo 1982.
Atlanta Symphony Orchestra; Louis Lane, conductor.
With: <u>Rodeo</u>; <u>Appalachian Spring</u>.

D126. Time-Life Records **STL** 570 stereo 1979 (previously recorded).
[Various ensembles and conductors].
With: <u>Appalachian Spring</u>; <u>Dance Symphony</u>; <u>Vitebsk</u>; <u>Piano Variations</u>; <u>The Tender Land</u>; <u>Billy the Kid</u>; <u>El Salón México</u>; <u>Quiet City</u>; Symphony No.3.
In: Copland.

D127. Turnabout TV 34169 stereo 1967.
Dallas Symphony Orchestra; Donald Johanos, conductor.
With: <u>Rodeo</u>; <u>Billy the Kid</u>.

D128. Vanguard VRS 1067 mono 1961.
Hartford Symphony Orchestra; Fritz Mahler, conductor.
With: Orchestral Variations.

D129. Vogt CSRV 2600 stereo 1978.
Crane Symphony Orchestra (New York State University College, Potsdam); the composer conducting.
With: <u>Canticle of Freedom</u>; <u>Letter from Home</u>; <u>Old American Songs, Sets I and II</u>, Symphonic Ode; <u>The Tender Land</u> (Suite).

D130. Westminster WL 5286 mono 1954; WL 18284 mono 1956; WST 14284 stereo 1968.
National Symphony Orchestra of Washington, D. C.; Howard Mitchell, conductor.
With: <u>Appalachian Spring</u>; <u>Billy the Kid</u>; <u>El Salón México</u>.

Four Piano Blues

D131. Columbia M2 35901 stereo 1979.
Leo Smit, piano.
With: <u>The Cat and the Mouse</u>; <u>Piano Variations</u>; <u>In Evening Air</u>; Passacaglia; Piano Sonata; Piano Fantasy; <u>Midsummer Nocturne</u>; <u>The Young Pioneers</u>; <u>Sunday Afternoon Music</u>; <u>Down a Country Lane</u>; <u>Night Thoughts</u>.
In: The Complete Music for Solo Piano.
See also: B982, B1157

D132. Concert Hall **CHC**-51 mono 1947? (Three Blues: Two Blues and <u>Sentimental Melody</u>).

Leo Smit, piano.
With: Danzón Cubano (arranged for two pianos); Our Town (Suite, arranged for piano).

D133. Dot DLP 3111 mono 1958.
Leo Smit, piano.
With: Tansman, Alexandre. Spiritual and Blues; Hindemith, Paul. Shimmy. Ragtime; Milhaud, Darius. Three Rag Caprices; Gershwin, George. Three Preludes; Stravinsky, Igor. Piano Rag Music.
In: The Masters Write Jazz.

D134. Golden Age Recording GAR 1008-1009.
Joan Singer, piano.
With: Passacaglia; Down a Country Lane; In Evening Air; The Cat and the Mouse; Piano Sonata; Sentimental Melody; Two Children's Pieces; Piano Variations; Night Thoughts; Piano Fantasy.
In: All the Piano Music.

D135. London LPS 298 mono 1950.
The composer, piano.
With: Barber, Samuel. Quartet, Strings, Op.11, B Minor; Adagio; Bloch, Ernest. From Jewish Life.

D136. New World Records NW 277 mono 1976 (previously recorded on Decca/London DK 2372 in 1949).
The composer, piano.
With: Piano Sonata; Piano Variations; Danzón Cubano (arranged for piano).
In: Works for Piano, 1926-1948.

D137. Nonesuch D-79006 stereo 1980.
Paul Jacobs, piano.
With: Bolcom, William. Three Ghost Rags; Rzewski, Frederic. North American Ballads.
In: Paul Jacobs Plays Blues, Ballads & Rags.
See also: B917

D138. Orion ORS 7280 stereo 1979.
Robert Silverman, piano.
With: Piano Sonata; Passacaglia; The Cat and the Mouse.

D139. Supraphon 1 11 1721-1 11 1722 stereo 1975.
Peter Toperczer, piano.

D140. Varèse Sarabande VC 81098 mono 1980 (previously released 1948).
Leo Smit, piano.
With: Concerto for Piano and Orchestra; Danzón Cubano; Our Town; Ukelele Serenade; Rodeo (Hoe-Down); Nocturne.
In: Copland Conducts and Plays Copland.

In Evening Air

D141. Columbia M2 35901 stereo 1979.
Leo Smit, piano.

With: The Cat and the Mouse; Piano Variations; Passacaglia; Piano
   Sonata; Piano Fantasy; Four Piano Blues; Midsummer Nocturne; The
   Young Pioneers; Sunday Afternoon Music; Down a Country Lane;
   Night Thoughts.
In: The Complete Music·for Solo Piano.
See also: B982, B1157

D142. Golden Age Recording GAR 1008-1009 stereo 1977?
   Joan Singer, piano.
   With: Passacaglia; Down a Country Lane; The Cat and the Mouse;
      Four Piano Blues; Piano Sonata; Sentimental Melody; Two Chil-
      dren's Pieces; Piano Variations; Night Thoughts; Piano Fantasy.
   In: All the Piano Music.

D143. Musical Heritage Society MHS 4126 stereo 1979.
   Walter Hautzig, piano.
   With: Bach, Johann Sebastian. Concerto, Harpsichord, S.974, D
      Minor: Adagio; Beethoven, Ludwig van. Sonata, Piano, No.14, Op.
      27, No.2, C# Minor; Schubert, Franz Peter. 20 Valses; Walker,
      George. Variations on a Kentucky Folksong; Debussy, Claude.
      Feux d'Artifice; Chopin, Frederick. Mazurka in C Major, Op.24,
      No.2. Polonaise in A-flat Major, Op.53.
   In: Walter Hautzig Peking Recital.

D144. Unicorn RHS 383 stereo 1978.
   Peter Dickinson, piano.
   With: Gershwin, George. A Foggy Day in London Town. They All
      Laughed. I Got Rhythm; Carter, Elliott Cook. Three Poems of
      Robert Frost. Voyage; Thomson, Virgil. Two by Marianne Moore.
      Portrait of F.B. (Frances Blood); Poet's Song (E. E. Cummings);
      Night Thoughts.
   In: An American Anthology; [Songs & Piano Music].

In the Beginning

D145. CBS Masterworks 32 11 0017 mono 1967; 32 11 0018 stereo 1967;
      Columbia M 30375 stereo 1970.
   Adele Addison, soprano; New England Conservatory Chorus; the
   composer conducting.
   With: Twelve Poems of Emily Dickinson; Las Agachadas; Lark.

D146. Everest LPBR 6129 mono 1965; SDBR 3129 stereo 1965.
   Gregg Smith Singers.
   With: Schuman, William Howard. Carols of Death; Barber, Samuel.
      Reincarnation, Op.16.
   In: An American Triplych.
   See also: B759

D147. Lyrichord LL 124 mono 1964; LLST 7124 stereo 1964.
   Whikehart Chorale; Lewis E. Whikehart, conductor.
   With: Thompson, Randall. The Peaceable Kingdom.
   See also: B426

D148. Music Library Recordings MLR 7007 mono 195-?
San Jose State College A Cappella Choir; William J. Erlendson,
conductor.
With: Four Sacred Chorales.

D149. Musical Heritage Society MHS 3167 stereo 1975.
Irene Weldon, soprano; Wartburg College Choir; James Fritschel,
conductor.
With: Martin, Frank. Mass for Double Chorus, a Capella; Fritschel,
James. Be Still.

Inscape

D150. Columbia MS 7431 stereo 1970.
New York Philharmonic; Leonard Bernstein, conductor.
With: Connotations for Orchestra.

John Henry

D151. Columbia M 33586 stereo 1975.
New Philharmonia Orchestra; the composer conducting.
With: The Red Pony (Suite); Music for Movies; Letter from Home;
Down a Country Lane.
In: Copland Conducts Copland.

Lark

D152. CBS Masterworks 32 11 0017 mono 1967; 32 11 0018 stereo 1967;
Columbia M 30375 stereo 1970.
New England Conservatory Chorus; the composer conducting.
With: Twelve Poems of Emily Dickinson; In the Beginning.

Letter from Home

D153. Columbia M 33586 stereo 1975.
London Symphony Orchestra; the composer conducting.
With: The Red Pony (Suite); Music for Movies; John Henry; Down a
Country Lane.
In: Copland Conducts Copland.

D154. Music Guild MS 858 stereo 1970; Westminster WST 17131 stereo 1967.
Vienna Radio Orchestra; Joseph Eger, conductor.
With: Korn, Peter Jona. In Medias Res; Riegger, Wallingford. New
Dance, Piano, 4 Hands & Percussion; Prokofiev, Sergey. Di-
vertisement, Orchestra, Op.43, C Major.

D155. Vogt CSRV 2600 stereo 1978.
Crane Symphony Orchestra (New York State University College,
Potsdam); the composer conducting.
With: Fanfare for the Common Man; Canticle of Freedom; Old Ameri-
can Songs, Sets I and II; Symphonic Ode; The Tender Land (Suite).

Lincoln Portrait

D156. **ASCAP CB** 179 mono 1954.
      John Ragin, narrator; Pittsburgh Symphony Orchestra; William
        Steinberg, conductor.
      With: Honegger, Arthur. Symphony No.5.
      In: Pittsburgh International Contemporary Music Festival.

D157. Columbia D3M 33720 stereo 1975.
      Henry Fonda, narrator; London Symphony Orchestra; the composer
        conducting.
      With: Fanfare for the Common Man; Appalachian Spring; Billy the
        Kid; Rodeo; Our Town; El Salón México; Dance Panels.
      In: A 75th Birthday Celebration.
      See also: B691

D158. Columbia M 30649 stereo 1971.
      Henry Fonda, narrator; London Symphony Orchestra; the composer
        conducting.
      With: Fanfare for the Common Man; Appalachian Spring.
      In: Copland Conducts Copland.

D159. Columbia ML 2042 mono 1949.
      Kenneth Spencer, narrator; New York Philharmonic Symphony Orches-
        tra; Artur Rodzinski, conductor.
      With: Gould, Morton. Spirituals for Orchestra.

D160. Columbia ML 5347 mono 1959; MS 6040 stereo 1959.
      Carl Sandburg, narrator; New York Philharmonic; Andre Kostelanetz,
        conductor.
      With: Schuman, William Howard. New England Triptych; Barber,
        Samuel. Vanessa: Intermezzo, Act 4.

D161. Columbia ML 6084 mono 1965; MS 6684 stereo 1965.
      Adlai Stevenson, narrator; Philadelphia Orchestra; Eugene Ormandy,
        conductor.
      With: Fanfare for the Common Man; Ives, Charles. Three Places in
        New England.

D162. Columbia MX-266 78 rpm mono 1946.
      Kenneth Spencer, narrator; New York Philharmonic Symphony Orches-
        tra; Artur Rodzinski, conductor.

D163. London CS 6613 stereo 1969.
      Gregory Peck, narrator; Los Angeles Philharmonic Orchestra; Zubin
        Mehta, conductor.
      With: Kraft, William. Concerto, Percussion & Orchestra.

D164. RCA Victor DM-1088 78 rpm mono 1947.
      Melvyn Douglas, narrator; Boston Symphony Orchestra; Serge
        Koussevitzky, conductor.

D165. RCA Victor LCT 1152 mono 1956.
      Melvyn Douglas, narrator; Boston Symphony Orchestra; Serge
        Koussevitzky, conductor.

With: Fauré, Gabriel U. Pelléas et Mélisande (Suite); Sibelius, Jean. Pohjola's Daughter; Stravinsky, Igor. Capriccio, Piano & Orchestra.

D166. RCA Victrola AVM1-1739 mono 1976 (previously recorded 1946).
Melvyn Douglas, narrator; Boston Symphony Orchestra; Serge Koussevitzky, conductor.
With: Appalachian Spring; El Salón México.

D167. Vanguard SRV 348 SD stereo 1975; VSD 2115 stereo 1968; VRS 1088 mono 1962.
Charlton Heston, narrator; Utah Symphony Orchestra; Maurice Abravanel, conductor.
With: Quiet City; An Outdoor Overture; Our Town.

Midsummer Nocturne

D168. Columbia M2 35901 stereo 1978.
Leo Smit, piano.
With: The Cat and the Mouse; Piano Variations; In Evening Air; Passacaglia; Piano Sonata; Piano Fantasy; Four Piano Blues; The Young Pioneers; Sunday Afternoon Music; Down a Country Lane; Night Thoughts.
In: The Complete Music for Solo Piano.
See also: B982, B1157

Music for a Great City

D169. CBS Masterworks 32 11 0001 mono 1966; 32 11 0002 stereo 1966; Columbia M 30374 stereo 1970.
London Symphony Orchestra; the composer conducting.
With: Statements.
See also: B753

Music for Movies

D170. Columbia M 33586 stereo 1975.
London Symphony Orchestra; the composer conducting.
With: The Red Pony (Suite); John Henry; Letter from Home; Down a Country Lane.
In: Copland Conducts Copland.

D171. M-G-M Records M-G-M E 3334 mono 1956.
M-G-M Chamber Orchestra; Arthur Winograd, conductor.
With: Weill, Kurt. Works: Selections.

D172. M-G-M Records M-G-M E 3367 mono 1956.
M-G-M Chamber Orchestra; Arthur Winograd, conductor.
With: Music for the Theatre; Music for Radio.

Music for Radio

D173. M-G-M Records M-G-M E 3367 mono 1956.
      M-G-M Chamber Orchestra; Arthur Winograd, conductor.
      With: Music for Movies; Music for the Theatre.

Music for the Theatre

D174. American Recording Society ARS-12 mono 1953; ARS-110 mono 1953.
      American Recording Society Orchestra; Walter Hendl, conductor.

D175. Columbia MG 30071 (Dance) stereo 1970.
      New York Philharmonic; Leonard Bernstein, conductor.
      With: Rodeo; Billy the Kid; Appalachian Spring; El Salón México.
      In: The Copland Album.

D176. Columbia ML 5755 (Dance) mono 1961; MS 6355 stereo 1961.
      New York Philharmonic; Leonard Bernstein, conductor.
      With: Appalachian Spring; El Salón México.

D177. Columbia ML 6098 mono 1965; MS 6698 stereo 1965.
      New York Philharmonic; Leonard Bernstein, conductor.
      With: Concerto for Piano and Orchestra.

D178. Desto DST 6418 stereo 1971.
      Vienna Symphony Orchestra; Walter Hendl, conductor.
      With: Barber, Samuel. Overture to the School for Scandal.

D179. M-G-M E 3095 mono 1954.
      M-G-M Symphony Orchestra; Izler Solomon, conductor.
      With: Weill, Kurt. Kleine Dreigroschen Musik. See also: B235

D180. M-G-M Records M-G-M E 3367 mono 1956.
      M-G-M Chamber Orchestra; Arthur Winograd, conductor.
      With: Music for Movies; Music for Radio.

D181. RCA Victor CM-744 78 rpm mono 1941.
      Eastman-Rochester Symphony Orchestra; Howard Hanson, conductor.

Night Thoughts (Homage to Ives)

D182. Columbia M2 35901 stereo 1979.
      Leo Smit, piano.
      With: The Cat and the Mouse; Piano Variations; In Evening Air;
         Passacaglia; Piano Sonata; Piano Fantasy; Four Piano Blues;
         Midsummer Nocturne; The Young Pioneers; Sunday Afternoon Music;
         Down a Country Lane.
      In: The Complete Music for Solo Piano.
      See also: B982, B1157

D183. Delos DEL 25436 stereo 1976.
      Charles Fierro, piano.
      With: Piano Fantasy; Passacaglia; Piano Variations.

D184. Golden Age Recording GAR 1008-1009 stereo 1977?
Joan Singer, piano.
   With: Passacaglia; Down a Country Lane; In Evening Air; The Cat
   and the Mouse; Four Piano Blues; Piano Sonata; Sentimental
   Melody; Two Children's Pieces; Piano Variations; Piano Fantasy.
   In: All the Piano Music.

D185. Unicorn RHS 383 stereo 1977; UN1-72017 stereo 1977.
Peter Dickinson, piano.
   With: In Evening Air; Poet's Song (E. E. Cummings); Gershwin,
   George. A Foggy Day in London Town. They All Laughed. I Got
   Rhythm; Carter, Elliott Cook. Three Poems of Robert Frost.
   Voyage; Thomson, Virgil. Two by Marianne Moore. Portrait of F.B.
   (Frances Blood).
   In: An American Anthology; [Songs & Piano Music].

Nonet for Strings

D186. Columbia M 32737 stereo 1974.
Columbia String Ensemble; the composer conducting.
   With: Sonata for Violin and Piano; Duo for Flute and Piano.
   In: Copland Performs and Conducts Copland.
   See also: B629, B983

Old American Songs, Sets I and II

D187. Argo ZRG 862 stereo 1977.
Robert Tear, tenor; Philip Ledger, piano.

D188. Colosseum 1008 mono 1951.
Randolph Symonette, bass-baritone.
   In: Americana.

D189. Columbia ML 2206 mono 1951.
William Warfield, baritone; the composer, piano.
   With: Dougherty, Celius. Five Sea Chanties. See also: B209

D190. Columbia ML 5897 mono 1963; MS 6497 stereo 1963.
William Warfield, baritone; Columbia Symphony Orchestra; the
   composer conducting.
   With: Concerto for Clarinet and String Orchestra.

D191. Golden Crest Records CRS 4187 stereo 1979 (The Boatman's Dance;
   Simple Gifts; Long Time Ago; I Bought Me a Cat).
   Antonio Perez, baritone; University of Kansas Symphonic Band;
   Robert E. Foster, conductor.
   With: Gounod, Charles François. Avant de Quitter Ces Lieux; Mozart,
   Johann Chrysostom Wolfgang Amadeus. Le Nozze di Figaro: Non Più
   Andrai; Massenet, Jules Émile Frédéric. Hérodiade: Vision
   Fugitive; Grainger, Percy Aldridge. Irish Tune from County Derry;
   Rossini, Gioacchino Antonio. Il Barbiere di Siviglia: Largo al
   Factotum; Boch, Jerry. Highlights from Fiddler on the Roof; Lake,
   Mayhew Lester. The Roosters Lay Eggs in Kansas.
   In: Music for the Baritone Voice and Wind Symphony.

D192. Her Magesty's Victrola DA-7038-9 78 rpm mono 1951.
    Peter Pears, tenor; Benjamin Britten, piano.

D193. Vogt CSRV 2600 stereo 1978.
    Crane Chorus; Crane Symphony Orchestra (New York State University
      College, Potsdam); the composer conducting.
    With: Fanfare for the Common Man; Canticle of Freedom; Letter
      from Home; Symphonic Ode; The Tender Land (Suite).

Orchestral Variations

D194. Columbia M 31714 stereo 1973.
    London Symphony Orchestra; the composer conducting.
    With: Symphonic Ode; Preamble for a Solemn Occasion.

D195. Louisville Philharmonic Society LOU-59-1 mono 1959.
    Louisville Orchestra; Robert Whitney, conductor.
    With: Letelier Llona, Alfonso. Ceculeo.

D196. Vanguard VRS 1067 mono 1967; VSD 2085 stereo 1967.
    Hartford Symphony Orchestra; Fritz Mahler, conductor.
    With: Fanfare for the Common Man; Bloch, Ernest. Poèms Juifs.

Our Town

D197. Columbia D3M 33720 stereo 1975 (previously released).
    London Symphony Orchestra; the composer conducting.
    With: Fanfare for the Common Man; Lincoln Portrait; Appalachian
      Spring; Billy the Kid; Rodeo; El Salón México; Dance Panels.
    In: A 75th Birthday Celebration.
    See also: B691

D198. Columbia MS 7375 stereo 1970.
    London Symphony Orchestra; the composer conducting.
    With: An Outdoor Overture; Two Pieces for String Orchestra; Quiet
      City.

D199. Concert Hall A2 78 rpm mono 1946 (arranged for piano).
    Leo Smit, piano.
    With: Piano Sonata.

D200. Concert Hall CHC-51 78 rpm mono 1947? (arranged for piano).
    Leo Smit, piano.
    With: Three Blues, from Four Piano Blues; Danzón Cubano (arranged
      for two pianos).

D201. Decca DL-7527 mono 1952.
    Little Orchestra Society; Thomas Scherman, conductor. See also: B1063

D202. Vanguard SRV 348 SD stereo 1975; VRS 1088 mono 1968; VSD 2115
      stereo 1968.
    Utah Symphony Orchestra; Maurice Abravanel, conductor.
    With: Lincoln Portrait; Quiet City; An Outdoor Overture.

D203. Varèse Sarabande VC 81098 mono 1980 (previously released 1948);
(Selections arranged for piano: Story of Our Town; Conversation
at the Soda Fountain; The Resting Place on the Hill).
Leo Smit, piano.
With: Concerto for Piano and Orchestra; Danzón Cubano; Four Piano
Blues; Ukelele Serenade; Rodeo (Hoe-Down); Nocturne.
In: Copland Conducts and Plays Copland.

D204. Vox 174 78 rpm mono 194-? (Story of Our Town, arranged for piano).
Andor Foldes, piano.
With: short works by Barber, Samuel; Bowles, Paul Frederick; Harris,
Roy; Piston, Walter; Schuman, William Howard; Sessions, Roger;
and Thomson, Virgil.
In: Contemporary American Piano Music.

An Outdoor Overture

D205. Boosey & Hawkes 2142 78 rpm mono 1948? (arranged for band).
Band of the Irish Guards.

D206. Columbia MS 7375 stereo 1970.
London Symphony Orchestra; the composer conducting.
With: Two Pieces for String Orchestra; Our Town; Quiet City.

D207. Deutsche Grammophon 2584 027 stereo 1971; Polydor 245006 stereo
196-?
Boston Pops Orchestra; Arthur Fiedler, conductor.
With: Shostakovich, Dmitriĭ Dmitrievich. Festive Overture;
Sullivan, Arthur Seymour, Sir. Overture Di Ballo; Goldmark,
Carl. Springtime Overture.
In: Fiedler's Favorite Overtures.

D208. Epic LC 3819 mono 1962; BC 1154 stereo 1962.
Cleveland Pops Orchestra; Louis Lane, conductor.
With: Menotti, Gian Carlo. Amahl and the Night Visitors; Riegger,
Wallingford. Dance Rhythms; Elwell, Herbert. The Happy Hypo-
crite; Shepherd, Arthur. Horizons (The Old Chisholm Trail).
In: Music for Young America.

D209. Vanguard SRV 348 SD stereo 1975; VRS 1088 mono 1962; VSD 2115
stereo 1968.
Utah Symphony Orchestra; Maurice Abravanel, conductor.
With: Lincoln Portrait; Quiet City; Our Town.

Passacaglia

D210. Columbia M2 35901 stereo 1979.
Leo Smit, piano.
With: The Cat and the Mouse; Piano Variations; In Evening Air;
Piano Sonata; Piano Fantasy; Four Piano Blues; Midsummer Noc-
turne; The Young Pioneers; Sunday Afternoon Music; Down a
Country Lane; Night Thoughts.
In: The Complete Music for Solo Piano.
See also: B982, B1157

D211. Delos DEL 25436 stereo 1976.
      Charles Fierro, piano.
      With: Piano Fantasy; <u>Night Thoughts</u>; Piano Variations.

D212. Disques Adès 14.002 stereo 1976.
      Walter Chodack, piano.
      With: Quartet for Piano and Strings; Gershwin, George. Preludes,
         Piano; Kalajian, Berge. Suite.
      In: Musique Americaine.

D213. Golden Age Recording GAR 1008-1009 stereo 1977?
      Joan Singer, piano.
      With: <u>Down a Country Lane</u>; <u>In Evening Air</u>; <u>The Cat and the Mouse</u>;
         Four Piano Blues; Piano Sonata; <u>Sentimental Melody</u>; Two Chil-
         dren's Pieces; Piano Variations; <u>Night Thoughts</u>; Piano Fantasy.
      In: All the Piano Music.

D214. Lyrichord LL 104 mono 1963.
      Webster Aitken, piano.
      With: Piano Variations; Piano Sonata.

D215. Orion ORS 7280 stereo 1972.
      Robert Silverman, piano.
      With: Piano Sonata; Four Piano Blues; <u>The Cat and the Mouse</u>.

D216. Walden 101 mono 1953.
      Webster Aitken, piano.
      With: Piano Variations; Piano Sonata.
      <u>See also</u>: B203, B795

<u>Piano Fantasy</u>

D217. Columbia M2 35901 stereo 1979.
      Leo Smit, piano.
      With: <u>The Cat and the Mouse</u>; Piano Variations; <u>In Evening Air</u>;
         Passacaglia; Piano Sonata; Four Piano Blues; <u>Midsummer Noc-
         turne</u>; <u>The Young Pioneers</u>; <u>Sunday Afternoon Music</u>; <u>Down a
         Country Lane</u>; <u>Night Thoughts</u>.
      In: The Complete Music for Solo Piano.
      <u>See also</u>: B982, B1157

D218. Columbia ML 5568 mono 1960; MS 6168 stereo 1960; Odyssey 32 16 0039
         mono 1967; 32 16 0040 stereo 1967.
      William Masselos, piano.
      With: Piano Variations.
      <u>See also</u>: B1178

D219. Delos DEL 25436 stereo 1976.
      Charles Fierro, piano.
      With: Passacaglia; <u>Night Thoughts</u>; Piano Variations.

D220. Golden Age Recording GAR 1008-1009 stereo 1977?
      Joan Singer, piano.
      With: Passacaglia; <u>Down a Country Lane</u>; <u>In Evening Air</u>; <u>The Cat
         and the Mouse</u>; Four Piano Blues; Piano Sonata; <u>Sentimental</u>

Melody; Two Children's Pieces; Piano Variations; Night Thoughts.
In: All the Piano Music.

D221. Unicorn RHS 323 stereo 1975.
Anthony Peebles, piano.
With: Bartók, Béla. Three Studies, Op.18; Dallapiccola, Luigi.
Musical Exercises for Annaliberia.
See also: B691

Piano Sonata

D222. Bis LP 52 stereo 1976.
Eva Knardahl, piano.
With: Sinding, Christian. Sonata, Piano, Op.91, B Minor.

D223. Columbia M2 35901 stereo 1978.
Leo Smit, piano.
With: The Cat and the Mouse; Piano Variations; In Evening Air;
Passacaglia; Piano Fantasy; Four Piano Blues; Midsummer Noc-
turne; The Young Pioneers; Sunday Afternoon Music; Down a
Country Lane; Night Thoughts.
In: The Complete Music for Solo Piano.
See also: B982, B1157

D224. Composers Recordings CRI 171 mono 1963.
Hilde Somer, piano.
With: Sonata for Violin and Piano; Vitebsk.
See also: B1112

D225. Concert Hall A2 78 rpm mono 1946.
Leo Smit, piano
With: Our Town (Suite, arranged for piano).

D226. Epic BC 1262 stereo 1963; LC 3862 mono 1963.
Leon Fleisher, piano.
With: Sessions, Roger. From My Diary; Kirchner, Leon. Sonata,
Piano; Rorem, Ned. Barcarolles.

D227. Golden Age Recording GAR 1008-1009 stereo 1977?
Joan Singer, piano.
With: Passacaglia; Down a Country Lane; In Evening Air; The Cat
and the Mouse; Four Piano Blues; Sentimental Melody; Two
Children's Pieces; Piano Variations; Night Thoughts.
In: All the Piano Music.

D228. Lyrichord LL 104 mono 1963.
Webster Aitken, piano.
With: Passacaglia; Piano Variations.

D229. New World Records NW 277 mono 1976 (previously recorded, RCA
Victor Vic 12-0681/3, 1947).
Leonard Bernstein, piano.
With: Piano Variations; Four Piano Blues; Danzón Cubano (arranged
for piano).
In: Works for Piano, 1926-1948.

D230. Orion ORS 7280 stereo 1972.
    Robert Silverman, piano.
    With: Passacaglia; Four Piano Blues; The Cat and the Mouse.

D231. RCA Camden CAL 214 mono 1952?
    Leonard Bernstein, piano.
    With: Ravel, Maurice. Concerto in G Major; Bernstein, Leonard.
     Anniversaries.

D232. RCA Victor DM-1278 78 rpm mono 1949.
    Leonard Bernstein, piano.
    With: Bernstein, Leonard. Anniversaries.

D233. Walden 101 mono 1953.
    Webster Aitken, piano.
    With: Passacaglia; Piano Variations.
    See also: B203, B795

Piano Variations

D234. Columbia M2 35901 stereo 1978.
    Leo Smit, piano.
    With: The Cat and the Mouse; In Evening Air; Passacaglia; Piano
     Sonata; Piano Fantasy; Four Piano Blues; Midsummer Nocturne;
     The Young Pioneers; Sunday Afternoon Music; Down a Country Lane;
     Night Thoughts.
    In: The Complete Music for Solo Piano.
    See also: B982, B1157

D235. Columbia ML 5568 mono 1960; MS 6168 stereo 1960.
    William Masselos, piano.
    With: Piano Fantasy.
    See also: B1178

D236. Columbia X-48 78 rpm mono 1935.
    The composer, piano.
    With: Two Pieces for Violin and Piano (Nocturne).

D237. Concert-Disc M-1217 mono 1960; 217 stereo 196--?
    Frank Glazer, piano.
    With: Shapero, Harold. Sonata, No.1, in D; Gottschalk, Louis
     Moreau. Le Bananier, Op.5; Dello Joio, Norman. Sonata No.3;
     Gershwin, George. Three Preludes.
    In: Frank Glazer Plays American Music. See also: B1178

D238. Delos DEL 25436 stereo 1976.
    Charles Fierro, piano.
    With: Piano Fantasy; Passacaglia; Night Thoughts.

D239. Dover Publications HCR 5265 mono 1966; HCR-ST 7014 stereo 1966;
    HCR-ST 7265 stereo 1966.
    Beveridge Webster, piano.
    With: Sessions, Roger. Sonata, Piano, No.2; Carter, Elliott Cook.
     Piano Sonata.
    In: Modern American Piano Music.

D240. Golden Age Recording GAR 1008-1009 stereo 1977?
    Joan Singer, piano.
    With: Passacaglia; Down a Country Lane; In Evening Air; The Cat
        and the Mouse; Four Piano Blues; Piano Sonata; Sentimental
        Melody; Two Children's Pieces; Night Thoughts; Piano Fantasy.
    In: All the Piano Music.

D241. Golden Crest CRSD-1, CRSTT-1 stereo 1977.
    Grant Johannesen, piano.
    With: Schumann, Robert Alexander. Six Intermezzi, Op.4; Debussy,
        Claude. Masques. L'Isle Joyeuse.
    In: Grant Johnson in Recital.

D242. Golden Crest CRS 4111 stereo 197-?
    Grant Johannesen, piano.
    With: Bergsma, William. Tangents; Dello Joio, Norman. Two Noc-
        turnes; Harris, Roy. American Ballads.

D243. Lyrichord LL 104 mono 1963.
    Webster Aitken, piano.
    With: Piano Sonata; Passacaglia.

D244. New World Records NW 277 mono 1976 (previously recorded, Columbia
        68320/D, 1945)
    Leo Smit, piano.
    With: Piano Sonata; Danzón Cubano; Four Piano Blues.
    In: Works for Piano, 1926-1948.

D245. Odyssey 32 16 0039 mono 1967; 32 16 0040 stereo 1967.
    William Masselos, piano.
    With: Piano Fantasy.

D246. Time-Life Records STL 570 stereo 1979 (previously recorded).
    [Various ensembles and conductors].
    With: Fanfare for the Common Man; Appalachian Spring; Vitebsk;
        Dance Symphony; The Tender Land; Billy the Kid; Rodeo; El Salón
        México; Quiet City; Symphony No.3.
    In: Copland.

D247. Vox SVBX 5303 stereo 1976.
    Roger Shields, piano.
    In: Piano Music in America, Vol.2: 1900-1945.

D248. Walden 101 mono 1953.
    Webster Aitken, piano.
    With: Passacaglia; Piano Sonata.
    See also: B203, B795

Preamble for a Solemn Occasion

D249. Columbia M 31714 stereo 1973.
    London Symphony Orchestra; the composer conducting.
    With: Symphonic Ode; Orchestral Variations.

Quartet for Piano and Strings

D250. Argo ZRG 794 stereo 197-?
    Cardiff Festival Ensemble.
    With: Ives, Charles. Trio for Piano and Strings.

D251. CBS Masterworks 32 11 0041 mono 1967; 32 11 0042 stereo 1967;
        Columbia M 30376 stereo 1970.
    Juilliard String Quartet; the composer, piano.
    With: Sextet for Clarinet, Piano, and String Quartet; Vitebsk.

D252. Columbia ML 4421 mono 1952; ML 4221 stereo 196-?
    New York Quartet.
    With: Concerto for Clarinet and String Orchestra. See also: B209

D253. Disques Adès 14.002 stereo 1976.
    Trio à Cordes de Paris; Walter Chodack, piano.
    With: Passacaglia; Gershwin, George. Preludes, Piano; Kalajian,
        Berge. Suite, Piano.

Quiet City

D254. Argo ZRG 845 stereo 1976.
    Michael Laird, trumpet; Celia Nicklin, cor anglais; Academy of St.
        Martin-in-the-Fields; Neville Marriner, conductor.
    With: Barber, Samuel. Quartet, Strings, Op.11, B Minor. Adagio;
        Ives, Charles. Symphony No.13; Cowell, Henry. Hymn and Fuguing
        Tune; Creston, Paul. A Rumor.

D255. Artist 100 mono 1950; JS-13 78 rmp mono 1949; Everest 6118 mono
        195-?; 3118 stereo 195-?
    Janssen Symphony of Los Angeles; Werner Janssen, conductor.
    With: Cowell, Henry. Ancient Desert Drone; Ives, Charles. Three
        Places in New England. The Housatonic at Stockbridge; Gilbert,
        Henry Franklin Belknap. The Dance in the Place Congo.
    In: Four American Landscapes.

D256. Cambridge CRS 2823 stereo 1970.
    Armando Ghitalla, trumpet; Chamber Orchestra of Copenhagen; John
        Moriarty, conductor.
    With: Anonymous Suite in D for Trumpet and Orchestra; Haydn,
        Michael. Trumpet Concerto (Sinfonia) in C Major, P.34; Selig,
        Robert. Mirage.
    In: Armando Ghitalla, Trumpet [Vol.2].

D257. Capitol P-8245 mono 195-?
    Harry Glantz, trumpet; Albert Goltzer, English horn; Concert Arts
        Orchestra; Vladimir Golschmann, conductor.
    With: Barber, Samuel. Adagio for String Orchestra, Op.11, B
        Minor; Diamond, David Leo. Rounds for String Orchestra; Creston,
        Paul. Two Choric Dances, Op.17b.
    In: Contemporary American Music.
    See also: B210

D258. Columbia MS 7375 stereo 1970.
    William Lang, trumpet; Michael Winfield, English horn; London
      Symphony Orchestra; the composer conducting.
    With: An Outdoor Overture; Our Town; Two Pieces for String
      Orchestra.

D259. Eastman Rochester Archives ERA 1001 stereo 1975?; Mercury MG 50076
    mono 1956 (originally issued under serial no. MG 40003).
    Sidney Mear, trumpet; Richard Swingley, English horn; Eastman-
      Rochester Symphony Orchestra; Howard Hanson, conductor.
    With: Barlow, Wayne. The Winter's Passed; Rogers, Bernard. So-
      liloquy for Flute and Strings; Kennan, Kent Wheeler. Night
      Soliloquy, for Flute and Strings; Keller, Homer. Serenade for
      Clarinet and Strings; Hanson, Howard. Serenade for Flute,
      Strings, and Harp. Pastorale for Oboe, Strings, and Harp.
    In: Americana for Solo Winds and String Orchestra.

D260. Mercury MG 50421 mono 194-?; SR 90421 stereo 1965.
    Sidney Mear, trumpet; Richard Swingley, English horn; Eastman-
      Rochester Symphony Orchestra; Howard Hanson, conductor.
    With: Symphony No.3; Harris, Roy. Symphony No.3.

D261. Time-Life Records STL 570 stereo 1979 (previously recorded).
    [Various ensembles and conductors].
    With: Fanfare for the Common Man; Appalachian Spring; Dance
      Symphony; Vitebsk; Piano Variations; The Tender Land; Billy the
      Kid; Rodeo; El Salón México; Symphony No.3.
    In: Copland.

D262. Turnabout TV-S 34398 stereo 1970.
    Buffalo Philharmonic Orchestra; Lukas Foss, conductor.
    With: Ruggles, Carl. Men and Mountains; Ives, Charles. From the
      Steeples and the Mountains; Mason, Daniel Gregory. Quartet,
      Strings, Op.19, G Minor.
    See also: B766

D263. Vanguard SRV 348 SD stereo 1975; VRS 1088 mono 1962; VSD 2115
    stereo 1968.
    Utah Symphony Orchestra; Maurice Abravanel, conductor.
    With: Lincoln Portrait; An Outdoor Overture; Our Town.

The Red Pony (Orchestral Suite)

D264. Columbia M 33586 stereo 1975.
    New Philharmonia Orchestra; the composer conducting.
    With: Music for Movies; John Henry; Letter from Home; Down a
      Country Lane.
    In: Copland Conducts Copland.

D265. Columbia ML 5983 mono 1964; MS 6583 stereo 1964; Odyssey Y 31016
    stereo 1972.
    St. Louis Symphony Orchestra; André Previn, conductor.
    With: Britten, Benjamin. Sinfonia da Requiem, Op.20.
    See also: B426

D266. Decca DCM 3207 mono 1962; DL 9616 mono 195-? (Children's Suite).
      Little Orchestra Society; Thomas Scherman, conductor.
      With: Thomson, Virgil. Louisiana Story. Acadian Songs and Dances.

Rodeo (Four Dance Episodes, unless otherwise noted)

D267. Boosey and Hawkes S-2095 mono 1948 (Hoe-Down, arranged for string
         orchestra).
      New Concert String Ensemble; Jay Wilber, conductor.

D268. CBS Records MY 36727 stereo 1981 (previously released, Columbia
         MS 6175).
      New York Philharmonic; Leonard Bernstein, conductor.
      With: Billy the Kid.

D269. Capitol L-8198 mono 195-?; P-8196 mono 195-?
      Ballet Theatre Orchestra; Joseph Levine, conductor.

D270. Capitol SP 8702 stereo 1969.
      Concert Arts Orchestra; Robert Irving.
      With: Appalachian Spring; Bernstein, Leonard. Fancy Free.
      In: Great American Ballets.

D271. Columbia D3M 33720 stereo 1975 (previously released).
      London Symphony Orchestra; the composer conducting.
      With: Fanfare for the Common Man; Lincoln Portrait; Billy the Kid;
         Appalachian Spring; Our Town; El Salón México; Dance Panels.
      In: A 75th Birthday Celebration.
      See also: B691

D272. Columbia M 30114 stereo 1971.
      London Symphony Orchestra; the composer conducting.
      With: Billy the Kid.

D273. Columbia M 31823 stereo 1973; ML 5575 mono 1960; MS 6175 stereo
         1960.
      New York Philharmonic; Leonard Bernstein, conductor.
      With: Billy the Kid.

D274. Columbia MG 30071 stereo 1970.
      New York Philharmonic; Leonard Bernstein, conductor.
      With: Billy the Kid; Appalachian Spring; El Salón México; Music
         for the Theatre.
      In: The Copland Album.

D275. Columbia MS 7521 stereo 1970 (Hoe-Down).
      London Symphony Orchestra; the composer conducting.
      With: Fanfare for the Common Man; El Salón México; Billy the Kid
         (Celebration); Appalachian Spring.
      In: Copland's Greatest Hits.

D276. Concert Hall CHC-58 mono 1951 (Hoe-Down, arranged for violin and
         piano).
      Louis Kaufman, violin; Annette Kaufman, piano.

With: Two Pieces for Violin and Piano; short works by Everett B. Helm, William Grant Still, Harold Triggs, and Robert G. McBride.

D277. Concert Hall H-1640 mono 195-? (Hoe-Down).
Louis Kaufman, violin; Annette Kaufman, piano.
With: Two Pieces for Violin and Piano; short works by John Alden Carpenter, Robert Guyn McBride, and William Grant Still.

D278. Mercury MG 50172 mono 1958; SR 90172 stereo 1958.
Minneapolis Symphony Orchestra; Antal Dorati, conductor.
With: El Salón México.

D279. Music Guild MS 164 stereo 1970; Westminster 8170 mono 1970; WST 14058 stereo 196-?
Utah Symphony Orchestra; Maurice Abravanel, conductor.
With: Billy the Kid.

D280. National Geographic Society 07819 stereo 1979.
National Geographic Society Orchestra; Dennis Burnside, conductor.
With: Appalachian Spring.

D281. RCA Victor LM 2195 mono 1958; LSC 2195 stereo 1958; AGL1-1335 stereo 197-?
Morton Gould Orchestra; Morton Gould, conductor.

D282. RCA Red Seal ARL1-0109 stereo 1973 (Hoe-Down).
Boston Pops Orchestra; Arthur Fiedler, conductor.
With: Billy the Kid (Street in a Frontier Town; Celebration);
Fanfare for the Common Man; El Salón México; Appalachian Spring.
In: Copland's Greatest Hits.

D283. RCA Red Seal ARL1-2862 stereo 1975.
Dallas Symphony Orchestra; Eduardo Mata, conductor.
With: El Salón México; Appalachian Spring.

D284. RCA Red Seal CHL3-3270 stereo 1979 (previously released).
[Various orchestras and conductors].
With: Kay, Hershy. Stars and Stripes; Gould, Morton. Fall River Legend; Rodgers, Richard. Slaughter on Tenth Avenue; Bernstein, Leonard. Fancy Free; Gould, Morton. Interplay; Ives, Charles. Variations on America; Gottschalk, Louis Moreau. Cakewalk (Suite) arranged by Hershy Kay; Appalachian Spring.
In: The Ballet Box; Favorite American Ballets.

D285. RCA Victor DM-1214 78 rpm mono 1948; LMX-32 mono 1950; WDM-1214 45 rpm 1950.
Dallas Symphony Orchestra; Antal Dorati, conductor.
With: Billy the Kid (Waltz).

D286. Seraphim S60198 stereo 197-?
Concert Arts Orchestra; Robert Irving, conductor.
With: Appalachian Spring.

D287. Telarc DG-10078 stereo 1982.
Atlanta Symphony Orchestra; Louis Lane, conductor.
With: Fanfare for the Common Man; Appalachian Spring.

D288. Time-Life Records STL 570 stereo 1979 (previously recorded).
[Various ensembles and conductors].
   With: Fanfare for the Common Man; Appalachian Spring; Dance
      Symphony; Vitebsk; Piano Variations; The Tender Land (Suite);
      Billy the Kid; El Salón México; Quiet City; Symphony No.3.
   In: Copland.

D289. Turnabout TV 34169 stereo 1967.
   Dallas Symphony Orchestra; Donald Johanos, conductor.
   With: Fanfare for the Common Man; Billy the Kid.

D290. Varèse Sarabande VC 81098 mono 1980 (Hoe-Down) (previously re-
      leased).
   Louis Kaufman, violin; Annette Kaufman, piano.
   With: Concerto for Piano and Orchestra; Danzón Cubano; Our Town;
      Four Piano Blues; Ukelele Serenade; Nocturne.
   In: Copland Conducts and Plays Copland.

D291. Westminster XWN 18840 mono 1958.
   Utah Symphony Orchestra; Maurice Abravanel, conductor.
   With: El Salón México; Billy the Kid.

El Salón México

D292. Angel S-37314 stereo 1978.
   Utah Symphony Orchestra; Maurice Abravanel, conductor.
   With: Grofé, Ferde. Grand Canyon Suite.

D293. Classics for CFP 40240 stereo 1976?
   London Symphony Orchestra; John Pritchard, conductor.
   With: Gershwin, George. An American in Paris. Porgy and Bess.

D294. Columbia CL 920 mono 1956.
   Columbia Symphony Orchestra; Leonard Bernstein, conductor.
   With: Bernstein, Leonard. Fancy Free; Milhaud, Darius. La
      Création du Monde.

D295. Columbia D3M 33720 stereo 1975.
   New Philharmonia Orchestra; the composer conducting.
   With: Fanfare for the Common Man; Lincoln Portrait; Appalachian
      Spring; Billy the Kid; Rodeo; Our Town; Dance Panels.
   In: A 75th Birthday Celebration.
   See also: B691

D296. Columbia M 33269 stereo 1975.
   New Philharmonia Orchestra; the composer conducting.
   With: Danzón Cubano; Three Latin American Sketches; Dance Panels.

D297. Columbia MG 30071 stereo 1970.
   New York Philharmonic; Leonard Bernstein, conductor.
   With: Rodeo; Billy the Kid; Appalachian Spring; Music for the
      Theatre (Dance).
   In: The Copland Album.

D298. Columbia ML 2203 mono 1951.
Columbia Symphony Orchestra; Leonard Bernstein, conductor.
With: Milhaud, Darius. La Création du Monde.

D299. Columbia ML 5755 mono 1961; MS 6355 stereo 1961.
New York Philharmonic; Leonard Bernstein, conductor.
With: Appalachian Spring; Music for the Theatre (Dance).

D300. Columbia ML 5841 mono 1963; MS 6441 stereo 1963.
New York Philharmonic; Leonard Bernstein, conductor.
With: Strauss, Richard. Till Eulenspiegel's Merry Pranks, Op.28;
Debussy, Claude. Afternoon of a Faun; Tchaikovsky, Peter Ilich.
Six Dances from the Nutcracker Suite.
In: Leonard Bernstein Conducts for Young People.

D301. Columbia MS 7521 stereo 1970.
New York Philharmonic; Leonard Bernstein, conductor.
With: Fanfare for the Common Man; Billy the Kid (Celebration);
Rodeo (Hoe-Down); Appalachian Spring.
In: Copland's Greatest Hits.

D302. M-G-M 30016 78 rpm mono 1947?
M-G-M Symphony Orchestra; Macklin Marrow, conductor.

D303. Mercury MG 50172 mono 1958; SR 90172 stereo 1958.
Minneapolis Symphony Orchestra; Antal Dorati, conductor.
With: Rodeo; Danzón Cubano.

D304. Music Guild MS 167 stereo 1970.
Utah Symphony Orchestra; Maurice Abravanel, conductor.
With: Gershwin, George. Porgy and Bess (Suite).

D305. RCA Red Seal ARL1-0109 stereo 1973.
Boston Pops Orchestra; Arthur Fiedler, conductor.
With: Fanfare for the Common Man; Billy the Kid (Street in a
Frontier Town. Celebration); Rodeo (Hoe-Down); Appalachian
Spring.
In: Copland's Greatest Hits.

D306. RCA Red Seal ARL1-2862 stereo 1978.
Dallas Symphony Orchestra; Eduardo Mata, conductor.
With: Appalachian Spring; Rodeo.

D307. RCA Red Seal LCT 1134 mono 195-?
Boston Symphony Orchestra; Serge Koussevitzky, conductor.
With: Appalachian Spring.

D308. RCA Red Seal LSC 3303 stereo 1972; RCA Victor LM 1928 mono 1955.
Boston Pops Orchestra; Arthur Fiedler, conductor.
With: Grofé, Ferde. Grand Canyon Suite.

D309. RCA Victor 28-0419 78 rpm mono 1947; 52-0065 45 rpm mono 1950?
Al Goodman Orchestra; Al Goodman, conductor.

D310. RCA Victor DM-546 78 rpm mono 1939.
       Boston Symphony Orchestra; Serge Koussevitzky, conductor.

D311. RCA Victrola AVM1-1739 mono 1976 (previously recorded 1938).
       Boston Symphony Orchestra; Serge Koussevitzky, conductor.
       With: Appalachian Spring; Lincoln Portrait.

D312. Time-Life Records STL 570 stereo 1979 (previously recorded).
       [Various ensembles and conductors].
       With: Fanfare for the Common Man; Appalachian Spring: Vitebsk;
        Dance Symphony; Piano Variations; The Tender Land (Suite);
        Billy the Kid; Rodeo; Quiet City; Symphony No.3.
       In: Copland.

D313. Vanguard VRS-439 mono 1953.
       Vienna State Opera Orchestra; Franz Litschauer, conductor.
       With: Appalachian Spring.

D314. Westminster 14063 stereo 196-?
       Utah Symphony Orchestra; Maurice Abravanel, conductor.
       With: Gershwin, George. Porgy and Bess.

D315. Westminster WL 5286 mono 1954; WL 18284 mono 1956; WST 14284
        stereo 1968.
       National Symphony Orchestra of Washington, D.C.; Howard Mitchell,
        conductor.
       With: Appalachian Spring; Fanfare for the Common Man; Billy the
        Kid; El Salón México.

D316. Westminster XWN 18840 mono 1958.
       Utah Symphony Orchestra; Maurice Abravanel, conductor.
       With: Rodeo; Billy the Kid.

The Second Hurricane

D317. Columbia ML 5581 mono 1960; MS 6181 stereo 1960.
       Soloists and chorus of the High School of Music and Art, New York
        City; New York Philharmonic; Leonard Bernstein, narrator and
        conductor.

D318. New World Records NW 241 stereo 1978 (Two Willow Hill. Sextet.
        Jeff's Song. Queenie's Song) (previously recorded).
       [Various performers and conductors].
       With: Herbert, Victor. Natoma. No Country Can My Own Outvie;
        Taylor, Deems. The King's Henchman; Gruenberg, Louis. The
        Emperor Jones; Hanson, Howard. Merry Mount; Menotti, Gian
        Carlo. The Consul; The Tender Land.
       In: Toward an American Opera, 1911-1954.

Sentimental Melody

D319. Golden Age Recording GAR 1008-1009 stereo 1977?
       Joan Singer, piano.

With: Passacaglia; <u>Down a Country Lane</u>; <u>In Evening Air</u>; <u>The Cat and the Mouse</u>; Four Piano Blues; Piano Sonata; Two Children's Pieces; Piano Variations; <u>Night Thoughts</u>; Piano Fantasy.
In: All the Piano Music.

Sextet for String Quartet, Clarinet, and Piano

D320. CBS Masterworks 32 11 0041 mono 1967; 32 11 0042 stereo 1967.
Harold Wright, clarinet; the composer, piano; Juilliard String Quartet.
With: Quartet for Piano and Strings.

D321. Columbia M 30376 stereo 1970.
Harold Wright, clarinet; the composer, piano; Juilliard String Quartet.
With: Quartet for Piano and Strings; Vitebsk.

D322. Columbia ML 4492 mono 1953.
David Oppenheim, clarinet; Leonid Hambro, piano; Juilliard String Quartet.
With: Kohs, Ellis B. Chamber Concerto for Viola and String Nonet.
See also: B679

Short Symphony (No.2)

D323. Columbia MS 7223 stereo 1969.
London Symphony Orchestra; the composer conducting.
With: <u>Dance Symphony</u>.
See also: B496

Sonata for Violin and Piano

D324. Allegro AL 33 mono 195-?; LEG 9001 mono 1964.
Fredell Lack, violin; Leonid Hambro, piano.
With: Hindemith, Paul. Sonata, Violin and Piano, Op.11, No.2, D Major.

D325. Columbia M 32737 stereo 1974.
Isaac Stern, violin; the composer, piano.
With: Duo for Flute and Piano; Nonet for Strings.
In: Copland Performs and Conducts Copland.
See also: B629, B983

D326. Composers Recordings CRI 171 mono 1963.
Carroll Glenn, violin; Hilde Somer, piano.
With: Piano Sonata; <u>Vitebsk</u>. See also: B1112

D327. Concert Hall C-10 78 rpm mono 1949.
Louis Kaufman, violin; the composer, piano.
With: Two Pieces for Violin and Piano (Nocturne).

D328. Crystal Records S-631 stereo 1970.
Myron Sandler, violin; Lowndes Maury, piano.

With: Maury, Lowndes. <u>Sonata in Memory of the Korean War Dead</u>;
Ives, Charles Edward. Sonata, Violin and Piano, No.2.

D329. Decca DL-8503 mono 195-?
Joseph Fuchs, violin; Leo Smit, piano.
With: Stravinsky, Igor. Duo Concertant for Violin and Piano.

D330. Desto DC 6439 stereo 1975.
Jaime Laredo, violin; Ann Schein, piano.
With: Ives, Charles Edward. Sonata, Violin and Piano, No.4;
Blinkerd, Gordon W. Sonata, Violin and Piano.

D331. RCA Victor LM 6092 mono 1959 (Lento).
Yehudi Menuhin, violin; Marcel Gazelle, piano.
With: Bartok, Béla. <u>Improvisations on Hungarian Peasant Songs</u>;
Berg, Alban. <u>Au Leukon. Nun Ich der Riesen Stärksten</u>; Bliss,
Arthur. <u>Conversations</u>; Dallapiccola, Luigi. Geothe-Lieder;
Debussy, Claude. <u>Cloches à Travers les Feuilles. Ballade que
Feit Villon à la Requeste de Sa Mère pour Prier Nostre-Dame</u>;
Falla, Manuel de. <u>Montañesa</u>; Hindemith, Paul. <u>Stilling Mariä mit
dem Auferstandenen</u>; Janacek, Leos. <u>Diary of One Who Vanished</u>;
Milhaud, Darius. Très Lent, from String Quartet No.6; Rawsthorne,
Alan. Quartet for Clarinet, Violin, Viola, and Cello (Poco Len-
to); Reger, Max. String Trio in A Minor (Larghetto); Roussel,
Albert Charles Paul. Trio for Violin, Viola, and Cello (Allegro
Moderato); Rubbra, Edmund. <u>Missa Cantuariensis</u>; Satie, Erik.
Trois Pièces Montrées; Schönberg, Arnold. String Quartet in F
Sharp Minor (Mässig). Serenade (March); Shostakovich, Dmitrii.
String Quartet No.2 (Valse); Skriabin, Aleksandr Nikolaevich.
Prelude. <u>Étrangeté</u>; Strauss, Richard. <u>Blindenklage</u>; Stravinsky,
Igor. Trois Pièces pour Quatuor à Cordes: No.1. <u>L'Histoire du
Soldat (Marche Royale)</u>.
In: History of Music in Sound.

<u>Song (E. E. Cummings)</u>

D332. New World Records NW 243 stereo 1977.
Bethany Beardslee, soprano; Robert Helps, piano.
With: Chanler, Theodore. <u>The Children</u>; Thomas Logge. <u>These, My
Ophelia</u>; Bowles, Paul Frederic. <u>Once a Lady Was Here. Song of an
Old Woman</u>; Duke, John Woods. <u>Poems by Edwin Arlington Robinson</u>;
Citkowitz, Israel. Five Songs from Chamber Music; Sessions,
Roger. <u>On the Beach at Fontana</u>; Barber, Samuel. <u>Sure on This
Shining Night</u>; Helps, Robert. <u>The Running Sun</u>.
In: But Yesterday Is Not Today.

D333. Unicorn RHS 383 stereo 1977; UN1-72017 stereo 1977.
Meriel Dickinson, mezzo-soprano; Peter Dickinson, piano.
With: Gershwin, George. <u>I Got Rhythm. A Foggy Day in London Town.
They All Laughed</u>; Carter, Elliott Cook. <u>Three Poems of Robert
Frost. Voyage</u>; Thomson, Virgil. <u>Two by Marianne Moore. Portrait
of F.B. (Frances Blood); In Evening Air; Night Thoughts</u>.
In: An American Anthology; [Songs & Piano Music].

Statements

D334. CBS Masterworks 32 11 0001 mono 1966; 32 11 0002 stereo 1966;
    Columbia M 30374 stereo 1970.
    London Symphony Orchestra; the composer conducting.
    With: Music for a Great City.
    See also: B753

D335. Everest LPBR 6015 mono 1958; SDBR 3015 stereo 197-?
    London Symphony Orchestra; the composer conducting.
    With: Billy the Kid.

D336. RCA Victor DM 1333 78 rpm mono 1950; WDM-1333 45 rpm mono 1950?
    (No.5: Jingo).
    RCA Victor Symphony Orchestra; Leonard Bernstein, conductor.
    With: Billy the Kid.

Symphonic Ode

D337. Columbia M 31714 stereo 1973.
    London Symphony Orchestra; the composer conducting.
    With: Preamble for a Solomn Occasion; Orchestral Variations.

D338. Vogt CSRV 2600 stereo 1978.
    Crane Symphony Orchestra (New York State University College,
    Potsdam); the composer conducting.
    With: Fanfare for the Common Man; Canticle of Freedom; Letter
    from Home; Old American Songs, Sets I and II; The Tender Land.

Symphony for Organ and Orchestra

D339. Columbia MS 7058 stereo 1968.
    E. Power Biggs, organ; New York Philharmonic; Leonard Bernstein,
    conductor.
    With: Bernstein, Leonard. Symposium After Plato.

The Tender Land

D340. Columbia ML 6214 mono 1966; MS 6814 stereo 1966 (the opera,
    abridged).
    Joy Clements, soprano; Claramae Turner, mezzo-soprano; Richard
    Cassilly, tenor; Richard Fredericks, baritone; Norman Treigle,
    bass-baritone; Choral Art Society; New York Philharmonic; the
    composer conducting. See also: B495

D341. New World Records NW 241 stereo 1978 (It Promises to be a Fine
    Night; The Promise of Living) (previously recorded).
    [Various performers and conductors].
    With: The Second Hurricane; Herbert, Victor. Natoma. No Country
    Can My Own Outvie; Taylor, Deems. The King's Henchman; Hanson,
    Howard. Merry Mount; Gruenberg, Louis. The Emperor Jones;
    Menotti, Gian Carlo. The Consul.
    In: Toward an American Opera, 1911-1954.

D342. RCA Victor LM 2401 mono 1960; LSC 2401 stereo 1960 (orchestral
      suite).
      Boston Symphony Orchestra; the composer conducting.
      With: Appalachian Spring.

D343. Time-Life Records STL 570 stereo 1979 (previously recorded).
      [Various ensembles and conductors].
      With: Fanfare for the Common Man; Appalachian Spring; Dance
      Symphony; Vitebsk; Piano Variations; Billy the Kid; Rodeo; El
      Salón México; Quiet City; Symphony No.3.
      In: Copland.

D344. Vogt CSRV 2600 stereo 1978.
      Crane Chorus; Crane Symphony Orchestra (New York State University
      College, Potsdam); the composer conducting.
      With: Fanfare for the Common Man; Canticle of Freedom; Letter
      from Home; Old American Songs, Sets I and II; Symphonic Ode.

Third Symphony

D345. CBS Records 6181 stereo 1979?
      New York Philharmonic Orchestra; Leonard Bernstein, conductor.
      With: Harris, Roy. Symphony No.3.

D346. Columbia M 35113 stereo 1978.
      Philharmonia Orchestra; the composer conducting.

D347. Columbia ML 6354 mono 1967; MS 6954 stereo 1967.
      New York Philharmonic; Leonard Bernstein, conductor.
      See also: B753

D348. Everest LPBR 6018 mono 1959; SDBR 3018 stereo 196-?
      London Symphony Orchestra; the composer conducting.
      See also: B754

D349. Mercury MG 50018 mono 1953; MG 50421 mono 194-?; SR 90421 stereo
      1965.
      Minneapolis Symphony Orchestra; Antal Dorati, conductor.
      With: Quiet City; Harris, Roy. Symphony No.3.
      See also: B203, B795

D350. Time-Life Records STL 570 stereo 1979 (previously recorded).
      [Various ensembles and conductors].
      With: Fanfare for the Common Man; Appalachian Spring; Dance
      Symphony; Vitebsk; Piano Variations; The Tender Land; Billy the
      Kid; Rodeo; El Salón México; Quiet City.
      In: Copland.

Three Latin American Sketches

D351. Columbia M 33269 stereo 1975.
      New Philharmonia Orchestra; the composer conducting.
      With: Danzón Cubano; El Salón México; Dance Panels.
      See also: B558, B624

Twelve Poems of Emily Dickinson

D352. CBS Masterworks 32 11 0017 mono 1967; 32 11 0018 stereo 1967;
        Columbia M 30375 stereo 1970.
        Adele Addison, soprano; the composer, piano.
        With: In the Beginning; Las Agachadas; Lark.

D353. Columbia ML 5106 mono 1956.
        Martha Lipton, mezzo-soprano; the composer, piano.
        With: Weisgall, Hugo. The Stronger.

Two Children's Pieces

D354. Columbia M2 35901 stereo 1978.
        Leo Smit, piano.
        With: The Cat and the Mouse; Piano Variations; In Evening Air;
          Passacaglia; Piano Sonata; Piano Fantasy; Four Piano Blues;
          Midsummer Nocturne; Down a Country Lane; Night Thoughts.
        In: The Complete Music for Solo Piano.
        See also: B982, B1157

D355. Golden Age Recording GAR 1008-1009 stereo 1977.
        Joan Singer, piano.
        With: Passacaglia; Down a Country Lane; In Evening Air; The Cat
          and the Mouse; Four Piano Blues; Piano Sonata; Sentimental
          Melody; Piano Variations; Night Thoughts; Piano Fantasy.

Two Compositions for Chorus of Women's Voices

D356. Vox PL-7750 mono 1953.
        Vienna State Academy Chamber Chorus; Ferdinand Grossman, conductor.
        In: Concert of American Music.

Two Pieces for String Orchestra

D357. Columbia MS 7375 stereo 1970.
        London Symphony Orchestra; the composer conducting.
        With: An Outdoor Overture; Our Town; Quiet City.

D358. M-G-M Records M-G-M 3117 mono 195-?
        M-G-M String Orchestra; Izler Solomon, conductor.

Two Pieces for String Quartet

D359. Vox SVBX 5305 stereo 1974.
        Kohon Quartet.
        With: Mennin, Peter. String Quartet No.2; Piston, Walter. String
          Quartet No.5; Gershwin, George. Lullaby for String Quartet;
          Thomson, Virgil. String Quartet No.2; Ives, Charles. Scherzo for
          Two Violins, Viola, and Cello; Schuman, William Howard. String
          Quartet No.3; Sessions, Roger. Second String Quartet; Hanson,
          Howard. Quartet in One Movement, Op.23.
        In: American String Quartets, Volume II: 1900-1950.

D360. Columbia 70092-D 78 rpm mono 1940.
    Dorian String Quartet.

Two Pieces for Violin and Piano

D361. Columbia X-48 78 rpm mono 1935 (Nocturne).
    Jacques Gordon, violin; the composer, piano.
    With: Piano Variations.

D362. Columbia X-68 78 rpm 1937 (Ukulele Serenade).
    Jacques Gordon, violin; the composer, piano.
    With: Vitebsk.

D363. Concert Hall C-10 78 rpm mono 1949 (Nocturne).
    Louis Kaufman, violin; the composer, piano.
    With: Sonata for Violin and Piano.

D364. Concert Hall CHC-58 mono 1951; H-1640 mono 195-?
    Louis Kaufman, violin; Annette Kaufman, piano.
    With: Rodeo (Hoe-Down); short works by various other composers.

D365. Orion ORS 74160 stereo 1974 (Ukulele Serenade).
    Diana Steiner, violin; David Berfield, piano.
    With: Creston, Paul. Suite for Violin and Piano, Op.18; Kodály,
    Zoltán. Adagio; Sarasate y Navascues, Pablo Martin Meliton de.
    Introduction et Tarantelle, Op.43; Suk, Josef. Four Pieces for
    Violin and Piano, Op.17; Engel, Carl. Sea-shell.
    In: Great Music for Violin Lovers.

D366. Varese Sarabande VC 81098 mono 1980 (previously released 1948).
    Louis Kaufman, violin; the composer, piano.
    With: Concerto for Piano and Orchestra; Danzón Cubano; Our Town;
    Four Piano Blues (No.1 and No.4); Rodeo (Hoe-Down).
    In: Copland Conducts and Plays Copland.

Vitebsk

D367. CBS Masterworks 32 11 0041 mono 1967; 32 11 0042 stereo 1967;
    Columbia M 30376 stereo 1970.
    Earl Carlyss, violin; Claus Adam, cello; the composer, piano.
    With: Quartet for Piano and Strings; Sextet.

D368. Columbia X-68 78 rpm mono 1937.
    Ivor Karman, violin; David Freed, cello; the composer, piano.
    With: Two Pieces for Violin and Piano (Ukulele Serenade).

D369. Composers Recordings CRI 171 mono 1963.
    Carroll Glenn, violin; Hilde Somer, piano; Charles McCracken,
    cello.
    With: Sonata for Violin and Piano; Piano Sonata.
    See also: B1112

D370. Decca DL 10126 mono 1966; DL 710126 stereo 1966.
    Nieuw Amsterdam Trio, consisting of Edith Mocsanyi, piano; John
        Pintavalle, violin; Heinrich Joachim, cello.
    With: Ives, Charles Edward. Trio, Piano and Strings; Bloch,
        Ernest. Nocturnes, Piano Trio.
    See also: B415

D371. Laurel LR 109 stereo 1979.
    Western Arts Trio, consisting of Brian Hanly, violin; David
        Tomatz, cello; Werner Rose, piano.
    With: Manziarly, Marcelle. Trilogue; Tcherepnine, Alexandre.
        Trio, Op.34, D Major; Turina, Joaquin. Trio, Piano, No.2.

D372. Oklahoma University Recordings No.1 mono 1953.
    University of Oklahoma Trio.
    With: Harris, Roy. Trio for Violin, Violoncello, and Piano;
        Kerr, Harrison. Trio for Violin, Violoncello, and Piano (revised
        version, 1949).
    In: 3 American Trios.

D373. RCA Victor LM 6167 mono 1966; LSC 6167 stereo 1966.
    Boston Symphony Chamber Players.
    With: Mozart, Johann Chrysostom Wolfgang Amadeus. Quartet in D,
        Flute and Strings, K.285. Quartet in F, Oboe and Strings, K.370;
        Brahms, Johannes. Quartet, C Minor, Piano and Strings, Op.60;
        Beethoven, Ludwig van. Serenade in D, Flute, Violin, and Viola,
        Op.25; Fine, Irving Gifford. Fantasia, String Trio; Carter,
        Elliott Cook. Woodwind Quintet (1948); Piston, Walter. Diverti-
        mento for 9 Instruments.
    In: The Boston Symphony Chamber Players.

D374. Time-Life Records STL 570 stereo 1979 (previously recorded).
    [Various ensembles and conductors].
    With: Fanfare for the Common Man; Appalachian Spring; Dance
        Symphony; Piano Variations; The Tender Land; Billy the Kid;
        Rodeo; El Salón México; Quiet City; Symphony No.3.
    In: Copland.

Vocalise

D375. Laurel Protone LP-14 stereo 1976 (arranged for flute and piano).
    Laila Padorr, flute; Anita Swearengin, piano.
    With: Duo for Flute and Piano; Dello Joio, Norman. The Developing
        Flutist (Suite); Piston, Walter. Sonata for Flute and Piano;
        Muczynski, Robert. 3 Preludes for Unaccompanied Flute.
    In: Music for Flute & Piano by Four Americans.

D376. New Music Quarterly Record 1211 78 rpm mono 1935?
    Ethel Luening, soprano; the composer, piano.

BIBLIOGRAPHY
BY COPLAND

B1. "Active Market in New Music Records." <u>Modern Music</u> 13 (January–February 1936): 45–47.
    Some of the most popular recent recordings are noted. Copland mentions various composers and their works in addition to the recording artists, but does not designate the recording labels and numbers. Critical comments are made about each of the recordings discussed. Copland feels "that the phonograph provides the acid test—a piece must 'have something' if it will withstand repeated playing."

B2. "The Aims of Music for Films." <u>New York Times</u>, March 10, 1940, XI, p.7:4.
    One of Hollywood's sayings is that a film score is good only when it does not draw attention to itself. Copland has composed the music for <u>Of Mice and Men</u> and does not like to think that all his work has gone unnoticed. His goal was "to strengthen and underline the emotional content of the entire picture."

B3. "The American Composer Gets a Break." <u>American Mercury</u> 34 (April 1935): 488–492.
    Copland examines the contemporary music scene in which many more contemporary American composers' works are being performed than in the past. In addition, music critics are not rejecting these contemporary works as they did during the past few decades. Also discussed are compositions of Copland's contemporaries, such as Roy Harris, Roger Sessions, Walter Piston, and Virgil Thomson.

B4. "The American Composer Today." <u>U.S.A.</u> (U.S. War Information Office) 2, no.10 (1945): 23–27.
    Copland comments on the status of American composers and how their status has increased during the past twenty years. During the first part of the twentieth century composers adopted musical idioms from Indian chants, spirituals, and jazz. These concepts were not satisfactory in general. American music in the 1940's is based on the styles of a number of American composers, such as Roger Sessions, Howard Hanson, Virgil Thomson, Samuel Barber,

Walter Piston, and Leonard Bernstein. Copland discusses major
contributions in orchestral music, opera, chamber music, ballet,
film, and radio music.

B5.   "America's Young Men of Music." Music and Musicians 2 (December
       1960): 11.

B6.   "America's Young Men of Promise." Modern Music 3 (March 1926):
       13-20.
          Seventeen young American composers are examined in this
       article. This is not a critical survey because none is over
       thirty-three years of age. These musicians are worthy of
       noting because their compositions are beginning to receive
       recognition. Among those mentioned are Howard Hanson, Randall
       Thompson, and Roger Sessions.

B7.   "Are My Ears on Wrong?" San Francisco Symphony Program Notes
       (February 1967): 6-7.

B8.   "The Art of Darius Milhaud." Saturday Review of Literature 31
       (June 26, 1948): 43.
          Copland reviews the Columbia album MM704 containing Milhaud's
       First Symphony and In Memoriam as well as the RCA Victor album
       DM1027 containing Protée--Symphonic Suite No.2. Copland feels
       that Milhaud has not been appreciated properly for his fine
       compositions. He states, "I continue to marvel at Milhaud's
       apparently inexhaustible productive capacity, at his stylistic
       consistency, at the sheer creative strength that the body of
       his work represents."

B9.   "At the Thought of Mozart." High Fidelity 6 (January 1956): 53.
          Copland admits that he and other composers are awed by
       Mozart's "works that seem so effortless and so close to
       perfection." This essay comments on the increased interest and
       respect that Mozart's compositions are receiving. Even atonal
       composers such as Schoenberg sometimes consider themselves
       disciples of Mozart.

B10.   "Benjamin Britten: The Rape of Lucretia." Music Library Associa-
       tion Notes 2nd Ser., v.4, no.2 (March 1947): 190-191.
          Copland reviews Britten's second opera and judges that it is
       better written than the first opera, Peter Grimes. Since
       Britten is only in his thirties, Copland expects that many more
       important works will be written in the future.

B11.   "A Businessman Who Wrote Music on Sundays." Music and Musicians
       9 (November 1960): 18.
          Charles Ives is the businessman who composed his music on the
       side. He has become an important contemporary composer in spite
       of the fact that he not a composer by profession.

B12.   "Carlos Chávez--Mexican Composer." New Republic 54 (May 2, 1928):
       322-323; In American Composers on American Music; a Symposium,
       edited by Henry Cowell, 102-106. New York: F. Ungar, 1962.
          Copland examines the music of the relatively unknown composer
       Chávez. His early musical training in Mexico and his subsequent

move to New York has given him a broad background on which to base his works. His Mexican ballet, The New Fire, incorporates Mexican Indian folk elements into his music. Although his compositions have limitations, "he is one of the few American musicians about whom we can say that he is more than a reflection of Europe."

B13.   "Claire Reis (1889-1978)." Musical Quarterly 64 (July 1978): 386-388.
      This eulogy for Reis cites her years of effort in bringing contemporary American music to the public. Copland reminisces about their friendship through the years. Her first efforts in promoting music centered about bringing concerts to New York settlement houses. Later she concentrated her efforts on small concerts for special groups as the League of Composers' chairman of the board. Her favorite cause was "the promotion and welfare of living composers."

B14.   "The Composer and His Critic." Perspectives of New Music 2, no.2 (1964): 22-23.
      This article originally appeared in Modern Music (May-June 1932). Copland suggests that music critics study the scores and music of contemporary composers if this is the field they are going to evaluate. A single hearing of a work at its premiere performance is hardly the best way to judge a composition's qualities. The ideal critic is one whose criticisms "are based upon a sound knowledge and comprehension of the music itself."

B15.   "Composer from Brooklyn." Magazine of Art 32 (September 1939): 522-523.
      This is a rather detailed article on Copland's beginnings in composition taken from his The New Music. His studies with Nadia Boulanger in France are recounted as well as his subsequent return to the United States. Some of his musical achievements are discussed, such as the RCA Victor Company award of $5,000. He received this for his Dance Symphony which consists of three movements from his ballet Grohg. Copland's latest works "embody the tendency toward an imposed simplicity." Billy the Kid and El Salón México are among these compositions. See also: B76

B16.   "Composer from Brooklyn: an Autobiographical Sketch." ASCAP Today 2, no.1 (1968): 4-8.
      This is an excerpt from The New Music. Copland recalls his early interest in becoming a composer and his educational studies in pursuing this dream. His studies with Nadia Boulanger in Paris produced several significant compositions, but it was not until he returned to New York in 1924 that he heard any of his own orchestrations. He reminisces about his difficulties in the beginning in regard to supporting himself. Fortunately he received a Guggenheim Fellowship to assist him in starting his career. See also: B76

B17.   "The Composer in America, 1923-1933." Modern Music 10 (January-
        February 1933): 87-92.
            "The decade 1923-33 definitely marks the influx of new music."
        In 1922 the International Composers' Guild was formed to present
        experimental contemporary works. Within two years the League of
        Composers was also formed. Publishers were reluctant to pub-
        lish too many scores by Americans, and there were few grants
        and competitions to provide economic assistance. The Guild and
        the League provided tremendous opportunities for modern American
        composers where there had been few before. Conductors such as
        Serge Koussevitzky had great influence in promoting the works of
        new composers such as Copland.

B18.   "Composers and Composing." Saturday Review 43 (August 27, 1960):
        33-35.
            This is an excerpt from Copland on Music in which Berlioz,
        Ravel, and Poulenc are discussed. Included also are some of
        Copland's own reactions to various aspects of music. For
        example, he states that "nothing pleases the composer so much
        as to have people disagree as to the movements of his piece
        that they like the best." See also: B24.

B19.   "The Composers Get Wise." Modern Music 18 (November-December
        1940): 18-21.
            Composers face economic difficulty and spend much of their
        time making money through other endeavors. This is changing
        as a new source of income has become available. Payment for
        performance rights is a new aspect of composer income in addition
        to the traditional commissions to write specific works and
        royalties from the sale of scores. ASCAP has been a collection
        agency for popular composers since 1914, but it is only recently
        that composers of serious music are demanding payment.

B20.   "The Composers of South America." Modern Music 19 (January-
        February 1942): 75-82.
            This is an overview of current composition efforts in various
        areas of South America including Argentina, Brazil, and Chile.
        Copland has been visiting composers there in an effort to bring
        contemporary American music to these countries as well as to
        learn more about their music. He is involved in bringing about
        better musical relations with these countries.

B21.   "Composer's Report on Music in South America." New York Times,
        December 21, 1947, II, p.9:3.
            After returning from a recent government cultural exchange
        tour in South America, Copland writes about his impressions of
        South American music. There is better name recognition of North
        American composers now than there was during his last visit six
        years ago. Copland conducted several concerts and gave forty-
        four talks on music during his visit.

B22.   "Contemporaries at Oxford, 1931." Modern Music 9 (November-
        December 1931): 17-23.
            The annual festival of the International Society for Contempo-
        rary Music was held in London recently. This year's program

featured the works of numerous young composers. This article
reviews some of the works performed and comments on the importance of the festival in regard to revolutionary and established
music.

B23. "The Contemporary Scene." <u>Saturday Review</u> 49 (June 25, 1966): 49.
This is an excerpt from a talk given in May regarding the
status of American composers in contemporary music.

B24. <u>Copland on Music</u>. 1960. Reprint. New York: Da Capo Press, 1976.
This is a collection of the author's articles written during
the years around 1930 to 1960. He addresses the American musical
scene in general and examines a number of young composers who
are becoming successful. Several reviews of works which he
critiqued are included along with an examination of contemporary
music.

B25. "Copland Salutes Boulanger." <u>New York Times</u>, September 11, 1977,
II, p.25:6.
Copland reminisces about his former teacher, Nadia Boulanger,
with whom he studied in the 1920's in France. He feels that
she had a tremendous influence on him and other well-known composers such as Virgil Thomson and Walter Piston because of her
interest in new ideas. When she was invited to perform in the
United States as an organ soloist in 1924, she encouraged
Copland to write a Symphony for Organ and Orchestra, which he
did. <u>See also</u>: W26

B26. "Copyright Revision and the U.S. Symphonic Composer." <u>ASCAP Today</u>
7, no.2 (1975): 9.
Copland, an ASCAP composer and member of the board, submitted
his proposal for revision of the U.S. Copyright Act of 1909 to
the U.S. House of Representatives Judiciary Subcommittee on June
3, 1975. He primarily addressed the problems of fair compensa-
tion for composers, citing the greater monetary benefits that
record companies and performers receive. Also, he noted that
the copyright protection in most places outside of the United
States is in effect at least fifty years after a composer's
death. He urged the Committee to extend the copyright term in
the United States.

B27. "The Creative Mind and the Interpretive Mind." In <u>Contemporary
Composers on Contemporary Music</u>, edited by Elliott Schwartz and
Barney Childs, 146-149. 1967. Reprint. New York: Da Capo Press,
1978.
This excerpt from Copland's book, <u>Music and Imagination</u>,
expresses the composer's view of his profession. One of the
questions he attempts to answer is, "Why is the creative impulse
never satisfied; why must one always begin anew?" <u>See also</u>: B65

B28. "Creativity in America." In <u>Proceedings of the American Academy of
Arts and Letters and the National Institute of Arts and Letters</u>.
Ser.2, no.3, p.33-40. New York: American Academy of Arts and
Letters, 1953.
Copland gave this address at the Blashfield Institute. He
feels that "the creative act affirms the individual, and gives

value to the individual." It is through creativity that people communicate in a different way. European countries have a tradition of respecting and preserving art, but the United States has an environment which is less accepting of artistic works. Copland would like to see increased support of the arts by the government so there would not be so much dependence upon private contributions.

B29. "Current Chronicle: United States: New York." Musical Quarterly 37 (July 1951): 394-396.
       The Juilliard String Quartet performed the New York premiere of William Schuman's String Quartet No.4 at a League of Composers' concert December 17, 1950. Copland reviews this work which he considers to be "one of Schuman's most mature works." Copland also suggests that Schuman is one of America's foremost contemporary composers.

B30. "Defends the Music of Mahler." New York Times, April 5, 1925, IX, p.6:1.
       In this letter to the editor Copland decries the music critics' assertion that "Gustav Mahler, as a composer, is hopeless." Copland agrees that some of the writers' criticisms are justified, but he defends the composer as a master of polyphonic writing and subtle changes.

B31. "The Essence Remained." New York Times, May 3, 1953, VII, p.7:1.
       Copland reviews Halsey Stevens' book The Life and Music of Béla Bartók. It is a thorough analysis of his work but not of his life. The book is well done, but it will appeal more to the professional than to the amateur musician.

B32. "Fauré Festival at Harvard." New York Times, November 25, 1945, II, p.4:5.
       The Harvard University Music Department will sponsor five free concerts at the end of November to celebrate the hundreth anniversary of Fauré's birth. He has not been popular outside of France, so Copland hopes that these concerts will acquaint listeners with the composer's works. Copland admires Fauré's compositions because he "knew how to extract an original essence from the most ordinary music materials."

B33. "Festival in Caracas." New York Times, December 26, 1954, II, p.9:6.
       A festival of music by Latin-American composers was recently celebrated in Caracas, Venezuela. The eight concerts were performed during the two and a half week festival. Prizes were awarded for the three best symphonic works.

B34. "Five Post-Romantics." Modern Music 18 (May-June 1941): 218-224.
       The five composers discussed are Richard Strauss, Gustav Mahler, Alexander Scriabine, Gabriel Fauré, and Jan Sibelius. Copland feels that these five were most important around 1910 because they used some of the techniques from the romantic period as well as new ideas. "Mahler gave most to the music of the future" in Copland's opinion. This article is from a chapter in Copland's Our New Music. See also: B84

B35. "Forecast and Review: Baden, Baden, 1927." Modern Music 5
      (November-December 1927): 31-34.
          Copland reviews the festival of Deutsche Kammermusik held in
      July. Four chamber operas were presented which proved to be the
      highlight of the festival. The music of well-established com-
      posers was presented as well as that of less-prominent and more
      radical composers.

B36. "From the '20's to the '40's and Beyond." Modern Music 20
      (January-February 1943): 78-82.
          Copland examines the influences of the last two decades and
      concludes "that we have come a particularly long way." One of
      the important improvements is that composers are receiving better
      economic support for their work. The government is becoming
      more aware of its role in the sponsorship of music through pro-
      grams to exchange music with other countries.

B37. "Gabriel Fauré, a Neglected Master." Musical Quarterly 10 (October
      1924): 573-586.
          Copland regards Fauré as the greatest living composer in France
      because he managed to incorporate modern trends in works that
      were based on the traditions of the past.

B38. "George Antheil." League of Composers' Review (Modern Music) 2,
      no.1 (January 1925): 26-28.
          Antheil's music and writings are examined in this article.
      Copland feels that Antheil is an "extremely talented young
      American composer."

B39. "The Gifted Listener." Christian Science Monitor, June 29, 1976,
      Home Forum, p.21:3; Saturday Review 35 (September 27, 1952): 41.
          This material is extracted from Copland's Music and Imagination.
      The article is written for the amateur listener and he suggests
      ways to improve listening skills. He discusses his interpreta-
      tion of the meaning of music. As a composer, Copland likes to
      think about the reaction his compositions will elicit from the
      amateur musician or listener. See also: B65

B40. "How the Composer Works." In The New Music Lover's Handbook,
      edited by Elie Siegmeister, 43-46. New York: Harvey House, 1973.
          This essay is the chapter "The Creative Process in Music" from
      Copland's What to Listen For in Music. Inspiration certainly
      plays a significant role in a composer's work, but some days
      Copland finds that he is more inspired than others. Copland
      feels that harmonies are so complex that one needs to use a
      piano to assist in the composition process. A composer starts
      with a musical idea and refines it. By changing the dynamics or
      the harmony, he can vary the theme. In addition, he can look for
      complimentary ideas to go with his musical theme as well as
      stretch out the idea and develop it. Copland's philosophy is
      that there must be "a sense of continuity from first note to last."
      See also: B108

B41. "In Memory of Marc Blitzstein (1905-1964)." Perspectives of New
      Music 2, no.2 (1964): 6-7.

This eulogy for Blitzstein describes his great attachment to the theater. His works for the stage, such as <u>The Cradle Will Rock,</u> used American idioms to give the music an American sound. "Most important of all, he was the first American composer to invent a vernacular musical idiom that sounded convincing when heard from the lips of the man-in-the-street."

B42. "An Indictment of the Fourth B." <u>New York Times</u>, September 21, 1952, VI, p.18; <u>Music Journal</u> 10 (November 1952): 13; <u>Music Journal</u> 22 (March 1964): 29.
       This material is reprinted from Copland's <u>Music and Imagination</u>. The major symphony orchestras present the same familiar concert works year after year. Copland decries this practice. Not only does he feel that audiences must be bored with it, but he asserts that there is no learning or intellectual stimulation to give life to the concert repertoire. Copland proposes that more contemporary music be performed. <u>See also</u>: B65

B43. "Influence, Problem, Tone." <u>Dance Index</u> 6, no.10-12 (1947): 249; In <u>Stravinsky in the Theatre</u>, edited by Minna Lederman, 121-122. 1949. Reprint. New York: Da Capo Press, 1975.
       Igor Stravinsky's music and influence is examined by Copland. His earlier style using "the displaced accent and the polytonal chord" has changed to one of neo-classicism. However, Stravinsky mixes techniques so it seems unlikely that he will be associated with one particular style in the future. His unique music "has never to my knowledge been adequately described, let alone imitated."

B44. "Is the University Too Much with Us." <u>New York Times</u>, July 26, 1970, II, p.13:7.
       It appears that most contemporary composers are associated with an institution of higher learning these days. Copland wonders if it is a desire to escape from the rigors of earning a living as a composer rather than as a faculty member. He concludes that most music composition is done on campuses and "that the university is where the action is."

B45. "Jazz Structure and Influence." <u>Modern Music</u> 4 (January-February 1927): 9-14.
       There is no analysis available on the influence of jazz on serious music. Copland proceeds to examine the structure of jazz and to project his opinion of its importance on future music. He feels that jazz elements will be found in many concertos and symphonies in the future.

B46. "John Cage and the Music of Chance." In <u>The New Music Lover's Handbook</u>, edited by Elie Siegmeister, 542-544. Irvington-on-Hudson, New York: Harvey House, 1973.
       This essay, taken from Copland's <u>The New Music</u>, examines the indeterminate music of Cage. "At present Cage has practically removed himself from the sphere of music, concentrating instead on public manifestations of noise-producing phenomena for which there is no exact precedent." As composers have moved further away from conventional music notation, all types of graphic symbols have resulted with each composer developing his own

method. Consequently, nothing is standardized. The question is whether or not it will remain an important musical force in the future. See also: B76

B47. "Leon Kirchner: Duo for Violin and Piano." Music Library Association Notes 7 (June 1950): 434.
      This is a review of Kirchner's score which was composed in 1947. Kirchner is a young American composer whose music has "an emotional impact and explosive power that is almost frightening in intensity." Copland finds these traits to be unusual because there is nothing unique about the structure of Kirchner's rhythms, harmonies, or melodies.

B48. "The Lyricism of Milhaud." Modern Music 6 (January-February 1929): 14-19.
      Milhaud's works have not been popular in America, Copland notes. In some cases audiences have been antagonistic toward this revolutionary's dissonant music. Copland analyzes Milhaud's compositions and asserts that "Milhaud's gift is clearly that of a lyricist."

B49. "Letters to Nicolas Slonimsky and to Arthur V. Berger." In Letters of Composers; an Anthology, 1603-1945, edited by Gertrude Norman and Miriam Lubell Shrifte, 401-404. New York: A. A. Knopf, 1946.
      Three letters from Copland are included. The first letter to Slonimsky in 1927 thanked Slonimsky for sending him reviews from the Boston newspapers after a performance of the Piano Concerto. Copland wrote to Berger in 1943 addressing articles Berger was publishing about Copland's Piano Variations and Piano Sonata. These letters were written in a friendly vein, but probing questions about some of Berger's comments are included.

B50. "Letters to the Editor." New York Times, September 4, 1966, VII, p.18.
      Copland responds to Richard Schechner's review of Harold Clurman's new book, The Naked Image. Schechner's statement that it takes more effort and work to write a review of a play than to write a play itself is disputed.

B51. "Letters to the Editor: Varèse." New York Times, August 13, 1972, VII, p.24.
      Copland disagrees with Joan Peyser's review of the accounts of the disagreement between Edgar Varèse and Claire Reis. He also disagrees with Peyser's statements about the purpose of the League of Composers. The book which was reviewed was Louise Varèse's Varèse: A Looking Glass Diary.

B52. "The Life of Music." Christian Science Monitor, January 27, 1976, Home Forum, p.25:5.
      This is reprinted from Copland's Music and Imagination. He credits the imaginative mind with being the most important trait necessary for musical enjoyment. The gifted listener is one to be envied. See also: B65

B53. "Listening to Polyphonic Music." In The Music Lover's Handbook,
      edited by Elie Siegmeister, 105-106. New York: W. Morrow, 1943.
         This excerpt is from Copland's chapter "Musical Texture" in
      What to Listen For in Music. It is more difficult to listen to
      polyphonic music than that which is harmonically conceived. The
      listener should hear a piece many times to be able to distinguish
      the various linear lines. Copland makes suggestions for train-
      ing the ear to hear the multiple lines. Repeated listening of
      this music is more interesting than that of homophonic textures.
      See also: B108

B54. "Making Music in the Star-Spangled Manner." Music and Musicians
      8 (August 1960): 8-9.

B55. "Marc Blitzstein." In The Music Lover's Handbook, edited by Elie
      Siegmeister, 761-764. New York: W. Morrow, 1943.
         This excerpt from Copland's Our New Music examines Blitzstein's
      stage works: The Cradle Will Rock and No for an Answer. These
      were designed for actors who can sing, not for opera singers.
      Copland finds the second work to be musically superior to the
      first. Copland admires Blitzstein's sense of energy and design.
      See also: B84

B56. "The Measure of Kapell." Saturday Review 36 (November 28, 1953):
      67.
         Copland's eulogy for William Kapell cites some of the pianist's
      outstanding qualities. Copland's music was a favorite of his
      and Copland thought that it was unusual that Kapell preferred
      Copland's most difficult music. Kapell had an affinity for music
      "that his audiences were least likely to fathom." Copland
      admired this performer because the man believed in performing
      contemporary music whether or not it was popular to do so.

B57. "Melody." In The New Music Lover's Handbook, edited by Elie
      Siegmeister, 54-56. Irvington-on-Hudson, New York: Harvey House,
      1973.
         This essay is abridged from Copland's What to Listen For in
      Music. Copland does not attempt to define what a good melody is,
      but gives some characteristics of one. Examples of melodies
      drawn from the works of Palestrina, Bach, and Schubert illustrate
      some varieties of excellent melodic lines. Contemporary com-
      posers using twelve-tone techniques base their music upon a dif-
      ferent type of tonal center than was common in earlier music.
      Copland urges listeners to seek out the melodic line and follow
      it throughout a work and not let accompanying material detract
      from it. See also: B108

B58. "Memorial to Paul Rosenfeld." Music Library Association Notes
      2d Ser., v.4, no.2 (March 1947): 147-148.
         Copland applauds Rosenfeld's work as a critic because of the
      sensitivity shown to composers in his criticisms. His involve-
      ment with Copland and other composers was important as they
      began their careers in music. Included is a bibliography con-
      sisting chiefly of books and articles written by Rosenfeld.
      This article was later reprinted as "A Verdict" in Paul
      Rosenfeld, Voyager in the Arts without the bibliography.
      See also: B106

B59. "Mexican Composer." New York Times, May 9, 1937, XI, p.5:2.
      Silvestre Revueltas and Carlos Chávez are two contemporary
      Mexican composers who are becoming well-known. Chávez has
      recently been a guest conductor of the New York Philharmonic.
      His works are heavily based on Mexican folk tunes and styles.
      Revueltas writes works that are "vivid tone pictures" and has
      composed the film score for The Wave or Redes.

B60. "Modern Music: 'Fresh and Different.'" In The Meaning in Reading,
      edited by Jacob Hooper Wise, J. E. Congleton, and Alton C.
      Morris. 4th ed., 243-245. New York: Harcourt, Brace, 1956;
      New York Times, March 13, 1955, VI, p.15.
      Copland's article is a defense against the views of Henry
      Pleasants, a noted music critic. Pleasants contends that serious
      music is a dead art but Copland asserts that serious music has
      been very much alive during the first half of the twentieth
      century. Although recent new compositions are not performed
      very much, there is growing acceptance of it. Copland argues
      that creativity will be stifled if composers only write music
      that is pleasing to the average listener and will bring in
      significant box office receipts.

B61. "Modern Orchestration Surveyed." Modern Music 8 (November-
      December 1930): 41-44.
      Egon Wellesz's book Die Neue Instrumentation is an overview
      of orchestration with little detailed analyses. There are
      problems in selecting representative contemporary works to
      analyze because modern orchestration appears to change with each
      new work. Copland concludes that this "is at best a disappoint-
      ing book but at least it makes a start in a much-neglected field."

B62. "The Modern Symphony." In The Music Lover's Handbook, edited by
      Elie Siegmeister, 125-126. New York: W. Morrow, 1943.
      This excerpt is taken from the chapter "Sonata Form" in
      Copland's What to Listen For in Music. It seems that most
      modern composers have not written symphonies. However, Mahler
      and Sibelius are notable exceptions. In his nine symphonies,
      Mahler increased the size of the symphony by adding to the
      orchestra and increasing the number of movements. Sibelius is
      noted for symphonies written in a freer form than previously.
      For example, his Seventh Symphony consists of one movement.
      Copland feels that, in general, composers are adhering to the
      usual three or more separate movements, but the differences
      appear within the movements. See also: B108

B63. "A Modernist Defends Modern Music." New York Times, December 25,
      1949, VI, p.11; Boston Symphony Orchestra Concert Bulletin 14
      (February 3, 1950): 760.
      Copland attempts to assist the listener in understanding
      contemporary music. He lists composers in four classifications
      from very easy to very tough. He responds to the problem of
      dissonance by indicating that "what sounds dissonant to you may
      sound quite mellifluous to me." Unfortunately, the public is
      not interested in a piece of music it does not understand or
      enjoy upon first hearing.

B64. "Music." In Man's Right to Knowledge; an International Symposium
      Presented in Honor of the Two-Hundredth Anniversary of Columbia
      University, 1754-1954. 2d Ser., 99-106. New York: H. Muschel,
      1954; Musical Courier 151 (February 1, 1955): 54-56.
      This is one of several radio broadcasts which was sponsored
      by Columbia University in commeration of its two hundredth
      anniversary. The theme, "Music as an Aspect of the Human Spirit,"
      is described as immense. Copland discusses music in relation to
      other arts, and the intangible aspects of the fascination it
      holds for most people. He also writes that most listeners are
      reluctant to listen to contemporary works and this has a serious
      effect on future music and its composers. He concludes, however,
      that "so long as the human spirit thrives on this planet, music
      in some living form will accompany and sustain it."

B65. Music and Imagination. Cambridge: Harvard University Press, 1952.
      The six lectures given at Harvard University by the composer
      while he was the Charles Eliot Norton Professor of Poetry in
      1951-1952 comprise this book. The first three lectures examine
      the imaginative mind in regard to listening and understanding,
      while the last three lectures discuss the relation of imagination
      to the contemporary musical scene. In summary, Copland believes
      that "one of the primary problems for the composer in an in-
      dustrial society like that of America is to achieve integration,
      to find justification for the life of art in the life about him."
      Music must move the average person to make the artist's job
      worthwhile.

B66. "Music in the Films." In The Music Lover's Handbook, edited by
      Elie Siegmeister, 628-635. New York: W. Morrow, 1943.
      Copland gives his opinions on the film music industry in this
      abridgement from his book Our New Music. Hollywood uses much
      contemporary music in movies now. The composer's limitations
      involve working with the producer, a limited amount of time to
      create the music, and the fact that the music should help the
      film. He discusses the procedures for setting music to film at
      length and cites some of the commonly used formulas for doing
      this. However, Copland laments the fact that music critics and
      the public alike do not seem to feel that film music is very
      important musically. See also: B84

B67. "Music Is the Message." Christian Science Monitor, July 22, 1976,
      Home Forum, p.2.
      This is a reprint of two paragraphs from Music and Imagination
      which considers the meaning of music and the theories that
      attempt to describe it. See also: B65

B68. "Music Out of Everywhere." New York Times, February 22, 1953,
      VII, p.7:1.
      Copland reviews Darius Milhaud's Notes Without Music: an
      Autobiography. Few recent composers have written about their
      feelings about music with the exception of Milhaud and Copland.
      This is a delightful, readable book. It is a translation of
      Notes sans Musique published in 1949 with supplementary material.

82   Bibliography

B69. "Music Since 1920." Modern Music 5 (March–April 1928): 16–20.
        Much music has been composed since 1920 and modern music "is
     no longer in the experimental stage." Among the contemporary
     composers working during this time were Hindemith and Milhaud.
     Their music, as well as that of others, basically uses rhythms
     and harmonies which were established during the preceding two
     decades.

B70. "The Musical Scene Changes." Twice a Year 5–7 (1940–1941): 340–343.
        Copland notes his perceptions of the musical changes that have
     occurred during the first three decades of the twentieth century.
     Rhythm and harmony began to experience change from the established
     nineteenth century norms. Copland's conclusion is that the
     changes have resulted in "a simplification of style for the sake
     of once more making contact with the large mass of listeners."
     His goal is to have more contemporary music presented to audiences
     so that listeners will not be so dependent on music of the past.
     He also plans to write music that he knows audiences will enjoy.

B71. "Musikalisches Schaffen in Amerika." Österreichische Musikzeit-
     schrift 20 (May–June 1965): 266–270.
        This translated excerpt, "Creativity in America," is taken
     from the composer's Copland on Music. In it Copland expresses
     his views on the American musical scene. The American styles
     and trends in music are contrasted with those of the past and
     with the European tradition. See also: B24

B72. "Nadia Boulanger: an Affectionate Portrait." Harper's Magazine
     221 (October 1960): 49–51.
        This is an extract from Copland on Music in which Copland
     reminisces about his composition studies with Mlle. Boulanger in
     France. Although she was teaching harmony and Copland had com-
     pleted his studies in this area, friends convinced him to visit
     her class. He was impressed with her knowledge and attitude.
     Although her list of compositions is short, Copland credits her
     with an unusually astute perception of flaws in compositions in
     progress. Among her other American composition students were
     Walter Piston, Virgil Thomson, and Roy Harris. See also: B24

B73. "Nadya Bulanzhe–-Uchitel' Kompozitsii." Sovetskaya Muzyka 28
     (June 1964): 120–122.
        An excerpt from Copland on Music on his composition teacher
     in Paris Nadia Boulanger. See also: B24

B74. "Neglected Works: a Symposium." Modern Music 23 (Winter 1946): 3–
     12.
        As part of a discussion on neglected compositions, Copland
     notes one example from each major category which he feels should
     have more publicity. Among these is Milhaud's opera Christopher
     Columbus which he suggests might be "a landmark in the field of
     modern opera."

B75. "New Electronic Media." In The New Music Lover's Handbook, edited
     by Elie Siegmeister, 430–433. Irvington-on-Hudson, New York:
     Harvey House, 1973.

This extract from Copland's The New Music reveals his feelings about the fact that "science and scientific calculation were injected into our musical thinking." The current detailed analyses of composers' works by critics in these terms often astound the composers. The technological aspect of musical design and construction appears to be gaining more emphasis than the emotional or human nature of music. Electronic music has a monotony not encountered in sounds produced by conventional means. Copland believes that musical styles must change and not remain static. His advice is to approach electronic music with an open mind. See also: B76

B76. The New Music, 1900-1960. Rev. ed. New York: W. W. Norton, 1968.
      This is a revised edition of Our New Music published in 1941. Some of the material is drawn from his articles and lectures. One section examines the music of contemporary European composers, and another section analyzes contemporary American composers' music. Included also is an autobiographical sketch and his impressions on electronic music and music of chance. See also: B84

B77. "The New 'School' of American Composers." New York Times, March 14, 1948, VI, p.18.
      Copland reports on the maturing composers of the 1940's such as Leonard Bernstein and John Cage. There is less European influence on American composers since few now study there. However, there is no uniform style evident. Biographical and stylistic information is given on seven representative composers.

B78. "None in the Same Way." Christian Science Monitor, September 19, 1979, p.21.
      Copland examines the motives involved in being a composer in this excerpt from Music and Imagination. He concludes that there is an inward drive that manifests itself in this type of expression. There is a compulsion to continue this type of self-expression, for the composer learns more about himself with each work. See also: B65

B79. "A Note on Young Composers." Music Vanguard 1, no.1 (March-April 1935): 14-16.

B80. "On Music Composition." In The Creative Mind and Method: Exploring the Nature of Creativeness in American Arts, Sciences, and Professions, edited by Jack D. Summerfield and Lorlyn Thatcher, 29-33. New York: Russell & Russell, 1964, c1960.
      Collaborative music, such as that involved in ballets and films, is writing that generally requires the script to be developed before the music. Copland feels that music for films should be considered a more important form than it is at the present. Copland revises his film music when he prepares it for a concert performance.

B81. "On the Notation of Rhythm." Modern Music 21 (May-June 1944): 217-220.
      Rhythm can be most clearly heard when the listener views the score. The equal division of meters is no longer the normal

situation. Rhythmic possibilities seem endless and contemporary composers are using unusual rhythms in new works.

B82. "One Hundred and Fourteen Songs." Modern Music 11 (January-February 1934): 59-64.
   Charles Ives originally had his songs printed in 1922 and recently several have been reprinted. In an essay he apologizes for these works because he composed them when he was working at his principal occupation as a businessman. The biggest problem with this collection is that "there is no order here--either of chronology, style or quality."

B83. "Orchestral Magic." Christian Science Monitor, January 30, 1980, p.20.
   This excerpt from Music and Imagination reviews the concept of the modern orchestra. Before Hector Berlioz, there was no blending of sounds in the modern orchestral sense. See also: B65

B84. Our New Music; Leading Composers in Europe and America. New York: McGraw-Hill, 1941.
   This book, drawn chiefly from Copland's writings and lectures, was revised and enlarged in 1968 as The New Music, 1900-1960. His impressions about contemporary European and American music are given, along with background about the events preceding twentieth century music. A selected list of recordings is included. See also: B76

B85. "Our Younger Generation--Ten Years Later." Modern Music 13 (May-June 1936): 3-11.
   Ten years ago Copland named seventeen young contemporary composers who he felt were going to be important in the future. He lists these composers again and briefly reviews their accomplishments during the past decade. In addition, a new list of promising young composers is named.

B86. "The Personality of Stravinsky." In Igor Stravinsky, edited by Edwin Corle, 121-122. New York: Duell, Sloan and Pearce, 1949.
   The essence of Stravinsky's personality is difficult to determine, Copland notes. Stravinsky's music is so unusual that it is rarely confused with anyone else's compositions. Copland agrees that the compositions are unique but he is unable to define why they are so different.

B87. "Piano Fantasy." Tempo 46 (Winter 1958): 13-14.
   Copland discusses his latest large-scale piano work which uses twelve-tone techniques. This extended work does not incorporate folk elements. The Piano Sonata and Piano Variations were also absolute music. Details of the construction of this composition are noted.

B88. "Pioneer Listener." New Republic 86 (April 15, 1936): 291-292.
   Copland's review of Paul Rosenfeld's Discoveries of a Music Critic finds the work to be of excellent quality. "He has lost none of his original zest and enthusiasm for 'pioneer listening' such as we came to expect of him fifteen or twenty years ago." This book of essays is drawn from Rosenfeld's writings in New Republic.

B89. "Playing Safe at Zurich." <u>Modern Music</u> 4 (November–December 1926):
      28–31.
           After attending the June festival of the International Society
      for Contemporary Music, Copland expresses his disappointment
      about the absence of new names among the composers presented.
      The first two festivals in 1923 and 1924 seemed to take more
      risks by presenting the works of little-known composers. In
      Copland's opinion there was no outstanding work presented at the
      most recent festival.

B90. "Pleasures of Music." <u>Saturday Evening Post</u> 232 (July 4, 1959):
      18–19.
           This talk was originally presented in the Distinguished
      Lecture Series of the University of New Hampshire, April 1959.
      Copland examines some of the specific elements of music as the
      rhythm, color, and musical flow. He feels that music "gives
      pleasure simultaneously on the lowest and highest levels of
      apprehension." He decries the reliance of the public on works
      of well-known composers and urges that unknown composers be given
      more opportunities to present their works.

B91. "Problemes de la Musique de Film." <u>Vie Musicale</u> 1 (March 1951):
      5–6.

B92. "A Quarter-Century Reflection." <u>American Composers Alliance Bul-
      letin</u> 11, no.2–4 (1963): 1.
           Copland helped establish the American Composers Alliance and
      reflects on its first twenty-five years. He asserts that it has
      helped give the composer "a new sense of pride in his profession,
      and a new urgency as to the need for group action."

B93. "Scherchen on Conducting and Ewen on Composers." <u>Modern Music</u>
      12 (January–February 1935): 94–96.
           Hermann Scherchen's <u>Handbook of Conducting</u> and David Ewen's
      <u>Composers of Today</u> are reviewed. The first is a successful
      "exhaustive study of the actual technique involved in the con-
      ducting of an orchestra." Ewen's book "is full of inaccuracies,
      one or more to the page."

B94. "Scores and Records." <u>Modern Music</u> 14 (November–December 1936):
      39–99.
           Reviews of recent recordings and scores which are expected to
      be of interest to readers are given. In addition, Copland
      mentions R. D. Darrell's <u>Gramophone Shop Encyclopedia of Recorded
      Music</u> which is a much needed addition to music literature.

B95. "Second Thoughts on Hollywood." <u>Modern Music</u> 17 (March–April 1940):
      141–147.
           Hollywood is a place where living composers are needed con-
      stantly to create music for films. Having written film scores
      himself, Copland acknowledges that the music must never dominate
      the scenes but should only assist the story. Nonetheless, he
      feels that film scores need more variety since almost every
      film uses "the late nineteenth century symphonic style."

B96. "Serge Koussevitzky and the American Composer." Musical Quarterly
      30 (April 1944): 255-269.
           Copland reminisces about his first meeting with Koussevitzky
      in Paris in 1923. The conductor was quite interested in Copland's
      score, Cortège Macabre, which he had brought along. Koussevitzky
      spent the past twenty years as conductor of the Boston Symphony.
      He is congratulated for his policy of performing the works of
      American composers including those of Copland.

B97. "Some Notes on My Music for the Theatre." Victor Record Review
      (March 1941): 6.

B98. "Stefan Wolpe: Two Songs for Alto and Piano." Music Library
      Association Notes 2d Ser., v.6, no.1 (December 1948): 172.
           Copland reviews Wolpe's new publication by Hargail Music Press.
      He finds these songs by the recent German immigrant, via
      Palestine, to be "intensely alive, deeply Jewish, and very per-
      sonal."

B99. "Stravinsky and Hindemith Premieres." Modern Music 9 (January-
      February 1932): 85-88.
           Stravinsky's Violin Concerto and Hindemith's Das Unaufhorliche
      both premiered in Berlin during the fall of 1931. Stravinsky's
      stylistic characteristics are examined. Copland feels that
      Stravinsky has been writing in a neo-classic style since about
      1920, although most critics assert that he has adopted a new
      style with each work.

B100. "Stravinsky's Oedipus Rex." New Republic 54 (February 29, 1928):
      68-69.
           This review of Stravinsky's recent opera-oratorio indicates
      that the public did not receive it with much enthusiasm. This
      work contrasts significantly with his Le Sacre du Printemps.
      The rhythm is ordinary three-four and four-four time and "for
      entire pages the harmony rests on a single major or minor
      triad." This style is "an example of the new impersonal approach
      to music."

B101. "Tanglewood's Future." New York Times, February 24, 1952, II, p.
      7:7.
           As assistant director of the Berkshire Music Center, Copland
      writes about the group's future plans. Among these are increased
      availability of scholarships for the students and provisions for
      shorter terms of study as well as the usual six-week terms.

B102. "Thomson's Musical State." Modern Music 17 (October-November 1939):
      63-65.
           Virgil Thomson's The State of Music discusses the composer's
      profession which he views as a capitalistic venture. He does
      not judge the works of others but emphasizes the role of the
      composer in society. This "is the wittiest, the most provocative,
      the best written, the least conventional book on matters musical
      that I have ever seen."

B103. "Tip to Moviegoers: Take Off Those Ear-Muffs." New York Times,
      November 6, 1949, VI, p.28-32.

Most movie patrons are unaware of the musical accompaniment, Copland observes. Some comments describing the good and bad points of noticing the musical background are given. Copland also outlines the mechanisms involved in setting music to film.

B104. "A Tribute to Franz Liszt." HiFi/Stereo Review 5 (October 1960): 46-49.

B105. "Twentieth Century: Reorientation and Experiment." In Music and Western Man: the Canadian Broadcasting Corporation, edited by Peter Garvie. New York: Philosophical Library, 1958.
Copland feels that there were two types of musical revolutions which occurred during the beginning of the twentieth century. One was the acceptance of new chords and rhythms and the other was an aesthetic difference in rejecting the German influence. An analysis of several composers' stylistic characteristics support these views. Suggestions are made to listen to specific recordings for better understanding of the twentieth century idiom.

B106. "A Verdict." In Paul Rosenfeld, Voyager in the Arts, edited by Jerome Mellquist and Lucie Wiese, 166-168. 1948. Reprint. New York: Octagon Books, 1977.
This compilation of writings by forty-nine contributors about Rosenfeld is unique in that the writers have a chance to comment on a music critic. This section by Copland originally appeared in Music Library Association Notes, March 1947 but does not contain the bibliography of Rosenfeld's works. Copland confirms the well-known disagreements that composers have with critics' opinions. However, in this case, Rosenfeld is an exception. Because of Rosenfeld's involvement and commitment to music, he did much to assist young composers such as Copland in their early careers. See also: B58

B107. "What Is Jewish Music?" New York Herald Tribune, October 2, 1949, Book Review Section, p.7.
Copland reviews The Music of Israel by Peter Gradenwitz.

B108. What to Listen For in Music. Rev. ed. New York: McGraw-Hill, 1957.
Originally published in 1939, this revised work contains two new chapters. One chapter is on film music and the other is on listening to current compositions. The book guides the reader in an examination of the elements and forms of music. This material is drawn from fifteen lectures that Copland presented at the New School for Social Research, New York. A bibliography and discography are included.

B109. "When Private and Public World Meet." New York Times, June 9, 1968, II, p.17:1.
This essays concentrates on composers who have conducted their own works. The hazards of being a composer-conductor are examined, and it is noted that most musicians do not combine the two areas of music. Copland, however, has been successful as a composer and conductor.

B110. "The World of A-Tonality." <u>New York Times</u>, November 27, 1949, VII, p.5:3.
    Copland reviews René Leibowitz's <u>Schoenberg and His School</u>. As one of Schoenberg's students, Liebowitz defends his teacher in a very dogmatic style. Much of the book concentrates on a breif analyzation of the works of Schoenberg, **Berg, a**nd Webern. Copland concludes that this is an authorative work on the style of Schoenberg.

B111. "World of the Phonograph." <u>American Scholar</u> 6, no.1 (1937): 27-37.
    Copland feels that recorded music can never replace a live performance, but that it does have its value in providing contact for many people with good music. Present recordings involve changing the record every four and a half minutes and these breaks cause the work to lose its continuity. Recording companies are attempting to remedy this situation. Dynamics are also a problem because it is not simply of matter of the composition being loud or soft. A bibliography of recommended recordings is included.

BIBLIOGRAPHY
ABOUT COPLAND

B112. "Aaron and Martha." Newsweek 25 (May 28, 1945): 106-107.
Copland's ballet, Appalachian Spring, received the Pulitzer
Prize for Music on May 7. The following week Martha Graham and
her ballet company presented it in New York for the first time.
The work had been commissioned by Graham and had its premiere
performance the previous fall at the Library of Congress in
Washington, D.C. See also: W73

B113. "Aaron Copland." Canon 13 (May-June 1960): 239-240.
This short biography stresses Copland's early compositions and
achievements. His musical training in the United States and
in France with Nadia Boulanger is related along with his various
awards. His many activities have included active participation
in the League of Composers, the Berkshire Music Center, and the
National Institute of Arts and Letters.

B114. "Aaron Copland." Composers of the Americas 1 (1955): 26-35.
In Spanish and English. This biographical sketch of the
composer's life notes achievements such as his $5,000 composition
prize from RCA Victor for his Dance Symphony. Copland has
traveled in Latin America as a composer, conductor, and lecturer
under the direction of the Coordinator of Inter-American Relations of the United States. The major portion of this article
is a classified chronological catalog of his works.

B115. "Aaron Copland." Film Music Notes 10 (March-April 1951): 3.
Copland has been selected as the chair at Harvard University
for the Charles Eliot Norton professorship beginning in the fall.
Currently he is the composer-in-residence at the American Acad-
emy in Rome. Scores which Copland has written for films include
The Red Pony and The Heiress.

B116. "Aaron Copland." Music and Musicians 12 (May 1964): 11; Musical
Events 17 (February 1962): 18-19; Musical Events 19 (May 1964):
24.

B117. "Aaron Copland." Musical Times 92 (August 1951): 372.
        Copland conducted the Jacques Orchestra in his Clarinet Con-
        certo on May 31 at the Victoria and Albert Museum. "The two-
        movement concerto . . . consists of a long andante of considerable
        melodic power and unforced expressiveness, and a vivacious rondo."

B118. "Aaron Copland." Pan Pipes of Sigma Alpha Iota 44 (January 1952):
        27.
        This is a list of recordings made of Copland's works during
        1951, without specific recording numbers. Also noted is the
        publication of his score for the orchestral suite taken from
        his film music for The Red Pony. In addition, his appointment
        as the Charles Eliot Norton Professor of Poetry at Harvard Univer-
        sity is recorded.

B119. "Aaron Copland." Pan Pipes of Sigma Alpha Iota 45 (January 1953):
        45.
        This is a list of Copland's scores published during 1952 by
        Boosey and Hawkes, including his Concerto for Clarinet and String
        Orchestra. In addition, his book, Music and Imagination, was
        published. See also: B65

B120. "Aaron Copland." Pan Pipes of Sigma Alpha Iota 47 (January 1955):
        37.
        This is a synopsis of important publications, recordings, and
        performances of Copland's works during 1954. His opera, The
        Tender Land, was commissioned by Rodgers and Hammerstein through
        the League of Composers and had its premiere at the New York
        City Center of Opera and Drama April 1, 1954. See also: W90

B121. "Aaron Copland." San Francisco Symphony Program Notes (March 1,
        1966): 11; Tempo 21 (Autumn 1951): 1-2.

B122. Aaron Copland, a Complete Catalogue of His Works. New York:
        Boosey & Hawkes, 1960.
        This is a chronological list of Copland's works up to 1960
        plus accompanying information on individual compositions. Also
        included are a classified list and an alphabetical list.

B123. "Aaron Copland 80 [Achtzig]." Musik und Gesellschaft 30 (November
        1980): 698-699.

B124. "Aaron Copland--America's Sunniest Musical Genius." San Francisco
        Chronicle, November 24, 1978, p.49:4.
        Copland has done more conducting than composing during the
        past few years. His optimistic outlook has been apparent
        throughout his long life. He has no plans to stop conducting
        or retire because of his energy and enjoyment of conducting.

B125. "Aaron Copland--Amerikas Førende Komponist." Norsk Musikerblad
        53 (November 1964): 5.

B126. "Aaron Copland--Articulate Composer." Musical Events 20 (November
        1965): 26.

B127. "Aaron Copland, by Arthur Berger." Music and Letters 35 (July 1954): 245-247.
This ninety-six page book by Berger examines the Piano Variations very closely but includes little detail about Copland's other works. The reviewer feels that "the book would have been more valuable if.it had covered less ground more thoroughly." Copland's experimentation is contrasted with that of his contemporaries, such as Charles Ives. See also: B200

B128. "Aaron Copland, by Arthur Berger." Music Clubs Magazine 33 (January 1954): 18-19; Musique et Radio 52 (December 1962): 403; Pan Pipes of Sigma Alpha Iota 46 (May 1954): 13.
Book reviews. See also: B200

B129. "Aaron Copland: Chronological Catalog of the Works of the American Composer." Boletin de Musica y Artes Visuales 57-58 (November-December 1954): 33-38.

B130. "Aaron Copland Elected to American Academy." Musical Courier 15 (January 1, 1955): 28.
Copland was one of four elected to membership in the American Academy of Arts and Letters recently. "Aaron Copland, widely recognized today as one of the leading American composers, is one of the very few composers who has been able to support himself entirely by his compositions." Biographical information is included.

B131. "Aaron Copland 75 [Funf und Siebzig]." Musik und Gesellschaft 25 (November 1975): 700.

B132. "Aaron Copland, His Life and Times, by Arnold Dobrin." Clavier 7, no.5 (1968): 6.
A short review of Dobrin's biography which is directed toward a young audience. The book contains "a lively survey of our musical era as well as a fine biography." See also: B429

B133. "Aaron Copland, His Life and Times, by Arnold Dobrin." Council for Research in Music Education Bulletin 13 (Spring 1968): 39.
A two-sentence review of Dobrin's biography which is called a "folksy biography." See also: B429

B134. "Aaron Copland: His 70th Birthday." Music Journal 29 (January 1971): 10.
Photos and their captions report on the birthday party given by the composer's publisher Boosey & Hawkes on Nov. 14, 1970 at the Essex House in New York.

B135. "Aaron Copland Honored at University of Bridgeport." School Musician 48 (February 1977): 16.
On December 5 and 6, 1976, Copland was present at the University of Bridgeport to attend a concert of his works given in his honor. He also discussed his compositions. He was the seventh contemporary American to participate in the annual Carlson Festival of the Arts at the University of Bridgeport.

B136. "Aaron Copland Ill." _Times_ (London), February 10, 1962, p.8g.
        The composer became ill while rehearsing for a performance
    with the London Symphony Orchestra on February 9. He is re-
    covering.

B137. "Aaron Copland in Brazil." _Pan American Union Bulletin_ 82 (May
        1948): 293-294.
        The United States Department of State sponsored Copland's visit
    to Brazil in 1948 as part of a good-will tour. Copland delivered
    lectures in various cities and some of his compositions were
    performed in his honor.

B138. "Aaron Copland Is Now Seventy Years Young." _School Musician_ 42
        (January 1971): 59.
        Copland celebrated his seventieth birthday on November 14, 1970.
    He has been an active composer since the 1920's when he went to
    Paris and studied with Nadia Boulanger. ASCAP President Stanley
    Adams noted his birthday by stating, "We in the Society are
    tremendously proud of his musical achievements, as well as his
    great contributions as educator and lecturer."

B139. "Aaron Copland, Jorge Donn, and Erick Hawkins to Receive 1979
        Dance Magazine Awards." _Dance Magazine_ 53 (March 1979): 4.
        Copland "has done more than any other creative musician of
    his generation to establish a truly indigenous American music."
    He has been active in bringing American music to the public and
    his stylistic characteristics "make it especially suited for the
    dance." He is one of three individuals selected to receive the
    1979 _Dance Magazine_ awards.

B140. "Aaron Copland on the Composer's Craft." _International Musician_
        47 (May 1949): 34.

B141. "Aaron Copland on the ELP Version of _Fanfare for the Common Man_."
        Contemporary Keyboard 3 (October 1977): 30.
        Copland allowed the popular group Emerson, Lake, and Palmer to
    use his _Fanfare for the Common Man_ in their music. Their rendi-
    tion "is really around the piece, I'd say, rather than a
    literal transposition," according to Copland.

B142. "Aaron Copland Photo Album, with Commentary by Mr. Copland." _High
        Fidelity/Musical America_ 20 (November 1970): 56-63.
        Twenty-two pictures chronicle Copland's childhood plus signifi-
    cant events in his musical career. Included are recollections
    by Copland about particular items.

B143. "Aaron Copland Reaches the Half-Century Mark." _Musical America_ 70
        November 15, 1950): 14.
        A brief background of Copland's life and musical style is
    given. He grew up in Brooklyn, studied in Europe for several
    years, and returned to the United States where he established
    his own identity in the musical world. He is noted for his use
    of American themes in works such as Appalachian Spring. Experi-
    ments with jazz idioms and spare-textured works were brief as
    his music style returned to realism in film scores, for example.

B144. "Aaron Copland Talks About American Music Today." <u>Times</u> (London),
      August 20, 1958, p.11a.
      Copland is in London to conduct two of his works at Albert
      Hall in a Promenade Concert. In this interview, he notes that
      music is always changing. He fears that composers in the future
      may never be heard in concert but only on recordings.

B145. "Aaron Copland Tours the U.S.S.R., Japan and the U.K." <u>World of
      Music</u> 3 (June 1960): 56.
      Information about the tour which Lukas Foss and Copland are
      taking is provided. They have been conducting their own works
      in these three countries since April when the cultural program
      began. Copland will return to the Tanglewood Summer School of
      Music in late June.

B146. "Aaron Copland w Warszawie." <u>Ruch Muzyczny</u> 10, no.5 (1966): 8.

B147. "Aaron Copland's Anniversary Year." <u>Music & Dance</u> 51 (April 1951):
      13-14.

B148. "Aaron Copland's 70th Birthday Honored Internationally." <u>ASCAP
      Today</u> 5, no.1 (1971): 17.
      Among the special celebrations in Copland's honor were con-
      certs by almost every major orchestra in the United States as
      well as in some other countries. On his birthday, Nov. 14,
      1970, a Juilliard concert concluded with a dinner afterwards
      hosted by his publisher, Boosey & Hawkes. The entire November
      1970 issue of <u>High Fidelity/Musical America</u> was devoted to his
      life.

B149. "Aaron Copland's 75th Birthday." <u>High Fidelity/Musical America</u>
      26 (February 1976): MA24-25.
      Copland's birthday celebration was held two days early on
      November 12 at Alice Tully Hall at the MacDowell Colony in
      Peterborough, New Hampshire. Copland spoke about the influence
      of the colony on his works. A concert of his works was presented
      to commemorate the occasion.

B150. "Aaron Copland's <u>The Red Pony</u>." <u>Times</u> (London), May 23, 1957,
      p.3g.
      On May 21, Bernard Hermann conducted the London Symphony
      Orchestra in a concert at Festival Hall which included Copland's
      <u>The Red Pony</u>. This suite, adapted from the film score, "makes
      an effective concert piece."

B151. Abel, David W. "Fallacies." <u>New York Times</u>, October 12, 1952,
      VI, p.6:3.
      In this letter to the editor Abel replies to Copland's recent
      article, "An Indictment of the Fourth B." Abel draws parallels
      between art and music and suggests that there are two opposing
      fallacies. One is that all modern work is worthless and the
      other is that all contemporary work is great. He concludes that
      time will be the judge of what has value. <u>See also</u>: B42.

B152. Adams, Val. "Copland Composing for TV." <u>New York Times</u>, August
      28, 1966, II, p.19:2.

        The "C.B.S. Playhouse" series has commissioned Copland to com-
pose a one-minute theme that will introduce and conclude the
television show. Copland stated that this assignment is very
difficult and that "'composing 10 minutes of music would be a
lot easier.'"

B153. "Las Agachadas (The Shake-Down Song)." Music and Letters 34 (July
        1953): 269.
        Copland's diatonic unaccompanied chorus consists of a smaller
group which contrasts with the larger chorus. It was recently
published by Boosey & Hawkes.

B154. Alexander, M. "Copland and the Dance Episodes from Rodeo."
        Music Teacher and Piano Student 59 (September 1980): 17-18.

B155. "All Red Ties Denied by Aaron Copland." New York Times, May 27,
        1953, p.18:2.
        Senator Joseph R. McCarthy, a Wisconsin Republican, questioned
Copland about his alleged Communist affiliations. This Senate
Investigations Subcommittee spoke with Copland for two hours in
closed session. Afterwards, Copland stated, "'I testified under
oath that I never have been and am not now a Communist.'"

B156. "American Composers--Aaron Copland." Musical Courier 159 (March
        1959): 39.
        A biography of Copland which records his early studies is
augmented by an examination of his stylistic characteristics.
An early interest in jazz rhythms was found to be too limiting
so he continued expanding his forms. He also gives advice to
high school students to help in understanding music.

B157. "The American Composers' Art; Lincoln Center Inaugural Season:
        Copland's Connotations for Orchestra." Pan Pipes of Sigma
        Alpha Iota 55, no.2 (1963): 6.
        On September 23 Connotations received its premiere performance
at the opening of Philharmonic Hall. The work had been commissioned for this opening at Lincoln Center by Leonard Bernstein
conducting the New York Philharmonic. See also: W98

B158. "American Composers Honored." New York Times, December 22, 1932,
        p.20:6.
        One of Copland's compositions was selected from among 160
others to be performed at an international music festival in
Amsterdam in the coming summer. The work selected is not named.

B159. "An American in London." Newsweek 63 (June 8, 1964): 88-89.
        Music for a Great City recently had its premiere in Festival
Hall in London. The London Symphony Orchestra commissioned it
for their diamond jubilee celebration. Most of the audience
felt that the work reflected New York City. Copland conducted
it and spoke about his ideas for the composition. "Wit, humor,
and, at times, touching tonal imagery characterize Copland's
Suite." See also: W101.

B160. "American Music Listed." New York Times, September 22, 1945, p.
        14:6.

The New York City Symphony will perform the New York premiere of Copland's Danzón Cubano during the concert season. Leonard Bernstein, conductor, also announced that Copland's An Outdoor Overture will be performed at the first concert of the season on October 8.

B161. "American Salute of France Called More Effective than Printed Propaganda." Musical America 75 (July 1955): 13.
Several of Copland's works were presented in Paris by the Philadelphia Orchestra and the Radio Symphony Orchestra. Copland was present to conduct some of his works including Old American Songs.

B162. Anderson, Dale. "Music Lover's Bookshelf." Etude 71 (February 1953): 16.
Anderson finds Copland's Music and Imagination to be "pleasantly provocative." This book, taken from the author's lecture series at Harvard, addresses the styles of individual composers such as Franz List and Nicolai Rimsky-Korsakoff. The book is suitable "for thoughtful musicians." See also: B65

B163. Anderson, Owen. "New York." Music Journal 25 (December 1967): 73.
The New York Philharmonic commissioned Inscape to help celebrate its 125th anniversary. Although the first performance was at the University of Michigan on September 13, the New York premiere was October 13. "The work is quiet and contemplative, with the composer's consumate technical mastery everywhere in evidence." See also: W103

B164. Anderson, Ruth. "Copland, Aaron." In Contemporary American Composers: a Biographical Dictionary, 106-107. 2nd edition. Boston: G. K. Hall, 1982.
A brief listing of major honors and achievements is noted plus a list of works.

B165. Anderson, William. "American Brass." Stereo Review 46 (February 1981): 6.
Copland is the seventh musician honored to receive a Certificate of Merit for his contributions to American music by Stereo Review. His music is considered to have an "American" quality, but he has not been the forerunner of any particular modern style. Still, his influence is important. One area where serious music was not common was in film scores. Copland has been a forerunner in contributing to this medium.

B166. "Appalachian Spring." Harrisburg Symphony Orchestra Program Notes (November 18, 1975): 19-20; Oklahoma City Symphony Orchestra Program Notes (January 30, 1962): 174.

B167. "Appalachian Spring, Three Places in New England." Down Beat 46 (May 3, 1979): 31.
This is a review of Sound 80 Digital Records DRL-101 with Dennis Russell Davies conducting the St. Paul Chamber Orchestra. This recording uses the thirteen instruments in Copland's original scoring. The conductor "does a splendid job of capturing the atmosphere of this work." See also: D32

B168. "Applauding 'Diversity of Excellence.'" Christian Science Monitor, November 26, 1979, p.24.
    This editorial notes the second Kennedy Center Honors Program to be held December 2 and which includes Copland this year. This type of national recognition helps the country say thank you for these individuals' talents.

B169. Aprahamian, Felix. "Unheroic Hero." Times (London), September 21, 1975, p.37c.
    Among the reviews cited in this article is Copland's appearance on September 19 as guest conductor with the BBC Symphony Orchestra. The program of American music included Copland's "own early, brittle, two movement, jazz-influenced Piano Concerto."

B170. Archibald, Bruce. "Aaron Copland: His Life and Times." Music Library Association Notes 24, no.3 (March 1968): 500.
    This review of Arnold Dobrin's biography indicates the work is designed for young people. There are descriptions of his styles instead of a detailed analysis of Copland's music. The best feature of this biography is the "author's ability to present to the layman clear and vivid descriptions of the world of music." See also: B429

B171. Ardoin, John. "Orchestras." Musical America 83 (April 1963): 33.
    The New York Philharmonic with Leonard Bernstein conducting gave its second performance of Copland's Connotations for Orchestra in February. It had presented the premiere performance the previous September. The work was not well received on either occasion. Ardoin cites the work's occasional beauty, but he feels "the balance and length of the score still come between the music and the listener."

B172. Arlen, Walter. "Copland Joins in Monday 'Concert.'" Los Angeles Times, November 1, 1978, IV, p.13:1R.
    The Los Angeles County Museum of Art's Bing Theater was the location for a performance of the Twelve Poems of Emily Dickinson October 30. Copland accompanied Karen Yarmat. "Copland's pianistic contribution proved amazingly spry, fluent, rhythmically articulated and expressive." The Piano Quartet was his other work on the program.

B173. _____ and Albert Goldberg. "Ojai Festival Revolves around Works of Copland." Musical America 77 (July 1957): 10.
    Copland's West Coast premiere of selections from The Tender Land took place in Ojai, California on May 26. Copland conducted this and other works at the three-day festival. He received a warm reception from the audience.

B174. "Arts and Letters Group Names Writer President." New York Times, January 20, 1956, p.7:2.
    Copland has been elected to vice president of the National Institute of Arts and Letters. Malcolm Cowley was elected president for this term.

B175. "Arts Honoured by Princeton." Times (London), June 13, 1956, p.10b.
    Princeton University awarded an honorary doctor of music degree to Copland at its 209th commencement.

B176. "ASCAP/Copland Scholarship at Tanglewood and Aspen." ASCAP Today (Fall 1981): 32.

B177. Ashwell, Keith. "Copland Gives Banff a Bicentennial Focus." Performing Arts in Canada 13, no.3 (1976): 18-19.
Banff, a fine arts school, celebrated the United States' Bicentennial during its sixth annual festival consisting of fifty-four programs in a nineteen-day period. Copland was featured conducting some of his own works with the Canadian Chamber Orchestra. "At least with his own music, Copland is an effective conductor." A symposium discussed his book What to Listen For in Music. See also: B108.

B178. "Audience Braves Rain to Enjoy the Opening of Goldman Band's Silver Jubilee Year." New York Times, June 18, 1942, p.24:2.
Edwin Franko Goldman and his band included Copland's band transcription of An Outdoor Overture at the Central Park concert June 17. This was the first of the season in the twenty-fifth year of outdoor concerts.

B179. Austin, William W. "Copland, Aaron." In The New Grove Dictionary of Music and Musicians, edited by Stanley Sadie, 719-725. Washington, D.C.: Grove's Dictionaries of Music, 1980.
This thorough biography of Copland notes his musical training and attempts to examine his position as a contemporary composer in America. His work, and especially his styles, are analyzed along with musical examples. A classified list of his works and a bibliography of his writings as well as writings about him accompany the text.

B180. "Awards and Grants." Music Journal 28 (June 1970): 14.
The Howland Memorial Prize from Yale University has been awarded to Copland because of his accomplishments in the fine arts. Ohio State University has also awarded him an honorary degree.

B181. "BBC SO/Copland: Albert Hall/Radio 3." Times (London), September 17, 1975, p.10g.
On September 16, Copland was the guest conductor for a twentieth century American music program by the BBC Symphony Orchestra. Although he will be seventy-five years old soon, he still is a vigorous, enthusiastic musician. Included on the program were two of his own works: the Piano Concerto and Four Dance Episodes from Rodeo. He is "the most widely known of living American composers and an engaging conductor of other people's music as well as his own."

B182. "BMI Replies to the Etude Editorial 'The Bill of Musical Rights.'" Etude 59 (March 1941): 152.
Copland, as well as many other notable composers, had been barred from membership in the American Society of Composers, Authors, and Publishers (ASCAP) for many years because of its policies eliminating serious musicians. However, in a political move, it was announced recently in the newspapers that Copland had been made a member to refute claims that theirs was a "closed corporation." Copland sent ASCAP a telegram stating that he was not a member and would not consider being a member.

B183. Babb, Warren. "Aaron Copland: His Work and Contribution to American Music." Journal of Research in Music Education 4 (Fall 1956):
139-140.
This is a review of Julia Smith's biography. Her adaptation
of her dissertation is the most extensive examination of Copland's
life and work available. "She has succeeded even in making the
numerous analyses readable by the layman." Although the book is
extensive, Babb feels that Arthur Berger's smaller biography has
"the edge in both evocation of Copland's style and analysis of
his techniques. See also: B200, B1042

B184. "Bach's Hand Seen in Modern Music." New York Times, October 8,
1950, p.95:1.
The Music Institute, backed by the Griffith Music Foundation,
met in Newark, New Jersey on October 7. Copland spoke about
contemporary music and the influence of earlier composers such
as Johann Sebastian Bach.

B185. Bakeless, Katherine Little. Story-Lives of American Composers,
265-271. Rev. ed. Philadelphia: Lippincott, 1962.
This biography of Copland, among other famous Americans, is
designed for young people. It includes numerous anecdotes to
illustrate Copland's development as a prominent American composer. Some of his most popular works are mentioned.

B186. Baker, Doy. "Aaron Copland: Close Up." School Musician 39 (August-
September 1967): 36-38.
Copland recently visited the Interlochen Arts Academy at
Interlochen, Michigan where he was a lecturer-pianist in a
series of visiting contemporary composers. He performed some
of his piano works and conducted the orchestra. In addition,
he gave critiques to some of the student compositions and met
informally with the students.

B187. "Ban on Copland Work at Inaugural Scored." New York Times, January 17, 1953, p.12:4.
Representative Fred E. Busbey, an Illinois Republican, con-
vinced the Inaugural Concert Committee to exclude Copland's
Lincoln Portrait from the inaugural concert to be held January
18. The reason given was "that the composer had allegedly
associated with Communist front groups." The League of Composers
protested this action in a statement listing Copland's achievements, such as the Pulitzer Prize, and his reputation as a
leading composer in American music.

B188. Barnard, Eunice. "In the Classroom and on the Campus." New York
Times, March 14, 1937, II, p.6:5.
Copland's Second Hurricane will have its premiere April 21 by
the Henry Street Settlement Music School at the Neighborhood
Playhouse. This opera "is the first written in the United
States for children." See also: W81.

B189. Barnes, Clive. "The Dance: Miss Graham's Americana." New York
Times, December 17, 1975, p.41:1.
The second of three programs took place December 16 at the
Mark Hellinger Theater. The American theme of the evening in-
volved Copland conducting his Appalachian Spring.

B190. Barnes, Patricia. "Aaron Copland on a Lifetime of Music." Times
      (London), November 22, 1980, p.11d.
          This interview was conducted in New York just before Copland
      was scheduled to leave for a European tour. On December 2 he
      will be the guest conductor of the London Symphony Orchestra in
      a program of his works to celebrate his eightieth birthday. He
      reminisced about his long career and predicted that new composers
      will have much greater opportunities than he had.

B191. "Bassist Faces Challenge." New York Times, December 1, 1980, II,
      p.8:3.
          Gary Karr has "planned the world premiere performance of a
      sonata written for him by Aaron Copland" on November 30 in a
      recital at Alice Tully Hall.

B192. Bauer, Marion. "Aaron Copland." In The Music Lover's Handbook,
      edited by Elie Siegmeister, 757-761. New York: W. Morrow, 1943.
          Copland's early training and awards, such as his Guggenheim
      Fellowship, are related. An examination of his styles follows.
      "He has gone from complexity to simplification, from harmonic
      harshness to a gentler and more amiable mode of procedure." His
      Piano Variations and Vitebsk are examples from his early period.
      Billy the Kid and The Second Hurricane illustrate his simpler,
      more melodic later style.

B193. Baumgarten, P. K. "New Music." New York Times, October 5, 1952,
      VI, p.6:3.
          In this letter to the editor the writer agrees with Copland's
      recent article, "An Indictment of the Fourth B." Baumgarten
      also feels that the classics have been performed so often that
      they become boring and he welcomes new music. See also: B42

B194. Bazelon, I. A. "The Heiress." Film Music Notes 9 (November-
      December 1949): 17-18.
          This is a review of Copland's film score.

B195. Beale, Jane Gutherie. "Seattle: Copland Conducts His Third
      Symphony." Music Magazine and Musical Courier 164 (April 1962):
      64.
          Copland was invited as a guest conductor of the Seattle
      Symphony in January and "it was a significant occasion for music
      in this growing city."

B196. "Beame Invokes Fame of 13 Sons of the City." New York Times, May
      30, 1975, p.9:3.
          Mayor Abraham D. Beame mentioned Copland's name in his budget
      address May 29. He was listing famous people who grew up in
      New York.

B197. "Beethoven Hall Is Rising in Bonn." New York Times, March 29,
      1956, p.24:3.
          At ceremonies to begin construction of a hall near Beethoven's
      birthplace in Bonn, Germany, a letter from Copland was read. It
      spoke of an international music center's value because Beethoven's
      importance in music is so great.

B198. Behrens, E. "Says Aaron Copland--'Take Off the Ear-Muffs.'" Music
      Clubs Magazine 29 (April 1950): 10-11.

B199. Belt, Byron. "Four Voices of America." Music Journal 25 (December
      1967): 89-90.
         Belt has selected four works which represent the American
      sound in his opinion. Among them is Appalachian Spring in
      which "Copland's tasteful use of the songs and dances of the
      people has resulted in a piece so atmospheric and of such in-
      tegrity that it survived in the concert hall."

B200. Berger, Arthur Victor. Aaron Copland. 1953. Reprint. Greenwood
      Press, 1971.
         This biography is divided into two sections. The first empha-
      sizes Copland's development and career along with his different
      styles of composition up to the 1950's. An analysis of his
      music is provided in the second section and it includes many
      musical examples. Two of his larger works are examined thor-
      oughly: the Third Symphony and the Piano Variations. A bibli-
      ography and a discography are included.

B201. _____. "An Aaron Copland Discography." High Fidelity 5 (July
      1955): 64-69.
         An annotated, chronological discography of Copland's major
      works is listed, beginning with his Passacaglia in 1922. Com-
      ments on the compositions themselves give the reader background
      material to assist in better evaluating the recording itself.

B202. _____. "Aaron Copland's Piano Fantasy." Juilliard Review 5
      (Winter 1957-58): 13-27.
         The Piano Fantasy had its premiere at the fiftieth anniversary
      of the Juilliard School of Music for which it was commissioned.
      The work is in one movement. An analysis with musical examples
      is included. Berger feels that Copland has a good "sense of
      proportion and a faculty for discovering unexpected resources
      in his material." See also: W93

B203. _____. "A Copland Landmark." Saturday Review 36 (October 31,
      1953): 74-75.
         The Minneapolis Symphony, under the direction of Antal Dorati,
      has produced the first recording of Copland's Third Symphony on
      Mercury MG 50018. In addition, the Piano Variations, Piano
      Sonata, and Passacaglia are available on Walden LP 101 played by
      Webster Aitken. See also: D216, D233, D248, D349

B204. _____. "The Home-Grown Copland." Saturday Review of Literature
      33 (November 25, 1950): 72.
         This article is based upon Berger's forthcoming book on Copland.
      Berger examines the composer's styles in regard to other serious
      music. "There has been a peculiar swing between periods when he
      has deliberately used colloquial material itself to Americanize
      his style and periods when this material has been absorbed into
      a technique synthesizing the colloquial." Berger notes that
      after a period of not using folk elements, Copland has returned
      to that style. Berger fears that the respect of other serious
      musicians may be lost if he continues to write in this vein.
      See also: B200.

B205. _____. "Music of Aaron Copland." Musical Quarterly 31 (October
1945): 420-447.
This is an extensive article in which Berger analyzes Copland's
musical development. Specific musical characteristics are noted
in the musical examples. Berger believes that Copland was "the
first of our composers to develop, back in his jazz period, a
genuine Americanism in which others have followed him since."
A list of works is included.

B206. _____. "La Musica de Aaron Copland." Nuestra Musica (May 1946):
97-134.
A list of Copland's works is included.

B207. _____. "On First Hearing Copland's Tender Land." Center 1
(May 1954): 6-8.
This review of The Tender Land presents an analysis and il-
lustrations of some of the melodic presentations in this opera
designed for students. The New York City Opera was lauded for
presenting this work. Berger considers this a "grass roots"
opera and feels that the beautiful orchestration follows a
common pattern "to merge opera with the Broadway musical."

B208. _____. "The Pot of Fat? Chamber Opera Receives Its Premiere--
New Copland Work at M.I.T." New York Times, May 15, 1955, II,
p.7:7.
Theodore Chanler's opera The Pot of Fat was presented the
evening following Copland's premiere of Canticle of Freedom at
the Massachusetts Institute of Technology May 8. Copland's
work had been commissioned for the opening of the M.I.T. Kresge
Auditorium. Berger feels that "the large percussion battery
(including vibraphone and tubular chimes) needs delicate attacks
to achieve the crystalline sonorities characteristic of Copland's
orchestration lately." See also: W91

B209. _____. "Reviews of Records." Musical Quarterly 38 (October 1952):
655-659.
Berger reviews both the Quartet for Piano and Strings as well
as the Concerto for Clarinet and String Orchestra recorded on
Columbia ML 4421. Also included is a review of Old American Songs
on Columbia ML 2006. Copland conducts and performs in these two
recordings. The Quartet has a sparseness this is developed by
"principles of serial treatment such as those to be found in
twelve-tone music." The Concerto was written for Benny Goodman
and contains jazz elements. William Warfield, baritone, performs the Old American Songs, Sets I and II. See also: D78,
D189, D252

B210. _____. "Second Views of Hindemith, Copland." Saturday Review 37
(March 27, 1954): 63.
Berger reviews the recording Capitol P-8245 which contains
Copland's Quiet City conducted by Vladimir Golschmann with
trumpeter Harry Glantz. The Concert Arts Orchestra performs
this as part of a contemporary American music series. See
also: D257

B211. _____. "Spotlight on the Moderns." Saturday Review 37 (October 30, 1954): 78.
  Various recordings, both old and new are discussed. Many composers' works are included along with those of Copland.

B212. _____. "Stravinsky and the Younger American Composers." Score (London) 12 (June 1955): 38-46.
  Copland's studies with Nadia Boulanger of France are noted. She "was a key figure in solidifying the kinship between Copland and Stravinsky." Stravinsky and other students of Boulanger have influenced each other to a certain degree.

B213. Berger, Melvin. "Aaron Copland." In Masters of Modern Music, 139-155. New York: Lothrop, Lee & Shepard Co., 1970.
  A biography of Copland is included in this study of fourteen contemporary composers designed for young people. Most of the emphasis is on Copland's early life and musical training. Anecdotes help make this an entertaining examination of this composer's increasing importance.

B214. Berges, Ruth. "New York: Bronx Opera Company." Opera Canada 17, no.2 (1976): 38.
  Copland revised and extended his opera The Tender Land from two to three acts for a performance at Hunter College Playhouse. "Copland's score sounded professional and attractive throughout, at times slightly old-fashioned and repetitious to the point of tedium, but always saved by an attention-seeking orchestral device."

B215. Berkowitz, Freda Pastor. Unfinished Symphony and Other Stories of Men and Music, 205-216. New York: Atheneum, 1963.
  Some material discusses Copland in this book designed for young people.

B216. "Berkshire Opens Center on July 5." New York Times, May 15, 1953, p.20:7.
  Copland is the assistant director of the Berkshire Music Center, Tanglewood, as it begins its eleventh session on July 5. He will also teach composition during the summer.

B217. Berlioz, Hector. Fantastic Symphony: an Authoritative Score; Historical Background; Analysis; Views and Comments, edited by Edward T. Cone. New York: W. W. Norton, 1971.
  Berlioz's score is accompanied by historical information plus comments by Copland and other notable composers.

B218. Bernheimer, Martin. "A Star Spangler at Ambassador." Los Angeles Times, January 17, 1976, II, p.9:1.
  Copland conducted the Los Angeles Master Chorale and Sinfonia Orchestra January 15 in a Bicentennial concert at the Ambassador Auditorium. Bernheimer felt that there are better works by Copland than the Canticle of Freedom and In the Beginning which were presented on the program.

B219. _____. "Television Celebrates Aaron Copland's 80th." Los Angeles Times, April 1, 1981, II, p.1:1-R.

A review of the KCET-TV production of the "Kennedy Center
Tonight" series noted that Copland's birthday was celebrated.
On hand to assist with this festive concert were Leonard Bernstein
and Hal Holbrook, the host. After all the platitudes were given,
Copland's response was not a speech, but a simple thank you. "'I
feel like an enormously lucky fellow,'" he said.

B220. Bernstein, Leonard. "A.C. (an Acrostical Sonnet, on His 80th
    Birthday)." Perspectives of New Music 19, no.1-2 (1981-82): 9.
    This is a poem written to commemorate Bernstein's long-time
    friend and associate as part of this issue which is devoted
    entirely to Copland. Bernstein refers to his own birthday party
    in 1937 which was the evening the two men first met.

B221. _____. "Aaron Copland—an Intimate Sketch." High Fidelity/Musical
    America 20 (November 1970):53-55.
    Two major events in Bernstein's life occured on November 14
    which is Copland's birthday. The first was in 1937 when he first
    met Copland. They became friends and Bernstein would bring his
    compositions to Copland for criticism for he was still a student.
    The second event was in 1943 when Bernstein was called upon to
    substitute as conductor for the New York Philharmonic in a
    nationally broadcast concert that afternoon. Excellent reviews
    appeared in the following day's newspapers. Copland's reaction
    was that everyone besides Bernstein himself knew that Bernstein
    would be successful.

B222. "Bernstein Conducts Copland and Harris Works." Musical America
    77 (February 1957): 232.
    Leonard Bernstein conducted the first New York performance of
    Copland's Short Symphony on January 24 at Carnegie Hall. The
    jazz-style rhythmic complexities of this work have prevented it
    from appearing on many concert programs. Several conductors
    cancelled performances of it because of the amount of rehearsal
    time which would have been required to meet their standards.
    Nevertheless, Bernstein conducted an admiral performance that
    "sounded perfectly spontaneous and secure in pace and accent."

B223. "Bernstein Conducts Symphony of the Air." Musical America 75
    (December 1, 1955): 17.
    Copland's new work, Canticle of Freedom, was presented by
    Leonard Bernstein conducting the Symphony of the Air recently.
    A description of this one-movement piece for orchestra and chorus
    is included. The reviewer finds this piece to be beautifully
    constructed and concludes that "this is a minor work, but
    masterfully wrought."

B224. "Bernstein Tells Story of U.S. Music." New York Times, February
    2, 1958, p.78:4.
    Bernstein's second New York Philharmonic Young People's Concert
    on February 1 was devoted to the sounds of American music.
    Copland was present at the Carnegie Hall concert to conduct one
    movement from his Third Symphony.

B225. "The Bernstein Years." Gramophone 60 (July 1982): 170.
    "The Bernstein Years" will be recorded on a six-disc set and

will include Copland's <u>The Second Hurricane</u>. Bernstein will
speak about the play-opera between acts. "The music itself is
not one of Copland's more memorable scores, although it has its
moments."

B226. Bessom, Malcolm E. "Conversation with Copland." <u>Music Educators
Journal</u> 59 (March 1973): 40-49.
      This interview with Copland was conducted at West Virginia
University at Morgantown. Copland was there for three days to
lecture and work with students in rehearsals and concerts of
his music. Copland relates that his first efforts at composition
using "American" elements involved jazz in his Music for the
Theatre. Copland confessed that one type of work he still wants
to do is a proper string quartet. Copland reminisces about many
of his fellow composers in this extensive interview. Lists of
recordings conducted by him and others plus a bibliography are
included.

B227. Biancolli, Louis. "<u>A Lincoln Portrait</u>." <u>San Francisco Symphony
Program Notes</u> (February 14, 1959): 15.
      Andre Kostelanetz suggested the idea for this work and con-
ducted the premiere by the Cincinnati Symphony Orchestra in
Cincinnati on May 14, 1942. A narrator uses selections from
Lincoln's letters and speeches. <u>See also</u>: W68

B228. "<u>Billy the Kid</u>: Suite from the Ballet." <u>Philadelphia Orchestra
Program Notes</u> (December 16, 1955): 67.

B229. Bird, David. "Aaron Copland and Miss Arroyo Honored at City U.
Ceremonies." <u>New York Times</u>, June 4, 1981, II, p.7:1.
      Martina Arroyo and Copland received honorary Doctor of Humane
Letters degrees from City University Colleges June 3. Copland's
award at Queens College in Flushing was enhanced by the renaming
of the music department to The Aaron Copland School of Music.
Copland responded that he felt that this "was a 'wonderful
compliment.'"

B230. "A Birthday Scrapbook for Aaron Copland." <u>Tempo</u> 135 (December
1980): 28.
      These four pages of photos from various periods in Copland's
life illustrate his long career as a composer. His pictures
range from three to seventy-eight years of age.

B231. Blake, A. "American Classical Releases." <u>Metronome</u> 78 (June 196):
27.

B232. Blanks, F. R. "Aaron Copland, a Vital Force in American Music."
<u>Canon</u> 12 (August 1958): 413-415.
      Blanks feels that Copland has been a major influence in the
development of music which is distinctively American. In
addition, his work is respected as being very important and
creative all over the world. The American flavor of many of his
works is evident. He has created many of his compositions for
specific events and occasions. He has been "a democratic composer, with something to give the masses as well as the con-
noisseurs."

B233. Bliss, Arthur. "Music and Imagination, by Aaron Copland." Musical Times 95 (January 1954): 21-22.
Copland's book consists of the six lectures he delivered at Harvard 1951-1952. He discusses the relationship of the composer, performer, and listener in regard to imagination in music. In the latter half of this short book Copland discusses European influences and the American musical scene. See also: B65

B234. _____ et al. "Benjamin Britten's Sixtieth Birthday." Tempo 106 (September 1973): 2-5.
Greetings from Copland and others were received by Benjamin Britten on his sixtieth birthday. Copland met Britten when Britten was in his twenties. Copland states, "'Few contemporary composers can match him for stylistic consistency and high level of accomplishment.'"

B235. Blitzstein, Marc. "Reviews of Records." Musical Quarterly 40 (July 1954): 454-456.
Blitzstein reviews Copland's Music for the Theatre which has been recorded on MGM E-3095 by the M-G-M Orchestra conducted by Izler Solomon. This work lends itself "with aptness and imagination to a delineation of the jazz-spirit of the twenties." It is abstract and has sparse orchestration. See also: D179

B236. Blumfeld, Harold. "A Discography of the Avant-Mainstream." Los Angeles Times, January 5, 1975, CAL, p.40:3.
This discussion of "radical" music includes information on Copland's works which were experimental modern music.

B237. Blyth, Alan. "Aaron Copland." Times (London), November 14, 1970, p.19e.
This is a brief assessment of Copland's impact on modern music as he reaches his seventieth birthday today. The interview reveals Copland's late interest in conducting and his optimism about life in general.

B238. _____. "The Tender Land; Chelsea Town Hall." Opera (London) 17 (February 1966): 165-166.
This review of The Tender Land in a London concert performance November 29 is not favorable. The libretto by Horace Everett has a "banality of expression" and "the plot creaks and cranks along by means of a rather colorless recitative." Blyth feels the work has too many deficiencies to be effective.

B239. "Book Corner." Symphony 6 (December 1952): 15.
This is a review of Copland's Music and Imagination which is a compilation of his lectures given at Harvard University. This book "provokes thought about those problems with which all serious musicians must concern themselves if their art is to fulfil its historic and true purpose." See also: B65

B240. "Book Guide: Aaron Copland, by Arthur Berger." Tempo 31 (Spring 1954): 34-35.
This is a review of Berger's biography which is basically divided into two sections. One is on Copland as a person and the second is an analysis of his music including many musical

examples. The book is "short, well-produced and worthwhile."
See also: B200

B241. "Book Guide: Music and Imagination, by Aaron Copland." Tempo 31
(Spring 1954): 35-36.
      Copland's lectures at Harvard University are published in this
book which examines "the imaginative mind and its relation to
the different aspects of music." The differences between the
composer, performer, and listener can vary considerably.
Copland's notes on how once can become a more "imaginative
listener are superb." See also: B65

B242. "Book Reviews: Music and Imagination." Musical Opinion 97
(November 1973): 73.
      This review of Copland's book finds the compiled lectures to
be thought-provoking and important reading. The composer's
desire is to have his work performed by a performer who under-
stands what the composer wants and ultimately to be understood
by the listener. See also: B65

B243. "Book Reviews: No Nonsense, No Evasion, No Pretense." American
Record Guide 28 (May 1962): 748-750.
      This reviewer finds Copland's book, Copland on Music, has
"sensitive reaction as well as prophetic appraisal." This work
is a compilation of his lectures and writings from the past
thirty years. One section is devoted to American composers and
he discusses developments on the American scene. See also: B24

B244. Bookspan, Martin. "The Basic Repertoire." Stereo Review 30 (February 1973): 55.
      Copland composed Fanfare for the Common Man and Lincoln
Portrait in 1942 when the United States was involved in World
War II. Eugene Goossens, the conductor of the Cincinnati
Orchestra asked eighteen composers "to create brief fanfares
on behalf of America's war effort." Andre Kostelanetz asked
three composers to contribute a work to reflect the national
spirit. Copland chose Lincoln. In his work a narrator provides
material from Lincoln's letters and speeches to the orchestral
accompaniment.

B245. "Boosey and Hawkes Concert: A Modern Program." Times (London),
February 28, 1944, p.8b.
      The first performance in London of Copland's Piano Sonata
took place at the Boosey and Hawkes' Concert on February 27 at
Wigmore Hall. The work "looks grim and gritty in print and fully
lives up to its appearance in performance."

B246. Boretz, Benjamin. "Music." Nation 195 (November 20, 1962): 314-
315.
      Connotations for Orchestra was commissioned for the opening of
Philharmonic Hall at Lincoln Center. An analysis of this work's
twelve-tone configuration is given and its relationship to his
earlier works in this vein, such as the Piano Fantasy and Piano
Quartet is shown. Boretz does not consider Connotations to be
twelve-tone music because it does not follow that pattern very
strictly. The work was not well received by the audience at its
premiere. See also: W98

B247. "Boston Symphony." Musical Courier 153 (March 1, 1956): 17.
   On February 8 Copland's revised Symphonic Ode had its New York
   premiere. It was commissioned by the Boston Symphony Orchestra
   for its seventy-fifth anniversary. The original version had
   also been commissioned by the Boston Symphony for its fiftieth
   anniversary. "It is a most effective piece of music." See
   also: W38

B248. Boston Symphony Heard at United Nations Concert." Musical America
   70 (January 1, 1950): 10.
   Copland's Preamble for orchestra and speaker was written for
   the United Nations' first anniversary of the Universal Declaration
   of Human Rights held on December 10, 1949. Sir Laurence Olivier
   was the speaker in this permiere performance. The reviewer ap-
   proved of the music, saying that it is "in Copland's familiar harmonic style, without undue dissonance." Leonard Bernstein conducted the Boston Symphony in this performance. See also: W84

B249. "Bostonians Defrost Australian Audience." New York Times, June 12,
   1960, p.46:4.
   The Boston Symphony Orchestra, with Copland as guest conductor,
   presented a concert in Centennial Hall, Adelaide, Australia.
   Three thousand people showed up even though the weather was very
   cold and the building had no central heating. Copland wore a
   topcoat during the performance.

B250. Brant, LeRoy V. "America, Involved in Music, Is Becoming Great in
   Music." Etude 71 (April 1953): 9.
   This interview with Copland illustrates Copland's enthusiasm
   for promoting American contemporary composers. He is quoted as
   saying, "'For a nation to become great musically she must come
   to understand the meaning of music, the importance of it in the
   daily lives of the people.'" Copland listed his suggestions for
   young composers to follow in becoming successful.

B251. Bredemann, Dan. "Audience Is First--Copland." Biography News 1
   (February 1974): 144.
   This interview is taken from the Cincinnati Enquirer, January
   13, 1974. Copland is quoted in this article saying, "'Music can
   only be really alive when there are listeners who are really
   alive.'" He feels that there is less audience resistance to new
   works now, and that provides more opportunities for new composers
   to have their works performed. There is still room for improve-
   ment in both of these areas, however. He is not certain whether
   or not his books on listening have helped audiences, but he
   hopes that it assisted in their musical education.

B252. Briggs, John. "Concert: at Tanglewood." New York Times, July 27,
   1959, p.21:2.
   Copland conducted his opera suite, The Tender Land, at the
   Berkshire Music Festival July 27. The Boston Symphony performed.
   "Although Mr. Copland's opera in theatre performance was felt by
   some observers to lack dramatic vitality, the Suite he has
   fashioned from it is an interesting and well-constructed work."

B253. Brodbin, John. "The Tender Land." Opera News 18 (April 5, 1954):
15.
      This new work "proves to be thoroughly American in expression
      and idiom, in its theme and music and in the way that Copland
      has achieved the integration of words and music." There seems
      to be renewed interest in opera in general among musicians and
      listeners. This may have influenced Copland as well as other
      Americans to attempt to write more for this medium.

B254. "Bronx Opera: The Tender Land." High Fidelity/Musical America
26 (May 1976): MA30.
      A revision of Copland's opera was presented at Hunter College
      in New York on January 16. The music "is in Copland's familiar
      'American' style, which is to say wide melodic intervals, open
      triadic harmony, and a certain emotive quality which has been
      taken to suggest the wide open spaces of the American heartland."
      It was not well received by the audience.

B255. Brook, Donald. "Aaron Copland." In Composers' Gallery; Biographical Sketches of Contemporary Composers, 133-136. London: Rockliff,
1946.
      This biography traces Copland's career through the mid 1940's
      when he was in the process of writing his Third Symphony as a
      memorial to the famous conductor Serge Koussevitzky's wife
      Natalie. Copland's major works are discussed with accompanying
      information on first performances.

B256. Brookhart, Charles Edward. "The Choral Music of Aaron Copland,
Roy Harris, and Randall Thompson." Ph.D. diss., George Peabody
College for Teachers, 1960.
      Brookhart did a harmonic analysis of Copland's Lark and In the
      Beginning. The interval of a third was found to be the most
      common aspect of Copland's choral style in these works. Melodic
      direction, chord root changes, and modulations frequently utilize
      thirds.

B257. Brown, Alan. "Copland: El Salón México." Music Teacher and Piano
Student 55 (June 1976): 17-18.
      This work grew out of Copland's desire to simplify his music
      and to make it more acceptable to audiences. This one-movement
      work lasts approximately eleven minutes and was composed in 1936.
      This article is an analysis of the rhythm, harmony, melody, or-
      chestration, and structure of the piece.

B258. Bryant, Celia. "Musical Drama--The Cat and the Mouse: Aaron
Copland's Humorous Scherzo." Clavier 7, no.9 (1968): 16-18.
      This piano piece was Copland's first composition to be pub-
      lished. It was first presented in a concert by him when he was
      studying in France. Jacques Durand, Debussy's publisher, offered
      to buy the rights to the work for twenty-five dollars and Copland
      accepted. A thorough discussion of the work is included. The
      piece appeals to young people by providing "a wide range of
      dynamics, a variety of touch, and the ability to move swiftly
      over the entire keyboard." See also: W14

B259. Bullock, Bruce Lloyd. "Aaron Copland's Concerto for Clarinet; a
    Lecture Recital, Together with Three Recitals of Music by Mozart,
    Rossini, Schumann, Brahms, and Contemporary European and North
    American Composers." Ph.D. diss., North Texas State University,
    1971.
        The lecture recital included a stylistic analysis of the Clari-
    net Concerto with an emphasis on rhythm and melody. This work
    is compared and contrasted to other works by Copland. A per-
    formance of the work with a piano reduction of the orchestral
    part concludes the lecture recital.

B260. Bumiller, Elisabeth, Donnie Radcliffe, and Joseph McLellan.
    "Kennedy Center Honors: the Movers Meet the Shakers." Washington
    Post, December 8, 1979, B, p.1:1.
        Copland was one of five honorees at the second annual honors
    tribute at the Kennedy Center for "lifetime achievements in the
    performing arts" on December 2.

B261. Burns, Mary T. "An Analysis of Selected Folk-Style Themes in the
    Music of Bedrich Smetana and Aaron Copland." American Music
    Teacher 25, no.2 (1975): 8-10.
        A brief history of Copland's works which embody folk themes is
    given. An analysis of the Tis the Gift to be Simple theme used
    in Appalachian Spring appears along with its variations in tempo,
    instrumentation, and rhythm.

B262. Burton, Humphrey. "The Art and Life of Aaron Copland." Listener
    74 (December 16, 1975): 987-990.
        Questions about Copland's developing abilities as a composer
    are asked in this interview from the British Broadcasting
    Corporation. Copland's interest in folk music and jazz is
    examined as he used these elements in his works. His method of
    composing has involved keeping notebooks with themes in them.
    He states that he consciously works at developing a theme be-
    cause it is not a spontaneous reaction as it is with some com-
    posers. He has recently been very interested in conducting, and
    his activities include lecturing and writing about music.

B263. Butterworth, Neil. "American Composers." Music (Schools Music
    Association) 2, no.1 (1967): 39-40.
        Copland's international fame began with his First Symphony
    after he returned from France and his studies with Nadia
    Boulanger. Copland realized that his music did not appeal to
    his audiences, so in the 1930's he consciously began writing
    material that he felt audiences would appreciate, such as Rodeo
    and Appalachian Spring.

B264. Caine, Milton A. "Comments on Copland." American Record Guide
    44 (November 1980): 4-6.
        This is an interview with Copland commenting on his eightieth
    birthday. He concedes that he has not been composing during the
    past few years, but he has been conducting. One of the things
    he regrets is that he has not composed an opera suitable for
    the Metropolitan Opera. Copland says in advance that he knew
    whether or not his music was going to be popular, so it was no
    surprise to him that the Piano Variations were not well received

and <u>Billy the Kid</u> was immediately accepted by audiences. His plans are to continue conducting as long as he is physically able but probably he will not compose any more.

B265. Cairns, David. "Aaron Copland." <u>Musical Times</u> 105 (July 1964): 520-521.
On May 26, Copland conducted the London Symphony Orchestra in his Clarinet Concerto, <u>Lincoln Portrait</u>, and <u>Music for a Great City</u>. "The accent was on Copland the prodigiously effective and resourceful functionalist rather than on the symphonic thinker or the folk-mystic." <u>Music for a Great City</u> is a new piece which was commissioned by the London Symphony Orchestra.

B266. Calta, Louis. "Copland Is Succeeded by Lynes as Head of MacDowell Colony." <u>New York Times</u>, January 30, 1969, p.39:1.
Russell Lynes took over the position of president from Copland who was retiring after having the post for seven years. The MacDowell Colony provides a quiet place for artists to work.

B267. Canby, Edward Tatnall. "Music and Electricity." <u>Saturday Review of Literature</u> 29 (August 17, 1946): 31.
"He is one of the few good composers in any land to write his best music in forms unplayable in the concert hall." Canby is referring to Copland's <u>Lincoln Portrait</u> which was commissioned for a radio broadcast and it consists of a narration of Lincoln's words with a musical background. This was very successful on radio, but in the concert hall, the amplification of the narrator made it sound "ludicrous" in Canby's opinion.

B268. "Captures Music Award." <u>New York Times</u>, May 22, 1950, p.16:2.
Copland is being succeeded by Mrs. Nicolai Berezowsky as the chairman of the League of Composers.

B269. Cariaga, Daniel. "Fullerton Does Copland Honors." <u>Los Angeles Times</u>, March 31, 1977, IV, p.1:4.
A three-day Copland Festival at the California State University, Fullerton honored the composer by presenting concerts of his music. A review of the performances follows. During the following week he will be honored again with a concert of his works at Occidental College.

B270. Carman, Judith Elaine. "A Comprehensive Performance Project in Solo Vocal Literature with an Essay: Twentieth-Century American Song Cycles: a Study in Circle Imagery." Ph.D. diss., University of Iowa, 1973.
Copland is one of the American composers whose song cycle is examined in this study.

B271. Carter, Elliott. "The Rhythmic Basis of American Music." <u>Score</u> (London) 12 (June 1955): 28-29.
"Copland maintains a direct relationship with jazz or other kinds of American dance music, especially in his fast movements." Other rhythmic elements have been utilized in his works.

B272. Carter, Richard. "National Symphony." <u>Washington Post</u>, August 6, 1979, B, p.7:1R.

Copland was a guest conductor of the National Symphony Orchestra in a concert consisting entirely of his works at Wolf Trap
on August 4. Some of his less well-know works were performed,
such as the Dance Symphony.

B273. "Celebrating 'Copland.'" Washington Post, March 26, 1981, D, p.
10:2
A premiere of the Public Broadcasting System show, "A Copland
Celebration," was shown March 25 at the Kennedy Center. Although
Copland was not present for the premiere, he saw the tapes later
and was reportedly reduced to tears during the Lincoln Portrait.

B274. Chanler, Theodore. "Aaron Copland." In American Composers on
American Music; a Symposium, edited by Henry Cowell, 49-56. New
York: F. Ungar, 1962.
Chandler analyzes Copland's style by examining several of his
major works, especially the Symphonic Ode. Chandler feels that
"in all preceding works, his essential personality has seemed
fragmentary, not wholly liberated." He finds the Ode to be much
more individual than any earlier work. This article was written
when Copland was only thirty-two years of age. Henry Cowell has
added a paragraph stating that in the past thirty years Copland's
compositions have changed significantly in style. A list of his
major works is included.

B275. Chapin, Louis. "Audience Lavishes Praises upon Youth." Christian
Science Monitor, February 2, 1963, p.11:6.
The January 31 concert included a repeat of Connotations which
had been commissioned for the New York Philharmonic, conducted
by Leonard Bernstein, for the opening of Philharmonic Hall at
Lincoln Center the previous fall. Chapin considers the work
"controversial" and says that he "found special difficulties
when once or twice a developmental idea is insisted on with
extended vehemence."

B276. _____. "Playright Composer in Campus Talks." Christian Science
Monitor, October 17, 1962, p.6:1.
Edward Albee and Copland were among the guest speakers at
Mount Holyoke College's 125th anniversary. Copland's feeling is
that a composer must compose because it "gives substance and
meaning to his and to others' lives."

B277. Chapman, E. "Copland and the L.S.O." Musical Events 19 (July
1964): 17.
Copland's Music for a Great City is being performed by the
London Symphony Orchestra.

B278. _____. "Copland and the L.S.O." Musical Events 20 (December
1965): 33-34.

B279. _____. "L.S.O.--L.P.O.--B.B.C." Musical Events 17 (April 1962):
12.
The London Symphony Orchestra, the London Philharmonic Orchestra, and the British Broadcasting Corporation are discussed.

B280. Chase, Gilbert. "Aaron Copland." In <u>The New Music Lover's Hand-book</u>, edited by Elie Siegmeister, 533-536. Irvington-on-Hudson, New York: Harvey House, 1973.

This excerpt is taken from Chase's book <u>America's Music</u> and related Copland's early musical training and stylistic changes. Copland's interest in American idioms resulted in two works which incorporate jazz techniques: <u>Music for the Theatre</u> and Concerto for Piano and Orchestra. Later he composed works which had an austere character, such as the Piano Variations. Realizing that the public did not appreciate his severe sounds, he consciously worked toward bringing simplicity to his music in such works as <u>Appalachian Spring</u>. In the 1950's his musical style included twelve-tone techniques in a return to his earlier austere style which resulted in Piano Fantasy, for example.

B281. _____. "Aaron Copland: His Work and Contribution to American Music." <u>Music Library Association Notes</u> 14 (March 1957): 256-257.

Julia Smith's dissertation was condensed to become this book. Chase finds the biography to be an important addition to the literature on American composers. She states that Copland is the foremost American composer. "Whatever authority her book possesses derives from her insights as a musician and the comprehensiveness of her information." <u>See also</u>: B1042

B282. _____. <u>The American Composer Speaks; a Historical Anthology, 1770-1965</u>. Baton Rouge: Louisiana State University Press, 1966.

One section of this book gives an overview of Copland's accomplishments throughout his long career as a composer. Most of the information is autobiographical and concentrates on his early introduction to music. Copland gives insight into his change in attitude toward music that the public finds pleasant and acceptable.

B283. _____. "The Americanists: Composer from Brooklyn--No.2" In <u>America's Music, from the Pilgrims to the Present</u>, 495-504. 2d ed. New York: McGraw-Hill, 1966.

Copland's career is related with an emphasis on the different styles he used. Shortly after beginning composing, he consciously tried to incorporate elements of Americanism into his works. At first he used jazz elements but later switched to folk and popular melodies. <u>Appalachian Spring</u> and <u>Billy the Kid</u> contain these popular themes. Earlier there was a period of austerity which resulted in works such as his Piano Variations. In the 1950's he incorporated twelve-tone techniques in works such as the Quartet for Piano and Strings.

B284. Chase, Mary Cole. "Sketches of Those Just Added to Roll of Pulitzer Prize Winners." <u>New York Times</u>, May 8, 1945, p.16:1.

Copland's score for the ballet <u>Appalachian Spring</u> received the Pulitzer Prize in Music this year. The work had its premiere with Martha Graham's Dance Company in Washington the previous fall. In addition, he has received two Guggenheim Fellowships and has authored numerous books and articles. It is noted also that many of his compositions deal with American themes.

B285. "Chatham Premieres Graham Ballet Film." Musical America 79 (March 1959): 37.
Martha Graham and Copland saw the world premiere of their filmed ballet, Appalachian Spring, at Chatham College, Pittsburgh on January 14. A concert of Copland's works was presented before the showing of the film. Although the ballet was first performed in 1944, it was not filmed until 1958.

B286. Chavez, C. "Ives y Copland." Clave 49 (August-September 1962): 19-23.

B287. "Cheerful Music by Mr. Copland." Times (London), May 27, 1964, p. 13a.
Copland was the guest conductor of the London Symphony Orchestra at Festival Hall May 26 in a concert of works by Britten, Stravinsky, and himself. His Music for a Great City which was commissioned by the London Symphony Orchestra had its premiere performance. "He is not a composer-conductor who exercises both faculties with equal brilliance." See also: W101

B288. "Children's Opera to Have Premiere." New York Times, March 14, 1937, VI, p.5:5.
The Henry Street Settlement Music School is planning to give the premiere performance of Copland's opera, The Second Hurricane, on April 21. This composition is designed for high school students. Edwin Denby is the librettist. See also: W51

B289. "Children's Suite." New York Philharmonic Program Notes (October 16, 1949): 2.
The New York Philharmonic under the direction of Leopold Stokowski performed the Children's Suite from The Red Pony at Carnegie Hall. This is from the film score for the movie by the same name and is based on John Steinbeck's story. A synopsis of the story of the film is included.

B290. Chissell, Joan. "The Sonata from 1778 to 1821." Times (London), October 4, 1968, p.13b.
This is a review of a performance of Copland's Organ Symphony by E. Power Biggs and the London Philharmonic Orchestra. Adrian Boult conducted the work at Festival Hall on October 3. This composition "is a curious medley of inconclusive material and muddled ideas."

B291. "Cincuentenario de dos Musicos." Revista Musical Chilena 6 (Spring 1950): 115-116.

B292. Citkowitz, Israel. "Aaron Copland--Personal Note." Boston Symphony Orchestra Concert Bulletin 2 (October 17, 1953): 68.
Citkowitz characterizes Copland's personality as one that contains many opposites. He feels that "Copland's insistance in the uncovering of new talent is an extraordinary phenomenon."

B293. _____. "Current Chronicle: New York." Musical Quarterly 40 (July 1954): 394-397.
Citkowitz wonders how The Tender Land could use procedures that

"are so confounding in their simplicity, in their confident
reliance on the humblest of musical materials" and be so successful as contemporary music. This simple music, embodying
folk elements, continues a style in which he consciously attempted
to appeal to a wide audience. In contrast, he has composed some
sparse, abstract music which some consider to be his "serious
music."

B294. "Clarence Adler in Mozart Series." New York Times, November 4,
1942, p.26:4.
    Copland spoke on "Mozart and Modern Music" at Adler's concert
    on November 3. Adler performed three of Mozart's piano concertos
    with the National Orchestral Association Alumni Orchestra con-
    ducted by Leon Barzin.

B295. Clark, B. "Cambridge." Music and Musicians 10 (April 1962): 40.
    Copland's opera, The Tender Land, was performed at Cambridge.

B296. "Classical or Modern: Aaron Copland Questions a Common Musical Dis-
tortion." Times (London), April 28, 1960, p.6e.
    This is an interview with Copland in which he decries the lack
    of interest in new music by modern audiences. They choose to
    hear familiar works and do not support modern, new compositions.

B297. "Cliburn Contest Set for September." New York Times, June 26, 1973,
p.54:2.
    One of the eight awards offered at the fourth Van Cliburn Inter-
    national Piano Competition is for the best performance of a new
    Copland piano solo. This event will take place September 17-30
    in Fort Worth, Texas. Night Thoughts was commissioned for this
    contest. See also: W111

B298. Clurman, Harold. "Aaron Copland." In Double Exposure, by Roddy
McDowall, 100-101. New York: Delacorte Press, 1966.
    Clurman recounts that in a letter he received from Copland in
    the 1920's, Copland indicated that his goal in life "was to be a
    great man to himself." Copland's outstanding personal attributes
    are noted in addition to his fame as a composer.

B299. _____. "Aaron Copland, by A. Berger." Saturday Review 36 (November 28, 1953): 36.
    Clurman reviews Arthur Berger's biography. The work is divided
    into two sections, one on the composer himself, and the other
    on an analysis of his music. Clurman feels that the most im-
    portant aspect of this book "is its attempt to relate the more
    popular or readily acceptable of the composer's work to the
    more difficult work." See also: B200

B300. Cole, Hugh. "Aaron Copland (I)." Tempo 76 (Spring 1966): 2-6.
    Cole analyzes Copland's styles by examining relatively little-
    known works as well as the most familiar ones. Musical examples
    illustrate his points on texture and voicing and contrasts are
    noted in styles from his different periods.

B301. _____. "Aaron Copland (II)." Tempo 77 (Summer 1966): 9-15.

Cole continues the analysis of Copland's works in this article which continues the previous entry. Twelve-tone techniques are particularly noted.

B302. _____. Popular Elements in Copland's Music." <u>Tempo</u> 95 (Winter 1970-1971): 4.

Nationalism in music was not in vogue when Copland began his career in the 1920's. Nonetheless, as a composer of serious music, he consciously attempted to infuse American feelings and tonalities into certain of his works. The jazz idiom is evident in his Piano Concerto. A detailed analysis of <u>El Salón México</u> in included along with musical examples. Copland incorporated popular music characteristics into his works in a sophisticated manner.

B303. _____. "El Salón Pimlico." <u>Guardian</u> 5 (October 1965): 9.

B304. Coleman, Jack. "The Trumpet: Its Use in Selected Works of Stravinsky, Hindemith, Shostakovich, and Copland." Ph.D. diss., University of Southern California, 1965.

Coleman extracted excerpts from eighty-four scores in analyzing trumpet parts in this study. He finds the frequent use of trumpet solos in Copland's orchestral works. One characteristic he notes is the tendency to switch the solo back and forth between members of the trumpet section. Copland's writing for trumpet is within normal ranges and is not unusually demanding.

B305. "College Commencements Honor 13 Here." <u>New York Times</u>, June 6, 1975, p.12:1.

An honorary Doctor of Humane Letters degree was awarded to Copland during Brooklyn College's commencement ceremonies.

B306. Commanday, Robert. "Cabrillo Festival: "Appalachian Spring's Eternal Appeal." <u>San Francisco Chronicle</u>, September 2, 1978, p.36:1R.

Copland was present at this festival to conduct his original version of <u>Appalachian Spring</u> for thirteen instruments. The revised, expanded version for orchestra is usually the version which is performed.

B307. _____. "The Direct Music of Aaron Copland." <u>San Francisco Chronicle</u>, August 29, 1978, p.40:2R.

This review finds Copland's works presented at the Cabrillo Festival on August 28 to be very appealing to audiences. Copland's enthusiasm is apparent in his conducting of his works, such as in <u>Dance Panels</u>. "Copland states what his music will be, and his music then says that, directly."

B308. "Committee Chosen for Hopkins Center." <u>New York Times</u>, May 27, 1962, p.96:2.

Copland is one of six composers selected to be on an advisory committee at Dartmouth University's Hopkins Center of Music, Drama, and Art.

B309. "Composer Aaron Copland Named to ASCAP Board of Directors." <u>ASCAP Today</u> 6, no.2 (1974): 5.

Copland was appointed to fill the unexpired term for Samuel
Barber who left to spend more time in Italy. A member of ASCAP
since 1946, Copland's many awards and achievements include the
Presidential Medal of Freedom for peacetime service in 1964.

B310. "Composer Aaron Copland Named to Serve on ASCAP Board of Directors."
School Musician 5 (December 1973): 53.
Copland received an appointment to the Board of Directors and
replaces Samuel Barber. Copland has been noted as a leading
American composer and has received numerous awards for his music
including the Pulitzer Prize for Appalachian Spring. His books
and lectures have brought him additional fame.

B311. "Composer Honored Here." New York Times, November 23, 1975, p.58:1.
A concert by pianist Leo Smit honoring Copland on his seventy-
fifth birthday was held November 22 at Cooper Union. Violinist
Delmar Stewart also performed.

B312. "Composer in Poetry Post." New York Times, March 11, 1951, p.78:5.
On March 10 Harvard University announced that Copland will be
the 1951-52 Charles Eliot Norton Professor of Poetry. Copland
has received a Pulitzer Prize and and Academy Award for his
scores.

B313. "Composers." Musical Courier 163 (April 1961): 30.
Copland's Nonet for Solo Strings is discussed.

B314. "Composers' Forum Opens Music Week." New York Times, May 8, 1939,
p.20:4.
The New York City Federal Music Project opened last week with
a concert in Carnegie Hall. Copland's An Outdoor Overture was
performed by the Federal Symphony Orchestra of New York. In
this work Copland "displayed his usual intelligence," but the
reviewer does not feel that the work is his best.

B315. "Composers Honor Copland at Age 50." New York Times, November 6,
1950, p.32:7.
An early birthday celebration was held November 5 by the League
of Composers with a concert of Copland's works at the Museum of
Modern Art. A critique of the various artists' performances is
included.

B316. "Concert and Opera Asides." New York Times, December 4, 1938, X,
p.11:8.
Among the current events noted is Copland's new work, An
Outdoor Overture, which he composed for the High School of Music
and Art, New York City. The premiere is scheduled by this
group on December 16 and 17. See also: W55

B317. "Concert in Englewood." New York Times, November 20, 1959, p.36:1.
Copland conducted his Tender Land Suite at Dwight Morrow High
School on November 19. The Boston Symphony Orchestra performed
this and other works for an audience of two thousand.

B318. "Concert Notes." Strad 80 (January 1970): 435.
Copland recently conducted the London Symphony Orchestra in a

concert of British works as well as his own compositions. Quiet
City is a "wistful essay in authentic Americana" and Billy the
Kid "showed virtuosity, fun and a certain pathos."

B319. "Concert Review: Aaron Copland Salute." Variety 281 (November 19,
1975): 55.
Copland's seventy-fifth birthday was celebrated by the Juilliard
Orchestra in Alice Tully Hall recently. Copland was present for
the occasion and conducted part of the all-Copland program.

B320. "Concerto for Clarinet and String Orchestra, with Harp and Piano."
Clarinet 1 (Fall 1950): 24-25; Houston Symphony Orchestra Program Notes (March 3, 1969): 19; London Musical Events 7 (November
1952): 32.

B321. "Concerto for Clarinet and String Orchestra, with Harp and Piano."
Music and Letters 33 (October 1952): 366.
This a review of Copland's score which includes elements of
ragtime. "It is an exciting hotchpotch of unpretentious
tomfoolery, reverently dedicated to Benny Goodman."

B322. "Concerto for Clarinet and String Orchestra, with Harp and Piano."
Philadelphia Orchestra Program Notes (November 24, 1950): 160-
163; San Antonio Symphony Program Notes (November 17, 1962): 17.

B323. "Concerto for Piano and Orchestra." Boston Symphony Orchestra
Concert Bulletin 2 (October 17, 1953): 64.

B324. Cone, Edward T. "Conversation with Aaron Copland." Perspectives
of New Music 6, no.2 (1968): 57-72; In Perspectives on American
Composers, edited by Benjamin Boretz and Edward T. Cone, 131-
146. New York: W. W. Norton, 1971.
This interview with Copland on November 13, 1967 gives insight
into his feelings about becoming a composer and about the various
influences upon his styles of music. The question and answer
session is chronological and follows Copland's long career. His
work in the League of Composers is noted.

B325. Conly, John M. "Aaron Copland Looks Ahead." Reporter 33 (August
12, 1965): 54.
Copland reports that he is enjoying conducting his works in
concerts and for recordings. His struggles as a beginning composer are recounted. He feels that composers who are just
starting out now have many more opportunities than he had, but
he is glad he was actively composing when he was because of other
factors. A list of Copland's favorite recordings of his own
works is included.

B326. "Connotations for Orchestra." National Symphony Program Notes
(February 21, 1967): 26.

B327. "Connotations for Orchestra." New York Philharmonic Program Notes
(September 23, 1962): 44-45.
The world premiere of this work took place in Philharmonic Hall,
Lincoln Center with Leonard Bernstein conducting the New York
Philharmonic on September 23. Copland's notes about this piece

indicate ' that he used twelve-tone techniques in its construction.
It resembles the Baroque chaconne in design. See also: W98

B328. "Connotations for Orchestra." New York Philharmonic Program Notes
(January 31, 1963): C-D.
Leonard Bernstein conducted the New York Philharmonic in the
second performance of Copland's Connotations. Its world premiere
was presented by the same group the previous September 23 at the
opening of Philharmonic Hall in Lincoln Center.

B329. Cook, Eugene. "Copland's Soundtrack." New York Times, October 1,
1961, VI, p.78.
Five photographs with captions picture Copland conducting his
score for the new movie Something Wild. Jack Garfein is the
director of this film which stars Carroll Baker.

B330. Coolidge, Richard. "Aaron Copland's Passacaglia: an Analysis."
Music Analysis 2, no.2 (1974): 33-36.
This article defines the differences between grounds, chaconnes,
and passacaglias. Coolidge feels that Copland's Passacaglia is
an excellent illustration of this form and he illustrates this
with a detailed analysis of the work.

B331. Cooper, Martin. "Copland, Aaron." In The Concise Encyclopedia of
Music and Musicians, 102. 4th edition. London: Hutchinson, 1978.
A brief sketch of Copland's major accomplishments is given. He
"has made use of regional American idioms to achieve a national
flavour."

B332. "Copland, Aaron." Current Biography 12 (March 1951): 21-23.
This article supercedes the previous one which appeared in
1940. This is a comprehensive biography detailing Copland's
background, compositions, and achievements. Among his many
achievements is the 1944 Pulitzer Prize in Music for Appalachian
Spring. He has always been active in promoting contemporary
American music. He helped organize the Copland-Sessions Concerts
has served in various offices in the League of Composers. His
writings in books and articles relate his philosophies of music.

B333. "Copland, Aaron." In The National Cyclopedia of American Biography,
vol. 1, 288-289. Chifton, New Jersey: J. T. White, 1971.
This is a brief biography listing Copland's works and achievements up to 1950.

B334. "Copland and Bloch Win Music Honors." New York Times, June 6,
1947, p.26:3.
Copland's Third Symphony and Ernest Bloch's Second Quartet
have just won the Music Critics Circle Award. These pieces were
selected from among orchestral and chamber works which had their
New York premieres during the past concert season.

B335. "Copland and Exxon Get Baton Awards." New York Times, June 10,
1978, p.9:1.
The American Symphony Orchestra League bestowed its prestig-
ious baton award for contributions to music and the arts to
Copland and the Exxon Corporation in Chicago during the League's
national conference.

B336. "Copland and Foss in Soviet Concert." New York Times, March 26, 1960, p.14:3.

Lukas Foss and Copland are on a four-week tour in the Soviet Union during which they are to meet with Russian composers as well as perform and conduct works of their own. On March 25 Copland conducted his Third Symphony which received a polite reception. In addition, Copland presented Dmitri Shostakovich with a National Institute of Arts and Letters' honorary membership.

B337. "Copland Appointed Professor." New York Times, January 25, 1957, p.16:3.

Copland has been designated the visiting Slee Professor of Music for one semester beginning next fall at the University of Buffalo.

B338. "Copland at 70." Tempo 95 (Winter 1970-1971): 1.

This entire issue is devoted to Copland who was seventy years old on November 14, 1970. His music includes a grandiose style seen in his Third Symphony as well as a sparce, economical style as depicted in his Piano Variations. "He is one of the great classicists of our time, in that he has conspicuously avoided both the hysteria and the complacency of much of the music of his generation, without withdrawing into triviality."

B339. "Copland at Sixty." Tempo 57 (Spring 1961): 1.

Boosey & Hawkes recently published a complete catalogue of Copland's works, most of which have been published by them. The list begins with The Cat and the Mouse (1920) and extends to the Nonet (1960). Details about the works, such as premieres, instrumentation, and dedications are included. See also: B122

B340. "Copland at Sixty." Time 76 (November 21, 1960): 93.

Copland's sixtieth birthday was celebrated by the New York Philharmonic in a performance in which he conducted his El Salón México and Symphonic Ode the previous week. Copland has varied his compositional styles over the years. At times his popular style has incorporated many American folk elements. He has been quite active as a guest conductor and is busy composing instrumental works.

B341. "Copland Collaborates with a Former Neighbor." New York Times, April 19, 1980, p.15:2.

Copland has been asked to conduct his Concerto for Clarinet and String Orchestra for the new movie Love and Money. James Toback, the writer-director, made the request. Copland has written the film scores for several movies.

B342. "Copland Conducts Concert with the Philharmonic." Musical Courier 162 (December 1960): 18.

Copland conducted the New York Philharmonic November 13 at Carnegie Hall. He conducted "with ardor, artistry, and authority." The Symphonic Ode and El Salón México were on the program as well as works by others.

B343. "Copland Conducts His Own Compositions." _Musical Events_ 15 (April 1960): 11.

B344. "Copland Conducts Little Orchestra." _Musical America_ 79 (January 15, 1959): 16.
    Copland was the guest conductor at New York's Little Orchestra Society performance recently of two of his own works at Town Hall. His conducting of _Music for the Theatre_ "brought out a new eloquence in this music, both in the rowdy jazz-inspired episodes and in the introspective sections." He also conducted his _Old American Songs, Sets I and II_.

B345. "Copland Conducts Own Music: First Rate Craftsman." _Times_ (London), April 20, 1960, p.16g
    On April 19, Festival Hall was the site for the beginning of the spring concerts by the London Symphony Orchestra. Copland was guest conductor for a concert of his works. He is "able to perform miracles with the most down-to-earth scraps of material."

B346. "Copland Conducts U.S. Music in London." _New York Times_, February 15, 1962, p.23:6.
    A concert of American works was presented in London on February 14. Copland was the guest conductor of the London Symphony Orchestra. Music critics in Britain wrote that they wished he had conducted a concert of his own works instead of the works of others.

B347. "Copland, Ella, 3 Others Get Kennedy Center Achievement Honors." _Variety_ 297 (December 5, 1979): 1.
    December 2 was the second annual Kennedy Center Awards at which Copland and others were honored for extensive contributions to the performing arts.

B348. "Copland Featured at Depauw U. Festival." _Diapason_ 62 (March 1971): 1.
    DePauw University's ninth annual Festival of Contemporary Music, held January 26 and 27, featured Copland as its guest artist. Copland conducted and met with students informally in this program designed to bring contemporary music closer to the students on campus.

B349. "Copland Feted by Composers' League." _Musical Courier_ 142 (December 1, 1950): 40.
    Copland's fiftieth birthday was celebrated November 5 by a concert in his honor at the Museum of Modern Art. The League of Composers sponsored this program which featured the composer playing the piano accompaniment for performance of seven of his _Twelve Poems of Emily Dickinson_.

B350. "Copland First Head of Composers' Group." _New York Times_, May 24, 1940, p.23:3.
    Members of the American Composers Alliance recently elected Copland as its president. This was the group's first general election.

B351. "Copland for Florida." Christian Science Monitor, April 15, 1966,
      p.4:2.
        The London Symphony Orchestra is slated to perform under the
      baton of Copland during July 28-August 21. The occasion is the
      Florida International Music Festival at Datona Beach. Some of
      Copland's compositions will be included on the programs August
      18 and 19.

B352. "Copland Gala." New Yorker 56 (December 8, 1980): 46-47.
        After a day chiefly devoted to performances of Copland's com-
      positions sponsored by Symphony Space, an evening program pro-
      vided the highlight of Copland's eightieth birthday celebration.
      Among the participants were Leonard Bernstein, Ned Rorem, and
      Morton Gould. At the conclusion of their speeches, Copland con-
      ducted his original thirteen-instrument version of Appalachian
      Spring. The event concluded with the audience singing Happy
      Birthday to him as a large cake with eighty candles was wheeled
      onto the stage.

B353. "Copland Gets MacDowell Medal." New York Times, August 20, 1961,
      p.80:4.
        The Edward MacDowell Medal was presented to Copland "for his
      contributions to American music." He has been associated with
      the MacDowell Colony since he first stayed there in 1925.
      President John F. Kennedy sent a telegram of congratulations.

B354. "Copland Gives First of 'One-Man' Concert." New York Times,
      October 12, 1935, p.13:3.
        A program of Copland's works was presented by the New School
      for Social Research October 11. Copland performed several of
      his works. El Salón México in a two-piano version was intro-
      duced. It remains to be seen whether or not this is a new
      direction in composition.

B355. "Copland Heads Colony." New York Times, January 25, 1926, p.25:1.
        The Edward MacDowell Association has named Copland as its
      president. The group is associated with the artists' residence,
      the MacDowell Colony, in Peterborough, New Hampshire.

B356. "Copland Honors Soviet Composer." Christian Science Monitor,
      march 26, 1960, p.14:2.
        While touring and conducting in Moscow, Copland honored Dmitri
      Shostakovich with a presentation at the end of a concert of works
      by both of them. Shostakovich received membership in the United
      States National Institute of Arts and Letters.

B357. "Copland in Harvard Poetry Post." Musical Courier 143 (March 15,
      1951): 19.
        Harvard University has announced the appointment of Copland as
      the Charles Eliot Norton Professor of Poetry for 1951-1952.

B358. "Copland Is Honored." New York Times, November 18, 1961, p.7:3.
        The Brooklyn Academy of Music presented Copland with "a
      citation describing him as a 'credit to the borough.'" The
      Occasion was a concert by the Boston Symphony Orchestra given
      at the Academy November 17.

B359. "Copland Is on Jury to Pick Best Music." New York Times, April 6, 1954, p.35:2.
       The three prize winners of the "Twentieth Century Masterpieces" will be selected by Copland and six others in Rome.

B360. "Copland Is Re-elected." New York Times, May 8, 1947, p.30:2.
       The League of Composers elected Copland to his second term as chairman during its annual meeting May 7.

B361. "Copland Night." Musical America 84 (September 1964): 36.
       The Lewisohn Stadium Series annually presents a concert devoted to a contemporary composer and July 16 was Copland night. Among the works performed were Old American Songs, with William Warfield as soloist, Lincoln Portrait, with Adlai Stevenson as narrator, and Quiet City. One might expect some monotony in a program composed entirely by one man, but the reviewer felt that "the brilliance and inventiveness of Copland's rhythmic thinking adds a neat enough twist to each piece to set it apart from its neighbor and imbue it with freshness."

B362. "Copland on Music." Instrumentalist 5 (December 1960): 20.
       This book by Copland is a compilation of his writings from numerous sources. "The significance of these essays varies according to the purpose for which they were written." See also: B24

B363. "Copland on Music." Metronome 78 (February 1961): 48-49.
       Book review. See also: B24

B364. "Copland on Music." Music and Letters 43, no.2 (1962): 138.
       Copland's essays were written several decades ago, but he has updated some earlier statements with footnotes. His outlook on life is optimistic and his sincerity is evident. See also: B24

B365. "Copland on Music." Music Educators Journal 47 (January 1961): 96.
       This book is chiefly composed of Copland's articles and lectures from the past three decades. His writings, as well as his music, is easy to comprehend. This work "constantly provokes thought and stimulates the attention." See also: B24

B366. "Copland on Music." Musical Events 17 (March 1962): 16.
       Book review. See also: B24

B367. "Copland on Music." Musical Leader 95 (August 1963): 17.
       This review contains the composer's views on various musicians in addition to the changing musical scene. He writes "with insight and warmth." See also: B24

B368. "Copland on Music." Showcase 41, no.2 (1961-62): 28-29.
       Book review. See also: B24

B369. "Copland on Music." Variety 221 (November 30, 1960): 50.
       Copland gives his views on "the position of music in our national cultural life with keen awareness of its many problems of survival." See also: B24

B370. "Copland Opera Sung." New York Times, April 23, 1954, p.23:4.
      The second performance of Copland's opera, The Tender Land,
was presented April 22 at City Center. This work was the first
half of a double bill.

B371. "Copland Pays a Homage to Stravinsky." Times (London), November
      5, 1965, p.16a.
      Copland was guest conductor for the London Symphony Orchestra
October 4 at Festival Hall. Works by Copland and Stravinsky
were on the program.

B372. "Copland Poetic and Copland Extroverted." HiFi/Stereo Review 6
      (February 1961): 72.

B373. "Copland Premiere at Juilliard." Juilliard Review (Fall 1957): 7.
      Copland's Piano Fantasy, performed by William Masselos, had
its premiere October 25. It is a work in one movement which is
approximately thirty minutes in length. It was performed twice
on the evening of its premiere, once before and once after the
intermission, and it was the only piece on the program. The
composition was commissioned by Juilliard to commemorate its
fiftieth anniversary. Masselos felt that the work sounds very
American and very Copland. See also: W93

B374. "Copland Recalls Criticism." New York Times, November 3, 1980,
      III, p.20:6.
      Copland, who will be eighty years old on November 14, reminisces
about an event that happened when he was in his early twenties
studying in Paris. He went to conductor Serge Koussevitzky's
home to play some of his ballet Grohg. Unfortunately Sergey
Prokofiev was there at the time and was the first to criticize
Copland's composition.

B375. "Copland Revises." Musical America 74 (September 1954): 29.
      Although Copland's premiere of his first opera, The Tender Land,
received mixed reviews, its revision and enlongation has resulted
in definite improvements according to this reviewer. It is
characterized as "a distinguished and moving, if imperfect,
piece of musical theater." Performances of the revised version
were given at the Berkshire Music Center August 2 and 3.

B376. "Copland Stirs Audience." New York Times, November 17, 1947): p.
      25:4.
      Copland conducted a concert of his works at the Colon Opera
House November 16 in Buenos Aires. This program was sponsored
by the United States Embassy and was enthusiastically received.

B377. "Copland Symphony in New Form." New York Times, March 1, 1935,
      p.17:4.
      Copland revised and expanded his Symphony for Organ and Orches-
tra as Symphony No.1 minus the organ part. The reviewer feels
that this work still has a contemporary sound because "it is
liberally dissonant and exhibits linear and rhythmic characteristics to identify it with the atonal-polytonal groups." The
composer's personal musical characteristics manage to pervade
the music, nonetheless.

B378. "Copland Symphony Premieres Here." New York Times, January 22,
1944, p.9:1.
   The New York premiere of Copland's Short Symphony took place
   January 9 at Radio City by the NBC Symphony Orchestra conducted
   by Leopold Stokowski. It is dedicated to Carlos Chávez who
   conducted it in Mexico City previously. See also: W43

B379. "Copland to be Feted." Musical Courier 142 (October 15, 1950): 12.
   Copland's fiftieth anniversary is to be celebrated by a concert at the Museum of Modern Art on November 5. The League of
   Composers will be opening their twenty-eighth season at that
   time. Copland's new string quartet will receive its New York
   premiere then.

B380. "Copland to Conduct." Christian Science Monitor, October 1, 1965,
p.4:1.
   The San Francisco Symphony Orchestra has invited Copland to
   be a guest conductor during a week of special concerts of contemporary music beginning March 1.

B381. "Copland to Lecture at Harvard." New York Times, January 22,
1944, p.9:1.
   Copland has received an appointment to present five lectures
   on modern music at Harvard University during the spring. The
   Horatio Appleton Lamb Fund will support this appointment.

B382. "Copland Wins Awards." Variety 260 (September 23, 1970): 68.
   The composer recently received the Commander's Cross of the
   Order of Merit of the Federal Republic of Germany. This
   award was presented in New York before he left to attend the
   Berlin Arts Festival.

B383. "Copland Wins Symphony Award." New York Times, January 10, 1947,
p.16:1.
   The Third Symphony received the first merit award given by
   the Boston Symphony Orchestra.

B384. "Copland Work Premiered." Musical Courier 156 (November 15,
1957): 29.
   The Juilliard School of Music commissioned the Piano Fantasy
   for its fiftieth anniversary. William Masselos gave the
   premiere performance on October 25 at The Juilliard Concert Hall.
   This one-movement work, lasting about thirty minutes, was the
   only piece on the program and was performed twice with an
   intervening intermission. "The work is introspective, percussive,
   beautifully lyrical, and excitingly pianistic." See also: W93

B385. "Copland's 80th Birthday Evokes Global Accolades." Billboard 92
(November 1, 1980): 52.
   More than a hundred special performances around the world are
   being devoted to the celebration of Copland's eightieth birthday.
   Among the orchestras honoring Copland are the National Symphony
   Orchestra, the American Symphony Orchestra, and the London
   Symphony Orchestra. Copland will participate by conducting at
   some of these tributes.

B386. "Copland's New Nonet: Combination Is Unusual." _Times_ (London),
      May 19, 1961, p.19c.
      The Nonet is scored for three violins, three violas, and three
      cellos. This was first performed in England at the B.B.C. Thurs-
      day Invitation Concert on May 18. This one-movement work's
      "richly clustering diatonic dissonances of the outer sections
      did not entirely avoid monotony."

B387. "Copland's New Work for L.S.O." _Times_ (London), April 27, 1964, p.
      6b.
      The premiere performance of _Music for a Great City_ will take
      place May 26. It was commissioned by the London Symphony Orches-
      tra, and Copland will be present to conduct his new work. _See
      also:_ W101

B388. "Copland's Sheepskin." _Variety_ 28 (January 28, 1976): 62.
      An honorary doctorate of music was awarded to Copland by the
      San Francisco Conservatory of Music on January 27.

B389. "Copland's Tender Land Issued in Vocal Score." _Musical America_
      76 (November 1, 1956.
      This opera was commissioned by Rodgers and Hammerstein for the
      thirtieth anniversary of the League of Composers. The chief
      flaw in this work is "the failure of the librettist and the
      composer to define the individual characters with sufficient
      sharpness and power." Horace Everett wrote the libretto. The
      reviewer feels that the work does contain sections of great
      beauty, but not enough to compensate for the opera's weak points.

B390. "Copland's Third." _Time_ 48 (October 28, 1946): 55.
      Serge Koussevitzky recently conducted the Boston Symphony
      Orchestra in the premiere performance of Copland's Third Symphony.
      Themes and tonal devices have been borrowed from his other works.
      "His technical competence far outshone his inventiveness." _See
      also:_ W77

B391. "Copland's Third Symphony." _Musical Times_ 99 (January 1958): 29.
      This review covers the November 13 concert of the BBC
      Symphony Orchestra conducted by Jascha Horenstein at Festival
      Hall. Included on the program was the Third Symphony which
      "proved to be an example of grandiloquence hiding sheer emptiness."

B392. Cornell University. Libraries. _Aaron Copland: a Bibliography of
      His Works in Cornell University Libraries_, compiled by Carolyn
      R. Owlett. Ithaca, New York: Cornell University Libraries,
      1971.
      This is a ten-page listing of Cornell's holdings on Copland.

B393. Cowell, Henry. "Current Chronicle." _Musical Quarterly_ 36 (July
      1950): 453.
      Copland's _Twelve Poems of Emily Dickinson_ are written "with his
      usual sophisticated simplicity with here and there an outburst
      of extreme dissonance." The song cycle uses some of the common
      devices such as repeated melodic passages but often changes one
      note unexpectedly.

B394. _____. "Current Chronicle: New York." Musical Quarterly 42 (January 1956): 90-92.
The Canticle of Freedom recently received its first New York performance with Leonard Bernstein conducting the Symphony of the Air. Cowell notes the influence of Stravinsky, but Copland's work is "music built on refinement and taste rather than on a system." The piece is chiefly diatonic with some characteristics of twelve-tone music.

B395. Cox, Ainslee. "Copland on the Podium." Music Journal 29 (February 1971): 27.
Copland recalls some advice he received about pursuing a new activity in his later years. He was advised to take up something new so that he would not be competing with his achievements earned while he was a young man. Consequently, he has devoted more time to conducting and less to composing during the past few decades. Although he is seventy, he has been engaging in conducting activities at a vigorous pace. He recently appeared with the London Symphony Orchestra and the Berlin Philharmonic Orchestra.

B396. Crankshaw, Geoffrey. "Aaron Copland." Chesterian 32, no.194 (Spring 1958): 97-101.
This discussion describes some of the early influences on Copland's compositions. Nadia Boulanger, the European music which he heard, and the jazz and folk music of America were all part of his development. An analysis of styles found in some of his prominent works is included. "What he has to say is new, and his manner of saying it is arresting, and, now that he has found his idiom, intensely personal."

B397. Cross, Milton John and David Ewen. "Aaron Copland." In The Milton Cross New Encyclopedia of the Great Composers and Their Music, v.1, 242-254. Revised edition. Garden City, New York: Doubleday, 1969.
This extensive entry on Copland gives ample biographical information as well as analytical notes on his orchestral and chamber music. His early musical training is related in detail. The transition from dissonant, complex music to a simplistic style, and then a return to dissonance is noted.

B398. Crowder, Charles. "Inter-American Fete." Musical America 81 (June 1961): 21.
Washington, D.C.'s second festival consisted of twelve free concerts and included numerous contemporary composers on its programs. Copland conducted his Nonet for Solo Strings which had its world premiere. It was written to celebrate the fiftieth wedding anniversary of Mr. and Mrs. Robert Woods Bliss and was commissioned by the Dumbarton Oaks Research Library. The work was enthusiastically received by the audience. See also: W96

B399. Crowther, Bosley. "The Screen: a Shattering Experience." New York Times, December 21, 1961, p.30:6.
This is a review of Something Wild for which Aaron Copland wrote the film score. Crowther feels the composer "puts some nice melodic phrases behind a few of the more reflective moments."

B400. "Current Chronicle: New York." <u>Musical Quarterly</u> 92 (January 1958):
92.
William Masselos gave a brilliant performance of the Piano
Fantasy recently. Copland composed this large piano work for
the fiftieth anniversary of the Juilliard School of Music. The
composition seems to be "a most serious attempt at finding a way
to peacefully co-exist with dodecaphony."

B401. Dahl, Ingolf. "Orchestral Music: Aaron Copland: <u>John Henry</u>, for
Orchestra." <u>Music Library Association Notes</u> 11 (March 1954):
277.
This is a brief review of the 1952 revised score by Copland.
It chiefly notes that the work consists of six variations on the
<u>John Henry</u> folk song theme.

B402. _____. "Orchestral Music: Aaron Copland: <u>Preamble for a Solemn
Occasion</u>." <u>Music Library Association Notes</u> 11 (March 1954):
276-277.
Dahl reviews Copland's score for orchestra with optional narrator. It was commissioned to celebrate the United Nations'
Declaration of Human Rights in 1949. "The tone is one of great
elevation, breadth, and power, as is befitting a 'solemn occasion.'"

B403. "<u>Dance Magazine</u> Awards 1979: Erick Hawkins, Aaron Copland, Jorge
Donn." <u>Dance Magazine</u> 53 (June 1979): 54-62.
Copland was one of three individuals selected to receive this
1979 award. Because of his contributions to the world of dance,
he has become a prominent composer in this field. His ballets
<u>Appalachian Spring</u> and <u>Billy the Kid</u> are well-known.

B404. "Dance Symphony." <u>New York Philharmonic Program Notes</u> (June 30,
1966): 3.
A performance of the <u>Dance Symphony</u> was given by the New York
Philharmonic with Leonard Bernstein conducting at Philharmonic
Hall, Lincoln Center June 30. Copland was planning to enter his
Symphonic Ode in a contest sponsored by RCA Victor Company but
he realized that he could not finish it in time. Instead, he
extracted three movements from his ballet <u>Grohg</u> and sent them in
as the <u>Dance Symphony</u>. <u>See also</u> W27

B405. "<u>Dance Symphony</u>, taken from <u>Grohg</u>." <u>Harrisburg Symphony Orchestra
Program Notes</u> (November 18, 1975): 18.

B406. "Danzón Cubano." <u>Music and Letters</u> 31 (January 1950): 92.
It is noted in this short review that this piece is not melodic.
"Such harmony as there is, is used rather as a rhythmic back-
ground."

B407. "Danzon Cubano." <u>Music Survey</u> 2 (Autumn 1949): 110.
<u>Danzón Cubano</u> and <u>Hoe-Down</u> from <u>Rodeo</u> are reviewed. The first
was written for two pianos, and the second was arranged for
violin and piano by Copland. Both are examples of Copland's
popular American style.

B408. Darrell, Robert Donaldson. "Learning to Listen." High Fidelity
      7 (July 1957): 75.
           Darrell reviewed Copland's book What to Listen For in Music.
      His writings were found to be "refreshingly concise, reliable,
      and free from both the banalities and hocus-pocus of too many
      elementary approaches." See also: B108

B409. Darter, Tom and Bob Doerschuk. "Profile of an Orchestral Pianist:
      Behind the Scenes at Carnegie Hall." Contemporary Keyboard 7
      (April 1981): 16.
           This interview with Elizabeth Wright is an account of the
      preparations for the American Symphony Orchestra's all-Copland
      program presented November 9, 1980 at Carnegie Hall. Copland
      was present for rehearsals during the days preceding this con-
      cert in honor of his eightieth birthday. The concert was chiefly
      noted from Wright's perspective as she viewed the proceedings
      from the grand piano.

B410. Daugherty, Robert Michael. "An Analysis of Copland's Twelve Poems
      of Emily Dickinson [with] Homage, a Score for Orchestra." Ph.D.
      diss., Ohio State University, 1980.
           An analysis of Copland's longest vocal work shows the stylistic
      techniques used in musically expressing the different lyrics
      found in the poems. These relationships are examined in terms
      of the whole, as well as individually.

B411. Davis, Dana. "A Copland Portrait." Instrumentalist 33 (March
      1979): 25-26.
           This interview was conducted at the California Institute of
      the Arts in Valencia when Copland was seventy-eight years old.
      Although his compositions are quite popular, he especially
      enjoys the excitement of conducting. Although he has never
      studied conducting formally, he has observed great conductors
      for decades. He says that he does not try to memorize scores,
      even his own, because it tends to limit a conductor in the num-
      ber of works available for him to conduct.

B412. Davis, Peter G. "America's Senior Composers--Why Was Their Impact
      Profound?" New York Times, September 28, 1980, II, p.25:1.
           Davis examines the role of major composers who are reaching at
      least their seventieth birthday, namely, Otto Luening, William
      Schuman, Samuel Barber, and Copland. "Mr. Copland's pre-eminence
      among his contemporaries is no accident." His diversity of
      styles makes it difficult to categorize his music. The extensive
      discography which is available, many of the recordings having been
      done with his assistance, substantiates his popular appeal.

B413. _____. "NY Philharmonic's Anniversary." Times (London), December
      23, 1967, p.16d.
           The 125th anniversary of the New York Philharmonic is being
      celebrated. Inscape was commissioned for this event. "Its
      chilly, uncompromising diamond-like sonorities and closely
      reasoned canonic writing is obviously not designed for easy
      listening. "

B414. Day, J. "Letters to the Editor: American Music." <u>Wall Street Journal</u>, December 8, 1980, p.29:2.
    This is a response to an earlier editorial concerning Copland's music in December. Day states that "Mr. Copland has failed to compose anything that sounds American to me."

B415. Dayton, Daryl. "Program Notes: Concerto for Clarinet with Harp and String Orchestra." <u>Los Angeles Philharmonic Orchestra Symphony Magazine</u> (November 15, 1951): 17.
    This concerto was written for Benny Goodman and was performed by him on November 6, 1950 with the N.B.C. Symphony Orchestra. Musical examples illustrate some of the program notes. Dayton feels that the piece "is a short, brilliant movement in one movement in free rondo form."

B416. Deane, James G. "Mrs. Coolidge Honored at Capital Festival." <u>Musical Courier</u> 142 (November 15, 1950): 3.
    The Elizabeth Sprague Coolidge Foundation's twenty-fifth anniversary celebration included the premiere performance of Copland's Piano Quartet. A series of concerts was held October 28-30 at the Library of Congress in Washington, D.C. "Despite a wide gamut of rhythmic and technical effects, it was a disappointment, especially in contrast with Copland's own <u>Appalachian Spring</u>, played on the final program." <u>See also:</u> W86

B417. "Decca's Nieuw Amsterdam Trio." <u>American Record Guide</u> 33 (October 1966): 142.
    This group, consisting of Edith Mocsanyi, piano, John Pintavelle, violin, and Heinrich Joachim, cello, has recorded <u>Vitebsk</u> on Decca DL-10126 and DL-710126. The trio is praised for its precise pitch despite the use of quarter tones and dissonances. <u>See also:</u> D370

B418. Del Rosso, Charles Francis. "A Study of Selected Solo Clarinet Literature of Four American Composers as a Basis for Performance and Teaching." Ph.D. diss., Columbia University, 1969.
    Del Rosso extensively analyzes Copland's Concerto for Clarinet and String Orchestra, along with three other compositions. The study concentrates on areas in the music which are complex performance problems as well as interpretative problems. <u>See also:</u> B603

B419. "Dello Joio Replaces Copland for Bicent." <u>Variety</u> 278 (April 2, 1975): 79.
    Copland had been commissioned to write a bicentennial work for the Wilmington, Delaware Grand Opera House performance in May 1976. He notified the underwriters that he will not be able to fulfill this commitment, so Norman Dello Joio will be the replacement.

B420. DeRhen, A. "Elaine Shaffer, Hephzibah Menuhin." <u>High Fidelity/ Musical America</u> 22 (January 1972): MA24.
    Shaffer, accompanied by Menuhin, performed Copland's Duo for Flute and Piano in Philadelphia and New York recently. This work was commissioned as a memorial to William Kincaid who had been the first flutist with the Philadelphia Orchestra. In contrast to some of the severe and complex tonalities found in

some of Copland's works, this seems mellower with a "greater
eloquence with increased economy of means." See also: W107

B421. Dickinson, Peter. "Copland at 75." Musical Times 116 (November
1975): 967.
This overview of the composer's long and varied musical career
emphasizes his early development. Major compositions are noted,
along with his writings. His most recent compositions of the
past decade are discussed, but he says he has no plans for any
future compositions. His seventy-fifth birthday is to be celebrated by a televised program of him talking, performing, and
conducting.

B422. _____. "Copland's View." Musical Times 110 (August 1969): 840.
Dickinson observes that Copland's new book, The New Music,
1900-60, is much more than a reprint of his earlier monograph,
Our New Music. The most important aspect of the revised version
is the additional material and views which expand his earlier
writing. Dickinson finds the book to be misleading at times
because some of the earlier material has not been updated. However, Copland's "breadth and vision show the American spirit at
its best." See also: B76, B84

B423. _____. "Music in London: Copland." Musical Times 106 (December
1965): 954.
Dickinson observes that American music is gradually being
performed more in England. Copland recently conducted the London
Symphony Orchestra at Festival Hall in a concert of his works and
the works of others. This visit "showed the distinguished composer's infectious enthusiasm for music, and provided authoritative performances of several of his orchestral pieces."

B424. Diether, Jack. "First Performance--Lincoln Center for the Performing Arts, Philharmonic Hall." American Record Guide 29 (January
1963): 332-334.
The premiere of Connotations occurred the previous fall at
the opening of Philharmonic Hall at Lincoln Center for the
Performing Arts. Columbia has issued this premiere performance
on L2l 1007 and L2S 1008. Leonard Bernstein conducted the New
York Philharmonic. See also: D90, W98

B425. _____. "Guide to Record Collecting: Aaron Copland Suggests a
Basic Mahler Library." Hi-Fi Music at Home 4 (March-April 1957):
26.
Diether comments on Copland's choice of five recordings that
the composer feels are especially notable. A segment on Gustav
Mahler's increasing importance is augmented by the recent recording of all of his works.

B426. _____. "1947-58 Copland--and Previn's Conducting Debut." Ameri-
can Record Guide 30 (August 1964): 1098.
Copland's In the Beginning has been recorded by the Whikehart
Chorale, conducted by Lewis E. Whikehart, on Lyrichord LL-124
and LLST-7124. The text is taken from Genesis, Chapters 1 and 2.
Also reviewed is Columbia ML 5983 and MS 6583 which has André
Previn conducting the St. Louis Symphony Orchestra in The Red
Pony. See also: D147, D265

B427. "Diplomat Extols Rhetoric's Power." New York Times, May 26, 1955,
p.62:1.
Eelco H. Van Kleffens, president of the United Nations General
Assembly, spoke at a meeting of the American Academy of Arts and
Letters and the National Institute of Arts and Letters. Copland
was inducted into membership during the meeting.

B428. Dispeker, Thea. "New Music: Munich." Music Journal 22 (January
1964): 112.
Dance Panels in Seven Movements had its premiere at the Munich
Opera Festival December 3, 1963. Copland was present to conduct
the music for his sixth ballet and received eight curtain calls.
See also: W95

B429. Dobrin, Arnold. Aaron Copland, His Life and Times. New York:
Thomas Y. Crowell Company, 1967.
This is an extensive biography designed for younger readers.
Copland's life and musical career are detailed along with details
about his most important compositions. A list of works and a
bibliography are included.

B430. Dorian, Frederick. "Notes on the Program: Statements for Orchestra." Pittsburgh Symphony Orchestra Program Notes (May 16,
1969): 857-861.
Details about the structure of Statements is given in these
program notes. Copland is to conduct this work on the program.

B431. _____. "Notes on the Program: Short Symphony." Pittsburgh Sym-
phony Orchestra Program Notes (October 7, 1966): 97.
Background information on the composition is related. The
Short Symphony was Copland's second symphony; the first was the
Symphony for Organ and Orchestra. His Sextet for String Quartet,
Clarinet and Piano is an arrangement of the Short Symphony. The
Sextet has been more popular and has been performed much more
than the Short Symphony.

B432. Douglas, John R. "The Composer and His Music on Record." Library
Journal 92, no.6 (March 15, 1967): 1117-1121.
This compilation of recordings includes eleven of Copland's
major works in which he is either the performer or the conductor.
The list is designed to assist librarians in selecting notable
recordings for their collections.

B433. Dower, Catherine. "Aaron Copland: Giant on the Contemporary Music
Scene." Musart 23, no.2 (1970): 10-11.
Celebrations of Copland's seventieth birthday will occur both
in the United States and Europe. This biographical sketch of
Copland's active career in music emphasizes his long association
with Tanglewood.

B434. "Down a Country Lane." Life 52 (June 29, 1962): 44-45.
This two-page piano piece is reproduced. It is one of the few
modern works designed for young piano students, but Copland
describes it as being more difficult than it appears. His compositions are "always stamped with directness and rhythmic
ingenuity."

B435. Downes, Edward. "Mitropoulos Bids Composers Relax." New York
      Times, June 16, 1956, p.12:1.
          Dimitri Mitropoulos, at a joint meeting of the American Sym-
      phony Orchestra League and the League of Composers, admonished
      the musicians to relax because more contemporary music was being
      performed in the United States than in Europe. Copland reported
      that only about eight percent of orchestral programs consisted
      of contemporary music during the past fifteen years.

B436. Downes, Olin. "American Composers and Critics." New York Times,
      May 8, 1932, VIII, p.6:1.
          Copland has expressed his feelings on newspaper criticism in
      a letter complaining of the intolerant attitude of music critics
      toward contemporary American music. This letter was a response
      to an earlier report on the recent conference between composers
      and critics at Yaddo. Although Copland was quoted as saying,
      "'Frankly I consider newspaper criticism a menace,'" he now
      writes that the critic "'is an absolute necessity.'"

B437. _____. "Le 50e [Cinquantième] Anniversaire de Aaron Copland."
      Vie Musicale 1 (March 1951): 4.

B438. _____. "A Composer States His Position." New York Times, Octo-
      ber 19, 1941, IX, p.7:1.
          Downes extensively reviews Copland's Our New Music. The
      theory that nineteenth century style romanticism in music is
      dead is questioned by Downes. See also: B84

B439. _____. "Copland at 50." New York Times, October 29, 1950, II,
      p.7:1.
          Downes notes Copland's fiftieth birthday in this article.
      Several performances are scheduled in his honor. One of these
      is the League of Composers' concert of his works to be performed
      November 5. Copland's importance as a contemporary American
      composer is noted. See also: 515

B440. _____. "Cultural Exchange." New York Times, October 20, 1946,
      II, p.7:1.
          The United States Department of Justice required visiting
      Ukrainian musicians to register as government agents while on
      their concert tour. Since the group had been invited to perform
      by the National Council of American-Soviet Friendship and other
      groups, they responded that they would not register as agents.
      The result was that they had to cancel their tour and return to
      their country. Copland and other prominent American musicians
      sent a letter of protest about this to the United States govern-
      ment.

B441. _____. "Music: Concert of Music and Films." New York Times,
      March 16, 1931, p.24:3.
          The Copland-Sessions Concert held at the Broadhurst Theatre on
      March 15 had film scores as its theme. Copland conducted his
      Music for the Theatre. Downes felt Copland's work showed more
      originality than most of the others performed.

B442. _____. "Music: Copland-Sessions Concerts." New York Times, April
14, 1930, p.24:7.
Downes reviews this Copland-Sessions Concert held at the President Theatre April 13. None of Copland's works was on the program. Most of the works performed were of little importance in
Downes' opinion.

B443. _____. "Music: More New Music." New York Times, May 7, 1928,
p.28:7.
Downes found the second of the Copland-Sessions Concerts at
the Edyth Totten Theatre May 6 to be excellent. Copland's Two
Pieces for String Quartet was one of the most significant works
on the program. It was "distinguished by simplicity, clearness
and, again, economy of material."

B444. _____. "Music: Premiere of One-Act Opera." New York Times,
April 2, 1954, p.24:1.
The first performance of The Tender Land took place April 1 at
City Center by the City Opera Company. "The composer often pro-
duces interesting music, not because of, but mainly in spite of
this flimsey and pseudo-dramatic material." Horace Everett
wrote the libretto. See also: W90

B445. _____. "Music: Presenting American Composers." New York Times,
April 23, 1928, p.20:4.
Downes reviews the first concert in the series sponsored by
Roger Sessions and Copland for the benefit of contemporary composers and listeners. This first Copland-Sessions Concert was
held April 22 at the Edyth Totten Theatre. Downes believes that
these concerts are an excellent idea but "found it hard to dis-
cover any very arresting personalities 'emerging' from their
cocoons last night."

B446. _____. Olin Downes on Music; a Selection from His Writings During
the Half-Century 1906 to 1955, edited by Irene Downes, 392-395.
New York: Simon and Schuster, 1957.
Downes, a music critic for the New York Times for many years,
wrote an article October 29, 1950 to honor Copland on his fiftieth
birthday. Many performances were being held to commemorate his
birthday. Copland's importance as a composer plus his efforts
to assist other contemporary composers are noted.

B447. Drew, David. "Aaron Copland Returns." New Statesman 59 (April
30, 1960): 620.
Copland was present to conduct the London Symphony Orchestra
in a concert of his works to celebrate his sixtieth birthday.
Among the compositions performed were El Salón México, the Piano
Concerto, Statements and the First Symphony. Drew feels that
these works lack "a scrupulous honesty and a rigorous attention
to detail."

B448. _____. "Old Frontiers." New Statesman 63 (March 9, 1962): 348.
The British premiere of The Tender Land by the Cambridge University Opera Group at the Cambridge Arts Theatre recently received a mixed reception. "Delicacy of a kind is the inner
strength of the opera—indeed, its only strength." Drew feels

that Copland uses old operatic clichés and the work is limited
so much that nothing happens.

B449. Dumm, Robert W. "Boston." Musical Courier 161 (February 1960):
41.
   Copland, "who transmits a large supply of kinetic energy
through his well-educated baton," conducted the Boston Symphony
Orchestra in several programs during the first week of 1960. He
is scheduled to accompany the group in its tour of the Orient in
the next few months.

B450. _____. "Boston." Musical Courier 163 (June 1961): 24.
   Staff members of Brandeis University recently presented the
Boston premiere of the Nonet for Strings and "it proved an
expressive and affable work." Dumm noticed some similarities
between this work and El Salón México.

B451. Durgin, Cyrus. "Copland Premiere, Revival of Debussy Work in
Boston." Musical America 76 (February 15, 1956): 193.
   Charles Munch conducted the revised version of Copland's
Symphonic Ode February 3 and 4. Copland had been commissioned
to write the work for the Boston Symphony's fiftieth anniversary
in 1930-31. He revised the work for their seventy-fifth anniversary. The size of the orchestra was decreased in the revision,
but the overall organization of the piece did not change. Durgin
found it to be "ponderous and cold, for all the obvious writing
skill." See also: W38

B452. _____. "Illness Causes Fiedler to Miss Opening of Pops 50th
Season." Musical America 75 (June 1955): 20.
   The first performance of the Canticle of Freedom was given
May 8 at the dedication of the Massachusetts Institute of Technology Kresge Auditorium and M.I.T. Chapel. This work for large
orchestra and chorus was commissioned for this dedication. The
instrumental introduction reminded Durgin of Copland's Appalachian
Spring with heavy percussion. Durgin was impressed with the
quality of this new piece. See also: W91

B453. East, Leslie. "Copland." Music and Musicians 21 (October 1972):
62.
   Copland conducted some of his works and those of others at
Albert Hall recently in Great Britain. His Red Pony Suite,
Danzón Cubano, and El Salón México were on the program. In the
latter two East feels that "the monotony of rhythmic pattern
needs enlivening." East believes the works should sparkle more.

B454. "East Harlem Unit Maps Drama Plans." New York Times, December 5,
1958, p.39:7.
   Copland is one of the sponsors of a new program called the
Edith J. R. Isaacs Theatre Arts Project. The organization's
aim is to have a regularly performing dramatic group in the
East Harlem community.

B455. Eble, Charles. "Iowa University Honors Copland." Musical America
78 (July 1958): 33.
   Copland was present at a concert given in his honor by the

University of Iowa Symphony under the direction of James Dixon.
Among his works performed were excerpts from The Tender Land
and Billy the Kid. A series of lectures and concerts were held
to commemorate the composer.

B456. "An Editorial." Down Beat 20 (June 3, 1953): 12S.
       This is an editorial reprinted from the April 29 Chicago Sun-
       Times criticizing Representative Busbey of Illinois who managed
       to have a composition by Copland withdrawn from the inaugural
       program for Eisenhower. A Lincoln Portrait was deleted from the
       ceremonies because "Copland had belonged to certain organizations
       unpleasing to the House Committee on Un-American Activities."
       The blackballing of Copland and other native composers, including
       Roy Harris and Leonard Bernstein, is a sad commentary on the
       nation's government according to the editorial.

B457. "Editorial Notes." Strad 62 (February 1952): 293; 71 (June 1960):
       53; 72 (April 1962): 437.

B458. "Editorial Notes." Strad 75 (July 1964): 85.
       Copland recently conducted the London Symphony Orchestra in
       his Music for a Great City. This four-movement piece was
       adapted from a film score and consisted chiefly "of blatant
       intrusive noise."

B459. "8 in the Arts Cited." New York Times, March 5, 1960, p.17:6.
       Copland received a gold medal and a grant of $1,500 from
       Brandeis University at ceremonies conducted by Dean Clarence
       Berger March 4.

B460. Ellsworth, Ray. "Americans on Microgroove." High Fidelity 6
       (August 1956): 64.
       A brief history of Copland's life and works is given. The
       "Americanism" that Copland's music exhibits was not always
       present. At times he veered toward atonality, but later he
       rejected it as too difficult for players and audiences alike.
       His major works are available on recordings, but few specific
       ones are mentioned.

B461. Engel, Lehman. This Bright Day; an Autobiography. New York:
       Macmillan, 1974.
       Lehman reminisces about his associations with many musicians
       such as Copland. For example, in describing the beginnings of
       the Arrow Music Press, he indicated that Copland, "who was the
       secretary, was a 'giggler'—a pushover for every kind of joke—
       but perfectly informed about every financial detail."

B462. Erickson, Raymond. "Copland Opera Sung at Youth Concert." Musical
       America 80 (May 1960): 35.
       The Second Hurricane was performed April 23 at Carnegie Hall
       by Leonard Bernstein conducting the New York Philharmonic in
       the Young People's Concert. Since this opera was designed for
       students, the vocal parts were performed by the Senior Choral
       Ensemble of the High School of Music and Art of New York. The
       scoring is generally simple, but the choral parts involve some
       intricate rhythmic applications

B463. _____. "Philharmonic Ventures into a Hall at Co-op City." New
York Times, June 19, 1971, p.18:1.
    Copland was the guest conductor for one of nine concerts
presented by the New York Philharmonic in community facilities.
The intent is to bring the orchestra to people in their own
communities for a nominal price.

B464. _____. "Youngsters Hear Music of Copland." New York Times,
November 13, 1960, p.87:3.
    Leonard Bernstein's Young People's Concert November 12 featured
the music of Copland. The composer was present for the occasion
and conducted his El Salón México. "Mr. Bernstein compared Mr.
Copland's works to a garden having all kinds of flowers, some
thorny and unbeautiful at first acquaintance." Excerpts from
several works were performed to illustrate Copland's varied
styles.

B465. "Erziehung zum Hören." Neue Zeitschrift für Musik 119 (June-
July 1958): 392.
    This is a short review of Copland's What to Listen For in
Music. The book is designed to assist the listener in becoming
more educated and aware of sounds. See also: B108

B466. Evans, Peter. "Aaron Copland." Musical Times 103 (March 1962):
169.
    Evans reviews Copland on Music which he finds to be a collection
of the composer's lectures and assorted thoughts. "Much of its
material was not worth preserving even in a bedside book." Evans
feels that there is nothing out of the ordinary to hold the
reader's attention. See also: B24

B467. _____. "Copland on the Serial Road: an Analysis of Connotations."
Perspectives of New Music 2, no.2 (1964): 141-149; Reprinted in
Perspectives on American Composers, compiled by Benjamin Boretz,
147-155. New York: W. W. Norton, 1971.
    This detailed analysis of Connotations and Copland's use of
serial techniques is supported with numerous musical examples.
References to earlier works such as the Piano Fantasy show his
growth in compositions of this nature. "The mastery with which
Copland has executed this splendidly logical structure is not
without parallel in his earlier work."

B468. _____. "First Performances: Copland's Connotations." Tempo 64
(Spring): 30-33.
    Connotations was commissioned for the opening of Philharmonic
Hall in Lincoln Center the previous September. The piece
utilizes tone-rows and other serials techniques. Musical examples
illustrate the material. See also: W98

B469. _____. "The Thematic Technique of Copland's Recent Works."
Tempo 51 (Spring-Summer 1959): 2-13.
    This is an analysis of Copland's current stylistic character-
istics as compared to his earlier styles. During the past
decade he has shown an interest in a new direction as seen in
works such as the Piano Quartet and Piano Fantasy. This is a
move away from his more recent popular functional music.

B470. Everett, Horace. "Scheme for an Opera: the Sources for the Con-
        struction of The Tender Land." Center 1 (March 1954): 14-16.
            The James Agee book, Let Us Now Praise Famous Men, which con-
        tained Walker Evans' photographs of sharecroppers, became the
        basis for the libretto for The Tender Land. Copland's goal was
        to produce a work suitable for college opera workshops. He was
        also interested in incorporating folk music in the work. Copland
        and Everett contend that it was not their intention to produce a
        folk opera, but "to use these elements without being committed
        to them." Everett's libretto centers around the maturation of
        Laurie, a high school senior.

B471. Evett, Robert. "The Brooklyn Eagle." Atlantic Monthly 224
        (October 1969): 135-136.
            Copland, born in Brooklyn sixty-nine years ago, is still
        active in music. His styles and techniques of composition have
        changed through the years. Emblems, for example, is "full of
        the hymn tunes and bits of fake Americana that have endeared
        Copland to the unenterprising listener." Copland has employed
        some serial techniques but Evett believes Copland has never been
        fully committed to this genre.

B472. Ewen, David. "Aaron Copland." In Composers Since 1900; a Bio-
        graphical and Critical Guide, 136-141. New York: H. W.
        Wilson Company, 1969.
            This is a short but thorough biography emphasizing Copland's
        works in a chronological style. This biographical entry
        covers his life through the 1960's. A supplement published in
        1981 covers the intervening years.

B473. _____. "Aaron Copland." In The World of Twentieth-Century Music,
        161-175. Englewood Cliffs, New Jersey: Prentice-Hall, 1968.
            This biography emphasizes Copland's stylistic characteristics.
        Critical evaluations of his major works constitute the major
        portion of the section on the composer. Premiere information
        and other circumstances regarding the creation of these major
        compositions are included.

B474. _____. "Aaron Copland: Biography." In The New Book of Modern
        Composers, 3d edition, revised, 131-147. New York: Knopf, 1961.
            Copland is one of thirty-two composers examined in this book.
        His biography is followed by an excerpt, "The Composer Speaks,"
        from his book Music and Imagination. Marion Bauer and Israel
        Citkowitz examine Copland's stylistic characteristics and his
        importance in American contemporary music. See also: B65

B475. _____. "Copland, Aaron." In American Composers: a Biographical
        Dictionary, 141-144. New York: G. P. Putnam's Sons, 1982.
            This biographical information traces the major events in
        Copland's career with particular attention to his early days.
        Included are his affiliations with various organizations as well
        as his awards. A small section written by the composer concludes
        the entry.

B476. Eyer, Ronald. "Copland Lectures issued in Book Form." Musical
        America 72 (November 1, 1952): 34.

This is a review of Copland's Music and Imagination which incorporates six lectures given at Harvard University as the Charles Eliot Norton Lectures. Eyer's opinion of this book is favorable. He especially agrees with Copland's feeling that there is too much emphasis on music of the past which results in too few opportunities for contemporary composers. See also: B65

B477. ______. "New Copland Opera." Musical America 74 (April 1954): 5.
The New York City Opera gave the premiere performance of The Tender Land April 1. Horace Everett wrote the libretto. Eyer describes the vocal music as simple and "built along almost conventional diatonic, chromatic and choral lines." He finds Copland's orchestral music "far more complex and sophisticated." See also: W90

B478. "Fanfare for the Common Man." Brass Quarterly 1 (March 1958): 187.
Eugene Goossens asked ten composers to write a fanfare in 1942 and these ten were published in 1944 as Ten Fanfares. Copland's Fanfare for the Common Man was one of these and it is now published separately. It sounds like a processional with a dramatic open sound. Copland used this fanfare in the last movement of his Third Symphony also.

B479. "Fantasia para Piano de Aaron Copland." Revista Musical Chilena 12 (January-February 1958): 82-83.

B480. "Fantasy for Piano; Composer Explains Its Particular Problems." New York Times, October 20, 1957, II, p.9:8.
This one-movement piano work lasts approximately thirty minutes and does not draw upon any folk elements. It is based on a sequence of ten notes from the chromatic scale.

B481. "February's Guest Artists." San Francisco Symphony Program Notes (February 1967): 9.
As Musica Viva's coordinator, Copland assists in planning the organization's activities. Copland is being featured during February's meetings and concerts as an author, lecturer, composer, conductor, and performer. A brief list of his achievements is included.

B482. Fenton, John H. "Harvard Hears Lord Home Urge West to Make Larger Sacrifices." New York Times, June 16, 1961, p.3:3.
Harvard University awarded an honorary Doctor of Music degree to Copland during its 310th commencement exercises.

B483. Fine, Irving. "Reviews of Records." Musical Quarterly 40 (October 1954): 622-623.
Fine reviews Capitol P-8382 which has Billy the Kid performed by the Ballet Theatre Orchestra conducted by Joseph Levine. This recording is compared to the one by the R.C.A. Victor Symphony conducted by Leonard Bernstein and Fine "misses the special qualities that Bernstein brings to the performance of Copland's music." This ballet is an important work in Copland's "American" style. See also: D42, D60

B484. _____. "Solo Songs." Music Library Association Notes 11 (December 1953): 159-160.
The Twelve Poems of Emily Dickinson are reviewed. These "songs
are Copland at his very best, his most inspired and his most
personal." These twelve pieces are barely related thematically
in the sense of most song cycles. However, the contrasts join
to form a type of dignified unity and sentiment.

B485. Finkelstein, Sidney. "Aaron Copland and American Music." Masses
and Mainstream 7 (March 1954): 50-56.
This review of Arthur Berger's Aaron Copland closely examines
Copland's attempts to help contemporary composers receive more
recognition. He has participated in cultural exchanges with other
countries and has had some success in having contemporary works
performed. "Copland himself has become a kind of 'dean' of
American composers, and the appearance of this book itself would
indicate the prestige he holds." See also: B200

B486. _____. "The Music of Aaron Copland." American Record Guide 17
(May 1951): 290-294.
The "Americanism" of Copland's music is examined in relation
to other serious music being composed during the first part of
the twentieth century. A biographical sketch describes his
beginnings as a composer.

B487. _____. "The Music of Aaron Copland." Music Parade 17 (June 1951):
329-333.
Finkelstein examines Copland's musical career and stylistic
changes. When Copland returned to the United States after his
studies in France, he soon adopted jazz elements in his works.
He began utilizing other folk characteristics for a time, then
switched to a style which excluded these elements. Biographical
information is included along with a list of his activities with
music organizations.

B488. Finney, Ross Lee. "A Reminiscence." Perspectives of New Music
19, no.1-2 (1981-1982): 21.
Finney recalls his first meeting with Copland in 1927 in France.
Copland spoke then of his interest in "being an AMERICAN composer,
about understanding your roots—where you come from." This issue
is devoted entirely to Copland.

B489. "First Performance." Musical America 70 (November 15, 1950): 5.
The Piano Quartet, first performed by the New York Quartet at
the Library of Congress the previous month, is based on six notes
of the whole tone scale with occasional semitones. The clashing
tonalities of this work contrasts sharply with the works such
as Billy the Kid although there are some sections which are
similar to his earlier works based on American musical idioms.
See also: W86

B490. "First Performances." World of Music 14, no.4 (1972): 86.
Three Latin American Sketches is included in this alphabetical
listing by composer of 1971-73 premieres. This work had its
premiere with Andre Kostelanetz conducting the New York Philharmonic June 7, 1972. See also: W109

B491. Fisher, Fred. "Contemporary American Style, How Three Representa-
      tive Composers Use the 'Row.'" Clavier 14, no.4 (1975): 34-37.
         Copland's Piano Fantasy is analyzed in terms of its relationship
      to a row, or in this case, "upon the circle of fourths and
      fifths." Fisher feels that music is composed with structure and
      relationships such as these in mind, rather than simply as an
      emotional expression. Carl Ruggles and Samuel Barber are the
      other two composers analyzed.

B492. "5 in Arts to be Honored." New York Times, September 13, 1979,
      III, p.11:1.
         The five honorees by the John F. Kennedy Center for the Per-
      forming Arts are Ella Fitzgerald, Henry Fonda, Martha Graham,
      Tennessee Williams, and Copland. These awards are given for
      "lifetime achievement in the performing arts." The awards are
      to be presented on September 16 at the Kennedy Center Opera House.

B493. "5 Pulitzer Prize Winners to Assess Literary Scene." New York
      Times, April 24, 1966, p.76:6.
         Five former award winners including Copland are to be featured
      May 10 as speakers at a fiftieth anniversary celebration.

B494. Flanagan, William. "Aaron Copland." HiFi/Stereo Review 16 (June
      1966): 43-54.

B495. _____. "Aaron Copland's Opera The Tender Land; Columbia's New
      Abridged Version Reveals a Work of Soaring Lyricism." HiFi/
      Stereo Review 16 (June 1966): 64-65.
         Columbia MS 6814 and ML 6214 contains an excellent rendition
      of Copland conducting the New York Philharmonic and the Choral
      Arts Society in his opera. The opera was not received well in
      the beginning but has gained popularity. "The recorded perfor-
      mance could scarcely be better." See also: D340

B496. _____. "Aaron Copland's Short (15') Symphony." Stereo Review
      22 (June 1969): 76-77.
         Although the Short Symphony was completed in 1934, this is
      its first appearance on a recording. Performance of this sparse
      work was cancelled by both the Philadelphia Orchestra and the
      Boston Symphony in the past "because its rhythmic difficulties
      required too much rehearsal time." The Dance Symphony is also
      on this Columbia Recording MS 7223 with Copland conducting the
      London Symphony Orhcestra. See also: D94, D323

B497. _____. "American Songs: a Thin Crop." Musical America 72 (Febru-
      ary 1952): 23.
         This is an overview of the authentically American art-song.
      Copland's Twelve Poems of Emily Dickinson, composed in 1950 is
      considered to be an outstanding example of this genre. Flanagan
      finds these songs to be simple and lyrical. He feels that the
      relationship of the text to the music could be better. "The
      words frequently seem to have been molded to the preconceived
      musical idea." The Second Hurricane has much greater prosodic
      value in Flanagan's opinion.

B498. Fleming, Shirley. "Philharmonic: Copland Premiere." High Fidelity/
Musical America 18 (January 1968): MA14.
The New York Philharmonic commissioned Inscape for its 125th
anniversary. Its New York premiere was October 19 at Philharmonic
Hall. This work has twelve-tone techniques incorporated in it
and has two tone-rows. The orchestration appears to be the most
important aspect of this work. There is "scarcely enough rhythmic
variety to cause a ripple on the sonic surface."

B499. Foldes, Andor. "Portraits: Aaron Copland 60 Jahre." Musica 14
(November 1960) 748-750.
This is a biographical sketch of the composer who will cele-
brate his sixtieth birthday on November 14. There is an emphasis
on his early training with Goldmark, and in France with Boulanger.
Some of his major works, as well as books, are examined.

B500. "Fonda, Graham, Copland, Fitzgerald and Williams to get Kennedy
Honors." Variety 296 (September 19, 1979): 2.
Copland is one of the artists slated to receive the second
annual Kennedy Center award for his contributions to the arts
on December 2.

B501. "For Aaron Copland at 80." Perspectives of New Music 19, no.1-2
(1980): 1-95
This entire issue has been devoted to Copland. Leonard Bernstein and Ross Lee Finney reminisced about their first meetings
with Copland in 1937 and 1927, respectively. Lawrence Starr
contributed a critical analysis of Copland's style. Many other
prominent musicians wrote about Copland and contributed music in
his honor.

B502. "For the People." Time 33 (June 5, 1939): 60.
Copland's ballet, Billy the Kid, was danced by Lincoln Kirstein's
Ballet Caravan at the American Lyric Theatre the previous week.
This work, "much of it based on cowboy songs, was close-knit [and]
percussive." A biographical sketch of Copland is included.

B503. Ford, Christopher. "Aaron's Rod." Guardian, May 30, 1972, p.10.

B504. _____. "Copland, the Conductor." Washington Post, June 15, 1972,
p.B15.
The transition from composer to conductor has been very easy
for Copland in his later years. At age seventy-two, he says
that he is slowing down in regard to composing. However, he
enjoys conducting, and believes that it helps keep him fit and
young. He reminisces about his long career in composition and
his activities in promoting contemporary American music.

B505. "Four Dance Episodes from Rodeo and Statements; Old American Songs
2nd Set." Music and Letters 35 (January 1955): 98-99.
These orchestra works show a marked contrast in Copland's
styles of composition. The episodes from Statements "are much
more severe in style" than the excerpts from Rodeo which incorporate folk elements. The Old American Songs are pleasant
works using "tunes that do not entirely avoid the commonplace."

B506. "Four New Members." New York Times, December 17, 1954, p.28:3.
       The American Academy of Arts and Letters has elected Copland
       to its membership. In the announcement on December 16, he was
       noted as being a leading composer in America.

B507. "Four Piano Blues." Music Survey 3 (Summer 1950): 50.
       This is a review of Copland's piano pieces which incorporate
       jazz elements. The reviewer wonders if this jazzy slickness
       has been established as an integral part of American folk music.

B508. Fowle, Farnsworth. "Princeton Gives 2 Women Honors." New York
       Times, June 13, 1956, p.41:3.
       In the citation awarding Copland the honorary Doctor of
       Music degree at Princeton University, it was noted that he has
       been "a tireless champion in the cause of contemporary music,
       especially in our own country."

B509. Fox, Charles Warren. "Aaron Copland: Sextet for String Quartet,
       Clarinet and Piano." Music Library Association Notes 6 (Septem-
       ber 1959): 634-635.
       This arrangement of Copland's Short Symphony is difficult for
       the performers because of the dissonances and the irregular
       rhythms. "It is chamber music only in instrumentation, not in
       idiom."

B510. Freedman, Guy. "A Copland Portrait." Music Journal 35 (January
       1977): 6-8.
       In this question and answer session with Freedman, Copland
       admits that he never was interested in composing electronic
       music. He said that he was happy when turned a light switch and
       the light came on! Copland discussed the problems composers face
       in having their music performed. Since there are more musical
       organizations now as well as more contemporary composers, there
       should be increased opportunities to have contemporary music
       performed.

B511. Freeman, John W. "New York." Opera News 40 (February 28, 1976):
       46.
       The Tender Land was performed recently by the Bronx Opera
       Company to celebrate Copland's seventy-fifth birthday which
       occurred the previous fall. The libretto by Horace Everett is
       not satisfactory in Freeman's opinion. Copland's music consists
       of "broad, poignant strands of melody and piquant bony rhythm."

B512. _____. The Reluctant Composer; a Dialogue with Aaron Copland."
       Opera News 27 (January 26, 1963): 8-12.
       In this interview Copland characterizes himself as one who
       considers composing an opera very carefully before going ahead
       with the project. He indicates that composing a successful opera
       is so difficult that it is considered "la form fatale." However,
       he states that he may write another one .

B513. French, P. "The London Concert Scene." Musical Opinion 91 (Novem-
       ber 1967): 71.
       Copland's Symphonic Ode is reviewed.

B514. Friedberg, Gertrude. "New Books on Music and Near-Musical Subjects." Music Clubs Magazine 35 (March 1956): 13.
This is a review of Julia Smith's Aaron Copland: His Work and Contribution to American Music. She traces his stylistic characteristics, especially his use of jazz, in his music. This is "an important source book in the history of American music."

B515. "From the Mail Pouch: Native Art." New York Times, November 5, 1950, p.9:2.
Three letters to the editor are in response to the recent article by Olin Downes which commemorated Copland's fiftieth birthday. See also: B439

B516. Frymire, Jack. "Copland 68." Music & Artists 1, no.5 (November 1968): 18-19.
This is an interview with Copland shortly before he reached his sixty-eight birthday on November 14. He is quite active conducting, and has appeared with the London Symphony Orchestra annually for the past four years. He is frequently asked to conduct his own works by various orchestras, but he likes to include the works of less well-known contemporary composers on his programs. Copland discusses his former teacher Nadia Boulanger as well as Martha Graham and Charles Ives.

B517. "Funds Obtained for Music Series." New York Times, November 15, 1961, p.51:7.
Copland is among those who have contributed donations to support Max Pollikoff's modern music concert series "Music in Our Time." The concerts are designed to present works by young composers.

B518. Furie, Kenneth. "Familiar Copland--with a Surprise. High Fidelity/ Musical America 24 (February 1974): 14.
Copland conducted a new recording of his Appalachian Spring for Columbia recently. The surprise was his addition of approximately eight minutes of music which he added just before the restatement of the Simple Gifts theme. A bonus disk of Copland rehearsing is to be issued along with this recording on Columbia M 32736. See also: D9

B519. Gagne, Cole and Tracy Caras. "Aaron Copland." In Soundpieces: Interviews with American Composers, 102-113. Metuchen, New Jersey: Scarecrow Press, 1982.
Copland is one of the twenty-four composers interviewed in this book. His interview took place January 6, 1975 in his home in Peekskill, New York. He relates his views on how he composes and notes some of the factors influencing his styles of writing. He did not want his music to be completely based on folk idioms so he is proud of writing in various styles. A short biography is included as well as list of his works.

B520. "A Gallery of Lifetime Achievers." Music Educators Journal 66 (April 1980): 45.
Copland, who is almost eighty, is listed among these older musicians. The synopsis of his major achievements included the Pulitzer Prize in Music in 1945 for Appalachian Spring.

B521. Gamarekian, Barbara. "Kennedy Center Honors Five for Life Achieve-
      ments in Arts." New York Times, December 3, 1979, III, p.14:1.
         On December 2 Henry Fonda, Martha Graham, Tennessee Williams,
      Ella Fitzgerald, and Copland were honored at an open house in
      Washington, D.C. Leonard Bernstein stated, "'Copland captured
      the texture of the American experience in his music.'"

B522. Gamer, Carlton. "Current Chronicle: Colorado Springs, Colorado."
      Musical Quarterly 59, no.3 (1973): 462-466.
         Copland's Piano Sonata was on the February 8 program performed
      by David Burge at the Colorado College. The work is chiefly
      diatonic and traditional in structure.

B523. Garvie, Peter. "Aaron Copland." Canadian Music Journal 6, no.2
      (1962): 3-12.
         Copland's development as a composer during the past six decades
      is noted. Some analysis of his major compositions and the
      different styles to which he has ascribed are examined. A
      description of the "American" elements found in his music is
      given. "Copland's is urban music, but with an intense hankering
      for the open spaces."

B524. _____. "Aaron Copland." Revista Musical Chilena 17, no.86 (1963):
      4-11.
         This article has biographical information and an analysis of
      some of Copland's most important works. His development and
      stylistic changes are chronicled.

B525. Gauntlett, Helen. "The Berkshire Festival." Musical Times 95
      (October 1954): 558.
         The Berkshire Music Center will present Copland's opera, The
      Tender Land, this concert season. Copland has revised the work
      since its premiere the previous April by the New York City
      Opera Company. The music is praised for its fine qualities, but
      Horace Everett's libretto is considered ineffective.

B526. Gebert, Armand. "Midland, Mich." Opera News 43 (August 1978): 45.
         The Matrix: Midland Arts Festival opened June 3 with Copland
      conducting The Tender Land. This work "has a wealth of musical
      subtlety, though its means are economical and its style simple."
      The Michigan Opera Theatre, under the direction of Michael Motel,
      performed the opera.

B527. Ginzburg, Leo. Dirizerskoe Ispolnitle'stvo: Praktika, Istorija,
      Estetika. Moskva: Muzyka, 1957.
         This book on conducting, its performance, practice, history
      and aesthetics, contains selections from various notable con-
      ductors' writings including those of Copland.

B528. "Give First Hearings of Chamber Music." New York Times, February
      10, 1930, p.21:1.
         The third season of the Copland-Sessions Concerts opened Febru-
      ary 9 at Steinway Hall. This series of performances is providing
      contemporary composers, especially American, an opportunity to
      have their works performed.

B529. Glueck, Grace. "First Private Foundation to Aid the Arts Is Set
      Up." New York Times, December 5, 1973, p.1:2.
      W. McNeil Lowry will direct a new foundation which will assist
      the arts in funding from private rather than government sources.
      Copland is listed among the foundation's incorporating members.

B530. Gold, Don. "Aaron Copland; the Well-Known American Composer Finds
      Virtues and Flaws in Jazz." Down Beat 25 (May 1, 1958): 16.
      In examining Copland's views on jazz, Gold notes that Copland
      found jazz to be a very important element in his music at one
      period in his life. Copland felt that jazz had "great attrac-
      tiveness, but with serious limitations." In his Music for the
      Theatre he attempted to use jazz elements, but only in a general,
      not a literal sense. His Piano Blues "are not a blues in
      structure, but in quality." Copland suggests that composers can
      use jazz characteristics in their music without actually following
      the typical jazz patterns.

B531. Goldberg, Albert. "Birthday Salute to Aaron Copland." Los Angeles
      Times, November 26, 1974, IV, p.1:2.
      Copland conducted the California Chamber Symphony on November
      24 in celebration of his seventy-fourth birthday. "He has
      become a rather good conductor--of his own music at least."

B532. _____. "Standard Fare." Musical America 81 (July 1961): 37.
      Copland's Nonet for Solo Strings had its West Coast premiere
      on May 1 by the Concertgebouw Orchestra of Amsterdam in Los
      Angeles. Goldberg's only criticism was "that it does not con-
      tain enough rhythmic variety to sustain its length.

B533. Goldberg, Isaac. "Aaron Copland." Disques 3 (September 1932);
      285-289.
      Goldberg examines several of Copland's most important works in
      light of Copland's own personal characteristics and style of
      living. Quotes from some of Copland's writings assist one in
      understanding the composer's feelings and thoughts when he was
      creating these works. Copland is only thirty-two years old now
      and he is becoming quite prominent.

B534. _____. "Aaron Copland and His Jazz." American Mercury 12
      (September 1927): 63-65.
      Although jazz is often associated with music of the American
      Negro, Goldberg feels that jazz has some of its origins in
      Jewish music as well. Copland, as George Gershwin, has incor-
      porated jazz elements in some of his compositions, such as
      Music for the Theatre.

B535. "Golden Baton Awards." Variety 291 (May 31, 1978): 2.
      The American Symphony Orchestra League of Washington, D.C.
      will present one of two gold baton awards to Copland in
      Chicago in early June. This honor is "for distinguished
      service to music and the arts."

B536. Goldman, Richard Franko. "Aaron Copland." Musical Quarterly 47,
      no.1 (1961): 1-3.

This biographical sketch examines Copland's stylistic characteristics at different stages of his career, from jazz to
austere to folk style. He has been successful in composing for
various musical classifications, as piano, voice, and instrumental. This tribute is in honor of Copland's sixtieth birthday.
It mentions his efforts on behalf of other musicians also.

B537. _____ . "Aaron Copland, His Work and Contribution to American
Music." Etude 74 (November 1956): 8.
    Goldman reviews Julia Smith's biography of Copland. He feels
that it is a good factual study of the composer but that the
details sometimes become tedious. He asserts that "her descrip-
tions of the music suffer from an odd combination of eagerness
and superficiality." See also: B1042

B538. _____ . "The Copland Festival." Juilliard Review 8, no.1 (1960-
1961): 14-16.
    A celebration of Copland's sixtieth birthday at the Juilliard
School of Music was a very sincere one, in Goldman's opinion.
Two concerts were held November 14 and 15 to present Copland's
works. Among those on the program were Music for the Theatre
and In the Beginning. No current American composer "has written
as effectively in every medium" as Copland has. His works range
from complex instrumental pieces to compositions suitable for
students.

B539. _____ . "Current Chronicle: New York." Musical Quarterly 37
(January 1951): 89.
    The League of Composers observed Copland's fiftieth birthday
with a concert of his works on November 5, 1950. Some of his
less well-known works were presented, including As It Fell upon
a Day and the Piano Quartet. Goldman feels "that no American
composer has made or is likely to make a deeper mark on his own
time."

B540. _____ . "Current Chronicle: New York." Musical Quarterly 49,
no.1 (1963): 91-93.
    Goldman believes that Connotations is the first composition
by Copland using twelve-tone techniques and he questions Copland's
motives in using the method. "Connotations is a harsh piece,
completely without charm."

B541. _____ . "Reviews of Books." Musical Quarterly 39 (January 1953):
107-109.
    Goldman finds Copland's Music and Imagination to be an
interesting, valuable book. The lectures that make up the book
were presented at Harvard University to musicians as well as
non-musicians. The object of the lectures is to encourage the
listener to realize that music is complex and to approach it
with an open mind. See also: B65

B542. _____ . "Reviews of Records." Musical Quarterly 42 (October
1956): 556-557.
    The Concert Hall Society recent recording contains the
Piano Concerto conducted by Copland with Leo Smit at the piano.
This work is also known as the Jazz Concerto and is a period
piece from the 1920's. Its vitality makes it successful.
See also: D84

B543. "Goldovsky-Copland-Schneider-Wilson Make Great NMC 1970 Team."
School Musician 42 (November 1970): 66.
Four well-known musicians participated in the Interlochen
National Music Camp during the past summer: Boris Goldovsky,
Alexander Schneider, George C. Wilson, and Copland. Copland
rehearsed the orchestra and conducted the group in an important
concert. In addition, the composer was presented with Phi Mu
Alpha Sinfonia's American Man of Music Plaque.

B544. Goldsmith, Harris. "N.Y. Phil., Gampel." High Fidelity/Musical
America 22 (September 1972): MA19-20.
Lilit Gampbel, a twelve-year old pianist, performed with the
New York Philharmonic June 7 with Andre Kostelanetz conducting.
Also on this program was Copland's Three Latin American Sketches
which Goldsmith described as "El Salón México without a liquor
license."

B545. "Goodman, Copland and Concertos." Woodwind Magazine 3 (November
1950): 14.
Benny Goodman commissioned Copland to write the Clarinet
Concerto for him. This is a review of Goodman's premiere
performance of it with the NBC Symphony on the radio which
resulted in much praise for Goodman's performance. However,
the reviewer "felt insecure about the value of the concerto."
See also: W79

B546. Goodwin, Noel. "Copland Conducts." Music and Musicians 14
(January 1966): 42.

B547. _____. "England." Musical Courier 161 (June 1960): 13.
The London Symphony Orchestra was recently conducted by Copland
in a concert of his works at the Royal Festival Hall. All of
the works on the program were written before 1937 so it was a
study of his early styles.

B548. _____. "Great City Blues." Music and Musicians 12 (July 1964):
27.
Copland's Music for a Great City is reviewed.

B549. _____. "LSO/Copland: Festival Hall." Times (London), December
3, 1980, p.14g.
The London Symphony Orchestra invited Copland to be the guest
conductor for a concert of his works and to celebrate his
eightieth birthday December 2. The composer "has repeatedly
distilled the voice of a specifically American music in works
which will never lose their exhilaration for export."

B550. _____. "The Quiet American." Music and Musicians 11 (February
1963): 16.

B551. _____. "Refractory Bernstein." Music and Musicians 11 (April
1963): 42.
Leonard Bernstein conducted the New York Philharmonic in the
premiere performance of Connotations at the opening of Philharmonic Hall in Lincoln Center this past September. Bernstein
also conducted it several more times during the following spring.
See also: W98

B552. Gorer, Richard. "Reviews of Music." <u>Music Review</u> 13 (May 1952): 158-159.
  <u>Danzón Cubano</u> for two pianos is reviewed. "Except for some rather unreal antiphony, there is a lack of characteristic effects." Gorer does not feel that Copland's reiteration of patterns develops the music as well as it should.

B553. Goss, Madeleine Binkley. "Aaron Copland." In <u>Modern Music-Makers, Contemporary American Composers</u>, 315-332. New York: Dutton, 1952.
  This biography emphasizes Copland's early interest and training in music. Information about the circumstances under which some of his most important compositions were written is given along with Copland's feelings about the works. A list of major events in the composer's life from 1900-1950 is included as well as a classified list of works.

B554. Gradenwitz, Peter. "Copland in Israel." <u>New York Times</u>, May 13, 1951, II, p.7:8.
  Copland was invited to head a conference for composers in Israel recently. The thirty-two Israeli composers conferred and examined Israeli works. While in the country Copland also conducted the Tel Aviv Chamber Choir in his choral work In the Beginning at the Ein Ger Festival.

B555. Gräter, Manfred. "Aaron Copland Besucht Europa." <u>Melos</u> 24 (April 1957): 108-110.
  Copland was interviewed by Gräter in Germany while he was visiting in Europe. In this question and answer session Copland discussed some of his major works and his feelings about these compositions.

B556. Greenfield, Edward. "Abe Lincoln in Britain." <u>High Fidelity</u> 19 (March 1969): 28.
  Copland recently conducted the London Symphony in his <u>Lincoln Portrait</u>. The composer admitted that it was difficult to convey his interpretation of this very American piece with the British orchestra. This was also the first time Copland conducted his <u>Down a Country Lane</u>.

B557. _____. "Copland by Copland." <u>High Fidelity/Musical America</u> 18 (January 1968): 14.
  An incident which occurred during Copland's recording of his Symphonic Ode is recounted. The composer was listening to the playback and was surprised by the sound of a triangle at one point. This did not appear on the conductor's score but it was written in the percussion part. His feeling was that it did not hurt anything, but he chose to delete the triangle part during re-recording because it was not in the composer's part.

B558. _____. "A Copland Premiere on Disc." <u>High Fidelity/Musical America</u> 22 (September 1972): 14.
  It is unusual for a premiere to be given at a recording studio but such was the case with <u>Latin American Sketches</u> conducted by the composer. These three pieces "with their cross-accents and uneven rhythms, are taxing enough for the players." The New York Philharmonic Orchestra recorded this for Columbia M 33269 in

June. Although Copland is seventy-one years old, he has been
handling an exhaustive conducting schedule recently. See also:
B109, D351

B559. _____. "Lobster Quadrille in London." American Musical Digest
1, no.4 (1970): 31-32.
This is abridged from the Guardian, November 26, 1969. Copland
conducted the London Symphony Orchestra in Quiet City and Billy
the Kid at Royal Festival Hall November 24, 1969. These two
works "are founded on music for the theatre, music intended to
evoke atmosphere and immediate emotion." Greenfield feels that
there is much to admire in this music. Also on the program was
David Del Tredici's Lobster Quadrille.

B560. _____. "Project Copland Nears Conclusion." High Fidelity/
Musical America 21 (February 1971): 13.
Copland is near the end of the project of conducting all of
his major works on recordings for CBS at London's EMI Studio.
The studio where this was taking place had recently been reno-
vated so the engineers had some problems to conquer. Copland
was pleased with the performance of the London Symphony Orchestra.

B561. Greenhaigh, John. "Copland's Mixed Bag." Music and Musicians 18
(February 1970): 53.
Copland appeared as conductor with the London Symphony
Orchestra November 25, 1969 at Festival Hall. Among the works
on the program were his Quiet City and Billy the Kid. The
latter composition illustrates Copland's excellent use of folk
elements in depicting the frontier tradition.

B562. Griffiths, Paul. "Copland, Aaron." In Makers of Modern Culture,
edited by Justin Wintle, 112. New York: Facts on File, 1981.
This is a brief biography of Copland emphasizing his cultural
contributions. Some of his major compositions were designed to
express American characteristics, such as Billy the Kid and
Appalachian Spring. Copland has always promoted the music of
other American composers in his work with the American Composers
Alliance and other organizations.

B563. Grigoriev, L. and L. Platek. "The American Composers in Moscow."
Music Journal 18 (June-July 1960): 60-61.
Lukas Foss and Copland are on a cultural good will tour in the
Soviet Union. Copland conducted his Third Symphony at the
Grand Hall of the Moscow Conservatory and presented Dmitrii
Shostakovich with an honorary membership in the American Academy
of Arts and Letters and the National Institute of Arts and
Letters.

B564. Grigson, Geoffrey and Charles Harvard Gribbs-Smith. "Sidewalk,
Glass, Steel and Prairie." In People: a Volume of the Good,
Bad, Great & Eccentric Who Illustrate the Admirable Diversity
of Man, 100-101. New York: Hawthorn Books, 1956.
Copland's short biography compares his early music to the
city: "complex, efficient and . . . goaded on by a mechanistic
frenzy." As the composer realized that the distance between
his music and audiences was growing wider, he changed his style

to one that would be more appealing to the average person by
employing folk themes and simplifying the musical line.

B565. Grove, George. "Copland, Aaron." Dictionary of Music and Musicians,
edited by Eric Blom, 5th ed., v.2, 428-429. New York: St.
Martin's Press, 1954.
    This short biography lists Copland's musical training and
achievements. An analysis of his different styles is included
as well as a complete classified list of his works.

B566. Gruen, John. "An Unconventional Showcase for Composers." New
York Times, September 27, 1981, II, p.19:1.
    Charles Schwartz, the founder and director of the Composers'
Showcase, has announced three special concerts to celebrate the
organization's twenty-fifth anniversary during September and
October. Copland will be present as narrator for L'Histoire du
Soldat during one of the concerts to be held at the Whitney
Museum of American Art.

B567. Günther, S. "USA-Sinfoniker des 20. Jahrhunderts." Orchester 10
December 1962): 39.

B568. Haberkorn, Michael H. "A Study and Performance of the Piano Sonatas
of Samuel Barber, Elliott Carter, and Aaron Copland." Ph.D.
diss., Columbia University Teachers College, 1979.
    The similarities among these three composers are noted in this
study. For example, each wrote a piano sonata between 1940 and
1950. The principal objective in the written portion of this
project was to examine the compositional styles and to make
performance suggestions.

B569. Häusler, Josef. "Aaron Copland in Deutschland." Musica 9 (November 1955): 559.
    Copland has been conducting the Southwest Radio Orchestra in
some of his compositions at Baden-Baden. Details about the
concerts are included.

B570. _____. "Musik von Drüben; Aaron Copland im Südwestfunk." Melos
22 (November 1955): 332.
    Copland have been visiting Germany and conducting the Southwest
Radio Orchestra in concerts of his works while there.

B571. Haggin, Bernard H. "Copland as Critic." New York Times, October
12, 1952, VII, p.7:1.
    Haggin reviews Copland's Music and Imagination and finds the
book well worth reading. It consists of lectures given while
he was at Harvard University. There are no musical examples so
the reader needs to either be acquainted with the music or be
able to secure the scores or recordings to fully appreciate this
book. See also: B65

B572. _____. "Music." Nation 177 (July 25, 1953): 79.
    Copland's book, Music and Imagination, contains his Harvard
University lectures from 1951-52 when he was the Charles Eliot
Norton lecturer. Copland notes that the public clings to the
classics. He encourages audiences to be more receptive to new

ideas and new sonorities which can be found in the music of contemporary composers. See also: B65

B573.   . "Music." Nation 182 (March 24, 1956): 247.
Copland's music seems to follow two stylistic directions. First, his more formal intellectual approach is exhibited in works such as his Symphonic Ode. In contrast, works such as Billy the Kid were the result of a decision "to write simpler, accessible music that would interest the general music public."

B574.   . Music in the Nation. 1949. Reprint. Freeport, New York: Books for Libraries Press, 1971.
As a music critic for the Nation, Haggin wrote two articles about Copland which are included in this compilation. The first commentary from February 14, 1942 examines some of Copland's ideas from his book Our New Music. Copland urges readers to listen to some modern music instead of always relying on the classics. However, Haggin stresses that all of his education about contemporary music has not altered his opinion of it. In the November 30, 1946 commentary, Haggin notes that he found the performance of the Piano Concerto by Leo Smit with the New York City Symphony conducted by Leonard Bernstein to be excellent. Haggin finds the composition itself to be "interesting only as part of the documentation of Copland's development as a composer." See also: B84

B575. Haines, Edmund. "N.Y. Philharmonic: Schuller Premiere." High Fidelity/Musical America 18 (September 1968): MA19.
The premiere performance of Gunther Schuller's Concerto for Double Bass and Chamber Orchestra plus works by Bernstein and Copland were presented at the Lincoln Center Summer Festival. Copland conducted his Third Symphony, and his "performance was controlled and strong." Haines finds the work to be a tightly-knit composition with "no extraneous material or uneven moments."

B576. Hall, David. "Copland & Ives." Stereo Review 42 (May 1979): 108.
The original version of Copland's Appalachian Spring for thirteen players is available on a new recording along with Charles Ives' Three Places in New England. Dennis Russell Davies conducts the St. Paul Chamber Orchestra on Sound 80 S80-DLR-101. Hall likes this version of Copland's suite because it is "wonderfully lean and lithe." See also: D32

B577. Hall, Roger. "Aaron Copland--an Interview." Journal of Church Music 24 (February 1982): 6-7.
Hall asks Copland about his church-related music in this short question and answer session. Two spirituals used in Copland's compositions are Simple Gifts and At the River. A list of Copland's vocal works is included.

B578. Hamilton, David H. "Aaron Copland: a Discography of the Composer's Performances." Perspectives of New Music 9, no.1 (1970): 149-154.
This is a list of recent recordings of most of Copland's works in which he is the pianist or conductor. A supplement to this discography includes recordings by other performers in some of the premieres of his works.

B579. _____. "Music." Nation 218 (January 19, 1974): 93.
        Connotations in a slightly revised version was recently per-
        formed by the New York Philharmonic. This group had commissioned
        the work in 1962.

B580. _____. "The Recordings of Copland's Music." High Fidelity/
        Musical America 20 (November 1970): 64-66.
        Copland's recordings are prolific and are continuing to
        increase as he does more conducting. His major works are listed
        with pertinent information on available recordings and comments
        about the works themselves. Important recordings which are no
        longer available are also noted.

B581. Haney, Daniel Q. "Copland Conducts on Center's 40th." Los Angeles
        Times, July 10, 1980, VI, p.6:1.
        The Berkshire Music Center at Lenox, Massachusetts celebrated
        its fortieth year with a concert by the Boston Symphony Orchestra
        with Copland conducting. Copland has been associated with the
        group for the past thrity-nine years and has been chairman of
        the faculty during much of that time.

B582. Hanson, Howard. "Flowering of American Music." Saturday Review
        of Literature 32 (August 6, 1949): 160-161.
        Hanson feels that both Gershwin and Stravinsky have had a
        great influence on Copland's music. "Of late, his music seems
        to have grown increasingly simple and direct." Appalachian
        Spring is written in this simplified style. Copland has been
        active as a composer and teacher at Tanglewood and his influence
        is being felt by new composers such as David Diamond and Marc
        Blitzstein.

B583. Hanson, John Robert. "Macroform in Selected Twentieth-Century
        Piano Concertos." Ph.D. diss., Eastman School of Music, Uni-
        versity of Rochester, 1967.
        Copland's Piano Concerto is one of thirty-three concertos
        analyzed in this study. The over-all formal organization of
        these concertos by twenty-six composers is compared.

B584. "Happy Impromptu." Time 58 (December 17, 1971): 68.
        A new ballet has been presented in New York by Jerome Robbins
        and the New York City Ballet. The Pied Piper uses Copland's
        Concerto for Clarinet and String Orchestra which is described
        as "plain and homely music."

B585. Harrington, Richard. "Cross Sweeps Grammys." Washington Post
        February 26, 1981, D, p.1:2.
        The twenty-third annual Grammy Awards hailed Christopher
        Cross as Best New Artist and awarded Copland the Trustee Award.

B586. Harrison, Jay S. "New Works at Lincoln Center." Show 2 (December
        1962): 39.
        Connotations for Orchestra had its premiere performance at the
        opening of Philharmonic Hall at Lincoln Center recently. The
        work was commissioned for this event and was performed by the
        New York Philharmonic under the direction of Leonard Bernstein.
        Connotations is based on serial methods and is quite dissonant.

Harrison thinks "that it is one of the few unsuccessful compositions America's leading composer has written." See also: W98

B587. _____. "The New York Music Scene." Musical America 84 (February
1964): 22-23.
   Copland's Concerto for Piano was performed by the New York
   Philharmonic with Leonard Bernstein conducting January 9. This
   work, with its jazz influences, was composed in 1926. Although
   Harrison considers it dated because of its stylistic characteristics, he also feels that "it still retains its charm and
   brashness."

B588. _____. "The New York Music Scene." Musical America 84 (May 1964):
30.
   On April 3 the Boston Symphony performed Copland's Symphony
   for Organ and Orchestra. Berj Zamkochian was the soloist and
   Erich Leinsdorf conducted. The work was written for a performance by his former teacher, Nadia Boulanger, and it is
   "thoughtfully conceived and handsomely tooled."

B589. Harrison, Max. "Music in London: Pianists." Musical Times 110
(March 1969): 289.
   This is a review of the January 14 concert by Bernard Roberts
   in which he performed Copland's one-movement Piano Fantasy.
   This work "grows not through variation proper so much as by
   dissection and reintegration."

B590. "Headliners of 1960." Musical America 81 (January 1961): 20.
   This is a pictorial review of important people in music during
   1960. Copland's sixtieth birthday was celebrated by the New
   York Philharmonic and the Boston Symphony. He also participated
   in a cultural exchange program with the Soviet Union and toured
   the Far East with the Boston Symphony.

B591. Heinsheimer, H. W. "Bugles and Bells." Musical Courier 149
(March 1, 1954): 5.
   American composers have written very few operas because there
   has been little market for them. Copland's first work for the
   professional stage, The Tender Land, will have its premiere in
   April. It is noted that other famous operatic composers, such
   as Gluck and Donizetti, had written approximately thirty operas
   by the time they were Copland's age which is now fifty-three
   years.

B592. Helm, Everett. "Die Eröffnung des Lincoln Center." Neue Zeitschrift für Musik 123 (December 1962): 564.
   Copland's Connotations for Orchestra was commissioned by the
   New York Philharmonic to celebrate the Lincoln Center concert
   hall opening. The premiere performance took place September 23,
   1962 with Bernstein conducting the New York Philharmonic. See
   also: W98

B593. _____. "Lincoln Center Opening." Musical America 82 (November
1962): 18.
   Copland's Connotations for Orchestra was commissioned for an
   opening in Lincoln Center by the New York Philharmonic. Leonard

Bernstein conducted the work during the opening concert. Helms considers the work "a sometimes unnecessarily strident piece which nevertheless contained some fine music." See also: W98

B594. Henahan, Donal. "He Made Composing Respectable Here." New York Times, November 8, 1970, II, p.17:3.
This interview with Copland at his home in Peekskill as he approached his seventieth birthday found him fit and happily reminiscing about his career. Although best known for his works written in a simple style, he indicated that it was unrealistic to expect him to always compose in the same manner. He has a number of atonal works to his credit, but he says that he has no interest in electronic music.

B595. _____. "Music: Copland Tribute." New York Times, November 19, 1970, p.42:6.
The seventieth birthday of Copland was celebrated November 17 by a concert of his works at the New York Cultural Center. Nella Girolo, mezzo-soprano, and Bruce Eberle, pianist, performed this tribute to the composer.

B596. _____. "Piano: Leo Smit's All-Copland Program." New York Times, November 18, 1980, III, p.13:1.
On November 16 Smit presented a recital of Copland's solo piano music. Copland was present for the performance of his works ranging from The Cat and the Mouse (1920) to Night Thoughts (1972). "Whatever else history says about Aaron Copland, it will not deny the breadth of his appeal."

B597. _____. "This Aaron Is a Musical Moses." New York Times, November 9, 1975, II, p.21:1.
The seventy-fifth birthday of Copland is to be observed on November 14. Henahan reviews the highlights of Copland's career and significant influences on his music. "His significance as the Moses of the modern-music movement . . . in this country over the last 50 years is unquestionable."

B598. Henderson, Robert. "Copland's Inscape." Tempo 87 (Winter 1968-1969): 29-30.
Inscape, commissioned for the New York Philharmonic Orchestra's 125th anniversary season, had its premiere at the University of Michigan September 13, 1969 with Leonard Bernstein conducting. This one-movement orchestral work employs serial techniques. "The writing bears the unmistakable imprint of Copland's mature personality." See also: W103

B599. Herbage, J. "Aaron Copland's Connotations for Orchestra." Musical Events 18 (February 1963): 13.
Connotations was commissioned for the opening of Lincoln Center's Philharmonic Hall the previous fall. Leonard Bernstein conducted the New York Philharmonic in the premiere performance and he will conduct it several more times in the spring. See also: W98

B600. Herrmann, Joachim. "Glanzvolle Wiederauferstehung des National-theaters." Musica 18, no.1 (1964): 16.

This is a review of recent German ballet performances which included Copland's Dance Panels.

B601. Hershowitz, Alan. "Aaron Copland: the American Composer Shares His Mind." Music Journal 39 (March-April 1981): 9-12.
In this interview with Copland who is eighty years old, Hershowitz asks about Copland's long life as a composer and more recently as a conductor. Copland concentrated on achieving a distinctly American sound in some of his works but feels it is no longer so important because it has been done. Copland's move away from simple, melodic music to works involving twelve-tone techniques was the result of his desire to explore new areas.

B602. Heylbut, Rose. "America Goes to the Ballet: a Conference with Aaron Copland." Etude 66 (July 1948): 401.
Ballet has received more interest recently, and music written by established composers who exhibit an American sound are especially valued. In this discussion with Copland he reminds the reader that the choreographer contributes the idea, and the composer provides the music to illustrate various segments of the story. Copland relates the various difficulties that a composer encounters in composing for this medium.

B603. Hilton, Lewis. "A Study of Selected Solo Clarinet Literature of Four American Composers as a Basis for Performance and Teaching." Council for Research in Music Education Bulletin 30 (Fall 1972): 38-40.
Hilton reviews this Ph.D. dissertation by Charles Francis Del Rosso which analyzes Copland's Concerto for Clarinet and Piano. The chief criticism Hilton finds is that the scores and the recital tape do not accompany the copy of the dissertation and this limits the researcher's information. The other problem concerns the score used for this analysis which is an arrangement of the original reduced for clarinet and piano. See also: B418

B604. Hitchcock, H. Wiley. "Aaron Copland, a Tribute." Virtuoso 2, no. 2 (1981): 16-18.
Copland's long career as a composer and more recently as a conductor is noted along with his major achievements.

B605. _____. "Nadia Boulanger and Copland." In Music in the United States: a Historical Introduction, 178-182. Englewood Cliffs, New Jersey: Prentice-Hall, 1969.
Copland studied with Nadia Boulanger in France during the early 1920's. Her influence on Copland and several other important American composers such as Virgil Thomson was significant. Copland sought to express an Americanism in his early work such as his Music for the Theatre. This was followed by more complex techniques involving tone-rows in works such as his Piano Variations in 1930.

B606. Hobson, Wilder. "The Finest Product of the Spirit." Saturday Review 35 (October 25, 1952): 34-35.
This is a review of Copland's Music and Imagination which consists of lectures delivered at Harvard University 1951-1952.

The book is directed toward the layman, especially the listener.
Copland "writes about his art with great warmth, intimacy, and
liveliness." See also: B65

B607. "Hoe-Down." Monthly Musical Record 79 (January 1949): 22.
      This is a short review of an excerpt from the score Rodeo.
The piece "needs experienced playing."

B608. Holland, Bernard. "College Names Division for Copland." New
      York Times, April 30, 1981, III, p.21:3.
      Queens College will honor Copland by giving its music depart-
ment the following name: Aaron Copland School of Music. The
composer was born in Brooklyn. The head of the school, Raymond
Erickson, says "'Aaron Copland symbolizes a coming of age in
American music.'"

B609. _____. "Music: Da Capo Toasts Copland." New York Times, March
      18, 1981, III, p.20:5.
      Copland was the guest of honor at a concert given by the Da
Capo Chamber Players at Carnegie Hall March 16. The group
performed his Threnody I and II in addition to his Sextet. "All
three pieces resonated with scrubbed-clean sounds."

B610. "Honors for Members." ASCAP Today 2, no.3 (1968): 34.

B611. Hosier, John. "The Musician's Bookshelf." Musical Times 98
      (December 1957): 667.
      Hosier reviews Copland's What to Listen For in Music which is
designed for the non-professional musician and listener. The
composer emphasizes active listening as opposed to performing as
a means to music appreciation. Hosier finds the book dis-
appointing in that "it could easily have achieved a lot more
than it has done." See also: B108

B612. Howard, John Tasker. "Aaron Copland." In Our Contemporary Com-
      posers; American Music in the Twentieth Century, 145-150. 1941.
      Reprint. Freeport, New York: Books for Libraries Press, 1975.
      Copland's use of jazz elements in his early works soon gave
way to styles that were very modern and complex. Later he moved
to a simplification of melody and texture. His career and background through the 1930's is noted, but no conclusion about his
work is offered. "The problem of judging Copland's recent works
is difficult; he is still developing his medium."

B613. _____. Our American Music; a Comprehensive History from 1620 to
      the Present. 4th ed. New York: T. Y. Crowell Company, 1965.
      Howard characterizes all of Copland's music as having "its own
sparse and lean character rather than with any borrowed style or
technique." The development of Copland's career and his compositions are detailed along with observations by other music
critics. This in-depth examination of his works for various
orchestrations includes information about some premiere performances as well. Copland's activities in music other than composing include conducting and writing.

B614. Hruby, Frank. "New Music and Old." Musical America 81 (January 1961): 185.
Copland's suite for orchestra, The Tender Land, was performed October 6 by the Cleveland Orchestra with George Szell conducting. "It had the typical Copland Americana sound—colorful, major-sounding, and extra-ordinarily competent." On October 12 the Indiana University Beaux Arts Trio performed Vitebsk at the first performance of the Cleveland Chamber Music Society.

B615. Hughes, Allen. "Conductor's Centennial Is Observed at Tanglewood in Concert Marathon." New York Times, July 28, 1974, p.42:6.
On July 27 Copland joined other well-known musicians in a concert honoring Serge Koussevitzky. Copland conducted the Boston Symphony in his Quiet City during this extensive concert at the Berkshire Music Festival.

B616. _____. "Empire Sinfonietta Is Led by Copland; Bartok Stands Out." New York Times, December 18, 1971, p.36:1.
Copland conducted the Empire Sinfonietta December 16 at Tully Hall in a concert which included his Clarinet Concerto. Bartók's Divertimento was the most successful piece on the program in the opinion of the author.

B617. _____. "4 Leading American Composers Draw Full House to the Whitney." New York Times, February 5, 1969, p.38:1.
Copland conducted his Nonet for Solo Strings at a Composers' Showcase Concert on February 4 at the Whitney Museum of American Art.

B618. _____. "Music: Copland Conducts." New York Times, November 12, 1960, p.15:3.
Copland is scheduled to be the guest conductor with the New York Philharmonic for three concerts in Carnegie Hall during the coming weekend. In the performance given on November 11, "the most stimulating part . . . was that in which Copland conducted Copland." He conducted his Symphonic Ode and El Salón México.

B619. _____. "Music: Copland Jubilee a Fine Salute." New York Times, November 16, 1975, p.72:4.
On Copland's seventy-fifth birthday on November 14, the Juilliard School of Music presented a program of Copland's works to celebrate the event. "It was a fitting salute." Copland has worked to bring contemporary music to the public since the 1920's.

B620. _____. "Music: Copland Revival." New York Times, January 18, 1976, p.44:2.
On January 16 the Bronx Opera Company presented The Tender Land at Hunter College. "The music was in Copland's consciously simplified style." Hughes felt that the libretto was still as weak as it was twenty-two years ago when the New York City Opera presented it.

B621. _____. "Work by Copland Hails Orchestra." New York Times, October 20, 1967, p.53:1.
Inscape was performed in Philharmonic Hall October 19. It was

commissioned by the New York Philharmonic to celebrate its
125th anniversary and had its premiere performance in September
when Leonard Bernstein presented it at the University of Michigan.
"The music is slow for the most part and so skillfully fashioned
that it has a familiar ring despite its dodecaphonic nature."
See also: W103

B622. Hume, Paul. "Aaron Copland." Washington Post, November 22, 1978,
B, p.3:3R.
    Copland celebrated his seventy-eighth birthday by conducting
the National Symphony Orchestra in several concerts at the
Kennedy Center. He included two of his own compositions on the
program: Three Latin American Sketches and Connotations. Connotations, written sixteen years ago, "no longer sounds as
forbidding as it did at first."

B623. _____. "Aaron Copland at 80--a Portrait in Music." Washington
Post, November 9, 1980, M, p.1:1.
    Copland, who will be eighty years old on November 14, has been
a significant factor in the course of American music during the
twentieth century. He has sometimes been called the dean of
American composers. There will be a concert of his works performed at the Kennedy Center on his birthday in his honor. He
will narrate while Leonard Bernstein conducts the National
Symphony Orchestra in the Lincoln Portrait.

B624. _____. "Aaron Copland Conducts." Washington Post, May 25, 1975,
L, p.4:1.
    Copland conducts the London Symphony Orchestra and the New
Philharmonia Orchestra in a newly released recording. Dance
Panels and Three Latin American Sketches have been recorded for
the first time on Columbia 33269. Dance Panels is "by design,
episodic, lean, but full of warmth." The Sketches "have a
fresh verve and rhythmic zest." See also: D93, D351.

B625. _____. "Bernstein's Bicentennial Dates." Washington Post, February 26, 1975, B, p.9:5.
    The National Symphony Orchestra will celebrate the Bicentennial
in the spring of 1976 with a series of concerts conducted by
guest conductors. Copland is scheduled to conduct several programs of his own works.

B626. _____. "Composer Aaron Copland's America: Taking the Audience
Home." Washington Post, April 7, 1975, B, p.7:1.
    On April 5 at the Kennedy Center Copland both conducted and
played the piano in a concert of his works. There were a
thousand people listening outside over speakers because the
auditorium was packed. The applause was very enthusiastic.
He stated, "'I'd like to take this audience home in my pocket.'"

B627. _____. "Copland at the Capitol." Washington Post, May 29, 1979,
B, p.1:1R.
    Copland conducted a number of his works in a Memorial Day con-
cert May 28 on the grounds of the Capitol. He narrated his
Lincoln Portrait and conducted the other works on the program
including his Fanfare for the Common Man. The National Symphony
Orchestra performed for approximately 22,000 people.

B628. _____. "Copland Conducts Copland." Washington Post, July 2, 1977, C, p.5:4.

On July 1 Copland conducted the National Symphony Orchestra at Wolf Trap in a concert of his own works. "Not only did he write the fascinating music, but also he does a terrific job of conducting its jazzy complexities."

B629. _____. "Copland: the Authentic Touch." Washington Post, May 12, Bookworld, p.4:3.

This is a review of the recording of Appalachian Spring on Columbia 32736 in which the original orchestration is used. Other recordings use the full score with large orchestra. "There is a tenderness in the clarity of the scoring for small orchestra." Also reviewed is the Duo for Flute and Piano with Elaine Shaffer, flutist, and the composer at the piano on Columbia 32737. Included in this recording is the Violin Sonata and the Nonet for Strings. See also: D9, D112, D186, D325

B630. _____. "Del Tredici's Captivating Quadrille, a Composition with a Surprise." Washington Post, March 29, 1978, B, p.12:5R.

David Del Tredici's Lobster Quadrille was part of the National Symphony Orhcestra's program March 28. Copland, the guest conductor, asked Del Trendici to conduct the Quadrille. Copland's Third Symphony was also on the program.

B631. _____. "Fitting Fanfare." Washington Post, November 15, 1980, F, p.1:5P.

Aaron Copland's eightieth birthday was celebrated on November 14 by a concert of his works at the Kennedy Center. Leonard Bernstein conducted the National Symphony Orchestra. There were many dignitaries present to greet Copland including President and Mrs. Jimmy Carter. Two scholarships in Copland's name were announced. They will be awarded to student composers at the Berkshire Music Center and the Aspen School of Music.

B632. _____. "A Gala Forecase of Programs to Come." Washington Post, August 23, 1978, D, p.3:5R.

A live broadcast of the National Symphony Orchestra on August 22 from Lisner Auditorium was designed to encourage ticket sales for the coming concert season. Mstislav Rostropouich, Leonard Bernstein, and Copland conducted this program and all three will conduct during the coming concert season. Copland's Fanfare for the Common Man was presented on the television broadcast.

B633. _____. "Happy Birthday, Dear Aaron." Washington Post, November 15, 1977, B, p.1:6.

Mstislav Rostropovich conducted the National Symphony Orchestra in a concert celebrating Copland's seventy-eighth birthday on November 14. Copland was present for this concert of his works.

B634. _____. "The Marvel of Copland." Washington Post, September 10, 1981, B, p.1:4R.

The Terrance Theater at the Kennedy Center was an occasion for Copland to speak about his fifty years as a composer on September 9. He participated in a series of concerts to celebrate the tenth anniversary of the Kennedy Center. Five of his works were performed.

B635. _____. "Natural Wonders." Washington Post, May 27, 1980, B, P.
1:4R.
     Copland conducted the National Symphony Orchestra on May 26 on
the Capitol lawn. Forty thousand people listened as he led his
Ceremonial Fanfare, Piano Concerto, Rodeo, and works by other
composers.

B636. _____. "Sensational Symphonies." Washington Post, January 19,
1977, B, p.11:5.
     Copland conducted his Fanfare for the Common Man and the
Dance Episodes from Rodeo at the inaugural concert January 18.
The National Symphony Orchestra performed.

B637. _____. "A Talk with Composers." Washington Post, October 10,
1974, 10B, p.13:6.
     Murry Sidlin moderated a discussion with William Schuman, Roy
Harris, and Copland at the Kennedy Center Concert Hall in the
first of a series of weekly seminars. The National Symphony
Orchestra commissioned each of them to write a symphony in
honor of the nation's Bicentennial. Copland did not want to
comment on the music he will compose.

B638. _____. "This Music Is Unmistakably American: NSO's Holiday
Downbeat." Washington Post, May 27, 1979, L, p.1:3.
     On May 28 Copland will conduct the National Symphony Orchestra
on the Capitol grounds. Among his works to be performed are
Fanfare for the Common Man and Lincoln Portrait which are ap-
propriate patriotic choices for a Memorial Day celebration. He
has written "some of our most characteristically American music."

B639. "In Memoriam Igor Stravinsky." Tempo 98 (1972): 22-23.
     This is twenty-one measures of music for flute, violin, viola,
and cello entitled Threnody--Igor Stravinsky: in Memoriam. It
is part of a collection of canons and epitaphs, set two, published in Tempo in memoriam to Igor Stravinsky.

B640. "In Memoriam 1945, Szeptember 26." Musika 13 (September 1970): 7.
     Copland is among several composers who wrote expressing their
views and feelings about Béla Bartók.

B641. "In the Beginning." Music and Letters 35 (January 1954): 77.
     This is a review of the score for mixed chorus with mezzo-
soprano solo which is based on the first chapter of Genesis.
The chorus is chiefly simple diatonic writing but occasionally
it is found "plunging into changes of key seemingly reckless
for unaccompanied singing."

B642. "Incorporators, Members." Washington Post, December 5, 1973, C,
p.11:1.
     Copland is the senior American composer among those original
members of W. McNeil Lawry's foundation. Lawry is fund raising
for the arts all over the United States.

B643. "Inscape." New York Philharmonic Program Notes (September 13,
1967): 1.
     Inscape was commissioned for the New York Philharmonic's

125th anniversary. The premiere performance was September 13
at the University of Michigan. <u>See also:</u> W103

B644. "Inter-American Plan." <u>New York Times</u>, December 21, 1941, IX, p.
7:6.
      Copland will complete his four-month cultural tour of Latin-
America as a United States representative soon. The music of
North America is performed very little in these countries because they do not have access to recordings, Copland states. He
proposes that centers of music be established and stocked with
North American music.

B645. "International Music Congress--Forum." <u>Music & Artists</u> 2, no.1
(1969): 23.
      Copland moderated a discussion on "The Sound of Things to
Come" at the International Music Congress held in New York and
Washington September 9-16, 1968. The consensus was that a composer can write any type of music he wishes and be accepted as
a serious musician. In the edited transcript from this forum
Copland states, "'I do see signs of an extraordinarily free and
open attitude toward all the many possibilities of music.'"

B646. "Ionian Quartet." <u>New York Times</u>, February 25, 1929, p.27:5.
      The second of the Copland-Sessions Concerts was held February
24 at New York's Little Theatre. The concert of contemporary
music was well attended.

B647. Isacoff, S. "Copland at 80: a Birthday Interview." <u>Virtuoso</u> 2,
no.2 (1981): 18-20.

B648. _____. "Playing Copland's Piano Music: William Masselos and
Leo Smit." <u>Virtuoso</u> 2, no.2 (1981): 21-23.

B649. "Italian Academy Names Five." <u>New York Times</u>, March 6, 1956, p.27:
1.
      On March 5 Copland was made an honorary member of the Academy
of St. Cecilia of Rome.

B650. Jablonski, Edward. "Copland, Aaron." In <u>The Encyclopedia of
American Music</u>, 215-217. Garden City, New York: Doubleday, 1981.
      This biography emphasizes Copland's major works and follows
his musical career. Copland's affiliations with organizations
such as the League of Composers is noted as well as his role
in the Copland-Sessions Concerts.

B651. Jacobs, Arthur. "<u>Music and Imagination</u>, by Aaron Copland." <u>Musi-
cal Times</u> 101 (March 1960): 160.
      This is a review of a new paperback edition of Copland's
Charles Eliot Norton lectures at Harvard University published by
Mentor Books. Copland's book should appeal to "the ordinary
concert-goer and the almost-hardened professional." <u>See also:</u>
B65

B652. Jacobs, Jody. "A Tribute to Aaron Copland." <u>Los Angeles Times</u>,
May 13, 1975, IV, p.2:1.

On May 10, Henri Temianka surprised Copland with a tribute in
honor of his approaching seventieth birthday in November. The
occasion was the Allegro Ball held at the Century Plaza Hotel
by the Chamber Symphony Society of California. Selections of
Copland's works were performed as well as film clips from The
Heiress for which Copland received an Academy Award for the film
score.

B653. Jacobson, Robert. "Viewpoint." Ballet News 2 (November 1980):4.
      Among various items of interest Jacobson notes that Copland
      will be reaching his eightieth birthday on November 14. Many
      concerts will celebrate this occasion. "Certainly, when the
      history of music and dance of the twentieth century is written,
      the name of Aaron Copland will be right up there, leading the
      pack."

B654. _____. "Viewpoint." Opera News 40 (November 1975): 5.
      Copland will reach his seventy-fifth birthday on November 14
      this year. His two major contributions to the stage have been
      The Second Hurricane in 1937 and The Tender Land in 1954.
      Jacobson feels that Copland's talents in this area should have
      been exercised more and he hopes that another opera will be
      forthcoming.

B655. Jennings, Vance Shelby. "Selected Twentieth-Century Clarinet Solo
      Literature: a Study in Interpretation and Performance." Ph.D.
      diss., University of Oklahome, 1972.
      Among the works analyzed is Copland's Concerto for Clarinet
      and String Orchestra. The performance aspects of each work is
      examined along with interpretation and suggested changes.

B656. Jirko, Ivan. "Vecery s Ceskou Filharmonit." Hudebni Rozhledy 26,
      no.12 (1973): 543.

B657. Johnson, Harriett. "Aaron Copland, Dean of American Composers."
      International Musician 75 (July 1976): 6.
      Copland, who will be seventy-six years old soon, related in
      this interview that he feels like a "glamour boy." His greatest
      joy in music is conducting. He defended the art of conducting
      by observing that there is much more to it than meets the eye.

B658. Johnston, Laurie. "Notes on People." New York Times, April 20,
      1976, p.27:1.
      Copland has resigned from the ASCAP Board after being on the
      committee for approximately thirty years.

B659. Jones, Charles. "Copland on Music." Musical Quarterly 47, no.1
      (1961): 125-127.
      Jones finds Copland's book, Copland on Music, to be an in-
      triguing and nostalgic view of the composer's observations.
      "From it one sees how completely aware Copland has been of the
      various stages of creative musical development in his lifetime."
      An index would have made the book more useful.

B660. Jones, Robert. "Musician of the Month." High Fidelity/Musical
      America 25 (November 1975): MA6.

In this interview Copland says that he does not feel seventy-
five years old possibly because he has been very active conducting
for the past fifteen years. He discussed the sonorities in his
compositions and his feelings about developing a national style.
He revealed that he was unhappy about unfavorable reviews of his
music in the beginning of his career, but he learned to accept
it. Although he would not say that he was working on any new
compositions, he denied that he had stop composing.

B661. "Joseph Fennimore, Piano." High Fidelity/Musical America 22 (February 1972): MA19.
Fennimore's piano recital at Tully Hall on November 14 honored
Virgil Thomson and Copland on their birthdays. He played the
Piano Fantasy which is based on serial techniques and is full
of contrasts. In the Fantasy "an amazing variety of sonic events
emerge, linked to one another by an inner logic."

B662. "June's Guest Artists." San Francisco Symphony Program Notes
(June 1968): 13.
The Musica Viva series is featuring Copland during June. He
will lecture and conduct several times during the concerts to be
held this month. A brief explanation of Copland's background
and achievements is given.

B663. "Kann ein Komponist vom Komponieren Leben?" Melos 36 (April 1969):
156.
In English and German. Copland, among others, wrote a short
reply to the question of whether or not a composer can make a
living by composing. He states that it is possible but not easy.
In fact, most composers earn their living through teaching.

B664. Karsh, Yousuf. "Aaron Copland." In Portraits of Greatness, 54.
London: T. Nelson, 1959.
A brief list of Copland's major awards and achievements and an
interview accompany the full-page photograph of him. Karsh
reminisced about photographing other prominent composers. Copland
expressed his desire that Karsh photograph Copland's former teacher in France, Nadia Boulanger.

B665. Kastendieck, Miles. "Copland Honored by N. Y. Philharmonic."
Christian Science Monitor, November 4, 1970, N4, p.4:1.
Approximately thirty orchestras will help celebrate Copland's
seventieth birthday soon. The New York Philharmonic Symphony
Society made him an honorary member after he conducted the
orchestra in a concert of his works recently.

B666. _____. "Copland's Americana." Christian Science Monitor, July
25, 1964, p.4:1.
Copland was recently honored at the Stadium Concerts at Lewisohn
Stadium. He was noted as "'the most internationally known of
contemporary American composers.'"

B667. Kaufman, Schima. "Aaron Copland: Music for Radio." In The Music
Lover's Handbook, edited by Elie Siegmeister, 233-234. New York:
W. Morrow, 1943.
This excerpt is taken from Kaufman's Everybody's Music. Music

for Radio was commissioned by the Columbia Broadcasting System. The subtitle, Saga of the Prairie, was added later after listeners wrote suggesting titles for it. Copland consciously simplified his musical style to achieve wider acceptance.

B668. Kaufmann, Helen Loeb. "Aaron Copland." In History's 100 Greatest Composers, 32–33. New York: Grosset & Dunlap, 1957.
A short biography of Copland is included in this compilation designed for children. Some of his compositions are listed.

B669. Kay, Norman. "Aspects of Copland's Development." Tempo 95 (Winter 1970–1971): 26–27.
Copland is credited with developing a national style for America. His style is contrasted with the prolific work composed by Charles Ives. Copland's first important composition after returning from his studies in Europe with Boulanger was the Organ Symphony. It was later that he consciously began writing in an open, simpler style which became characteristically American. After 1950 he returned to a more chromatic complex style.

B670. _____. "Copland, All-American Composer." Music and Musicians 14 (September 1965): 21–24.

B671. Keener, Andrew. "Gramophone Perspective: Aaron Copland." Gramophone 58 (February 1981): 1072.
This is an interview with Copland in which he reminisces about his development as a composer and conductor. Copland is eighty years now and has not composed anything for the past nine years. He is delighted that there are so many composers of contemporary music now.

B672. Kelen, Emery. "Copland, Aaron." In Fifty Voices of the Twentieth Century, 29–31. New York: Lothrop, Lee & Shepard, 1970.
Some quotations from lecturers and writings are included in this brief biography of Copland. He stated that he hopes for inspiration every day. This book is designed for young readers.

B673. Keller, Hans. "Dartington Summer School." Musical Opinion 82 (October 1958): 15.

B674. _____. "Film Music: From an Old and a New Culture." Music Review 13 (August 1952): 38–39.
Copland's music for the film The Red Pony has been arranged as an orchestral suite. Keller is pleased to see art music such as this being used in films.

B675. _____. "First Performances." Music Review 12 (November 1951): 309.
Copland's Concerto for Clarinet and String Orchestra was recently performed in England for the first time. Copland was present to conduct the work. Keller finds the first movement to be more satisfactory musically because of the harmonic clashes in the second movement.

B676. Kenyon, Nicholas. "Musical Events: Marriages." New Yorker 58 (August 9, 1982): 76–77.

The Santa Fe Chamber Music Festival's "Celebration of American Music" included Copland's Piano Quartet. Copland was present for an open rehearsal and he spoke about the serial techniques he used in this work. Kenyon states that the work "rarely strays from some feeling of tonality or tonal center."

B677. _____. "The Scene Surveyed." Music and Musicians 24 (November 1975): 22-23.
Copland who is going to be seventy-five years old this month is interviewed. He notes that Koussevitzky was one of the few conductors who presented the works of little-known composers when Copland was beginning his career. Temperament was a factor in whether or not early twentiety-century composers attempted to write music that sounded American. Copland regrets that some of his styles of music were not readily accepted by the public. He is now composing less and conducting more.

B678. Kerman, Joseph. "Aaron Copland: The Tender Land." Music Library Association Notes 14 (December 1956): 56-57.
This opera in three acts "includes much of the most attractive Copland: hoe-downs, hymns, and 'prairie' sounds." The folksy score is noted for its quality, but Horace Everett's libretto is criticized as boing too narrow and uninspired.

B679. _____. "American Music: the Columbia Series (II)." Hudson Review 14 (Fall 1961): 408-418.
Copland is among the thirty-eight composers whose forty-three chamber music works have been recorded in Columbia's Modern American Music Series on Columbia ML 4492. The Juilliard String Quartet with David Oppenheim, clarinet, and Leonid Hambro, piano, have recorded the Sextet for String Quartet, Clarinet, and Piano. See also: D322

B680. Kern, Fred. "Ragtime Wins Respectability." Clavier 15, no.4 (1976): 24-30.
The ragtime elements in the four movements of Copland's Four Piano Blues are discussed. These four were composed from 1926-1948. The fourth blues piece was actually composed first in 1926 and is the "closest to the actual rag period." This analysis of ragtime includes the music of Scott Joplin's Gladiolus Rag.

B681. Kerner, Leighton. "Music: Aaron Copland's Time and Place." Village Voice 25 (December 10, 1980): 95-96.
Celebrations in honor of Copland's eightieth birthday on November 14 are noted.

B682. _____. "Music: Business Better than Usual." Village Voice 26 (March 18, 1981): 70.
This is a commentary on the generally uninspired programs planned for the new concert season by the New York Philharmonic. Kerner finds the recent concerts containing some of Copland's works to be aesthetically pleasing and musically important.

B683. "Kid from Brooklyn." Newsweek 76 (November 23, 1970): 139.
This is a biographical sketch of Copland who has just reached his seventieth birthday. Included are quotations in which he

comments on his age, his music, and his popularity. He states
that he has lived in a very exciting time musically and feels
"'lucky to have had a first-row seat.'"

B684. Kirkpatrick, John. "Aaron Copland's Piano Sonata." Modern Music
19 (May-June 1942): 246-250.
Kirkpatrick analyzes Copland's most recent composition which
begins and ends with slow movements and is not difficult to perform. "There is considerable sharp dissonance, but the harmony
is predominantly constant."

B685. Klein, Howard. "Copland Is Heard in Central Park." New York Times,
August 25, 1965, p.29:1.
The concert August 24 in Central Park's Sheep Meadow was the
site for 70,000 people to listen to Copland play his Piano Concerto composed in 1926. The New York Philharmonic performed
with Alfred Wallenstein conducting.

B686. _____. "Music: Copland Conducts." New York Times, July 29, 1965,
p.19:2.
Copland conducted a performance of The Tender Land in the
French-American Festival sponsored by the New York Philharmonic
on July 28. "The music in unpretentious and not very dramatic
but sincere and open." Klein observed some awkward vocal lines.

B687. _____. "Music: Stravinsky's Own." New York Times, July 16, 1966,
p.15:2.
Elliott Carter, John Cage, and Copland were featured at an
all-Stravinsky program July 15 at Philharmonic Hall. The principal work of the evening was L'Histoire du Soldat in which the
three composers read parts.

B688. _____. "Music: the B.B.C. Symphony's Finale." New York Times,
May 17, 1965, p.43:5.
The B.B.C. Symphony presented the New York City premiere of
Copland's Music for a Great City September 15. The music is
drawn from his score for the film Something Wild. "The music is
kaleidoscopic." Copland was present for the performance.

B689. _____. "Philharmonic Takes on the Avant-Garde." New York Times,
January 5, 1964, II, p.9:5.
Copland will play his Piano Concerto this week with Leonard
Bernstein conducting the New York Philharmonic. This work will
be presented as part of a five-week avant-garde concert series.
Copland declined to guess the direction or form that newer music
will take because there are too many possibilities.

B690. Kolodin, Irving. "Appalachian Spring." New York Philharmonic
Program Notes (February 4, 1954): p.1.
The New York Philharmonic, under the direction of Dimitri
Mitropoulos, performed the orchestral suite from Copland's
ballet Appalachian Spring at Carnegie Hall. This work was
written for Martha Graham. Various sections in the suite are
described. This orchestral suite has had wide recognition in
the concert world.

B691. _____. "Copland (and others) on Copland." Stereo Review 36
(March 1976): 106-107.
Two recordings of Copland's works in Great Britain have received
good reviews. The Piano Fantasy, played by Antony Peebles on
Unicorn RHS 323 and the Clarinet Concerto with Bernard Jacob con-
ducting the London Mozart Players on Unicorn RHS 314 are discussed.
Copland is also conducting some of his works on Columbia. See
also: D7, D44, D82, D92, D118, D157, D197, D221, D271, D295

B692. _____. "Music to My Ears." Saturday Review of Literature 33
(December 9, 1950): 31.
The Concerto for Clarinet and String Orchestra was commissioned
by Benny Goodman and received its concert premiere with Eugene
Ormandy conducting the Philadelphia Symphony Orchestra and Ralph
McLane as soloist. Columbia is planning to release a recording
of this work with Goodman as soloist. See also: W79

B693. _____. "Music to My Ears." Saturday Review 50 (November 4, 1967):
50.
The New York Philharmonic commissioned Inscape for its 125th
anniversary season. Copland uses twelve-tone techniques in this
work whose title is taken from Gerard Manley Hopkins.

B694. _____. "Music to My Ears." Saturday Review 53 (November 14,
1970): 48-49.
This is a short critique of several of Copland's works which
were recently presented with Copland conducting. His Appalachian
Spring was judged the best of the selections.

B695. _____. "Music to My Ears: Celebrating Aaron Copland." Saturday
Review 7 (August 1980): 80-81.
During the past summer the Tanglewood Music Festival celebrated
its fortieth anniversary and Copland's approaching eightieth
birthday. The composer conducted the Boston Symphony Orchestra
in a program of his works. Copland has been closely involved
with this group since it began. The composer's efforts in
assisting other contemporary musicians is noted.

B696. _____. "Music to My Ears: Copland at the Bowl, Samuel at
Cabrillo." Saturday Review 50 (September 9, 1967): 48.
The Hollywood Bowl was the site of a second concert of Copland
conducting his works recently. Among the compositions on the
program were the Dance Symphony and the Piano and Clarinet
Concertos. He is "unique among those composers who are generi-
cally 'serious' as well as American."

B697. _____. "Music to My Ears: I Cannot Sing the New Songs." Saturday Review 33 (June 3, 1950): 27.
Among the songs presented at Columbia University's recent
festival of contemporary American music was Copland's Twelve
Poems of Emily Dickinson. Although there is evidence of some
inspired writing, Kolodin "felt a lack of identity between
written word and musical setting." Helen Thigpen was accompanied
by David Allen in this performance.

B698. _____. "Music to My Ears: Mödl as Isolde, Copland as Conductor."
Saturday Review 41 (February 15, 1958): 31.
    Copland recently conducted the New York Philharmonic for the
first time. He led the group in his Outdoor Overture and his
Third Symphony. His "preference in sound is a simple, candid
tone neither lacking in vibrato nor wavery with overtones."
Kolodin hopes to see him often as a conductor.

B699. _____. "Music to My Ears: Nadia Boulanger and Her Dynasty."
Saturday Review 6 (December 1979): 46-47.
    Boulanger died recently at the age of ninety-three. She had
considerable influence on several prominent American composers
who studied with her. Virgil Thomson, Elliott Carter, Roy Harris,
Walter Piston, and Copland are among her students. Copland was
the first of these to begin studies with her in France when he
was twenty-one. After one visit to her class he realized that
she was "informed, specific, and above all, alive with a new
point of view on music and composition."

B700. _____. "Music to My Ears: Toscanini, Backhaus, the Tender Copland." Saturday Review 37 (April 17, 1954): 25.
    The City Center Opera presented the premiere performance of The
Tender Land last week. The libretto by Horace Everett is considered "a rather inept script." Although Kolodin does not
really consider this to be an opera, he feels that "Copland has
written honestly, in his own style, and in [a] way which does him
credit as a craftsman." The audience's reception of this new
work was polite but unenthusiastic. See also: W90

B701. Koons, Walter E. "On Various Fronts: Copland Premiere on Air."
New York Times, November 27, 1938, IX, p.8:5.
    In this letter to the editor Koons states that the United
States premiere of Copland's El Salón México was on May 14 with
Adrian Bouet conducting the N.B.C. Symphony Orchestra instead of
a recent reviewer's claim that the Boston Symphony first per-
formed it on November 19.

B702. Kostelanetz, Richard. "Modern Music Criticism and the Literate
Layman." Perspectives of New Music 61, no.1 (Fall-Winter 1967):
119-133.
    Kostelanetz is unhappy that music critics view contemporary
music in general as very unsatisfactory. Little intelligent
writing about this music is available he believes. Some artists
and composers have published their thoughts about modern music
as Copland has done. Kostelanetz describes Copland's style as
"both engaging and condescending, tough and tolerant, enthusiastic and yet apologetic."

B703. Koussevitzky, Serge. "American Composers." Life 16 (April 24,
1944): 55-56.
    Koussevitzky, conductor of the Boston Symphony for many years,
reminisces about composers with whom he has worked during the
past two decades. In a discussion about Copland he recalls that
he performed Music for the Theatre in the 1925-26 season and
that it received poor reviews in New York. This work is now
widely accepted by major symphony orchestras.

B704. Krebs, Albin. "Notes on People." New York Times, December 9,
1971, p.59:3.
Copland has been elected president of the American Academy of
Arts and Letters. He succeeds George F. Kennan in this position.

B705. _____. "Notes on People." New York Times, February 9, 1974, p.
34:1.
Copland reveals that he added the title Appalachian Spring to
his ballet after he wrote the music. He composed it for Martha
Graham and she suggested the title. However, Copland finds it
amusing that people "'tell me they can see the Appalachian
Mountains and hear the spring in the music.'"

B706. Kremenliev, Boris. "Los Angeles." Musical Courier 163 (June 1961):
60.
On May 1, Copland's Nonet was performed in Plummer Park. This
twelve-tone composition is similar to his Piano Fantasy in style.
"The Nonet marks a happy return to writing that is typically
Copland in concept, feeling, and style."

B707. Kriegsman, Alan M. "Aaron Copland at Intersection of American
Musical Currents." Los Angeles Times, May 20, 1973, CAL, p.46:1.
This is an interview discussing Copland's long career in music
as a composer and his more recent interest in conducting. In
addition, he has lectured at colleges and universities and has
written several books and numerous articles. He shows no signs
of slowing down in his musical efforts.

B708. _____. "Aaron Copland: Interpreting His Own Works." Washington
Post, July 28, 1975, B, p.9:2.
Copland led the National Symphony Orchestra July 26 in a program of his works at Wolf Trap. "Copland's conducting had many
of the same virtues as his music—briskly differentiated sonorities, rhythmic acuity, sharply articulated lines of ortanization."

B709. _____. "Copland: Perennial Renewal." Washington Post, February
8, 1974, B, p.6:1.
On February 5 Copland conducted the National Symphony Orchestra
at the Kennedy Center. His Clarinet Concerto and First Symphony
were on the program. Although he is seventy-three years old,
he continues to conduct when invitations are issued. His conducting "is clear and forthright, without any marked tendency
toward histrionics."

B710. _____. "Finding Music in Books." Washington Post, January 28,
1973, L, p.9:2.
Copland's What to Listen For in Music is an introductory work
which "stands out as a model equalled by very few of its suc-
cessors." The layman can understand the concepts which are
described because of the clear way Copland conveys the information. See also: B108

B711. _____. "Honoring Koussevitzky at Tanglewood." Washington Post,
July 29, 1974, B, p.1:2.
Copland was one of the conductors in the nine-hour orchestral
tribute to Serge Koussevitzky recently. Koussevitzky, who died

in 1951, did much to assist in the growth and development of the
Berkshire Music Festival at Tanglewood.

B712. _____. "If America Ever Had a Composer Laureate..." Washington
Post, April 8, 1973, L, p.1:3.
This interview with Copland at his home in New York stressed
his contributions to American music over the past fifty years.
Kriegsman feels that Copland would probably be the composer
laureate if the United States had one. This extensive article
traces his musical career. His works have been considered
American in nature and he broke the ties with European influence.

B713. Kroeger, Karl. "Piano Music." Music Library Association Notes
26, no.2 (December 1969): 363.
Kroeger reviews Copland's arrangement of Danza de Jalisco for
two pianos. Originally written for chamber orchestra in 1959 as
one of Two Mexican Pieces, it was commissioned for Spoleto,
Italy's Festival of Two Worlds. The work has frequent rhythmic
changes and is somewhat dissonant.

B714. Kuppenheim, Hans F. "Louisville." Musical Courier 157 (April
1958): 37.
The Louisville Orchestra commissioned a work by Copland and
it received its premiere on March 5. The audience's reception
of the Orchestral Variations was divided. See also: W92

B715. Kyle, Marguerite Kelly. "AmerAllegro." Pan Pipes of Sigma Alpha
Iota 43 (December 1950): 111-113.
Performances in honor of Copland's fiftieth birthday included
one sponsored by the Coolidge Foundation in Washington, D.C. on
October 29. The group had commissioned the Piano Quartet and
observed the premiere performance on this day. Other premieres
during the year included Copland's Four Piano Blues performed by
Leo Smit in New York March 13 and the Twelve Poems of Emily
Dickinson May 18 in New York by Alice Howland with piano ac-
companiment by the composer. See also: W80, W86, W89

B716. _____. "AmerAllegro." Pan Pipes of Sigma Alpha Iota 52, no.2
(1960): 43.
Recent publications of scores and recordings are listed. Among
numerous awards Copland received were two honorary Doctor of
Music degrees from the University of Hartford and Temple University.

B717. _____. "AmerAllegro." Pan Pipes of Sigma Alpha Iota 53, no.2
(1961): 47.
During the past year Copland traveled to the Philippines,
Japan, England, and the Soviet Union where he conducted orchestras which performed his works. Copland on Music was published
and he was awarded the Brandeis University Creative Arts Medal
in Music. See also: B24

B718. _____. "AmerAllegro." Pan Pipes of Sigma Alpha Iota 54, no.2
(1962): 42.
Premieres of recent Copland works included the movie Something
Wild December 1961 for which Copland composed the music. His

Clarinet Concerto and Third Symphony were performed on a United
States State Department tour of Europe. In addition, Harvard
University granted him an honorary Doctor of Music degree. See
also: W96, W97

B719.   _____. "AmerAllegro." Pan Pipes of Sigma Alpha Iota 55, no.2
         (1963): 43.
         Connotations for Orchestra was commissioned for the opening of
         Philharmonic Hall, Lincoln Center, September 23, 1962. Leonard
         Bernstein conducted the New York Philharmonic in the premiere
         performance. Numerous new scores and recordings are noted.
         See also: W98

B720.   _____. "AmerAllegro." Pan Pipes of Sigma Alpha Iota 56, no.2
         (1964): 49.
         Copland's Ballet in Seven Movements had its premiere per-
         formance December 3 when he conducted the Bavarian State Opera
         in it. Also during 1963 the University of Chile, Santiago,
         elected him to a position of honorary professor. See also: W96

B721.   _____. "AmerAllegro." Pan Pipes of Sigma Alpha Iota 57, no.2
         (1965): 51.
         Music for a Great City was presented for the first time by the
         London Symphony Orchestra with the composer conducting on May
         26, 1964. It was presented in the United States on October 13
         at Constitution Hall, Washington, D.C. Copland also received
         three honorary doctorates in 1964 from the University of Michi-
         gan, the University of Rhode Island, and Syracuse University.
         He was the recipient of the Presidential Medal of Freedom
         September 14 from President Lyndon B. Johnson. See also: W101

B722.   _____. "AmerAllegro." Pan Pipes of Sigma Alpha Iota 58, no.2
         (1966): 57.
         Among Copland's concert activities in 1965 was a program of his
         works at the Hollywood Bowl which he conducted. He performed as
         soloist with his Piano Concerto which was presented by the New
         York Philharmonic in its free park concerts. In the fall of 1965
         he toured Europe conducting at various concerts.

B723.   _____. "AmerAllegro." Pan Pipes of Sigma Alpha Iota 59, no.2
         (1967): 68.
         Scores and recent recordings of Copland are listed.

B724.   _____. "AmerAllegro." Pan Pipes of Sigma Alpha Iota 60, no.2
         (1968): 66.
         Inscape had its premiere August 13, 1967 at Ann Arbor, Michigan.
         The work was commissioned by the New York Philharmonic for its
         125th anniversary. The composer was awarded honorary doctorates
         from Rutgers University and Jacksonville University. See also:
         W103

B725.   _____. "AmerAllegro." Pan Pipes of Sigma Alpha Iota 61, no.2
         (1969): 48.
         Copland's recent activities center on his frequent appearances
         as guest conductor with the Buffalo Philharmonic, New York Phil-
         harmonic, Cleveland Orchestra, and the Boston Symphony.

B726. _____. "AmerAllegro." Pan Pipes of Sigma Alpha Iota 64, no.2
       (1972): 49.
       The Duo for Flute and Piano received its premiere performance
       by Elaine Shaffer and Hephzibah Menuhin in Philadelphia in
       October 1971. Honorary degrees were given to Copland by York
       University in England and Columbia University. See also: W107

B727. _____. "AmerAllegro." Pan Pipes of Sigma Alpha Iota 65, no.2
       (1973): 37.
       Scores and recent recordings of Copland are listed.

B728. _____. "AmerAllegro." Pan Pipes of Sigma Alpha Iota 66, no.2
       (1974): 46.
       The Van Cliburn Piano Competition commissioned Night Thoughts
       and the contestants performed it beginning September 17, 1973
       in Fort Worth, Texas. Threnody II had its premiere at the Ojai,
       California Festival in June 1973. See also: W111-W112

B729. _____. "AmerAllegro." Pan Pipes of Sigma Alpha Iota 67, no.2
       (1975): 60.
       Leo Smit performed the Piano Sonata, Four Piano Blues, as well
       as Danzón Cubano with Michael Root at the Cleveland Institute of
       Music November 8, 1974.

B730. _____. "AmerAllegro." Pan Pipes of Sigma Alpha Iota 70, no.2
       (1978): 36.
       Copland has been active conducting programs of his music in
       California, Oklahoma, Colorado, Mexico, and Pennsylvania.

B731. _____. "AmerAllegro." Pan Pipes of Sigma Alpha Iota 71, no.2
       (1979): 29.
       During 1978 ballets using the music from El Salón México and
       Danzón Cubano were presented and choreographed by Eliot Feld.

B732. Lade, John. "Aaron Copland Concert." Musical Times 101 (June
       1960): 372.
       The London Symphony Orchestra presented a program of Copland's
       works on April 19 at Festival Hall. El Salón México was the most
       popular work performed since the others such as the Piano Con-
       certo, First Symphony, and Statements have been performed less.

B733. Lampert, Vera. "Koncert Kronika." Muzsika 16 (December 1973):
       24-28.
       This is a brief review of a concert in which Copland was the
       guest conductor.

B734. "Language and Function in American Music." Scrutiny 10 (1942):
       346-357.
       An examination of the elements that separate European and
       American music points toward rhythms and harmonies. Copland's
       change of style from complexity to simplicity is seen as a major
       element in the nationalization of his music. An analysis of
       several of his most important compositions is included.

B735. Lardner, James. "On State for the Stars." Washington Post, De-
       cember 3, B, p.1:3.

Five prominent Americans in the performing arts were honored
for their achievements at the Kennedy Center December 2. Leonard
Bernstein gave the tribute to his long-time friend, Copland, and
conducted some of Copland's music.

B736. "Lead Roles Filled in Juvenile Opera." New York Times, April 8,
1937, p.20:4.
The Second Hurricane will have its world premiere under the
auspices of the Henry Street Settlement Music School on April
21 at The Playhouse. Lehman Engel will conduct and Orson Wells
will be the stage director. The librettist is Edwin Denby.
See also: W51

B737. "A Leading Composer Looks at American Music Today." U.S. News and
World Report 81 (October 4, 1976): 68.
This interview with Copland examines some of the changes in
music which have occurred during his extensive career as a composer. He feels that Americans have established their own
style of music and no longer have the inferiority feelings that
were evident in regard to European music during the first part
of this century. Cultural exchanges between the United States
and Communist countries are helping to promote peace in some ways,
because musicians have much in common.

B738. "Letter from Composer." New York Times, October 10, 1954, II, p.
9:1.
Copland comments on an article October 3 entitled "Premiere in
News." Copland asserts that conductors need to include works on
their programs written by young contemporary composers. Without this support, new talent will not flourish.

B739. "Letters." New York Times, March 27, 1955, VI, p.4:4.
These letters to the editor address the Henry Pleasants-
Copland debate on the issue of serious music which Pleasants
feels is dead. Copland asserts that there have been changes in
the manner of expressing oneself through music, but that serious
music is very much alive. See also: B60

B740. Levant, Oscar. "Boys Are Marching." In A Smattering of Ignorance,
213-248. Garden City, New York: Garden City Publishing Co., 1942.
Copland was one of the earliest composers to develop an American sound in his compositions. Previously, music and musicians
were from Europe. Copland worked to change this European tradition through the League of Composers. Copland realized that
audiences were not interested in his early music because of its
complexity and difficulty. Levant reminisces about a composers'
conference at Yaddo where his music and the works of other contemporary American composers was heard. Copland was the chairman of the meetings.

B741. Levine, Joseph. "Appraisal of the Ballet Conductor's Art." Musical America 75 (April 1955): 8.
Levine discusses the Agnes de Mille ballet, Rodeo, which uses
Copland's music. The ballet was presented on television one
time, and the problems associated with using such a medium were
tremendous. In this case there was no room for the orchestra

in the room for the dancers, so the orchestra performed in a
separate room. Consequently, the essential eye contact between
the conductor and dancers was not possible.

B742. Levinger, Henry W. "World Premiere." Musical Courier 149 (April
15, 1954): 21.
    The premiere performance of The Tender Land is reviewed. The
New York City Opera Company performed it April 1. "It is a
thoroughly American opera." Horace Everett's libretto tells the
story of a farming family whose daughter is about to graduate
from high school. See also: W90

B743. Levy, Alan Howard. "A Nice Jewish Boy from Brooklyn." In Musical
Nationalism: American Composers' Search for Identity, 105-127.
Westport, Connecticut: Greenwood Press, 1983.
    Levy examines Copland's stylistic development and his break
from European traditional characteristics in establishing an
American school of music. In addition, the influence of his
Jewish heritage on his writing is discussed in relation to early
twentieth-century New York life. The impact of his studies in
France and his stylistic changes between simple and complex is
related.

B744. "Lincoln Center Festival 68 Opens." New York Times, June 22,
1968, p.24:2.
    Among the speakers at the opening of Lincoln Center on June
21 was Copland. He encouraged attendance at upcoming concerts
honoring his long-time friend and supporter Serge Koussevitzky.

B745. "A Lincoln Portrait." Boston Symphony Orchestra Concert Bulletin
12 (January 7, 1949): 623-624; Cincinnati Symphony Orchestra
Program Notes (February 20, 1953): 472-477.

B746. "A Lincoln Portrait." Southwestern Musician 18 (July 1952): 3-4.
    Boosey & Hawkes Publishing Company's Score of the Month Club
has chosen Copland's A Lincoln Portrait to honor on the work's
tenth anniversary. Andre Kostelanetz and the Cincinnati Symphony
Orchestra first performed it in 1942. It has become a staple in
symphonic literature since that time. The composition consists
of excerpts from Abraham Lincoln's writings and speeches. The
orchestra accompanies Lincoln's words.

B747. Lipman, Samuel. "Copland as American Composer." Commentary 61
(April 1976): 70-74.
    Copland's career is recounted and the styles of music which he
favored during different periods of his life are examined. He is
seventy-five years old now and is recognized as one of America's
foremost composers.

B748. "Listening." Christian Science Monitor, November 18, 1980, p.24.
    This editorial tribute to Copland as he reaches his eightieth
birthday examines a quote about how important the role of the
listener is in music.

B749. Livingston, Herbert. "Piano Music: Aaron Copland: Four Piano
Blues." Music Library Association Notes 6 (June 1949): 492.

This is a review of Copland's short piano pieces which incorporate jazz elements. "The scoring is precise and economical, the rhythms subtle and complex, the melodic material simple, the harmony sometimes static but always transparent."

B750. Lockett, David. "From the Mail Pouch." New York Times, October 26, 1941, IX, p.8:5.
   This is a letter to the editor commenting on Olin Downes' recent article, "A Composer States His Position" which reviewed Copland's book Our New Music. Downes disagrees with Copland's premise that Mahler is a better composer than Richard Strauss and Sibelius. Lockett writes in support of Mahler. See also: B84, B438

B751. Lockspeiser, Edward. "The Musician's Bookshelf." Musical Times 97 (March 1956): 135-136.
   Julia Smith's Aaron Copland: His Work and Contribution to American Music is a condensation of her dissertation. Lockspeiser disagrees with Smith's assessment "that the versatile and gifted musician is 'America's first great composer.'" Copland's music and writings are analyzed in this book. See also: B1042

B752. "The London Concert Scene." Musical Opinion 84 (September 1961): 729.
   Copland's Statements for Orchestra is reviewed.

B753. Luten, C. J. "The Competition Is Obliterated: Bernstein's Copland's Third." American Record Guide 33 (June 1967): 933.
   Luten finds the latest recording of Copland's Third Symphony on Columbia ML 6354 and MS 6954 to be exceptionally well done. Leonard Bernstein conducts the New York Philharmonic. Also reviewed is Music for a Great City and Statements on CBS 32 11 0001 and 32 11 0002. The composer conducts the London Symphony Orchestra in these two works. "Copland's conducting is good, but it could do with a little more dash." See also: D169, D334, D347

B754. _____. "A Revelation from Everest: Copland's Third by Copland." American Record Guide 26 (October 1959): 98.
   A new recording of the Third Symphony has been released on Everest SDBR-3018. Copland conducts the London Symphony. This disc is "a revelation of an important composition, and it is therefore one of the most outstanding events of the year." See also: D348

B755. Mabry, Sharon Cody. "Twelve Poems of Emily Dickinson by Aaron Copland: a Stylistic Analysis." Ph.D. diss., George Peabody College for Teachers, 1977.
   All aspects of the song cycle are analyzed. The melodic and harmonic aspects as well as the musical setting of the text are studied along with specific performance problems.

B756. Macauley, Ian T. "Copland, at 80, Looks to the Future." New York Times, November 9, 1980, XXII, p.1:1.
   In this interview he says, "'I consider myself very lucky to have reached this far.'" Celebrations in honor of his eightieth birthday are noted. Copland admits that he is not doing much

composing recently, but he is spending his time conducting. He
mentions that the piano is his favorite instrument, and that
his favorite composition is probably the Piano Fantasy.

B757. McCandless, William Edgar. "Cantus Firmus Techniques in Selected
    Instrumental Compositions, 1910-1960." Ph.D. diss., Indiana
    University, 1974.
        Copland's Appalachian Spring is one of ten works analyzed for
    its cantus firmus techniques.

B758. McCarty, Clifford. "Book on Copland Misses Target on His Filmusic."
    Down Beat 21 (June 16, 1954): 15.
        Arthur Berger's biography of Copland devoted five pages to the
    composer's music for films. McCarty criticizes Berger's asser-
    tion that movies generally have very large orchestras because
    the average number of orchestral players is around forty. Copland
    has written the music for five films and his efforts have received
    much acclaim because of its excellent quality. In general, scores
    are quickly written and added to the film after all the action
    is completed and little time is allowed. See also: B200

B759. Macdonald, Calum. "Recordings." Tempo 101 (July 1972): 54-56.
        An excellent recording of Copland's In the Beginning by the
    Gregg Smith Singers is available on Everest SDBR 3129. "It is
    absolutely personal in its harmonic simplicity, the light and
    space of its textures, and the sublimated jazz inflexions of
    such passages as 'Let there be lights in the firmament of the
    heaven.'" See also: D146

B760. "MacDowell Colony Names President." New York Times, February 12,
    1975, p.50:4.
        It has been announced that a new fellowship fund will be
    established in Copland's name at the MacDowell Colony. Details
    of it will be given when the Colony celebrates his seventy-fifth
    birthday in November.

B761. Machlis, Joseph. "Aaron Copland." In American Composers of Our
    Time, 114-125. New York: Crowell, 1963.
        This biography concentrates on Copland's early musical train-
    ing and experiences. Details about the writing and performance
    of later compositions the noted as well as his efforts to assist
    other American composers. Suggestions are made to assist the
    reader in the selection of appropriate compositions to become
    acquainted with Copland's most popular works. "In the eyes of
    the world he is the foremost American composer of our time."

B762. "McLane Is Soloist in Copland Concerto." Musical America 70
    (December 15, 1950): 27.
        Copland's Concerto for Clarinet and String Orchestra was per-
    formed by Eugene Ormandy conducting the Philadelphia Orchestra
    November 28. Ralph McLane was the soloist. The reviewer felt
    that because of the work's lack of rhythmic interest and manu-
    factured sound "it is second-rate Copland." Copland's other
    works show more inspiration in the opinion of the reviewer. The
    orchestra and soloist received a good review for their performance.

B763. McLellan, Joseph. "Aaron Copland." _Washington Post_, July 26, 1976, B, p.5:5.
　　　Copland conducted the National Symphony Orchestra in six of his works at Wolf Trap on July 25. Included on the program were _Billy the Kid_ and the Clarinet Concerto. "All of the music was performed well . . . and the composer's presence on the podium naturally gave the interpretation special authority."

B764. _____. "Celebrating Copland." _Washington Post_, November 9, 1975, E, p.1:1.
　　　This article honors Copland for his upcoming seventy-fifth birthday on November 14. His musical style is contrasted with that of Charles Ives. Major works are listed as well as recent recordings of his works.

B765. _____. "Copland: Both Sides Now." _Washington Post_, October 25, 1975, A, p.17:6.
　　　This review of a concert at the Library of Congress mentions the two styles of Copland's music which were performed. Most audiences are familiar with the works incorporating folk tunes, as in _Appalachian Spring_. However, the more austere Quartet for Piano and Strings provided contrast.

B766. Maconie, Robin. "Recordings." _Tempo_ 103 (December 1972): 54-55.
　　　The Buffalo Philharmonic conducted by Lukas Foss recorded Copland's _Quiet City_ on Turnabout TV 34398. "Copland's self-possession . . . seems to owe less to confidence of outlook than to the intervention of a benign nocturnal spirit." _See also_: D262

B767. Mann, William S. "Reviews of Music." _Music Review_ 14 (August 1953): 249-250.
　　　Mann reviews the _Twelve Poems of Emily Dickinson_ and finds that "a lot of the piano writing is in the treble register and nearly all of it [is] contrapuntal." The songs are difficult and require an experienced vocalist. Mann observes that the songs are of very high quality.

B768. "Many Happy Returns for Barber, Copland et al." _Symphony Magazine_ 31, no.6 (1980): 45-46.
　　　Copland, who celebrated his eightieth birthday on November 14, had over one hundred concerts given in his honor during October through December 1980 all over the world. Copland was guest conductor of the National Symphony in a concert of his works on his birthday. In addition, a National Press Club Symposium on November 12 featured Copland along with a discussion of his recordings.

B769. Marcus, Leonard. "Some Copland Incidentals." _High Fidelity/ Musical America_ 20 (November 1970): 4.
　　　This short article explains Copland's significance as an American composer. In discussing the American sound in his works such as _Billy the Kid_, it was theorized that any child growing up in the United States absorbs this national culture, even if he was reared in the city.

B770. Marcus, Omar. "Old Music." New York Times, October 5, 1952, VI,
p.4:5.
     In this letter to the editor Marcus responds to the recent
Copland article, "An Indictment of the Fourth B." He disagrees
with Copland's suggestion that concert repertoires are repetitious and that contemporary music should be offered to provide
variety. See also: B42

B771. Marsh, Robert C. "As High Fidelity Sees It; a Note from Timbuktu."
High Fidelity 11 (May 1961): 29.
     Copland, interviewed on his sixtieth birthday, was distressed
about the overdependence of the public on discs and tapes.
These recorded materials never vary in contrast to live performances which never sound exactly the same. He feels that
recordings are best suited for people living in Timbuktu without
access to live performances. Marsh defends the recording industry
because no city could present the variety and amount of musical
material which listeners would want.

B772. _____. "The First Recordings from Philharmonic Hall." High
Fidelity 13 (February 1963): 73.
     Among the first recordings made in Philharmonic Hall in New
York's Lincoln Center is Copland's Connotations for Orchestra.
Its premiere was at the September 23, 1962 opening of Philharmonic Hall and is recorded on Columbia L2S 1008. Marsh finds
this twelve-tone technique "to be yet another of his contrived
pieces . . . too uneven for the length of the work." The orchestra conducted by Leonard Bernstein received a good review
for its performance. See also: D90, W98

B773. Maskey, Jacqueline. "The Dance." High Fidelity/Musical America
22 (April 1972): 10-11.
     The ballet Rodeo has recently been revived, but it appears to
be dated now. It was commissioned by the Ballet Russe de Monte
Carlo in 1942. The story centers around a cowgirl who finally
gets her man. One of the most important parts about the music
"is its feel for the American Southwest and how successfully it
communicates that landscape."

B774. Mason, E. "The Composer Speaks." Music and Musicians 14 (January 1966): 36.

B775. Matthews, David. "Copland and Stravinsky." Tempo 95 (Winter 1970-
1971): 10-14.
     Igor Stravinsky's influence on Copland is examined. Examples
of music from Copland's Dance Symphony show definite similarities
to Stravinsky's The Rite of Spring. Musical examples from the
Short Symphony appear to be close to the style of Stravinsky,
but they are simpler in design. Important events in the lives
of both men are noted and the parallels are examined. Some of
differences are noted as well, for they composed in two quite
different societies.

B776. Mayer, William. "The Composer in the U.S. and Russia: a Frank Talk
Between Copland and Khachaturian." ASCAP Today 3, no.1 (1969):
22-25.

Aram Khachaturian and Copland attended a question and answer session moderated by Mayer, a former Guggenheim fellow. The men discussed nationalism in music which both composers agreed was an element in their respective compositions. The financial aspect of the composers' lives in the two countries illustrated one of the biggest differences between them. Khachaturian noted that most Russian composers do not have to teach because they are subsidized. Their Union of Composers provides room and board for some composers as they do their work. Copland cited the advantage of U.S. composers who have "a very permissive atmosphere in so far as style is concerned in the United States."

B777. _____. "Copland & Khachaturian--Historic Meeting." Music Journal 27 (March 1969): 25-27.
       Khachaturian and Copland had an informal discussion about the status of contemporary music in their respective countries. Both men have been composers as well as conductors. Khachaturian described the Russian manner of state support for artists. The two men discussed common problems they have confronted in their similar careers.

B778. _____. "Interview with Aaron Copland and Aram Khachaturian." Composer (US) 2, no.2 (1970): 44-47.
       This is an extract from Mayer's article "The Composer in the U.S. and Russia," published in ASCAP Today in 1969. Mayer conducted a question and answer session between Khachaturian and Copland. Both spoke of the respective freedoms each has in his country. Nationalism is one element each felt was present in his compositions. See also: B776

B779. Mellers, Wilfrid. "Cambridge: The Tender Land." Musical Times 103 (April 1962): 245-246.
       Copland's opera is compared to his ballets Appalachian Spring and Billy the Kid. The first performance of The Tender Land in Europe was not successful because the production was not professionally done. Mellers finds the simpleness of the work makes it "a more important work in his career and in modern music than its unpretentious nature superficially suggests."

B780. _____. "Homage to Aaron Copland." Tempo 95 (Winter 1970-1971): 2-4.
       Copland celebrated his seventieth birthday November 14, 1970 and continues to conduct orchestras when invited. Out of his beginnings in Brooklyn he has combined the sounds and influence of the city with the openness of the prairie. A comparison with Charles Ives shows that they both have written music that the public did not accept. However, Copland concentrated on writing simpler music that would receive public approval at certain times in his career. "Copland's music still irradiates not only a steely courage but also an agelessly boyish charm."

B781. _____. "Music for 20th-Century Children." Musical Times 105 (July 1964): 502.
       Copland's opera for children, The Second Hurricane, "is in character inseparable from his grown-up music, different only in degree, not kind." This work is analyzed and includes musical examples.

B782. Mitchell, Donald. "London Music: Some First Performances." Musi-
       cal Times 97 (September 1956): 483.
           The London Symphony recently performed a number of works by
       Americans including Copland's Third Symphony heard for the first
       time in Great Britain. The work "possesses certain homespun
       (homestead?) qualities, expressed as rough-hewn counterpoint or
       a quasi-folk idiom."

B783. "Modern Music." International Music News 1 (November 1952): 5.
           This article is in response to Copland's assertion that per-
       formances of contemporary music are too rare.

B784. "Modern Music Given." New York Times, March 17, 1930, p.20:4.
           The Copland-Sessions concerts have had their second presenta-
       tion at Steinway Hall on March 16. Among the contemporary works
       presented was Copland's Vitebsk. Copland "has something to say
       and knows how to say it musically."

B785. "Modern Piano Music: Compromise and Charm." Times (London), Febru-
       ary 11, 1944, p.6d.
           Copland's Piano Sonata is cited as being impossible to play.
       Written "in five flats but no easily definable key," the work
       has bunched dissonances.

B786. Monaco, Richard A. "Orchestral Music." Music Library Association
       Notes 23, no.4 (June 1967): 833.
       The new score Music for a Great City is reviewed. The four-
       movement work has sharply contrasting sections. Monaco hopes
       "that it is programmed with the frequency that it deserves."

B787. Monson, Karen. "Ojai: a Profusion of Premieres." High Fidelity/
       Musical America 23 (September 1973): MA21.
           The twenty-seventh annual Ojai, California Festival was held
       June 1-3. Michael Tilson Thomas conducted the premiere of
       Copland's Threnody I and II. The works were "short, amiable,
       simply constructed elegies for flute, violin, viola, and cello."
       Threnody I was written in memoriam to Igor Stravinsky and Threnody
       II to Beatrice Cunningham.

B788. Montgomery, Paul L. "Dinner Salutes Pulitzer Prizes." New York
       Times, May 11, 1966, p.33:2.
           Copland was one of five former award winners to speak at this
       fiftieth anniversary celebration at the Plaza Hotel May 10.
       Copland commented on modern music including electronic composi-
       tions.

B789. Moor, Paul. "Aaron Copland: Dean of American Composers." Theatre
       Arts 35 (January 1951): 40-45.
           An examination of Copland's extensive background in music shows
       that he has been quite active composing and conducting. He has
       done much through his association with the League of Composers
       to assist other composers in having their works performed. Most
       of his recent compositions have been commissioned and he is con-
       cerned that composers be properly compensated for their work.
       He has been doing more conducting than composing recently.

B790. _____. "Festival de Berlin 1970." Buenos Aires Musical 25,
no.422 (1970): 5.

B791. Morgan, Robert P. "Towards a More Inclusive Musical Literacy,
Notes on Easy Twentieth Century Piano Music, Part II." Musical
Newsletter 2 (April 1971): 13.
In this survey of contemporary piano music, Morgan finds the
first and third pieces of Copland's Four Piano Blues suitable
for piano students who are not too advanced. Those with small
hands may have difficulties in reaching some of the chords, but
the pieces are simple technically.

B792. Morris, Bernadine. "Fashions That Pass the Test of Time." New
York Times, November 19, 1965, p.45:2.
Women's fashions are featured in this report on the two-piano
benefit concert performed by Leonard Bernstein and Copland. The
program at the Plaza Hotel on November 17 was given to raise
money for the MacDowell Colony.

B793. Morton, David. "Program Note for Appalachian Spring." Etude 69
(May 1951): 57.
This is a poem which Morton wrote expressing his feelings about
Appalachian Spring.

B794. Morton, Lawrence. "Aaron Copland, by Arthur Berger." Musical
Quarterly 40 (January 1954): 93-98.
This is a review of Berger's biography on one of America's
foremost composers. Berger's "own career has been a part of the
general movement resulting from Copland's diversified activities."
Morton observes that the work should have been longer and more
detailed. See also: B200

B795. _____. "Copland." Musical Quarterly 40 (April 1954): 294-296.
Two recordings of Copland's works are reviewed. The first
is the Piano Sonata, Piano Variations, and Passacaglia performed
by Webster Aitken on Walden Records 101. Morton feels the rhythm
should have been observed more strictly by Aitken than it was.
The second recording is the Third Symphony performed by the
Minneapolis Symphony Orchestra with Antal Dorati conducting on
Mercury Classics MG 50018. Morton thinks that the Minneapolis
Symphony is a good orchestra but has "room for general improve-
ment, for refinement and polish." See also: D216, D233, D248,
D349

B796. _____. "Copland on Music, by Aaron Copland." Music Library
Association Notes 18, no.3 (1961): 412-413.
Morton notes that this book contains thirty of Copland's
collected writings from the past thirty or more years taken from
journals and newspapers. Copland has directed his efforts
toward the education of the public in accepting contemporary
music. See also: B24

B797. _____. "Music and Imagination, by Aaron Copland." Music Library
Association Notes 20 (December 1952): 95.
Copland's six lectures at Harvard University 1951-1952 became
the six chapters in this book. Copland analyzes the stylistic

trends in twentieth century music as he urges listeners to give
all new music a chance to be heard and understood. See also:
B65

B798. _____. "The Red Pony: a Review of Aaron Copland's Score." Film
Music Notes Special issue (February 1949): 2-8.
Morton's extensive review of this film adapted from John
Steinbeck's story includes excerpts from the music score to
illustrate his points. The dissonances become evident during
the stormy periods in the movie. Morton's analysis results in
much praise for the quality of the score. He feels that the
music is well suited to the movie medium "without any sacrifice
of artistic integrity."

B799. _____. "Southern California Activities." Symphony 5 (July-
August 1951): 4.
This is a review of the Quartet for Piano and Strings.

B800. "Mrs. Carter Narrates the Lincoln Portrait." New York Times,
October 9, 1976, p.8:3.
Rosalynn Carter will be the narrator for Copland's composition
this evening at a Democratic fund-raising concert at Constitution
Hall in Washington, D.C.

B801. "Munch Conducts Copland Ode." Musical America 76 (February 15,
1956): 225.
On February 8 at New York's Carnegie Hall Charles Munch conducted the Boston Symphony in Copland's revised Symphonic Ode.
Originally commissioned for the Boston Symphony's fiftieth anniversary, it has now been revised for the group's seventy-
fifth anniversary. It "remains a curiously uneven work." See
also: W38

B802. "Music and Imagination." Crescendo 3 (January-March 1953): 16.
A review of Copland's book. See also: B65

B803. "Music and Imagination." High Fidelity 2 (November-December 1952):
23.
This is a review of Copland's monography in which he encourages
contemporary composers to write more and he attempts to educate
the public to be more adventurous in their listening habits. In
this book he shows amateurs how they can sharpen their listening
skills. See also: B65

B804. "Music and Imagination." Monthly Musical Record 83 (December 1953):
253-255.
A review of Copland's book. See also: B65

B805. "Music and Imagination." Music and Letters 35 (January 1954): 50-
52.
Copland's six lectures given while he was the Charles Eliot
Norton Lecturer at Harvard University 1951-1952 comprise this
book. In the first part of the book Copland emphasizes the
necessity of listening to music other than that which has been
identified as masterpieces. He also examines the contemporary
music scene and the influences upon it. See also: B65

B806. "Music and Imagination." Musical Opinion 77 (January 1954): 221;
        Southwestern Musician 20 (November 1953): 4.
        A review of Copland's book. See also: B65

B807. "Music: Composers Get a Chance to Exhibit in One-Man Shows."
        Newsweek 6 (November 2, 1935): 41.
        Copland, with anonymous philanthropic aid, planned five con-
        certs, each to feature the works of one American. Copland's
        goal is to provide more visibility for American composers as well
        as to educate concert audiences. The five composers selected
        were Roy Harris, Virgil Thomson, Roger Sessions, Walter Piston,
        and Copland.

B808. "Music: Copland's Dirge in Woods." New York Times, March 29, 1955,
        p.34:2.
        The premiere in the United States of Copland's song took place
        March 28 at Carnegie Hall by Adele Addison. It was first heard
        in Paris and was composed in honor of Nadia Boulanger's fiftieth
        anniversary of teaching. "The vocal line is long and floating
        and the piano accompaniment ripples gently under it." See also:
        W89

B809. "Music for a Great City." Philadelphia Orchestra Program Notes
        (April 22, 1965): 15; Pittsburgh Symphony Orchestra Notes (May
        10, 1968): 853-857.

B810. "Music from Manhattan." Time 83 (June 5, 1964): 60.
        Music for a Great City, commissioned by the London Symphony
        Orchestra, had its premiere in London last week. It seemed
        obvious to the audience that the city in the music was New York.
        See also: W101

B811. "Music Group Seeks Copyright Treaty." New York Times, February
        17, 1946, p.36:6.
        Among the speakers at the first American-Soviet Music Society
        meeting February 16 was Copland. The Society hopes to reach
        agreement on a copyright treaty in the future. Copland stressed
        the organization's commitment to better relations and increasing
        cultural exchanges.

B812. "Music in London." Musical Times 103 (April 1962): 242.
        The London Symphony Orchestra, conducted by Copland, pre-
        sented a concert of American music on February 13. Included on
        the program were his Billy the Kid Suite and Orchestral Vari-
        ations. The reviewer admires the latter work because "the
        scoring is masterly."

B813. "Musical Voice of America." Times (London), November 12, 1965,
        p.15e.
        London has been the scene for many concerts featuring the works
        of Copland. He has also visited there many times. His different
        styles are discussed, from the serious tone-row idioms to the
        light-hearted choruses in The Tender Land.

B814. "Muzyka: Voobrazhenie." Sovetskaya Muzyka 32 (February 1968): 108-
        113; (March 1968): 108-113; (April 1968): 117-122.

These are excerpts from Copland's book <u>Music and Imagination</u>. See also: B65

B815. "Names, Dates and Places." <u>Opera News</u> 42 (June 1978): 7.
The Michigan Opera Theatre will open its Matrix: Midland Arts Festival with <u>The Tender Land</u> on June 3. On June 16 Copland will conduct a concert of his works at Wolf Trap Farm Park.

B816. National Federation of Music Clubs. <u>Study Outline for Use with Aaron Copland's What to Listen For in Music</u>. New York: McGaw-Hill, 1939.

B817. Naylor, P. "Aaron Copland at College." <u>RCM Magazine</u> 57, no.3 (1961): 72.
This is a discussion of Copland's visit to the Royal College of Music in Great Britain.

B818. "Neglected U.S. Composer." <u>Times</u> (London), November 2, 1965, p. 13b.
Copland was the guest conductor for the BBC Symphony Orchestra concert November 1. He included a work by Carl Ruggles on the program. He feels that Ruggles is a neglected American composer. Copland included his <u>Music for the Theatre</u> which is "a brilliant, vivacious essay in the jazz idiom."

B819. "New Books." <u>Monthly Musical Record</u> 84 (November 1954): 243-244.
This is a review of Arthur Berger's biography <u>Aaron Copland</u>. The reviewer feels that the subject is covered very thoroughly. However, he believes that the book would have been better if someone had "pruned away both the pretentiousness and the naïveté." <u>See also</u>: B200

B820. "New Books on Music Include Biographies: Copland Seen by Arthur Berger." <u>Musical Courier</u> 148 (December 15, 1953): 10.
Berger's <u>Aaron Copland</u> is reviewed. This biography contains detailed information about his works and premiere performances. <u>See also</u>: B200

B821. "New Books Reviewed." <u>Music Teacher and Piano Student</u> 41 (January 1962): 39.
<u>Copland on Music</u> is a compilation of Copland's views especially on other contemporary composers. Many of these commentaries were written some time ago and he has attempted to bring them up to date by adding footnotes. He discusses the problem faced by contemporary composers in having their works performed. Copland states that he does not have the answer as to why audiences do not want to hear contemporary music. <u>See also</u>: B24

B822. "'New Kid' Christopher Cross Dominates Grammy Awards." <u>Chicago Tribune</u>, February 26, 1981, 2, p.4:1P.
Copland and Count Basie received a special Trustees Award given by the National Academy of Recording Artists at the twenty-third annual Grammy Awards on February 25 in New York.

B823. "<u>The New Music</u>." <u>Piano Quarterly</u> 18, no.70 (1969-1970): 21.

This is a brief review of the 1968 revised and enlarged edition
of Copland's book. In this monograph Copland examines contemporary composers and music in Europe and America. See also: B76

B824. "The New Music, 1900-1960." American Music Teacher 20, no.3 (1971):
33.
Originally published as Our New Music in 1941, this revision
updates the current trends in contemporary music. See also.
B76, B84

B825. "The New Music, 1900-1960." American Record Guide 36 (June 1970):
846.
This is a review of the 1968 edition of Copland's Our New Music.
Sections on contemporary music are updated because there have
been dramatic changes during the past few decades. See also:
B76, B84

B826. "New York Concerts." Musical Courier 142 (December 15, 1950): 12.
Copland's Concerto for Clarinet and String Orchestra was
recently performed for the first time in New York by Ralph
McLane who was the soloist. "The two-movement composition makes
for pleasant listening."

B827. "New York Philharmonic." Musical Courier 157 (March 1958): 15.
Copland was guest conductor January 30 for two of his works:
Outdoor Overture and Third Symphony. The second composition does
not draw upon any familiar material but it has Copland's distinct
characteristics which are associated with an American sound.

B828. "New York Philharmonic Young People's Concert." Musical Courier
161 (May 1960): 19.
The final Young People's Concert April 23 featured Copland's
play-opera designed for high school students, The Second Hurricane. "The work is simple and melodious." Leonard Bernstein
narrated and conducted.

B829. "Newcomer's Grammy Awards Sweep." San Francisco Chronicle, Febru-
ary 26, 1981, p.57:1.
The twenty-third annual Grammy Awards on February 25 in New
York honored Copland with a special Trustees Award given by the
National Academy of Recording Artists.

B830. Newlin, Dika. "The Piano Music of Aaron Copland." Piano Quarterly
28, no.111 (1980): 6-8.
Newlin provides an overview of Copland's piano works beginning
with his first published composition, The Cat and the Mouse. A
brief analysis of Copland's works, including the Piano Concerto,
Four Piano Blues, Piano Sonata, and Piano Fantasy, illustrates
some of the harmonies employed by Copland. A short bibliography
of major works citing Copland is included.

B831. Newman, Bill. "Aaron Copland." Gramophone 36 (February 1959):
396.
Newman interviewed Copland in England and found that "he has
much praise for the British professional musician. When asked
about his success in composing, he indicated that concentration
of ideas is quite important.

B832. Newman, William S. "What to Listen For in Music." Music Library
Association Notes 15 (December 1957): 116.
      This is a review of Copland's revised edition of his book.
      Although the first edition was quite successful, Newman feels
      that some of its original shortcomings were not remedied. Among
      these are Copland's "failure to pinpoint most definitions" and
      the book's "lack of planned comprehensiveness." See also: B108

B833. "News: America." Opera (London) 5 (August 1954): 495-499.
      The world premiere of The Tender Land was given by the New
      York City Opera Company. The performance was not well received
      by the audience or the press. The libretto by Horace Everett
      received the most criticism. "The text is pervasively immature."
      The reviewer feels that the words and music do not combine to
      to make an interesting and dramatic opera. See also: W90

B834. Nichols, Lewis. "Talk with Aaron Copland." New York Times, October 19, 1952, p.47.
      In this interview, Copland speaks of his latest book, Music
      and Imagination, which is a compilation of his six lectures as
      the Charles Eliot Norton Professor of Poetry at Harvard Univer-
      sity. He supports contemporary composers and regrets that there
      are too few opportunities available for them to have their works
      performed. See also: B65

B835. Noble, J. "Musical Survey." Musical Events 15 (June 1960): 14.

B836. "Nonet for Strings." Music and Letters 43, no.4 (1962): 378.
      The Nonet is based on serial techniques and "has reaffirmed
      his old faith in added-note diatonicism." There is a serious-
      sounding opening which is followed by lighter ideas as well as
      a complexity of harmonies.

B837. "Nonet for Strings." Music and Letters 11 (November 1962): 65.

B838. Northcott, Bayan. "Composers of the Sixties." Music and Musicians
18 (January 1970): 36.
      Copland's music is almost always based "upon simple, often
      slowly-moving variation techniques." However, serialism is
      evident in his Dance Panels and Connotations composed in the
      early sixties. Further experiments in this area are evident in
      Music for a Great City and Inscape.

B839. _____. "Copland in England." Music and Musicians 18 (November
1969): 34-36.
      An analysis of the various styles of Copland is given along
      with specific qualities of selected compositions. Northcott
      concludes that English audiences should hear more of Copland's
      lesser-known works and he suggests combinations of music and
      performers which he would like to hear recorded. Sleep Is Sup-
      posed to Be, no. 1 from Twelve Poems of Emily Dickinson, for
      voice and piano is reproduced here.

B840. _____. "Notes on Copland." Musical Times 122 (November 1980):
686-687.
      Northcott attempts to assess Copland's significance in the

development of American music as the composer reaches eighty years
of age. Examinations of his varying styles of composition are
noted and some of his techniques are mentioned. Copland is no
longer composing but is compiling his memoirs.

B841. Norwood, Ann Bussert. "Letters: New and Old." New York Times,
January 15, VI, p.4:3.
  Norwood is responding to Copland's recent article, "A Modernist Defends Modern Music," which has created some controversy.
She suggests offering more contemporary music on concert programs. However, she thinks that romantic, less controversial
music should be programmed also. See also: B63

B842. "Notes Here and Afield: Town Hall Schedules Forum Series to be De-
voted to Modern Composers." New York Times, December 20, 1942,
VIII, p.6:3.
  On February 17 Copland will perform his Piano Sonata in its
U.S. premiere at Town Hall. In addition, his Music for Movies
and Music for the Theatre are scheduled on this program.

B843. "Notes of the Day." Monthly Musical Record 83 (December 1953):
252-255; 84 (January 1954): 1-3.
  Copland's Music and Imagination is reviewed. The first reviewer
is unsure about Copland's nineteenth-century view about inspiration occurring spontaneously. The second reviewer challenges the
validity of Copland's view that a score should be open to various
interpretations by performers and that it can still be stylisti-
cally correct. See also: B65

B844. "Notes on People: an Ode to Aging." New York Times May 17, 1980,
p.26:5.
  Copland, E. Y. (Yip) Harburg, lyricist, and Chaim Gross, artist,
will tell the American Jewish Committee about "the role Judaism
has played in their lives." They have taped their thoughts for
the William E. Weiner Oral History Library and will speak to the
group at a Waldorf-Astoria luncheon on May 17.

B845. "Notes on People: Copland 79, Going on 90." New York Times, August
27, 1980, p.21:1.
  At a sixty-second birthday celebration for Leonard Bernstein,
Copland related his feelings about writing his autobiography. He
stated that he remembered events far in the past very easily, but
he says he has difficulty remembering recent ones. A slip of the
tongue was responsible for his statement that he would be ninety
instead of eighty on his next birthday.

B846. Novik, Ylda. "The New Music, 1900-1960." American Music Teacher
18, no.3 (1969): 44.
  Novik's favorable review of Copland's book indicates that the
revision is beneficial to the reader. The original material is
supplemented. See also: B76

B847. Oakes, James Alfred. "An Analysis of Aaron Copland's Piano Fantasy."
Ph.D. diss., Catholic University of America, 1976.

B848. O'Connor, John J. "Copland in Limelight on Two PBS Programs."
      New York Times, March 17, 1976, p.83:1.
         The program "Copland Conducts Copland" will be presented on
      the Public Broadcasting System this evening. The hour-long con-
      cert was taped this past November at the Los Angeles County Music
      Center. Benny Goodman is soloist in the Concerto for Clarinet
      and Orchestra which he commissioned in 1948. Bill Moyers will
      interview Copland in a program to be aired March 20.

B849. _____. "Strike Up the Band (and the Chamber Group)." New York
      Times, April 25, 1971, II, p.15:1.
         Copland will be the guest conductor with the Empire Sinfonietta
      on television soon. It is hoped that this concert will help
      pave the way for more concerts to be presented on television.
      Copland's Quiet City is one of the works to be performed.

B850. _____. "TV: 'Copland Celebration' and Winter Olympics." New
      York Times, April 1, 1981, III, p.31:1.
         The ninety-minute "Kennedy Center Tonight" program featuring
      Copland and his music was taped last November 14 on Copland's
      eightieth birthday. This tribute "is more of a television essay,
      complete with interviews, rehearsal footage and extensive nar-
      ration."

B851. Oja, Carol J. "The Copland-Sessions Concerts and Their Reception
      in the Contemporary Press." Musical Quarterly 65 (April 1979):
      212-229.
         These concerts were organized by Roger Sessions and Copland in
      1928 to bring the music of contemporary composers to the public.
      The programs emphasized the music of Americans because European
      composers were gaining exposure through the League of Composers'
      concerts. Although both Copland and Sessions were young, they
      had already established themselves as important composers at
      that time. An appendix lists the programs presented at these
      concerts.

B852. "Old American Songs." Music and Letters 33 (January 1952): 94.
         These five songs represent different rural areas of the United
      States. The last song relates "entirely to animals and their
      respective noises." The reviewer considers these works very
      effective.

B853. "Old American Songs." Repertoire 1 (October 1951): 37.

B854. "Old American Songs, Second Set." London Musical Events 9 (Novem-
      ber 1954): 42.

B855. "Old American Songs Set by Aaron Copland." Musical America 75
      (November 15, 1955): 20.
         The second set of Old American Songs was finished in 1952, two
      years after the first set. The reviewer felt that Copland has
      kept the original flavor and emotions of the folk music in his
      adaptations and he does "not hesitate to enhance the tunes with
      sophisticated rhythmic and harmonic touches in the accompaniments."
      The second set consists of five songs as does the first set.

B856. "Opera by Children to be Sung April 21." New York Times, April 1, 1937, p.19:5.
    Copland's Second Hurricane will have its world premiere at the Playhouse on April 21. The Henry Street Settlement Music School is sponsoring the event. The work is designed for young people from age eight to eighteen. Edwin Denby is librettist, Orson Wells is stage director, and Lehman Engel will conduct. See also: W51

B857. "Opera That Gets to the Heart of the Matter." Times (London), February 27, 1962, p.13a.
    The Cambridge University Opera Group gave the continent's first performance of The Tender Land. "Tonight's production, for all its stiff cardboard actors and musical imperfections . . . still conveyed something of this moving power."

B858. Oppens, Kurt. "Opernabende in New York." Opernwelt 3 (March 1976): 37-39.
    This is a review of The Tender Land which was performed by the Bronx Opera Company January 17 in New York.

B859. "Orchestral Variations." Cleveland Orchestra Program Notes (April 9, 1970): 974-977; Harrisburg Symphony Orchestra Program Notes (November 18, 1975): 19.

B860. "Orchestral Work as a Challenge: Copland's Variations." Times (London), August 21, 1958, p.12c.
    On August 20 Copland was guest conductor for a performance of his Orchestral Variations at the Promenade Concert at Albert Hall. This work was recently adapted from his Piano Variations (1930). The Louisville Orchestra granted Copland a commission to transcribe this work for orchestra.

B861. Orga, Ates. "American in London." Music and Musicians 17 (December 1968): 49-50.
    Copland conducted his Inscape in its British premiere on October 24 with the London Symphony Orchestra. It was commissioned by the New York Philharmonic Orchestra for its 125th anniversary season. "It is a remarkably fresh work, with all the hallmarks of Copland's maturity." Copland also conducted Rodeo as well as works by other contemporary composers on the program.

B862. _____. "Anglo-American." Music and Musicians 16 (December 1967): 46.
    Copland recently conducted the London Symphony Orchestra on September 29 in works of his own as well as others. Among his works performed was the Symphonic Ode which involves complex orchestration. In the Dance Symphony "the rhythmic confusion and bad brass work in the closing pages was avoided in the more expansive preceding two movements."

B863. _____. "Copland." Music and Musicians 19 (February 1971): 68-69.
    Copland, celebrating his seventieth birthday this past November, has slowed his compositional efforts. He has not produced a major new composition since 1967 with Inscape. However, he

"is currently working on a Duo for flute and piano, and contem-
plating a String Quartet." A pre-birthday concert was given for
him November 11 by the Royal Philharmonic Society. He participated as composer, conductor, and pianist.

B864. Orrego Salas, Juan. Aarón Copland, un Músico de Nueva York."
Revista Musical Chilena (Julio-Agosto 1947): 6-14.

B865. _____. "Aaron Copland's Vision of America." Américas 7 (June
9155): 17-21.
Orrego Salas, a Chilean composer, feels that "Aaron Copland's
music is genuinely and unmistakably an expression of the United
States." Various works by Copland are examined for their national
as well as other important elements.

B866. Osborne, Charles. "Copland, Aaron." In The Dictionary of Composers, 92-93. London: The Bodley Head, 1977.
Biographical information is brief regarding Copland's early
music studies, but expands as major compositions are discussed
chronologically. Although he has not always written simple
music designed for public acceptance, he has become well-known
because of works such as Billy the Kid and Appalachian Spring.
"What emerges basically from his music is a gentle and lovable
personality, unashamed of his romanticism."

B867. _____. "A Copland Work Hailed in London." New York Times, May
27, 1964, p.47:1.
The world premiere of the commissioned Music for a Great City
occurred May 26 at London's Festival Hall. Copland was guest
conductor of the London Symphony Orchestra for this event. The
audience perceived New York to be the city Copland expressed in
his music. "Mr. Copland's attitude to New York is revealed as
one of ironic and exasperated affection." See also: W101

B868. Ottaway, Hugh. "Aaron Copland at 75." Listener 94 (November 27,
1975): 723-724.
Copland's attributes as a person and as a composer are discussed.
Some of his more rigid serial works, as the Piano Variations, appeal to a small audience but his fame has been garnered from compositions such as Billy the Kid which appeal to a much larger
audience. Many of Copland's works have been performed recently
in England in honor of his seventy-fifth birthday.

B869. _____. "Radio Notes." Musical Opinion 82 (October 1958): 35;
84 (July 1961): 621.

B870. "Our Day with Aaron Copland." Triangle of Mu Phi Epsilon 75, no.2
(1981): 11.
Copland was guest conductor for the Indianapolis Symphony
Orchestra. The Indianapolis Arts Chorale, with Elise Marshall,
conductor, invited Copland to attend a concert in his honor to
commemorate him on his upcoming eightieth birthday. He met with
the group for brunch and spoke with them informally.

B871. "An Outdoor Overture." Music and Letters 33 (July 1952): 266-267.
This overture is an optimistic-sounding work in which the

"material is pulled together in ingenious combinations and ends
with flags flying and guns blazing."

B872. Overmyer, Grace. "Aaron Copland." In <u>Famous American Composers</u>,
192-202. New York: Thomas Y. Crowell, 1944.
This is a thorough study of Copland's early musical training.
His <u>Dance Symphony</u> was one of five winners in a contest early
in his career. He has composed music for ballets, as <u>Billy the
Kid</u>, and for films, as <u>Our Town</u>. Copland has lectured widely
and has written books to aid listeners in the enjoyment of music.

B873. Overton, H. "Copland's Jazz Roots." <u>Jazz Today</u> 1 (November
1956): 40-41.

B874. Overton, James L. "It's a Very Lively Scene . . . We're in Good
Shape." <u>San Francisco Chronicle</u>, March 12, 1978, WOR, p.49:1.
While being interviewed in Houston, Copland admitted that his
compositional efforts "'seem to have bogged down a bit.'" He
has been busy as a conductor lately. He stated that because
there are so many composers today the nation has a greater chance
of developing composers who will have a significant impact on
future music.

B875. "PBS' Capital Copland." <u>Washington Post</u>, April 1, 1981, B, p.3:4R.
The Public Broadcasting System will air "Aaron Copland: a
Celebration" in its series "Kennedy Center Tonight" on April 1.
Pictures of the Lincoln Memorial and other monuments will be
shown while Copland's music is performed by the National Symphony
Orchestra with Leonard Bernstein conducting.

B876. Palmer, C. "Aaron Copland as Film Composer." <u>Crescendo Inter-
national</u> 14 (May 1976): 24-25.

B877. Parmenter, Ross. "Music: an Anniversary." <u>New York Times</u>, May 12,
1958, p.25:1.
The thirtieth anniversary of the Copland-Sessions concerts was
celebrated at the Composers Showcase Series at the Nonagon Art
Gallery. William Masselos performed Copland's Piano Fantasy.
Both Sessions and Copland were present and reminisced about their
early concert series. Copland was asked about the financing of
those concerts and "he replied with characteristic wit: 'The
way all things are financed nowadays. Some nice lady gave us
the money.'"

B878. _____. "Music: Orchestra of America Opens 2d Season." <u>New York
Times</u>, November 17, 1960, p.45:4.
Copland's sixtieth birthday was celebrated along with the
birthdays of Wallingford Riegger and Samuel Barber on November
16 by the Orchestra of America at Carnegie Hall. Copland's
Clarinet Concerto was performed with Benny Goodman as soloist.
Copland was present for the festivities.

B879. _____. "Portrait of an American Composer." <u>New York Times</u>,
August 24, 1941, IX, p.6:6.
Biographical information about Copland's musical career is
given. Because of his prominence in American music he has been

chosen to represent the United States in a cultural tour of
Latin America soon. He will lecture and participate in concerts.

B880. _____. "The World of Music." New York Times, June 1, 1947, II,
       p.7:7.
       Copland revealed his acceptance of a commission from Benny
       Goodman to write a Clarinet Concerto.

B881. _____. "World of Music: Copland Opera." New York Times, Janu-
       ary 17, 1954, II, p.7:1.
       Copland's The Tender Land will be presented by the New York
       City Opera at City Center in the spring. Little information
       about the work has been released, but the League of Composers
       indicated that the work was commissioned by Richard Rodgers and
       Oscar Hammerstein.

B882. _____. "The World of Music: Symphony Dedicated to U. N. Sought."
       New York Times, February 16, 1947, II, p.9:2.
       Copland has been offered a commission to write a symphony in
       honor of the United Nations. Andre Kostelanetz contacted the
       composer because of the success of A Lincoln Portrait.

B883. Patterson, Frank. "Letters: Less Modern." New York Times, Janu-
       ary 8, 1950, VI, p.6:5.
       In this letter to the editor responding to Copland's article,
       "A Modernist Defends Modern Music," Patterson feels that Copland
       "'has become much less modern'" in his recent works. The public
       appreciates this change. See also: B63

B884. Pavlakis, Christopher. "Book Reviews." Music Journal 35 (April
       1977): 36-37.
       Pavlakis reviews Copland on Music which has been reprinted in
       1976 by Da Capo Press. The book consists of the composer's
       writings from over a thirty year period beginning in the late
       1920's. "The lucidity of Copland's music is reflected in his
       literary style." See also: B24

B885. Peare, Catherine Owens. Aaron Copland, His Life. New York: Holt,
       Rinehart & Winston, 1969.
       This biography is designed for children. It includes a bibli-
       ography and a list of works.

B886. Peerce, Jan. "Letters: Music Debate." New York Times, April 3,
       1955, VI, p.4:4.
       This letter to the editor expresses the reader's views on the
       Henry Pleasants-Copland debate in which Copland defends modern
       music as being a viable art while Pleasants writes that serious
       music is a dead art. See also: B60

B887. Penchansky, A. "Barber, Copland, Walton Win; Most Performed by
       Major Orchestras." Billboard 91 (October 27, 1979): 82.
       A compilation of the number of works of various living composers
       was taken during the 1979-1980 concert season. Samuel Barber,
       Aaron Copland, and Sir William Warton were the three whose works
       received the greatest number of performances.

B888. "Performing Arts: Aaron Copland." Washington Post, June 29, 1981,
C, p.7:4R.
Copland, who is eighty years old now, recently conducted the
National Symphony Orchestra in some of his works at Wolf Trap.
"Copland once wrote that composers do not necessarily make good
conductors of their own music because they lack a dispassionate
heartbeat." The reviewer felt that Copland's conducting at
this concert was excellent.

B889. Persichetti, Vincent. "Current Chronicle: Concerto for Clarinet
and String Orchestra." Musical Quarterly 37 (April 1951): 260-
262.
Benny Goodman commissioned Copland's Clarinet Concerto. It
was recently performed by Ralph McLane with Eugene Ormandy conducting the Philadelphia Orchestra. The performance received an
excellent review.

B890. Peterson, Melody. "Copland Time at Northridge." Los Angeles
Times, May 9, 1975, IV, 17, 1.
This is a review of a performance at the California State
University, Northridge given by the Chamber Singers and Wind
and Symphony Orchestras. Copland directed them in his Dance
Symphony and In the Beginning. In addition, Emblems, Lark, and
Las Agachadas were presented. "Directing in an expansive manner
with a no-nonsense clarity of beat, Copland drew both gentle
reflection and soaring vibrance from the University Singers."

B891. Peterson, Melva. "Books." Pan Pipes of Sigma Alpha Iota 61, no.
2 (1969): 31.
Peterson reviews Copland's The New Music, 1900-1960 which is
a revision of his earlier Our New Music. Sections dealing with
the dodecaphonic school and certain composers have been rewritten.
More space is devoted to electronic music and music of chance.
He "knows how to use words and he writes from a composer's experience." See also: B76, B84

B892. "Philadelphia Hears Callas and Cliburn." New York Times, January
25, 1959, p.70:7.
The Academy of Music recently had a celebration featuring
Maria Meneghini Callas, soprano, and Van Cliburn, pianist. The
announcement was made that Copland had been selected "as the
winner of the academy's international award for 'distinguished
contributions to music.'"

B893. Phillips, Harvey E. "Sarah Caldwell's New Idea: a Tale of the
Hazards and Happiness of Community Involvement." High Fidelity/
Musical America 27 (September 1977): MA17-19.
Caldwell's goal was to involve communities in presenting
Copland's The Second Hurricane. Most of the personnel were to
be provided by the community. The venture was not entirely successful partially because of the bitter New England winter.
Phillips felt that the opera was not "strong enough to command
the respect and imagination of the participants and the enthusiasm of the audience. It was noted that some of the technical
problems could have been eliminated with more planning.

B894. "Piano Quartet." Strad 63 (February 1953): 330.

B895. Picoto, J. C. "Aaron Copland e o Jazz." Arte Musicale 33, no. 25 (1967): 37-39.

B896. Pisciotta, Louis Vincent. "Texture in the Choral Works of Selected Contemporary American Composers." Ph.D. diss., Indiana University, 1967.
      Representative choral works by Copland and nine other Americans are examined in this analysis of texture as it relates to form.

B897. Plaistow, Stephen. "Some Notes on Copland's Nonet." Tempo 64 (Spring 1963): 6-11.
      The Nonet was written during a period when Copland had moved away from functional music and music which incorporated folk elements. Comparisons between the Nonet and other of his compositions are made and musical examples illustrate the text.

B898. Porter, Andrew. "Aaron Copland." London Musical Events 9 (December 1954): 33-34.
      This is a biographical sketch of Copland's career plus a discussion of some of his major works.

B899. _____. "Aaron Copland's Theatre and Film Music." London Musical Events 10 (January 1955): 31-32.
      Copland's scores for stage and film are noted and the discussion includes a discography of his ballet music.

B900. _____. "Musical Events: Java Sparrows." New Yorker 51 (February 2, 1976): 75-78.
      The Tender Land was performed recently by the Bronx Opera Company to commemorate Copland's seventy-fifth birthday. This opera "is a Midwestern idyll--not a realistic drama but a romantic, pastoral fairy tale." This performance did not receive a good review.

B901. _____. "New Music at the Proms." London Musical Events 9 (August 1954): 22.

B902. Posell, Elsa Z. "Aaron Copland." In American Composers, 16-20. Boston: Houghton Mifflin, 1963.
      This biography of Copland discusses the major events in his musical career with an emphasis on his early music. After Copland's initial studies in piano and composition in Brooklyn, he studied with Nadia Boulanger in France. After his return to the United States he managed to become an established and respected composer in a very short time. His awards are many and include a Pulitzer Prize in music.

B903. "Preamble for a Solemn Occasion." Boston Symphony Orchestra Concert Bulletin (November 2, 1962): 331-332; Musical Opinion 76 (June 1953): 543.

B904. "Premiere Performances." Musical Courier 156 (November 1, 1957): 5.
　　　The world premiere of Piano Fantasy was given by William Masselos at the Juilliard School of Music October 25. It was the only work on the program and was performed twice with an intermission in between. See also: W93

B905. "Premieres." ASCAP Today (Fall 1979): 42.
　　　Copland's Four Motets are discussed.

B906. "Premieres." Music Journal 25 (October 1967): 54.
　　　The premiere performance of Inscape was given by the New York Philharmonic Orchestra September 13 at the University of Michigan at Ann Arbor. See also: W103

B907. "Premieres." Symphony News 23, no.3 (1972): 31.
　　　The premiere performance of Three Latin American Sketches was performed by the New York Philharmonic June 7, 1972. See also: W109

B908. "Previously Unpublished Composers' Letters as Written to Claire R. Reis." Musical America 83 (January 1963): 14.
　　　Reprinted are portions of a letter written by Copland to Reis. After twenty-five years in the League of Composers, Copland stated that he no longer felt the need for a name change to keep the organization avant-garde. In earlier times he had pressed for renaming the group.

B909. "Professional Materials." Music Educators Journal 56 (January 1970): 11.
　　　Copland's The New Music, 1900-1960 is briefly reviewed. It is a revised edition which now contains additional material on electronic music and contemporary composers. See also: B76

B910. "Program." Juilliard Review 8, no.1 (1960-1961): 8-13.
　　　The programs from the November 14-15, 1960 performances are printed. Among the works presented was Copland's The City. Included also are copies of newspaper articles and photographs of the events which marked Copland's sixtieth birthday.

B911. "Programs of the Week." New York Times, March 5, 1933, IX, p.6:4.
　　　Copland was recently elected to the executive board of the League of Composers. He has been active in the organization for many years.

B912. "Queens to Dedicate Copland Music School." New York Times, November 1, 1981, p.80:6.
　　　On November 5 Queens College will honor Copland by renaming its music department the Aaron Copland School of Music. A dedication concert will include works by Copland.

B913. "Quiet City." Boston Symphony Orchestra Concert Bulletin 21 (April 6, 1951): 1049-1050; Philadelphia Orchestra Program Notes (April 10, 1953): 674-675.

B914. "Rachmaninoff Concert." New York Times, January 16, 1946, p.18:7.
Melvyn Douglas will narrate during the performance of A
Lincoln Portrait at Carnegie Hall on February 12. The actor is
contributing his services in the fundraiser for the Rachmaninoff
Fund, Inc.

B915. Ramey, Phillip. "Copland and the Dance." Ballet News 2 (November
1980): 8-12.
Ramey's interview reveals Copland's surprise when Martha
Graham expressed interest in dancing to his most complex,
dissonant compositions. The Piano Variations and Appalachian
Spring were both used by her with her company. Copland felt
that the first ballet he wrote, Grohg, was never staged because
its style became unfashionable too soon.

B916. "Record Reviews: Appalachian Spring, Three Places in New England."
Down Beat 46 (May 3, 1979): 31.
This is a review of Sound 80 Digital Records DLR-101 with the
St. Paul Chamber Orchestra conducted by Dennis Russell Davies.
It includes Charles Ives' work on one side. See also: D32

B917. "Record Reviews: Blues, Ballads & Rags." Down Beat 49 (January
1982): 42-43.
This is a review of Copland's Four Piano Blues on Nonesuch
Records D-79006 played by Paul Jacobs. Jacobs' performance is
critiqued rather than the composition. See also: D137

B918. "Record Throngs at Fete in Lenox." New York Times, August 9,
1957, p.11:2.
The Berkshire Music Center celebrated its fifteenth anniversary
August 8 with an all-day Tanglewood on Parade Series. Copland
conducted the Boston Symphony in his Our Town suite and portions
from The Tender Land.

B919. "The Red Pony." Musical Opinion 74 (September 1951): 651.

B920. "Red Scare Easing, Truman Observes." New York Times, June 10,
1957, p.18:5.
Former President Harry S. Truman was commencement speaker
June 9 at Brandeis University. Copland received an honorary
Doctor of Letters degree at the ceremony.

B921. Redlich, Hans F. "Music from the American Continent." Music
Review 19 (August 1958): 247-248.
The Short Symphony is analyzed and musical examples are included. Redlich's belief that Copland's works reached an early
maturity is noted in his observations. This and other scores
"prove that Copland's unmistakable fingerprint of style . . .
was firmly established by 1933."

B922. _____. "New Music: a Critical Interim Report." Music Review 16
(August 1955): 264.
In the Beginning is designed for mixed chorus, a capella, with
a mezzo-soprano solo. It has a motet-like nature and uses
Genesis as its text. "It is a glorious piece of word-inspired
madrigalian music."

B923. _____. "New Music: a Critical Interim Report." Music Review 16 (August 1955): 268.
    The second set of Old American Songs illustrates Copland's "life-long attachment to his native folk music." Redlich cites the quality of the piano accompaniment and the beauty of the choral harmonies.

B924. _____. "New Music: a Critical Interim Report." Music Review 16 (August 1955): 161.
    Preamble for a Solemn Occasion and John Henry are analyzed. The introduction of the first work reminds Redlich of the Piano Variations. The second work is based on the folk tune of the same name.

B925. "Reference Articles on American Composers; an Index." Juilliard Review 1 (Fall 1954): 24-25.
    Six annotated references to articles about Copland from the journals Modern Music and Musical Quarterly are listed.

B926. Reif, Rita. "MacDowell Gala Adds to Birthday Tributes for Copland." New York Times, November 26, 1970, p.60:2.
    The MacDowell annual Artists' Gala honored Copland's seventieth birthday at the St. Regis-Sheraton on November 24. A mini-fugue entitled Aaron's Canon by Leonard Bernstein was performed. The event is a traditional fund-raiser for the artists' residence at Peterborough, New Hampshire.

B927. Reinthaler, Joan. "A Concert for Nadia Boulanger." Washington Post, September 30, 1977, C, p.10:1.
    Boulanger, who recently celebrated her ninetieth birthday, was honored at a concert September 29 at the Library of Congress. Copland was one of her former students. He was present for this occasion and conducted his Nonet for Strings.

B928. Reis, Claire Raphael. "Aaron Copland." In Composers in America; Biographical Sketches of Contemporary Composers with a Record of Their Works, 77-80. Revised. New York: Macmillan Company, 1947.
    This is a short biography which gives the highlights of Copland's development as a composer. A classified list of compositions through the 1940's is included.

B929. RePass, R. "American Composers of Today." London Musical Events 8 (December 1953): 25.

B930. "Reviews." Musical Courier 153 (January 15, 1956): 30.
    Julia Smith's biography is reviewed. Aaron Copland: His Work and Contribution to American Music is taken from her doctoral dissertation and is very thorough. "It is painstaking, accurate-- and dull." See also: B1042

B931. Reyer, C. and R. Fullerton. "Copland Conducts in Appalachia." Music Journal 30 (Annual 1972): 4.

B932. Rich, Alan. "Composer's Showcase." Musical America 81 (March 1961): 47.
    A program of Copland's vocal works was presented at New York's

Museum of Modern Art on January 26. Among those presented were
As It Fell upon a Day and Vocalise. Copland narrated in The
Second Hurricane as he conducted. Rich found the first two
songs to be "angular, chromatic and rather tricky pieces."

B933. _____. "Most Valuable Composer." New York 14 (February 16, 1981):
51.

B934. "Richard Wilbur Will Head Arts and Letters Academy." New York
Times, December 7, 1974, p.21:1.
Wilbur, a poet, will succeed Copland who served his three
year term as president of the American Academy of Arts and Letters.

B935. Rickman, Michael Lee. "Aaron Copland's Piano Fantasy, a Lecture
Recital, Together with Three Recitals of Selected Works." Ph.D.
diss., North Texas State University, 1977.
Rickman performed and discussed the Piano Fantasy at a recital
June 20, 1977. This recital, plus three earlier recitals, are
recorded and are available with the written part of the dissertation.

B936. Riley, Robert. "Copland Conducts Copland at the Bowl." Los Angeles
Times, August 26, 1976, II, p.18:1.
The Hollywood Bowl performance August 26 consisted of Copland
conducting the Los Angeles Philharmonic in a concert of his works.
The Third Symphony and the Concerto for Clarinet and Strings
were among the works on the program. Copland's "angular and
essentially clear-cut guidance" resulted in a satisfying program.

B937. Roca, Octavio. "Aaron Copland." Washington Post, June 30, 1980,
C, p.9:2R.
On June 28 Copland conducted the National Symphony Orchestra
in a concert of his works at Wolf Trap. "While Copland's view
of the American West is that of a native New Yorker, it has
proved hardy, fashionable, and at times very moving." Roca
feels that Copland's Latin American themes are not as successful.

B938. Rockwell, John. "Concert: Sessions and Copland Works." New York
Times, August 14, 1980, III, p.17:3.
The first half of this Copland-Sessions Concert was devoted to
Copland's works presented at Tanglewood's Festival of Contemporary Music August 11. Rockwell reviews the compositions
presented, and asserts that "the Piano Variations are Copland
at his best: intent, concise, yet still enlivened by the personality that infuses all his work."

B939. _____. "Copland, at 75, Is Still Copland the Kid." New York
Times, November 12, 1975, p.48:1.
Copland is to be honored by a concert of his works on November
12 by the MacDowell Colony and on November 14 by the Juilliard
School of Music, both at Alice Tully Hall.

B940. _____. "5 Brooklyn Composers Grace Philharmonia Concert." New
York Times, February 16, 1976, p.28:1.
The Brooklyn Philharmonia presented a concert entitled "A
Gathering of Brooklyn Composers" on February 14 at the Brooklyn

Academy of Music. The five composers honored who were born or
grew up in the area were Elliott Schwartz, Talib Rasul Hakim,
Elie Siegmeister, Roger Sessions, and Copland.

B941.   _____. "Free 13-Hour Marathon Celebrates American Music." New
York Times, November 21, 1980, III, p.1:1.
Symphony Space will present its "Wall-to-Wall" concert featuring
eighteen compositions by Copland. He will conduct Appalachian
Spring. Although other Americans are to be featured on the
program, Copland is being emphasized because he has done so much
to bring contemporary music to the attention of the public.

B942.   _____. "Music: Copland Conducts Copland." New York Times, July
7, 1980, III, p.11:1.
The Boston Symphony, under the baton of Copland, presented an
all-Copland concert July 6 at the 1980 Tanglewood Festival in
Lenox, Massachusetts. The Berkshire Music Center celebrated its
fortieth anniversary this summer as well as Copland's long
association with it as music director and chairman of the faculty.

B943.   _____. "Philharmonic: Copland." New York Times, November 21,
1980, III, p.25:1.
Copland's Third Symphony was performed November 20 at Avery
Fisher Hall with Zubin Mehta conducting the New York Philharmonic.
This orchestral piece is "a busy web of contrapuntal academicism."

B944. "Rodeo." Harrisburg Symphony Orchestra Program Notes (November 18,
1975): 20.

B945. "Rodeo: Saturday Night Waltz and Hoe Down." Repertoire 1 (January
1952): 141-142.
This is a review of the two-piano arrangement of these excerpts
from Rodeo which have been arranged by Arthur Gold and Robert
Fizdale.

B946. "Rodeo: Three Dance Episodes." San Francisco Symphony Program
Notes (March 31, 1955): 647-648.
Quotations from Agnes de Mille's Dance to the Piper are recorded. Her thoughts as she prepared her ballet for the performance of Rodeo are noted.

B947. Rogers, Harold. "Copland's Touch." Christian Science Monitor,
April 20, 1965, p.14:2.
The performance of Music for a Great City in Boston last week
"galvanized most of the listeners out of their indifference."
Copland conducted the Boston Symphony on this occasion.

B948.   _____. "Two New Works in a New Hall." Christian Science Monitor,
September 26, 1962, p.4:1.
The New York Philharmonic commissioned Connotations for Orchestra for the opening of Philharmonic Hall in Lincoln Center.
Leonard Bernstein conducted the work which was not enthusiastically
received by the audience. Copland uses "the twelve-tone technique
as his idiom." Rogers feels that "the quality of inspiration is
inferior." See also: W98

B949. _____. "Varied Program Includes His Own First Symphony." Christian Science Monitor, January 2, 1960, p.7:6.
    Copland has been conducting the Boston Symphony and he will be
    touring with them in the Far East in May. He included his First
    Symphony on a recent program and "the middle scherzo is a delight
    of syncopated rhythms."

B950. "The Role of the Composer." Canadian Composer 63 (October 1971):
24-35.
    Copland discussed the pecularities of being a composer in
    this extensive article. In earlier times, a composer was often
    the servant of a wealthy patron. He states that composers do a
    lot more than put dots on pieces of lined paper. Composing is
    a type of language in which he attempts to communicate to others.

B951. Romero, Hector Manuel. "Aaron Copland, el Compositor a Quien le
Vaticinaron ser Criminal." Orientacion Musical (July 1941): 6-7.

B952. Rorem, Ned. "Copland's Birthday." In Pure Contraption: a Composer's Essays, 88-93. New York: Holt, Rinehart and Winston,
1974.
    This article was written November 1970 to commemorate Copland's
    seventieth birthday. It relates the association Rorem and Copland
    had for the past twenty-seven years. Rorem is a music critic.
    In discussing Copland's five film scores he notes the high
    quality of the music in a field where speed is of the essence.

B953. _____. "Where Is Our Music Going?" In Music and People, 211-213.
New York: G. Braziller, 1968.
    Rorem records some of Copland's observations on the direction
    in which he feels music is going. As always, Copland would like
    to see more contemporary music performed, but major symphonies
    do not present many new works partially because of the lack of
    enough rehearsal time. The universities are more likely to
    present works such as Connotations or Inscape and they are less
    likely to perform his more popular works such as Billy the Kid.

B954. Rosenberg, Deena and Bernard Rosenh ʒ. "Aaron Copland." In The
Musicmakers, 31-38. New York: C ibia University Press, 1979.
    These interviews with Copland t place in 1975 and 1977. He
    notes that critics have commented on his diversity of styles,
    but it was a normal progression for him. Many of his works were
    commissioned for specific events and groups so often the medium
    for which he composed was previously determined. In recent
    years he has spent most of his time conducting.

B955. Rosenfeld, Paul. "Aaron Copland." In Musical Impressions: Selections from Paul Rosenfeld's Criticism, 248-256. New York:
Hill and Wang, 1969.
    Rosenfeld expresses his reactions to Copland's earliest musi-
    cal styles such as that found in the First Symphony and in Music
    for the Theatre. Rosenfeld notes that "his gift is decidedly
    proficient but small." Some comparisons are made to George
    Gershwin and William Grant Still.

B956. _____. "Aaron Copland's Growth." New Republic 67 (May 27, 1931): 46-47.
Rosenfeld examines Copland's music. The composer is thirty-one years old and is becoming more important as a serious musician.

B957. _____. "American Premieres: Symphonic Ode." New Republic 70 (April 20, 1932): 274.
Koussevitzky conducted the Boston Symphony in the first performance of Copland's Symphonic Ode recently. The composition has five sections which remind Rosenfeld of New York without resolution until the end. Copland's music "is the work of a maturing, solid force." See also: W38

B958. _____. "Copland." In Discoveries of a Music Critic, 332-337. New York: Harcourt, Brace and Company, 1936.
As a music critic for Disques, Modern Music, Musical Review, and New Republic, Rosenfeld has a broad acquaintance with contemporary music. After hearing Copland's early works, he notes that he found them "excessively austere, in places very bare and bleak."

B959. _____. "Copland Without the Jazz." In By Way of Art; Criticisms of Music Literature, Painting, Sculpture, and the Dance, 266-272. 1928] Reprint. New York: Books for Libraries Press, 1967.
This article, written when Copland was twenty-eight years old, examines his music. Rosenfeld was impressed with the composer's "brilliance and burlesquerie, the tastefulness of the material and method." However, Rosenfeld felt that the use of jazz elements in works such as Music for the Theatre lessened the worth of the composition.

B960. _____. "Current Chronicle: Copland--Harris--Schuman." Musical Quarterly 25 (July 1939): 372-376.
Rosenfeld comments on works by Roy Harris, William Schuman, and Copland. Three of Copland's recent compositions are An Outdoor Overture, Billy the Kid, and The City. Rosenfeld feels that "Copland probably is the most generously gifted composer among living Americans."

B961. _____. "In the Adolescent's World." New Republic 91 (May 19, 1937): 48.
Copland's The Second Hurricane is an opera for young people to perform. Edwin Denby wrote the libretto. This score is "clean-cut, refreshingly unhackneyed" and is very effective for adolescent performances.

B962. _____. "Musical Chronicle." In The Dial, edited by William Wasserstrom, 310-312. Syracuse: Syracuse University Press, 1963.
Rosenfeld finds Copland's Concerto for Piano and Orchestra to be a major American work. Performed by Copland with the Boston Symphony February 3, 1927 in New York, the work "has daringly utilized jazz polyrhythms and colourations in an interest entirely transcending that of the commercial jazz composers." The strength of this work places Copland among the important American composers of this time even though he is only twenty-seven years old.

B963. _____. "New American Music." Scribner's Magazine 89 (June 1931):
          624-632.
          Among the composers discussed is Copland whose music Rosenfeld
          describes as "slender, wiry, full of stony and metallic effects."
          Copland overdoes the use of a theme occasionally, but in general
          the scores are clear and carefully constructed.

B964. Rosenteil, L. "Remembrances of Nadia Boulanger (1887-1979)."
          Virtuoso 1, no.3 (1980): 34.
          Copland studied with Boulanger in France during the early
          1920's. Her insight and enthusiasm for new music was an im-
          portant factor in Copland's training.

B965. Rosenwald, H. "Contemporary Music." Music News 43 (January 1951):
          7.

B966. Rosenwald, Peter J. "Aaron Copland Talks about a Life in Music."
          Wall Street Journal, November 14, 1980, p.31:1.
          Copland celebrated his eightieth birthday and spoke about his
          desire to create a new sound in his compositions. He wanted to
          "give serious music a truly national character." As a successful
          composer and conductor, his work has had great influence on
          American music. His compositions are performed all over the
          world.

B967. _____. "The Loneliness of a Great Artist." Wall Street Journal,
          November 28, 1975, p.4:4.
          Copland is among a number of artists discussed. He is cele-
          brating his seventy-fifth birthday soon. When he was just
          beginning his career as a composer, he received much encouragement
          from Serge Koussevitzky who was conductor of the Boston Symphony
          Orchestra. Koussevitzky performed Copland's orchestral works
          and encouraged him to write more compositions.

B968. Rothstein, Edward. "Copland at 80: Still THE American Composer."
          San Francisco Chronicle, November 23, 1980, Review, p.19:1.
          Copland's eightieth birthday is being commemorated in this
          article detailing his achievements and honors. In this inter-
          view Copland describes his desire to create a sound that could
          be identified as American. Although his early compositions
          earned him the reputation as a modernist, he later consciously
          wrote works for the public to enjoy. The desire to write serious
          and appealing music has presented some conflict, so his styles
          have vascilated between simple and complex.

B969. _____. "Fanfare for Aaron Copland at 80." New York
          Times, November 9, 1980, II, p.21:1; New York Times Biographical
          Service 11 (November 1980): 1526-1528.
          This interview took place just before Copland's eightieth
          birthday on November 14. The composer reminisces about his
          musical development and some of the events relating to his com-
          positions. Biographical information about his extensive career
          is provided. Copland is being honored with numerous celebrations
          as he reaches his eightieth year.

B970. Russell, Margaret. "The Journal Reviews: Books." Music Journal
21 (October 1963): 76.
This review of Copland on Music notes that the book is a compilation of personal viewpoints about music first published in
1944. "It is an interesting, if brief, glimpse into the world
of a composer." See also: B24

B971. "S Pozitsii Obyvatelya--Ili?" Sovetskaya Muzyka 36 (October 1972):
129-130.

B972. Sabin, Robert. "Copland Fantasy." Musical America 77 (November 15,
1957): 24.
The premiere performance of Copland's Piano Fantasy by William
Masselos at the Juilliard Concert Hall on October 25 was a sell-
out. Sabin feels that the Fantasy is "by far the freshest and
most powerful thing that he has composed in recent years."
Copland's piece was enthusiastically received by the audience.
The work was commissioned for the fiftieth anniversary of the
Juilliard School of Music and was dedicated to the late William
Kapell. Copland was present for the performance. See also: W93

B973. _____. "New Biography of a Contemporary Composer." Musical
America 74 (January 1, 1954): 28.
Arthur Berger's book Aaron Copland received a favorable
review. The first part of the book is devoted to Copland's life
and the second to his music. A bibliography and discography are
included. Although Sabin feels that Berger's own convictions
cause him to sometimes unjustly criticize Copland's works,
Berger is felt to have done a thorough analysis of some of
Copland's music. See also: B200

B974. _____. "Philharmonic Marks Copland's Birthday." Musical America
80 (December 1960): 37.
The Young People's Concert given by Leonard Bernstein conducting the New York Philharmonic on November 12 was in honor
of Copland's sixtieth birthday. The composer conducted some of
his works himself. This all-Copland program included selections
from Our Town, Rodeo, and Old American Songs.

B975. Sadie, Stanley. "Music in London." Musical Times 109 (December
1968): 1131.
Sadie comments on Copland's October visit to London. Copland's
Inscape was performed and it begins very well, but near the end
the one-movement work "loses its sense of direction, its integrity." Other works on the program included his Rodeo and Orchestal
Variations.

B976. _____. "Strong Contrasts in New Copland Work." Times (London),
October 25, 1968, p.8f.
A recent concert at Festival Hall conducted by Copland was
the occasion for his performance of three of his own works:
Inscape, Rodeo, and Orchestral Variations.

B977. Safford, Laura Tappen. "Tanglewood Crosses the Centuries." Opera
News 19 (November 1, 1954): 16-17.
The revised version of The Tender Land was first performed

August 2 and 3 at Tanglewood. It had its premiere earlier in
the year. This work is "essentially simple and in the spirit of
folk music." Richard Rodgers and Oscar Hammerstein II provided
a grant which permitted the League of Composers to commission
Copland to compose this opera. <u>See also</u>: W90

B978. Sahr, Hadassah Gallup. "Performance and Analytic Study of Selected
Piano Music by American Composers." Ph.D. diss., Columbia
University, 1969.
    Copland's Piano Sonata is one of five works analyzed particu-
larly in regard to interpretative aspects of performance. The
American sound present in Copland's piece is examined.

B979. Saleski, Gdal. "Aaron Copland." In <u>Famous Musicians of Jewish
Origin</u>, 36-41. New York: Bloch Publishing Company, 1949.
    This biographical study of Copland emphasizes his early
development as a composer. His switch from using jazz idioms
to employing folk elements is examined. Achievements and
awards are chronicled along with a partial list of his works.

B980. "El Salón México." <u>New York Philharmonic Program Notes</u> (February
22, 1951): 3.
    The New York Philharmonic with Leonard Bernstein conducting
performed Copland's <u>El Salón México</u> at Carnegie Hall February
22. After a visit to Mexico in 1932 Copland decided to translate
his memories into music.

B981. Salzman, Eric. "Aaron Copland: the American Composer is Eighty."
<u>Stereo Review</u> 46 (February 1981): 66-69.
    An interview with Copland as he approaches his eightieth
birthday reveals his optomistic approach to his career as a
composer. He is not currently writing any new works but he says
that one must always live in hope for tomorrow, and he may have
ideas then. Copland discusses the "Americanism" in his works
and the music of others by indicating that it was a conscious
desire to have a national style in addition to the jazz and
popular style at that time. Copland is in demand as a conductor,
especially of his own works, and he especially enjoys presenting
some of his less popular favorites such as <u>Inscape</u> and <u>Statements</u>.

B982. _____. "Aaron Copland's Solo Piano Works in Illuminating Performances by Leo Smit." <u>Stereo Review</u> 44 (April 1980): 87.
    Smit performs these solo piano works on a two-disc release
on Columbia M2 35901. Salzman groups the three larger works
into Copland's more serious style. These are the Piano Variations, the Piano Sonata, and the Piano Fantasy. The other
shorter works which Salzman considers to be a more popular style
include <u>The Cat and the Mouse</u>, Passacaglia, Four Piano Blues,
<u>The Young Pioneers</u>, <u>Sunday Afternoon Music</u>, <u>Midsummer Nocturne</u>,
<u>Down a Country Lane</u>, <u>In Evening Air</u>, and <u>Night Thoughts</u>. <u>See
also</u>: D73, D110, D131, D141, D168, D182, D210, D217, D223, D234,
D354

B983. _____. "Copland's <u>Appalachian Spring</u>--Columbia Records the Whole
Thing." <u>Stereo Review</u> 32 (April 1974): 108.

Thirty years after this ballet was written Columbia Records has released the original version for small orchestra under the direction of the composer himself on Columbia M 32736. Soon after he wrote this, Copland transcribed the work into a shorter version for large orchestra. The Columbia Chamber Orchestra performs the work. Also offered on disc are three less popular works on Columbia M 32737: Sonata for Violin and Piano, Duo for Flute and Piano, and Nonet for Strings. See also: D9, D112, D186, D325

B984. _____. "Dean of Our Composers at 60." New York Times, November 13, 1960, VI, p.51.
An examination of Copland's influence on American music is undertaken. In addition to his own compositions, books, articles, lectures, and conducting, he has actively worked to assist other young composers in having their works performed. Details of his career are noted.

B985. _____. "A Few Notes on the Score." New York Times, November 13, 1960, VII, p.7.
This is a review of Copland's book Copland on Music. In it are essays from his long career as an important American composer. He will be sixty years old on November 14. Copland notes that after the second world war, American composers in general reverted to European styles. See also: B24

B986. _____. "Records: Copland." New York Times, March 29, 1959, II, p.15.
Salzman feels that the public views Copland's music as one-sided because they only hear his popular works and not the serious ones. Recent recordings by Everest and Mercury include some of his less familiar works.

B987. _____ and Paul Des Marias. "Aaron Copland's Nonet; Two Views." Perspectives of New Music 1, no.1 (1962): 172-179.
Salzman and Des Marias separately examine the serial techniques in the Nonet for Solo Strings for three violins, three violas, and three cellos. Salzman finds the work carefully constructed "with extraordinary care and artistry." Des Marias concludes that the work "is serial only periodically."

B988. Sargeant, Winthrop. "Musical Events." New Yorker 33 (February 8, 1958): 115-116.

B989. _____. "Musical Events: A New Opera." New Yorker 30 (April 10, 1954): 74.
The Tender Land had its premiere last week by the New York City Opera Company. Sargeant was not impressed with the work and states that the composer "seems incapable of suggesting the passionate and poetic feelings of his characters." See also: W90

B990. _____. "Musical Events: Copland as Conductor." New Yorker 36 (November 19, 1960): 150.
Copland, who is sixty years old now, recently conducted the New York Philharmonic in a concert at Carnegie Hall. Included

on the program were El Salón México and the Symphonic Ode.
Although Sargeant is not an enthusiastic admirer of Copland's
work, he concedes that the composer "has a well-defined style
of his own and is very experienced at manipulating it."

B991. _____. "Musical Events: Mr. Harris and Mr. Copland." New Yorker
32 (February 2, 1957): 72-73.
Sargeant reviews a recent Carnegie Hall concert by the New
York Philharmonic with Leonard Bernstein conducting. Roy Harris'
Third Symphony and Copland's Short Symphony were on the program.
Sargeant's opinion of Copland's work is that the composer is
simply "demonstrating his ingenuity in arranging notes on paper."

B992. Schmidt-Garre, Helmut. "Vier Komponisten in Eigener Sache." Neue
Zeitschrift für Musik 125, no.2 (1964): 69.
This is a review of four of Copland's works performed recently
in Germany along with stylistic information about them.

B993. Schonberg, Harold C. "Annual Tanglewood on Parade Attracts Record
Crowd of 14,588." New York Times, August 8, 1958, p.9:1.
On August 7 Copland was the pianist for the performance of his
Piano Concerto. It was the first time he had been the soloist
since 1927. "It is a rather dated work, with its echoes of
Gershwin and jazz of the Nineteen Twenties." The performance
was with the Boston Symphony Orchestra, Richard Burgin conducting,
at the Berkshire Music Festival.

B994. _____. "He Wanted to Reach Us." New York Times, February 28,
1971, II, p.15:1.
This tribute to Copland as he reached his seventieth birthday
discusses his long career as a composer. His position as leader
of an American style was undisputed. As styles changed, his and
that of the music world in general became less influential.
However, "Copland remains the most popular and the most-played
of serious American composers."

B995. _____. "Music: Birthday Party for Copland." New York Times,
November 15, 1960, p.47:4.
The Juilliard School of Music celebrated Copland's sixtieth
birthday on November 14 by presenting a concert of his works
to be followed by a second concert on November 15. Copland was
present for his birthday celebration.

B996. _____. "Music: Copland Plays at Philharmonic." New York Times,
January 10, 1964, p.19:2.
On January 9 Copland played his Piano Concerto with the New
York Philharmonic conducted by Leonard Bernstein. It was part
of an avant-garde series. Although written in 1926, the Piano
Concerto uses jazz elements within the context of serious music.

B997. _____. "Music: Copland Salute." New York Times, October 31,
1970, p.35:1.
On October 29 Copland conducted the New York Philharmonic in
a concert of his works. Copland, who will be seventy years old
soon, was also presented with an honorary membership in the
Philharmonic Symphony Society of New York. He was cited for

being "'a pioneer in placing American music in the mainstream of twentieth-century creation.'"

B998. _____. "Music: Copland Tribute." New York Times, August 18, 1965, p.39:1.
At a Tanglewood Festival of Contemporary Music on August 17 it was announced that Copland would retire from his post as head of the faculty and composition department after twenty-five years of association with the organization. Copland was present for an all-Copland concert on this occasion.

B999. _____. "Music: Finale at Lenox." New York Times, August 15, 1960, p.18:1.
The final concert of the Berkshire Music Festival season was given August 14 at Lenox, Massachusetts. On August 13 Copland conducted his First Symphony which "is a mixture of styles and ideas."

B1000. _____. "Music: the Occasion." New York Times, September 24, 1962, p.34:4.
Copland's Connotations was commissioned for the opening of Philharmonic Hall in Lincoln Center September 23. Leonard Bernstein conducted the New York Philharmonic in this twelve-tone work. "Parts of it actually sounded tonal, despite a lavish use of dissonant harmonies." See also: W98

B1001. _____. "Rise of an American Tradition: from Gottschalk to Copland." In The Lives of the Great Composers, 579-583. Revised edition. New York: W. W. Norton, 1981.
Copland is cited as "the composer who best represented the United States in the public and professional eye." A discussion of the various influences on Copland's style includes references to specific works.

B1002. _____. "Russian Composers Hear Copland Work." New York Times, November 22, 1959, p.83:4.
On November 21 several visiting Russian composers were present at the Carnegie Hall concert given by the Boston Symphony Orchestra. Copland conducted his suite The Tender Land in its first New York performance. This music "is the product of a fine technician, and many sections have the authentic Copland touch."

B1003. Schubart, Mark A. "U.S. Music Festival planned in Paris." New York Times, March 1, 1945, p.23:4.
The United States Information Service and the French government will sponsor a festival of music in Paris in June. Leonard Bernstein and Copland are two of the prominent Americans who will be in Paris to participate in the festival.

B1004. Schuman, William. "A Birthday Salute to Aaron Copland." Juilliard Review 8, no.1 (1960-1961): 6-7.
This article was reprinted from the New York Herald-Tribune, November 30, 1960. Copland was honored on his sixtieth birthday by the Juilliard School of Music November 14 and 15, 1960 with two concerts of his music. His struggle to bring other American

composers' works to the public was noted. The Americanism in
his music has enriched the sound of this contemporary art.

B1005. _____. "More Comments on Copland." American Record Guide
44 (November 1980): 6-8.
    A composite of short articles written by Copland and others
    gives insight to Copland the composer. Elements of his back-
    ground and development are discussed as well as his influence
    on American music.

B1006. _____. "The Place of Composer Copland." New York Times, November 8, 1953, VII, p.3:3.
    This review of Arthur Berger's Aaron Copland is quite compli-
    mentary. "Mr. Berger's own thoughtful commentary weaves
    through the text, adding a welcome philosophic dimension."
    Many musical examples accompany the text and analysis. Works,
    bibliography, and discography are listed. See also: B200

B1007. Scott-Maddocks, D. "Aaron Copland." Music and Musicians 8
(June 1960): 25.

B1008. "Second Hurricane in World Premiere." New York Times, April 22,
1937, p.18:4.
    Copland's play-opera for children received its world premiere
    on April 21 at The Playhouse. The Henry Street Settlement
    Music School was in charge of the event. Edwin Denby contributed
    the libretto. The reviewer found this performance to be "pretty
    dull fare." Most of the choral singing was in unison, the
    orchestra sat on the stage behind the performers, and the stage
    was devoid of scenery with the exception of a few props. See
    also: W51

B1009. "The Second Hurricane Issued in Vocal Score." Musical America
79 (December 1, 1959): 40.
    Boosey & Hawkes recently published the vocal score separately
    for this opera for students. "The music is sturdy, melodic,
    spontaneous, and it never becomes patronizing or cheap."

B1010. "Second in Our Poll of America's Most Distinguished Composers We
Salute--Aaron Copland." Music Clubs Magazine 36 (January 1957):
7.

B1011. "II [Second] Inter-American Music Festival." Inter-American Music
Bulletin 23 (May 1961): 8.
    The world premiere of Copland's Nonet for Solo Strings was
    conducted by him at the April 25 Inter-American Music Festival
    in Washington, D.C. in Howard University's Cramton Auditorium.
    The work was commissioned in honor of the fiftieth wedding
    anniversary of Mr. and Mrs. Robert Woods Bliss in 1958 and was
    dedicated to his teacher Nadia Boulanger. See also: W96

B1012. Seroff, Victor I. "Musicians in Covers: Aaron Copland." Saturday
Review 39 (April 7, 1956): 17.
    Julia Smith's biography Aaron Copland, His Work and Contribu-
    tion to American Music is taken from her dissertation at New
    York University. Copland's music is thoroughly analyzed.

Included also are lists of his music, recordings, and writings.
The book is best suited for the professional musician and not
the layman because of its technical approach.

B1013. "Sextet, for String Quartet, Clarinet and Piano." Music and
Letters 33 (October 1951): 371.
"The rhythmic treatment . . . helps to give the work immense
vitality." The reviewer believes that the work is not as
successful as it could be if it had not been adapted from
another medium.

B1014. Shanes, Estelle M. "Letters: New Music." New York Times, January 15, VI, p.2:5.
In this comment on Copland's recent article, "A Modernist
Defends Modern Music," Shanes offers two reasons that account
for the lack of interest in contemporary music. One is that
there is too much difference in the styles from the Classic and
Romantic Periods, and the second is that people cannot force
themselves to appreciate a style of music. See also: B63

B1015. Shawe-Taylor, Desmond. "The Arts and Entertainment: Aaron
Copland." New Statesman 41 (June 9, 1951): 648.
Copland's premiere of his Concerto for Clarinet in England
occurred last week at the Victoria and Albert Museum. This
work was written for Benny Goodman. "The key is C major, the
colors soft, pure and brilliant, the texture simple and
beautifully spaces." The previous fall the ballets Billy the
Kid and Rodeo were performed in London by the New York City
Ballet. The orchestra suite of Appalachian Spring has often
been performed in England, but not the ballet. "As an orchestral
piece it is entrancingly fresh and brilliant."

B1016. _____. "Musical Events; Connotations for Orchestra Performed
by the New York Philharmonic." New Yorker 49 (January 7,
1974): 63.
Connotations for Orchestra, written a decade ago, was not
well received in the beginning because it "seemed too tough and
demanding a piece." Now the work is receiving much interest.
This twelve-tone composition "represents the severe, intellectual side of this warm and genial man."

B1017. Shepard, Richard F. "The Brooklyn Crowd on Mount Parnassus."
New York Times, February 21, 1971, p.75:6.
Copland, among other famous artists, is noted for his early
days in Brooklyn. Copland recalls that for one "coming from
that background, the arts constituted a discovery.'"

B1018. _____. "TV: 'Kennedy Center Honors' Celebrates the Performing
Arts." New York Times, December 29, 1979, p.42:4.
A tape of the December 2 affair will be shown on CBS Television
on the evening of December 29. Five individuals were honored for
their life achievements in art: Ella Fitzgerald, Henry Fonda,
Martha Graham, Tennessee Williams, and Copland.

B1019. Sherman, Robert. "Music: Salute to Copland." New York Times,
November 23, 1975, p.58:4.

On November 21 Martin Josman and his National Chorale presented the first of three Bicentennial concerts. Many Copland
works were included in this sampling of America at the Carnegie
Recital Hall.

B1020. Shneerson, G. "Amerikanskie Kompozitory v Moskve." Sovetskaya
Muzyka 24 (May 1960): 135-137.
This is a discussion of the cultural visit of Copland and
other Americans to Moscow.

B1021. "Short Symphony." New York Philharmonic Program Notes (October
7, 1966): 97.

B1022. "Short Symphony No.2." Musical Opinion 78 (June 1955): 545.
This is a review of the miniature score now available from
Copland's publisher Boosey & Hawkes.

B1023. "Shura Cherkassky." Musical Opinion 83 (March 1960): 385.
A performance by Cherkassy including Copland's Piano Fantasy
is discussed.

B1024. "Shy Venture." Time 63 (April 12, 1954): 65-66.
The first performance of Copland's opera, The Tender Land,
was given in New York. He had planned to have the opening at
a less cosmopolitan area, but he did not want to pass up the
New York setting when it was offered. The work was politely
received but the music "held as little punch as the libretto."
See also: W90

B1025. Siebert, F. Mark. "Choral Music." Music Library Association
Notes 13 (June 1956): 529-530.
Siebert reviews the following scores: Stomp Your Foot and
The Promise of Living, both from The Tender Land, as well as
Ching-a-Ring Chaw and Canticle of Freedom (choral finale).
The first three pieces "are examples of the genre in which Copland
excels--the musical pictorialization of rural America." The
Canticle of Freedom is quite complex rhythmically and harmoni-
cally.

B1026. Siegmeister, Elie. "Night Thoughts (Homage to Ives) by Aaron
Copland." Pan Pipes of Sigma Alpha Iota 66, no.2 (1974): 29.
This piano piece was commissioned for the fourth Van Cliburn
International Piano Competition. Vladimir Vladimirovich Viardo
from the Soviet Union was the winner of the competition where
the work was first performed the week of September 17-30 at
the Texas Christian University in Fort Worth. See also: W111

B1027. Silverman, Robert. "Aaron Copland: Happy Birthday." Piano
Quarterly 28, no.111 (1980): 5-6.
An interview was conducted with Copland at his home in
Peekskill, New York as he approached his eightieth birthday.
He states that he is no longer composing, but he expressed a
lot of musical ideas over the past five decades. He admits
that he is no longer in close contact with contemporary music.
He still prefers live performances over recordings because the
live performance provides an excitment that is lacking on discs.

He agrees that recordings have the advantage of being available to play repeatedly. Copland also asserts that new composers have an advantage because of the recording industry and the accessibility people have to music.

B1028. Simmons, David. "London Music." Musical Opinion 92 (December 1968): 119.
   On October 24 Copland was the guest conductor with the London Symphony Orchestra. On his program were compositions of his own plus works by other contemporary composers. Inscape had its London premiere.

B1029. _____. "London Music." Musical Opinion 93 (January 1970): 182-183.
   Visiting musicians from America have been performing with the London Symphony Orchestra during the previous month. Copland conducted his Quiet City and Billy the Kid as well as works of other contemporary composers.

B1030. _____. "London Music." Musical Opinion 94 (January 1971): 175-176.
   Appalachian Spring, the Piano Concerto, and the Third Symphony were included on a recent London Symphony Orchestra program to celebrate Copland's sixtieth birthday. Copland was the soloist in the Piano Concerto while André Previn conducted.

B1031. _____. "London Music." Musical Opinion 95 (July 1972): 510.
   Copland recently was the guest conductor for the New Philharmonia Orchestra at Albert Hall. Simmons believes this orchestra does not understand the American style as well as the London Symphony Orchestra. El Salón México, Danzón Cubano, and The Red Pony were on the program.

B1032. "Sinfonia of London: from Film Studio to Concert Platform." Times (London), September 23, 1958, p.3d.
   Copland conducted the Sinfonia of London in his suite Appalachian Spring on September 22. "This is simple, direct Copland, in keeping with the scene and the period."

B1033. Singer, Samuel L. "Philadelphia." Musical Courier 159 (March 1959): 28.
   Copland accepted the golden lyre from the Philadelphia Academy of Music for musical distinguished service recently. It was said that he received over two-thirds of the ballots.

B1034. "Six on the State of Music." Music Magazine and Musical Courier 163 (October 1964): 23-24.
   The CBS Radio Network recently invited six musicians to discuss their views on the future of symphonic orchestras. The six were Richard Burgin, Arthur Fiedler, Erich Leinsdorf, Leonard Bernstein, Gary Graffman, and Copland. They debated the issue of presenting non-standard contemporary works and still managing to attract audiences. Also noted in this program entitled "The Direction of Music in America" was that the newest composers are not writing works for symphonies. Copland explained that few symphonic works are written because there is little chance for the new composer to have the work performed.

B1035. Skladatelé o Hudební Poetice 20 Století: Copland [et al.], edited
by Ivan Vojtěch. Praha: Československý Spisovatel, 1960.
This is a collection of articles and writings by twentieth
century composers and musicians, especially Copland.

B1036. Skovran, D. "Beograd." Zvuk 49-50 (1961): 551-552.

B1037. Slonimsky, Nicolas. "The Six of American Music." Christian
Science Monitor, March 17, 1937, Mag, p.8-9.
The American composers whose works are discussed are Roy
Harris, Walter Piston, Roger Sessions, Henry Cowell, George
Antheil, and Copland. Slonimsky notes that Copland's Music for
the Theatre is historically important because "it gives ex-
pression of jazz music in a classical dance form for the first
time."

B1038. Smit, Leo. "Editorial." Piano Quarterly 28, no.111 (1980): 1.
A short list of Copland's compositions is given along with a
tribute to the composer for the outstanding contributions he
has made to music. He "has given new expression and direction
to American music."

B1039. _____. "For and About Aaron on His 75th." Saturday Review 3
(November 29, 1975): 49.
This tribute to Copland notes his importance in American contemporary music. Smit uses the cuckoo as a bird with which to
identify Copland and other influential musicians.

B1040. _____. "Interpreting Conversation at the Soda Fountain."
Virtuoso 2, no.2 (1981): 23-26.
This excerpt from the music for the film Our Town is arranged
for piano. Music is included in this analysis.

B1041. Smith, Cecil. "League of Composers Program Celebrates Copland
Birthday." Musical America 70 (December 1, 1950): 18.
The first League of Composers concert for the 1950 season
was given in honor of Copland's fiftieth birthday. Among his
works performed were As It Fell upon a Day and the Twelve Poems
of Emily Dickinson. This concert concentrated on Copland's
small forms. Smith feels that Copland's widest recognition
has come from his compositions in large forms, such as ballets
and orchestral works as Billy the Kid and Appalachian Spring.
Smith thinks the Piano Quartet is an important new development
in Copland's career and believes "it is likely to provide a
stimulus toward important growth."

B1042. Smith, Julia Frances. Aaron Copland, His Work and Contribution
to American Music. New York: Dutton, 1955.
This book is taken from Smith's dissertation at New York
University in 1953 which was subtitled: a study of the development of his musical style and an analysis of the various
techniques of writing he has employed in his works. The material is arranged chronologically with most of the biographical
information centering around the early part of his career.
This is a detailed study of his compositions up to the early
1950's and includes numerous musical examples. A list of works,
discography, and his critical writings are included.

B1043. "Smith, Julia Frances. Aaron Copland, His Work and Contribution to American Music." Musical America 76 (May 1956): 29.
    This book is "a penetrating, if not exactly scintillating, study of a colleague and elder statesman." The format is chronological and analyzes his works as his life progresses. This causes some incontinuity in the biographical information. Smith's analysis of Copland's work is very thorough and perceptive. See also: B1042

B1044. "Smith, Julia Frances. Aaron Copland, His Work and Contribution to American Music." School Musician 27 (June 1956): 23.
    This reviewer finds Smith's book to be a well written, critical examination of Copland's styles. This is especially difficult to do while a composer is still living. She "has written authoritatively in combining autobiographical material with an illuminating study of Copland's music." See also: B1042

B1045. Smith, Patricia Beach. "Matrix Midland Festival." Opera Canada 19, no.3 (1978): 29-30.
    Midland hosted an arts festival June 3 at which Copland conducted his opera The Tender Land. The Michigan Opera Theatre performed.

B1046. Smith, Patrick J. "N.Y. Philharmonic: Copland Tribute." High Fidelity/Musical America 21 (February 1971): MA26.
    Copland's seventieth birthday was honored by the New York Philharmonic on October 29, 1970. Copland conducted five of his works written from 1925 (Music for the Theatre) to 1967 (Inscape). Smith, a music critic, was outraged because some members of the audience walked out during the final part of the concert. He felt these individuals gave a "direct affront to a major American composer."

B1047. Smith, Rollin. "American Organ Composers." Music (American Guild of Organists) 10 (August 1976): 18.
    Among the composers discussed is Copland. His first work which included an organ was the Symphony for Organ and Orchestra. Nadia Boulanger, his composition teacher in France, was invited to perform with the New York Orchestra. She encouraged Copland to write a work for her and the result was his symphony. Episode is an organ solo he wrote which has, "for the organ, a rather incredible range of dynamic contrasts."

B1048. Soria, Dorle J. "Artist Life." High Fidelity/Musical America 20 (November 1970): MA4-5.
    This interview commemorates Copland's seventieth birthday. He reminisces about his early compositions such as The Cat and the Mouse which he sold for about twenty-five dollars. Lincoln Portrait and Appalachian Spring are the two most performed works. Copland still conducts on occasion but spends most of his time at his home in the country outside of New York City.

B1049. _____. "Artist Life." High Fidelity/Musical America 26 (March 1976): MA6-7.
    Walter Cronkite's rehearsal as narrator in Lincoln Portrait is reviewed. This was in preparation for a performance with the

New York Philharmonic with Andre Kostelanetz conducting. In
November of 1975 the New York Times hailed the composer as
"Copland the Kid." Asked about his activities, Copland replied
that he had a great capacity for celebrating birthdays so he
had no problem with growing older.

B1050. _____. "Copland P.S." High Fidelity/Musical America 20 (December 1970): MA32.
    A reference is made to the November 1970 article by Soria in
which Copland's seventieth birthday was noted. The composer
was honored by the German Consul General, Count von Posadowsky-
Wehner, who presented him with the German Republic Cross of
the Commander of the Order of Merit. Among the guests at this
luncheon presentation were Virgil Thomson and Claire Reis.
See also: B1048

B1051. _____. "The Devil and Aaron Copland." High Fidelity/Musical
America 16 (November 1966): MA14.
    Copland has been commissioned to write a one-minute theme
for the CBS Playhouse television drama series. His remuneration
was ample, but he found this assignment to be quite difficult.

B1052. _____. "A Tree of Many Branches." High Fidelity/Musical America 15 (November 1965): 196.
    Copland resigned at the age of sixty-five from his positions
as chairman and head of the Department of Composition at
Tanglewood's Berkshire Music Center. He had held these positions
since 1940 and 1957, respectively. He intends to devote more
time to composing and conducting.

B1053. Spicknall, Joan Singer. "The Piano Music of Aaron Copland: a
Performance-Tape and Study of His Original Works for Piano
Solo." Ph.D. diss., University of Maryland, 1974.
    The thirty-three page written portion of this project examines
Copland's piano works and analyzes them in relation to the
American sound which is evident in some of the pieces.

B1054. "Stadium Summer Plans." New York Times, April 1, 1928, IX, p.
10:2.
    Among the announcements of upcoming musical events is a new
series of Concerts of Contemporary Music. Roger Sessions and
Copland are organizing these performances for the benefit of
contemporary composers, especially Americans.

B1055. Stambler, B. "Four American Composers." Juilliard Review 2
(Winter 1955): 7-16.
    The four composers examined are William Schuman, Samuel Barber,
Charles Ives, and Copland. Many aspects of their development
as composers are compared, such as the age at which they decided
to become composers and their educational background in Europe
and the United States. The divergent paths they followed are
examined as well. Copland is noted for working very hard to
have his music and that of others performed in public. His
"was a world of coming to grips with the practicalities of
music, performers, conductors, and publishers."

B1056. Starin, Dennis. "An Art Center Gets Involved." New York Times,
       September 23, 1973, p.118:3.
       The Hampton Art Center, Quogue, Long Island, is a new gallery
       designed to promote art in this community. Marcos Blahove, one
       of the artists involved in this project, "recently did a com-
       missioned portrait of Aaron Copland, the composer, that is now
       in the permanent collection of the Smithsonian Institution."

B1057. Starr, Lawrence. "Copland's Style." Perspectives of New Music
       19, no.1-2 (1981-1982): 68-89.
       Starr examines Copland's stylistic characteristics in this
       article which is an issue devoted exclusively to Copland.
       Musical examples illustrate Starr's points in his critical
       analysis of some of Copland's major works.

B1058. "Statements for Orchestra." Boston Symphony Orchestra Concert
       Bulletin 5 (November 18, 1949): 270-271.

B1059. Stern, Walter H. "Music on the Air: Opening Night." Musical
       Leader 94 (October 1962): 6.
       Copland's Connotations for Orchestra was commissioned for the
       opening of the Philharmonic Hall in Lincoln Center for the
       Performing Arts. It had its premiere performance September 23
       and was conducted by Leonard Bernstein. This dissonant twelve-
       tone work did not receive a warm reception. See also: W98

B1060. Sterne, Michael. "Notables Open Oral History Venture." New York
       Times, May 26, 1978, II, p.3:5.
       Columbia University celebrated the thirtieth anniversary of
       its Oral History Project May 25. Copland was one of the guests
       of honor and is among the 4,000 contributors to this program.

B1061. Sternfeld, Frederick W. "Aaron Copland." Music Library Associ-
       ation Notes 11 (March 1954): 306-307.
       This is a review of Arthur Berger's biography. It includes
       bibliographies about and by Copland as well as a list of works
       and recordings. An analysis of a few major works is included
       along with musical examples. Sternfeld states that he does not
       agree with some of Berger's opinions expressed in this book,
       but he feels that the book is an important one. See also: B200

B1062. _____. "Copland as a Film Composer." Musical Quarterly 37
       (April 1951): 161-175.
       Sternfeld critiques Copland's compositions for film. Although
       most composers reduce their scores to the barest essentials,
       Copland "never forsakes the tradition or the vocabulary of
       serious music." Copland's music for Our Town and Of Mice and
       Men has been considered quite successful.

B1063. _____. "Reviews of Records." Musical Quarterly 39 (April 1953):
       307-308.
       This is a review of Our Town on Decca DL 7527 which was
       originally a film score. Since the movie was a slow, quiet
       one, the music is much the same, and Sternfeld notes that there
       is "hardly enough contrasting material for the concert hall."
       See also: D201

B1064. Stevens, Elizabeth Mruk. "The Influence of Nadia Boulanger on
Composition in the United States: a Study of Piano Solo Works
by Her American Students." Ph.D. diss., Boston University,
1975.
Boulanger was Copland's composition teacher during the early
part of the 1920's in France. Her influence on his work is
examined, particularly in his piano work Passacaglia.

B1065. Stevenson, J. "A Conversation with Aaron Copland." Your Musical
Cue 1, no.2 (1973): 21-22.

B1066. "Stevenson Cast as Concert 'Star.'" New York Times, February
20, 1962, p.31:1.
United Nations Delegate Adlai E. Stevenson will narrate
Copland's Lincoln Portrait September 23 in a concert series
celebrating the opening of Philharmonic Hall in Lincoln Center.
Copland's Connotations has been commissioned for this opening
and will be heard for the first time. See also: W98

B1067. Stoddard, Hope. "Book Notes." International Musician 59 (February 1961): 47.
Copland on Music is a compilation of the composer's thoughts
and views. Quotes are given as examples of his ability to
express his opinions clearly. The book is written "with an
understanding and an acuteness rare even in the writer born
and bred." See also: B24

B1068. Strauss, Theodore. "What Music Has Charms?" New York Times,
June 23, IX, p.3:3.
Although Copland has composed film scores before, the consensus among critics is that he has done an excellent job with
the music for Thornton Wilder's Our Town which recently
premiered. Copland commented on his role as a film composer.
He strongly feels that the music score should assist and
enhance the story but not dominate it.

B1069. Strongin, Theodore. "Copland Prevails at Tanglewood." New York
Times, July 26, p.49:4.
On July 25, Copland conducted the Boston Symphony Orchestra
in two of his works: Dance Panels and the Clarinet Concerto.
The first work is for ballet and "although it is typical
Copland--sensitively, economically scored with a nice sense of
angular fantasy--it is relatively uneventful."

B1070. _____. "Mrs. King Narrates Lincoln Portrait." New York Times,
February 17, 1969, p.30:1.
Coretta Scott King, widow of Dr. Martin Luther King, Jr.,
narrated Copland's Lincoln Portrait at Philharmonic Hall February 16. Copland was guest conductor for the concert presented
by the Washington National Symphony Orchestra. Copland also was
soloist in his Piano Concerto and he "knew better than many
fulltime pianists exactly what kind of sound to get from his
instrument in order to set forth its jazzy passages to best
advantage."

B1071. _____. "Music: Copland Conducts." New York Times, July~17,
1964, p.16:1.
On July 16, Copland conducted the Stadium Symphony at the
Lewisohn Stadium in a concert of his works. United Nations
Representative Adlai Stevenson narrated the Lincoln Portrait
and William Warfield was the vocal soloist.

B1072. Swan, Annalyn. "Copland's American Dream." Newsweek 96 (December 1, 1980): 97.
Copland recently conducted the American Symphony Orchestra
at Carnegie Hall. A birthday cake was brought on stage to
celebrate his eightieth birthday. Numerous celebrations are
being held all over the world in his honor. Included is a
synopsis of his career.

B1073. Swickard, Ralph. "All-Copland Concert Honors 60th Birthday."
Music of the West 16 (December 1960): 10.
A concert in Hancock Auditorium at the University of Southern
California in Los Angeles on November 14 honored Copland on
his sixtieth birthday. The program consisted of his Piano
Fantasy, Vitebsk, El Salón México, In the Beginning, and
Danzón Cubano. Copland's telegram of appreciation was read at
the conclusion of the concert.

B1074. Swift, Richard. "Piano Solo." Music Library Association Notes
3, no.1 (September 1974): 158-159.
Copland's Night Thoughts is reviewed. A description of this
piano work indicates that "its bell sonorities and gentle hymn-
like melodies form a mild meditation." It is a brief work,
but it is also well done.

B1075. "Symphony No.3." Chicago Symphony Orchestra Program Notes (Novem-
ber 14, 1950): 13; Detroit Symphony Orchestra Program Notes
(February 24, 1966): 412; Seattle Symphony Orchestra Program
Notes (January 15, 1962): 9.

B1076. Szmolyan, Walter. "Gespräch mit Aaron Copland." Österreichische
Musikzeitschrift 22 (October 1967): 612-613.
Copland, who will be sixty-seven years old on November 14, is
interviewed while visiting in Wien. Many of his most important
works are mentioned and he expresses some of his views on contemporary American music.

B1077. Tarvin, Ronald Dean. "History of the Violin Scordatura: Lecture
Recital Together with Three Recitals of Music by Albinoni,
Copland, Beethoven, Haydn, Arensky, Vitali, Prokofiev, and
Grieg." Ph.D. diss., North Texas State University, 1976.

B1078. Taubman, Howard. "Copland Conducts His Work in London." New
York Times, June 1, p.20:6.
Copland conducted the Jacques Orchestra in his Clarinet Con-
certo May 31 at the Victoria and Albert Museum as part of a
Festival of Britain concert. Frederick Thurston was the soloist.
It was noted that British audiences, as well as American ones,
do not attend concerts of contemporary music in large numbers.

B1079. _____. "Copland Fantasy for Piano Heard." New York Times,
October 26, 1957, p.18:3.
The premiere performance of the Piano Fantasy was given by
William Masselos October 25. It was the sole work on the pro-
gram and was performed twice. It had been commissioned for the
Juilliard School of Music's fiftieth anniversary and was dedi-
cated to William Kapell's memory. He "uses twelve-tone devices,
but he does not follow them slavishly." See also: W93

B1080. _____. "Copland on Lincoln." New York Times, February 1, 1953,
II, p.7:7.
Copland's Lincoln Portrait was recently removed from the
inaugural concert program because an Illinois representative
felt that Copland had been associating with Communists. The
League of Composers and others have protested this blacklisting.
Most of the article is devoted to Copland's description of how
he composed this work.

B1081. _____. "Copland's New Opera." New York Times, March 28, 1954,
II, p.7:7.
Copland relates the events that resulted in his decision to
write an opera. He has written a children's work called The
Second Hurricane earlier. He discusses some of the problems
he faced in writing for this medium. The premiere of The
Tender Land will occur on April 1 and will be presented by the
City Opera Company at City Center. See also: W90

B1082. _____. "Copland's Opera Sung at Festival." New York Times,
August 3, 1954, p.15:1.
The Berkshire Music Center presented a revised version of
The Tender Land at a performance August 2. Copland and Horace
Everett, the librettist, are commended for their "courage and
wisdom to concede that their opera was weak in dramatic con-
flict." Some of the announced revisions are a changed in the
time period of the opera and a change from two to three acts.

B1083. _____. "Music: Aaron Copland." New York Times, January 31,
1958, p.24:6.
Copland was present at the New York Philharmonic concert
January 30 as guest conductor for the first half of the program
at Carnegie Hall. He led the Philharmonic in his Outdoor
Overture and Third Symphony. Taubman feels that this symphony
is one of the best written by an American. "It represents an
assimilation of the abstract and folk periods that had marked
his music."

B1084. _____. "Music: Copland Premiere." New York Times, February 9,
1956, p.37:2.
The Boston Symphony commissioned Copland to write a work for
its seventy-fifth anniversary. Copland revised his Symphonic
Ode which he had written for the group's fiftieth anniversary
twenty-five years earlier. The premiere of the revision took
place February 8 at Carnegie Hall with Charles Munch conducting.
It is a twenty-minute one-movement work with a reduced orchestra.
The work "seems somewhat overblown—too big, long and insistent
for its content." See also: W38

B1085. _____. "Prizes Awarded at Fete in Lenox." New York Times,
August 15, 1954, p.77:1.
　　Copland presented awards and scholarships to outstanding
students who had studied and performed at the Berkshire Music
Center. These were distributed during the intermission of a
concert held there August 14.

B1086. _____. "Revised Opera." New York Times, August 8, 1954, II,
p.7:8.
　　Taubman reviews the revised version of Copland's opera The
Tender Land. It was recently performed at the Berkshire Music
Center. These "revisions, though they are relatively slight,
strengthen the piece as compared with the version seen at the
New York City Center last season." Taubman states that he hopes
Copland will write more operas because he feels that the next
one would be better.

B1087. _____. "Scored for Americans." New York Times, January 1, 1956,
VII, p.5:1.
　　This is a review of Julia Smith's biography Aaron Copland,
His Work and Contribution to American Music. The book, enlarged
from her doctoral dissertation, is very complete but "is over-
burdened with detail." The scope of the work is significant
and Copland's styles are analyzed thoroughly. See also: 1042

B1088. _____. "Second Hurricane." New York Times, July 26, 1936, IX,
p.5:1.
　　In early 1937 the Music School of the Henry Street Settlement
will produce a play-opera by Copland and librettist Edwin Denby.
The work is designed for children and the number of performers
can vary. Portions of the libretto are printed in this article.
"The music is, according to those who have examined it, clear,
dramatic, humorous and simple enough for the children who are to
perform it, but with the personality of the composer unmistakably discernible." See also: W51

B1089. _____. "6,000 at Concert in the Berkshires." New York Times,
August 8, 1938, p.9:1.
　　Music for the Theatre, written in 1925, was presented at the
Berkshire Symphonic Festival August 7 at Lenox, Massachusetts.
Copland performed the piano part and Serge Koussevitzky con-
ducted the Boston Symphony Orchestra.

B1090. _____. "Style Is the Man." New York Times, February 10, 1957,
II, p.9:1.
　　"When a composer writes music difficult to perform and grasp,
is he deliberately talking to himself and, with luck, to a
sympathetic clique?" Taubman specifically is referring to
Copland's difficult Short Symphony which has been dropped from
some orchestral programs because of the amount of rehearsal
time required to master the difficult rhythms. It has rarely
been performed. This work was composed in the nineteen thirties
and soon afterwards Copland adopted a more simplistic style.

B1091. _____. "To Benefit Composers." New York Times, June 8, 1952,
II, p.7:8.

The League of Composers has commissioned Copland to write a
short opera for television. This commission is being financed
by Richard Rodgers and Oscar Hammerstein II. Copland's commission is one of few being granted during the League's thirtieth year. This resulted in The Tender Land. **See also:** W90

B1092. _____. "A Week for Youth; Plan for Orchestras to Give Some Time
Each Season to Young Composers." New York Times, August 11,
1957, II, p.7:1.
Copland has formulated a plan which would permit young composers, age twenty to thirty-five, to have their works performed
by major symphony orchestras. He proposed that an additional
week be added to the regular concert season to rehearse and
present the works of these young Americans. The major obstacle
for this plan is financing it since most orchestras already
operate at a deficit. There is hope that some organization
might underwrite this project.

B1093. Taylor, M. "Aaron Copland." Music and Musicians 10 (March 1962):
41.

B1094. "Ten Works Are Commissioned by the Philharmonic for 1962-63."
New York Times, January 25, 1962, p.24:4.
Among the ten commissioned works is one for Copland who will
compose an orchestral work for the New York Philharmonic to
perform at the opening of Philharmonic Hall in Lincoln Center
in September 1962. Connotations was the result of this commission. **See also:** W98

B1095. "The Tender Land." Opera (London) 13 (May 1962): 345-346.
Copland's opera for students received its premiere European
performance February 20 by the Cambridge University Opera
Group. It "was more warmly received by the English critics
than by the American." It is an opera with simple melodic lines
as well as a simple romanticized plot set in the mid-West.

B1096. "The Tender Land." Tempo 31 (Spring 1954): 10-16.
A synopsis of this opera is given. Horace Everett, the librettist, writes about his basis for the story. James Agee's
photographs of share croppers in Let Us Now Praise Famous Men
was the inspiration for this drama.

B1097. "The Tender Land at Cambridge." Musical Opinion 85 (May 1962):
461.

B1098. "Tender Land Gets Tough Going Over as Copland's First Opera Makes
Bow." Variety 194 (April 7, 1954): 57.
The production of Copland's opera by the New York City Opera
Company on April 1 was not received favorably. It "was defeated
by a static, undramatic libretto by Horace Everett and a single-
mood, unexciting score by Copland."

B1099. "The Tender Land; Royal Academy of Music." Opera (London) 19
(August 1968): 685-686.
A performance of Copland's opera at the Royal Academy of
Music on June 6 and June 11 was not well received. Horace

Everett's libretto was considered uninspired by not confronting
the conflicts evident in the plot. Copland's music was desribed
as characterless.

B1100. "Tender Land Suite." Pittsburgh Symphony Orchestra Program Notes
(May 16, 1969): 875.
Program notes for a performance of the orchestral suite taken
from the opera The Tender Land give a synopsis of the opera plot.
This suite has folk idioms used in expressing its farm theme.
"Thematic building stones, that are simple and even raw, are
cemented in Copland's personal, sophisticated manner."

B1101. Terry, Kenneth. "Caught!" Down Beat 47 (May 1980): 60-61.
Paul Jacobs and Copland recently performed the two-piano
work Danzón Cubano in New York City. Jacobs also performed
Copland's Four Piano Blues which combine "reminiscences of
rural America with flashes of big city sophistication."

B1102. "Thank You, Aaron Copland." American Record Guide 32 (November
1965): 196-201.
A number of friends, colleagues, and former students have
commemorated Copland's sixty-fifth birthday by writing one or
two paragraphs of thanks. Among the group are Roger Sessions,
Harold Clurman, and Olga Koussevitzky.

B1103. "13 Hours of a Musical Marathon Mark Aaron Copland's 80 Years."
New York Times, November 23, 1980, p.45:1.
On November 22, Symphony Space presented a thirteen-hour
"Wall-to-Wall concert of American music, especially that of
Copland who was present." Mayor Edward I. Koch had declared
it "Wall-to-Wall Copland Day" and a great number of the com-
poser's works were presented.

B1104. "30 Receive Freedom Medal at the White House." New York Times,
September 15, 1964, p.15:3.
Copland was one of thirty notable people who received the
nation's highest civilian honor, the Presidential Medal of
Freedom, presented by President Lyndon B. Johnson on September
14.

B1105. "This Month's Personality." Music and Musicians 8 (April 1960):
5.

B1106. Thompson, Howard. "Copland Accepts Film Assignment." New York
Times, March 15, 1961, p.44:1.
Copland has agreed to compose the music for the film Something
Wild. It has been twelve years since the composer has composed
any film scores because he has been busy with other projects.
"'I've always felt that audiences will really be conscious of
a good score, unless they're tone-deaf, no matter how well-
integrated to the rest of the picture,' he said."

B1107. Thompson, Oscar. "Aaron Copland." In Great Modern Composers,
41-48. New York: Dodd, Mead & Company, 1941.
This biography has been revised since its first appearance in
the author's International Cyclopedia of Music and Musicians.

A classified list of works follows the biographical information. The synopsis of the composer's life is quite thorough.

B1108. Thomson, Virgil. "Aaron Copland." In American Music Since 1910, 49-58. New York: Holt, Rinehart and Winston, 1971.
    Copland is one of the major American composers examined in this study of twentieth century music. An analysis of his stylistic trends shows the varied forms that American music took. Copland is noted for his associations with other American composers and for his efforts to have their music performed. "He has never turned out bad work, nor worked without an idea, an inspiration."

B1109. _____. "Aaron Copland." Modern Music 9, no.2 (January-February 1932): 67-73; Perspectives of New Music 2, no.2 (1964): 21-22.
    This discussion of the composer's work has little technical analysis. Thomson feels that Copland's ideas are usually based on religious subjects. Copland's musical style is examined and Thomson vividly describes his perception in areas such as harmonies and orchestration.

B1110. _____. "Hollywood's Best." In Music, Right and Left, 120-123. 1951. Reprint. New York, Greenwood Press, 1969.
    This article, originally published in the New York Herald Tribune, April 10, 1949, examines Copland's music for films. The score for The Red Pony is considered to be of high quality and this is rare in the film industry. "Whenever Copland has provided landscape music, action music, or a general atmosphere of drama he has worked impeccably."

B1111. _____. "Two Ballets." In The Art of Judging Music, 161-164. 1948. Reprint. New York: Greenwood Press, 1969.
    This article reviews Appalachian Spring and originally appeared in the New York Herald Tribune May 20, 1945. Martha Graham and her dance company recently presented it at the National Theater. Thomson finds the work to be much better writing than most ballets for nonclassical dancers. "Every aspect of the work is musically interesting, though all of it is not equally intense as expression." The harmonies and simple melodic line evoke a rural feeling which helps express the mood of the story.

B1112. "Three by Copland from CRI." American Record Guide 30 (September 1963): 43.
    The reviewer of Composers Recordings CRI-171 finds this to be an excellent disc. Hilde Somer, piano, Carroll Glenn, violin, and Charles McCracken, cello, have recorded Copland's Piano Sonata, Violin Sonata, and Vitebsk. See also: D224, D326, D369

B1113. "Throw Potatoes—Don't Sit and Take It, Composer Tells Modern Music Victims." New York Times, April 21, 1950, p.25:6.
    Gian Carlo Menotti suggest that audiences rebel against music they do not like. Menotti and Copland were speakers at the Women's City Club's luncheon April 20 at the New Weston Hotel. Copland suggested restraint and felt that one should give unfamiliar music a fair hearing.

B1114. "Thumb Nail Notes on American Composers." Music Teacher 35 (March
       1956): 159.

B1115. Timbrell, Charles. "Baltimore." Opera News 41 (October 1976):
       65-66.
           On June 26 the Hartford Opera performed The Tender Land under
       the direction of Richard Getke. The cast and the Baltimore Sym-
       phony conducted by Saul Lilienstein gave an excellent performance.

B1116. Tippett, Michael. "The American Tradition." American Musical
       Digest 1 (October 1969): 21.
           This article is abridged from the Listener June 5, 1969. It
       is a discussion of James Goodfriend's article on nationalism in
       music in the United States. Tippett feels Charles Ives and
       Copland have exhibited nationalism in some of their compositions.
       Goodfriend's list of works embodying an American sound does not
       include enough jazz in Tippett's opinion.

B1117. Tircuit, Heuwell. "Tokyo; Copland: Most Popular Composer."
       Music Magazine and Musical Courier 164 (April 1962): 41.
           "Copland is the best-known American composer here, outside of
       Gershwin." Copland, among others, is currently touring in
       Japan and he is presenting some of his works in concerts.

B1118. _____. "The Year of the American Composer." San Francisco
       Chronicle, December 25, 1979, p.54:1.
           Tircuit believes that Copland is one of America's greatest
       composers and feels that his works are not presented as much
       as they should be in concerts. He suggests that local orches-
       tras invite Copland to conduct since he has not conducted in
       the San Francisco area since 1966. Tircuit indicates that
       the composer is a better conductor than some of the conductors
       of the past who were considered to be great conductors.

B1119. Tischler, Hans. "Aaron Copland, by Arthur Berger." American
       Musicological Society Journal 7 (Summer 1954): 157-158.
           This book review notes that the biography contains "an ex-
       cellent analysis of the elements of Copland's style as they
       have evolved over the years." Berger gives Copland's music much
       praise which he supports with his analyses. Included is a
       chronological list of works, records, and a bibliography. See
       also: B200

B1120. "Town Hall Club 'Hausmusik.'" New York Times, February 17, 1941,
       p.11:1.
           Copland spoke and performed the piano part of his Vitebsk at
       the Town Hall Club concert February 16. He was the guest of
       honor on this occasion.

B1121. Tracey, Edmund. "Concerts." Musical Times 104 (April 1963):
       265-266.
           Leonard Bernstein conducted the New York Philharmonic in a
       concert at Festival Hall February 13 for the Royal Philharmonic
       Society. Copland's Connotations was presented in Great Britain
       for the first time. "It was a shapely set of free variations,
       generally with tonal implications."

B1122. "Trail Blazer from Brooklyn." Time 56 (November 20, 1950): 50-52.
        This is a synopsis of Copland's career up to his fiftieth
        birthday. His changing stylistic characteristics are noted,
        such as his early interest in jazz. Copland's plans for the
        coming year include teaching in Tel Aviv and consulting in Rome
        at the American Academy.

B1123. "Tribute to Aaron Copland." Pan Pipes of Sigma Alpha Iota 68,
        no.1 (1975): 20.
        Copland was guest conductor in a program of his works with
        the National Symphony Orchestra April 5 at the Kennedy Center.
        Among the recent honors bestowed on the composer was Syracuse
        University's Chancellor's Medal for Distinguished Achievement.
        He also received the Brandeis University Commission Award for
        Notable Achievement and an honorary doctorate from Brooklyn
        College. His publisher, Boosey & Hawkes, and the MacDowell
        Colony celebrated Copland's seventy-fifth birthday with a
        concert and a party.

B1124. "Tribute to Copland." Billboard 92 (December 6, 1980): 12.
        ASCAP established two scholarships of one-thousand dollars
        each in honor of Copland's eightieth birthday. Morton Gould
        presented these at special programs held in the composer's
        honor recently in Washington and New York.

B1125. Trimble, Lester. "Copland Birthday Concerts." Musical America
        80 (December 1960): 84-85.
        On November 14 and 15 at the Juilliard School of Music, two
        concerts were given which were devoted to the works of Copland.
        Criticism of several of his works is included. Trimble found
        The City to be "one of the finest documentaries around."
        William Masselos performed the Piano Sonata, Piano Variations,
        and Piano Fantasy and received favorable reviews.

B1126. _____. "Copland Guest with Philharmonic." Musical America 80
        (December 1960): 37.
        Copland led the New York Philharmonic in two of his works
        on November 13 at Carnegie Hall as part of his sixtieth birthday
        celebration. The Symphonic Ode was "almost violently declamatory
        in sections, and vividly brassy." Trimble found El Salón México
        to be "even more ingratiating and infectious than usual as
        Copland conducted it."

B1127. _____. "Music." Nation 185 (November 16, 1957): 375-376.
        The Piano Fantasy performed by William Masselos recently had
        its world premiere at the Juilliard Concert Hall. This work,
        based on a twelve-tone system, contains a "successful com-
        bination of vigorous logic and free fantasy." It differs from
        his earlier work such as the Piano Variations and the Piano
        Sonata by its "almost neutral stylistic sheath." See also: W93

B1128. _____. "Music." Nation 192 (February 11, 1961): 127.
        Copland was the featured composer at the Composers' Showcase
        Concert at the Museum of Modern Art recently. On the program
        were four of the Twelve Poems of Emily Dickinson sung by Dorothy
        Renzi and a concert version of The Second Hurricane performed

by Students in the High School of Music and Art, New York. Copland participated in the opera by providing the narration between the choral sections of the work. Copland's songs are "highly attractive and display the same cleanliness of line and texture that characterize his instrumental music."

B1129. _____. "Profile at 60." Musical America 80 (November 1960): 13.
A brief history of Copland's musical background and achievements is given in honor of his sixtieth birthday on November 14. Copland states his current views on music. In this interview Copland discusses contemporary music and states that he has a permissive attitude. If a piece interests him, he is not concerned about who wrote it or why. The situation in the 1920's when he was starting his career was quite unlike that faced by composers today. He thinks that there are so many composers now that few are noticed.

B1130. Tuck, Lon. "Another Side of Copland: Opera." Washington Post, August 29, 1979, B, p.11:R.
The Tender Land will be performed over the Public Broadcasting System this evening under Copland's baton. The text by Horace Everett consists of "predictable action and banal verse."

B1131. Turok, Paul. "The Journal Reviews: Books." Music Journal 26 (March 1968): 101.
Copland's The New Music: 1900-1960 is a revised and enlarged edition of an earlier book written twenty-six years ago. In it he comments on some of his earlier views and opinions. Turok feels "Copland has added little to its original strengths but much to its basic weakness—that it has a kind word for everyone." See also: B76

B1132. "Twelve Poems of Emily Dickinson, First Sung by Alice Howland." Music News 42 (August 1950): 15.
The premiere took place at Columbia University with the composer accompanying Alice Howland. See also: W87

B1133. "Twelve Poems of Emily Dickinson, for Voice and Piano." Music and Letters 33 (July 1952): 274.
These songs are based on topics in which Dickinson was interested but the twelve are generally unrelated to one another. "The eager buoyancy of Copland's style, with its wide leaps and bracing diatonic dissonances, is indeed a match for the picturesque and impetuous poetry." Although it has been more than twenty years since the composer has written solo songs, the reviewer feels that these are very successful.

B1134. "Twentieth Century Music: Copland and Fricker." Times (London), April 8, 1952, p.2f.
Copland's Sextet and Peter Fricker's Four Piano Impromptus had their premiere performances in England on April 7. The Society for Twentieth Century Music sponsored the concert at Hampton Town Hall. The Sextet (1937) "is a violently dissonant, metrically intricate work."

B1135. "25 Men and 5 Women to Receive President's Medals of Freedom."
New York Times, July 4, 1964, p.1:7.
President Johnson announced the recipients of the nation's
highest civilian honor, the Presidential Medal of Freedom.
Copland was among those being honored and was listed as "a
leading force in development of the modern American school of
composition."

B1136. "Two Arts Groups Make 24 Awards." New York Times, May 24, 1956,
p.25:1.
The American Academy awarded the Gold Medal for Music to
Copland during its fifteenth annual ceremonies May 23.

B1137. "$250,000 Fellowship Fund Honoring Aaron Copland Set Up for
MacDowell Colony." Music Clubs Magazine 55, no.3 (1976): 22.
Copland's seventy-fifth birthday is being honored by this
endowment. Copland has been a board member and president of
the MacDowell Colony in the past.

B1138. "$250,000 to MacDowell to Mark Copland's Day." New York Times,
November 13, 1975, p.51:1.
The Norlin Foundation has presented this grant to the MacDowell
Colony to commemorate Copland's seventy-fifth birthday on Novem-
ber 14. Copland has been both a board member and a president of
the MacDowell Colony during the past fifty years. The grant
was presented at a concert in Copland's honor at Alice Tully
Hall on November 12.

B1139. "Two Music Groups Announce Merger." New York Times, December 2,
1954, p.38:1.
Copland is composer-chairman of the merged League of Composers
and the International Society for Contemporary Music, United
States Section. Details of the organization's new policies are
related.

B1140. "2 U.S. Composers Will Visit Soviet." New York Times, March 8,
1960, p.38:4.
Lukas Foss and Copland will spend a month in the Soviet Union
in a cultural program under the auspices of the U.S. State
Department. The two will perform and conduct their own works
in concerts. Copland will also conduct in the Far East and in
London before returning the the United States.

B1141. "U.S. Awards to British Writers." Times (London), May 24, 1956,
p.3a.
A gold medal was presented to Copland by the American Academy
of Arts and Letters and the National Institue of Arts and Letters.

B1142. "U.S. Composers in a Bright Era." Life 40 (May 21, 1956): 145.
Copland is cited as being a major influence in creating
increased opportunities for American composers. Some composers
have followed the Copland style which is described as having a
"percussive craggy harshness."

B1143. "U.S. Musicians in Soviet." New York Times, March 17, 1960, p.
25:4.

Lukas Foss and Copland are currently on a four-week tour of
Russia during which they will meet with Russian composers as
well as perform and conduct some of their own works in concerts.
It was reported that Copland "was pleased that meetings between
Soviet and American composers had become a regular routine."

B1144. "U.S. Seen Snubbing 2 Russian Singers." New York Times, October
20, 1946, II, p.7:1.
Copland was one of four well-known musicians who sent pro-
tests to the United States Department of Justice. Visiting
Ukrainian musicians were being required to register as foreign
agents. The Americans protested that these individuals were
invited to the U.S. for a cultural exchange and not as government agents.

B1145. "U.S. Subsidizing of Arts Is Urged." New York Times, May 29,
1952, p.24:1.
The meeting of the American Academy and the National Institute of Arts and Letters featured Copland as a speaker May 28.
He urged the government to support the arts more. He feels
that "'the obvious dangers of bureaucratic control' are worth
risking for Government sponsorship of the arts."

B1146. Ulanov, Barry. "Music." In The Two Worlds of American Art, the
Private and the Popular, 16-35. New York: Macmillan, 1965.
Copland's place as a favored American composer is examined in
relation to his contemporaries.

B1147. Unger, Arthur. "The American Genius of Aaron Copland." Christian
Science Monitor, March 30, 1981, p.17:1.
The Public Broadcasting System is attempting to bring more
musical culture to its television viewers. A live performance
of Copland as a conductor will be aired April 1 as part of the
"Kennedy Center Tonight" series. There will be background
information provided to accompany the performance.

B1148. _____. "JFK Center Tribute: It Was Better on TV." Christian
Science Monitor, December 28, 1979, p.15:1.
The "Kennedy Center Honors: a Celebration of the Performing
Arts" took place December 2 but will be broadcast on December
29 on PBS television. Five distinguished Americans were at this
second annual event and Copland was among the five. Unger
notes that the television program shows details not seen at
the live performance.

B1149. Valencia M., Ernesto. "Aaron Copland, el Hombre el Musico, la
Leyenda." Heterofonia 4, no.24 (1972): 9-11.
This is an interview with Copland during one of his visits
to Mexico. His Salón México was composed four years after he
visited Mexico for the first time. He wrote this piece based
on a popular dance hall there. Copland expressed some of his
views on contemporary composers. He noted that some followed
the styles of prominent composers such as Schoenberg and Cage,
but he preferred traditional composition techniques. Copland
encouraged all composers to follow their own feelings and not
to be influenced by others.

B1150. Varga, Bálint András. "Ketten Aaron Copland-Rŏl." *Muzsika* 13
(January 1970): 34-36.
This biographical sketch of Copland includes information on
his principal works.

B1151. "Venture in Opera." *Newsweek* 43 (April 12, 1954): 63.
The first performance of Copland's second opera, *The Tender
Land*, took place last week and was performed by the New York
City Opera Company. Horace Everett's libretto "is weak and
implausible." Richard Rodgers and Oscar Hammerstein II com-
missioned this work through the auspices of the League of
Composers. See also: W90

B1152. "Vienna, Virginia." *Woodwind World--Brass and Percussion* 17, no.
5 (1978): 25.
A Gold Baton award by the American Symphony Orchestra League
has been given to Copland for his contributions to the arts.

B1153. Vincent, John. "Music Mailbag: Where It Is." *New York Times*,
August 30, 1970, II, p.30:4.
In this letter to the editor Vincent of the UCLA Department
of Music replies to Copland's article, "Is the University Too
Much with Us." Vincent feels that most important composers of
Copland's generation were not as isolated as Copland contends
they were, and most were associated with an institution.
Economically, it is very difficult not to be associated with
an institution while being a composer. See also: B44

B1154. "Visit to Peekskill." *Newsweek* 56 (November 14, 1960): 98.
Copland is interviewed at his new residence in Peekskill
overlooking the Hudson River. His sixtieth birthday is being
celebrated by many honors. Columbia Records is releasing
three anniversary albums and Leonard Bernstein and Copland will
prepare a program for television. Copland plans to stay home
and work on new compositions after these birthday celebrations
are over.

B1155. "Vom Richtigen Anhören der Musik." *Musikhandel* 18, no.6 (1967):
306; *Orchester* 16 (March 1968): 141.
What to Listen For in Music is reviewed. See also: B108

B1156. Von Rhein, John. "Copland: Nearing 80, Still as Fresh as His
Music." *Chicago Tribune*, November 9, 1980, 6, p.7:1p.
This interview gives details of Copland's musical career
since the 1920's. Although he has not recently been active
in producing new compositions, he does not say that he no
longer composes. He has been quite active as a conductor
during the past several decades and appears to enjoy this role
in music very much.

B1157. _____. "Lineup for Listening." *Chicago Tribune*, December 16,
1979, 6, p.26:2r.
Columbia's two-disk set of Copland's complete piano music
performed by Leo Smit is almost ready to be issued [as M2
3590]. Smit had performed these works at Harvard earlier.

"Smit plays everything with brilliance, panache, and a sharp-edged sense of rhythm." See also: D73, D110, D131, D141, D168, D182, D210, D217, D223, D234, D354

B1158. Voss, Ruth Hemmert. "Industrialist Serves Music: Cincinnati's Mr. Corbett." Music Journal 22 (March 1964): 78.
J. Ralph Corbett founded the Corbett Music Lectures at the University of Cincinnati College-Conservatory of Music. He has gathered well-known musicians to speak and Copland was one of the recent lecturers. Copland spoke on "New Trends in Contemporary Music" on February 3.

B1159. "Wall-to-Wall Program to Honor Copland." New York Times, November 18, 1980, II, p.8:2.
A thirteen-hour marathon program entitled "Wall-to-Wall Copland/America" will be presented by Symphony Space on November 23.

B1160. Walsh, Stephen. "Aaron Copland: Festival Hall." Times (London), November 12, 1970, p.13f.
Copland will reach his seventieth birthday on November 14, but he still shows great vigor in his performances. On November 11 he conducted the last in a series of concerts with the London Symphony Orchestra. The audience enjoyed his Appalachian Spring the most and his Third Symphony and Piano Concerto were not as well received.

B1161. _____. "Book Reviews." Tempo 88 (Spring 1969): 63.
Copland's The New Music is a revised edition which adds updated material to his personal views on music. Copland "writes with the profound insight of one whose own creative experience is part of the subject he seeks to explain." See also: B76

B1162. _____. "NPO/Copland: Albert Hall." Times (London), May 31, 1972, p.12d.
As guest conductor May 30 at Albert Hall, Copland led the New Philharmonia Orchestra in a concert of American works. Walsh considers Copland's music to be rather simple and conservative and this made for a rather monotonous evening.

B1163. Ward, Robert. "Aaron Copland: Four Dance Episodes from Rodeo." Music Library Association Notes 2d ser., 4, no.2 (March 1947): 191.
Ward reviews Copland's suite which was extracted from his ballet Rodeo. The suite is not as effective as the suite taken from his ballet Billy the Kid in Ward's opinion. This new score was selected as Boosey & Hawkes' February "Score of the Month."

B1164. Waters, Edward N. "Harvest of the Year; Selected Acquisitions of the Music Division." Quarterly Journal of the Library of Congress 24, no.1 (January 1967): 56.
Donors recently have contributed a large number of letters and manuscripts to the Library of Congress Archives. Among them were two manuscripts which Copland presented: Fanfare for

the Common Man and Vitebsk. The first work, completed in 1942,
includes a preliminary outline for piano. The second larger
work, composed in 1929, is the rough pencil score.

B1165. _____. "Variations on a Theme; Recent Acquisitions of the Music
Division." Quarterly Journal of the Library of Congress 27,
no.1 (1970): 58.
The concert Listed are donations of letters and manuscripts of important
musicians to the Library of Congress. Copland has recently
donated four more manuscripts: Connotations, Emblems, Music
for Radio, and Something Wild.

B1166. Watt, Douglas. "Musical Events: Something for Everyone." New
Yorker 26 (December 9, 1950): 140-141.
The concert premiere of Copland's Clarinet Concerto was
performed recently by Eugene Ormandy conducting the Philadelphia
Orchestra. Ralph McLane was soloist. This composition actually
had its first performance over a radio program earlier with
soloist Benny Goodman for whom the work was written. Watt was
not impressed with the work and found it empty and devoid of
interest. See also: W79

B1167. Weinberg, Henry. "Piano Music: Aaron Copland: Piano Fantasy,
1954-57." Music Library Association Notes 15 (September 1958):
660.
The Piano Fantasy is a half-hour work not based on traditional
patterns of form. Detailed notations, including the composer's
remarks, are included in the score.

B1168. Werlé, Frederick. "General Reviews." Musical Courier 153 (June
1956): 52.
Richard Rodgers and Oscar Hammerstein II commissioned Copland
to write the opera, The Tender Land, for the League of Composers'
thirtieth anniversary. Its premiere was April 1, 1954 at the
New York City Center of Music and Dance. See also: W90

B1169. _____. "Publishers' Mart: Books." Musical Courier 163 (February 1961): 36.
Werle reviews Copland on Music which is written "in a simple,
direct and warm-hearted style." Copland examines other notable
musicians and analyzes American contemporary music. See also:
B24

B1170. "What to Listen For in Music, by Aaron Copland." Monthly Musical
Record 88 (July-August 1958): 149.
The reviewer finds Copland's book to be unsatisfactory for
"he tends to be eloquent about little, digressing often." The
reviewer also feels that some of Copland's chapters are in-
correctly labeled because of some confusion between design and
structure. See also: B108

B1171. "What to Listen For in Music, by Aaron Copland." Music Teacher
and Piano Student 36 (May 1957): 243.
See also: B108

B1172. White, Chappell. "Atlanta." American Choral Review 10, no.3
(1968): 135.

Copland revised his <u>Canticle of Freedom</u> for the October 19, 1967 performance by the Atlanta Symphony with Robert Shaw as conductor. White found the work to be pleasing, but he feels that "only at the final climax does the composer build to a peroration that involves the listener emotionally."

B1173. Whitten, Sammie Gayle. "A Stylistic Comparison of Aaron Copland's Passacaglia, Piano Variations, and Four Piano Blues." Ph.D. diss., North Texas State University, 1981.

Whitten's study of these three piano pieces shows some marked differences in influence and stylistic characteristics from the French neo-classic school to jazz to twelve-tone idioms. Copland retains his characteristic short thematic material throughout all these works.

B1174. Whitwell, David. "The Enigma of Copland's <u>Emblems</u>." <u>Journal of Band Research</u> 7, no.2 (Spring 1971): 5-9.

This is an analysis of Copland's <u>Emblems</u> (1964) for symphonic band. A discussion of the problems encountered in interpreting and performing this work is included.

B1175. "Wicked Music." <u>New Republic</u> 128 (January 26, 1953): 7.

Representative Fred E. Busbey, a Republican from Illinois, had Copland's composition, <u>Lincoln Portrait</u>, removed from the inaugural concert "on the grounds that Copland had identified himself with Communist-front organizations."

B1176. Wiedrich, Bob. "Aaron Copland's Musical Legacy." <u>Chicago Tribune</u>, November 18, 1980, 5, p.4:1c.

Copland celebrated his eightieth birthday on November 14 and he is remembered in this article commemorating his works. Wiedrich reflects about Copland's most popular and familiar works such as <u>Appalachian Spring</u> and <u>Billy the Kid</u>. His artistry has achieved "an enduring place in a society of so many diverse cultures."

B1177. Wier, Albert Ernest. "Copland, Aaron." In <u>The Macmillan Encyclopedia of Music and Musicians</u>, 376. New York: Macmillan Company, 1938.

This is a biographical sketch of the highlights of Copland's musical background and works up to the age of thirty-eight. He was well established as a notable American contemporary composer by 1938.

B1178. "William Masselos and the Copland Piano Fantasy." <u>American Record Guide</u> 27 (December 1960): 315.

This is a review of Columbia ML 5568 and MS 6168 which contains Copland's Piano Fantasy and Piano Variations performed by Masselos. "Copland uses dodecaphonic techniques generously but inconsistently." Also reviewed is Frank Glazer's recording of the Piano Variations on Concert-Disc. See also: D218, D235, D237

B1179. Willinger, Edward. "Copland Ballet Music on LP." <u>Ballet News</u> 2 (November 1960): 42.

A listing of various records which have been made of Copland's ballets is printed. Background information is related about

the works as well as performers and conductors who were involved
in the recordings.

B1180. Wilson, Gladys M. "Books." Pan Pipes of Sigma Alpha Iota 48
(March 1956): 11-12.
Wilson reviews Julia Smith's Aaron Copland, His Work and
Contribution to American Music. This biography is adapted
from her Ph.D. dissertation. The book is chronologically
written and Copland's stylistic changes are noted throughout
his career. "The book is very comprehensive." See also: B1042

B1181. Wimbush, Roger. "Here and There." Gramophone 46 (December 1968):
823.
Copland regularly visits in London and has returned to conduct the London Symphony Orchestra in Rodeo and Orchestral
Variations. Some of Copland's development as a composer is
recorded. Copland reveals that he waits for inspiration before
composing and that he does all his work at the piano.

B1182. Winer, Linda. "Uncommon Man at Grant Park." Chicago Tribune,
July 3, 1972, 2, p.6:1.
Copland conducted the Grant Park Symphony Orchestra in a
concert during the previous weekend. Although he is almost
seventy-two years old, his enthusiasm abounds. "While always
more composer than conductor, he lets pitches slip a bit these
days." The concert agenda was designed for easy listening so
the performance did not have the preciseness that many have.

B1183. Wolffers, Jules. "Boston." Musical Courier 153 (March 1, 1956):
25.
The premiere performance of the Symphonic Ode which was revised for the Boston Symphony Orhcestra's seventy-fifth
anniversary has resulted in some criticism. The Symphonic Ode
was originally commissioned twenty-five years ago for the Boston
Symphony's fiftieth anniversary. "To receive one commission
and then to dish up the same work for another commission with
the thin excuse that this is, after all, a first performance of
a somewhat revised version, is totally inexcusable." See also:
W38

B1184. "Works by Copland Stolen." New York Times, May 30, 1941, p.17:3.
Manuscripts of completed and partially completed works and
an extensive collection of themes were stolen from his car
May 28. He was packing for his trip to Lenox, Massachusetts
to teach composition at Tanglewood.

B1185. "World of Music." Etude 74 (October 1956): 5.
Copland was honored recently by three organizations. Princeton University gave him an honorary doctorate of music, the
National Institute of Arts and Letters gave him the Gold Medal
for Music, and the National Academy of St. Cecilia of Rome
made him an honorary member.

B1186. Wyatt, Lucius Reynolds. "The Mid-Twentieth-Century Orchestral
Variation, 1953-1963: an Analysis and Comparison of Selected
Works by Major Composers." Ph.D. diss., University of Rochester,
1974.

Copland's Orchestral Variations (1957) is included in this study of styles and form.

B1187. Yarustovsky, Boris. "Journey to America." Journal of Research in Music Education 10, no.2 (1962): 124.
Yarustovsky, a musicologist, reports on the cultural exchange between the United States and the Soviet Union. Copland was one of the American who made the trip. The Tender Land was performed and reported to be of high quality. It is "contemporary in character and genuinely national."

B1188. Young, Douglas. "Copland's Dickinson Songs." Tempo 103 (1972): 33-37.
Young finds Copland's Twelve Poems of Emily Dickinson for solo voice and piano to be similar in style to early works of Charles Ives. A technical analysis of various phrases illustrate the techniques used in setting the music to Dickinson's words. His song cycle "emphasizes the regular pulse of the poetic thought and helps give the musical line directness and concentration." Young believes that this is excellent music.

B1189. _____. "The Piano Music." Tempo 95 (Winter 1970-1971): 15-22.
Young has done a detailed analysis of Copland's three major piano works: Piano Variations, Piano Sonata, and Piano Fantasy. The first two show his "ability to build his music from very simple basic elements." The third work involves the use of a ten-note row as its basis.

B1190. Young, Percy Marshall. "Aaron Copland." In Biographical Dictionary of Composers, 89-90. New York: Crowell, 1954.
This is a short biography along with a suggestion to listen to the composer's Passacaglia and The Cat and the Mouse. Copland's books are listed in the bibliography.

B1191. _____. Music Makers of Today, 149-160. New York: Roy, 1958.
A section of this book for young people gives biographical information on Copland.

B1192. Zoff, Otto. "Copland-Uraufführung in New York." Melos 21 (July-August 1954): 232-233.
This is a review of the premiere performance of Copland's opera The Tender Land in New York recently. The work was composed for the League of Composers' thirtieth anniversary. Richard Rodgers and Oscar Hammerstein II commissioned it. See also: W90

Appendix I:

ALPHABETICAL LIST
OF COMPOSITIONS

Numbers following each title, e.g. W40, refer to the "Works and
Performances" section of this volume.

Agachadas, Las, W65
Appalachian Spring, W73
As It Fell upon a Day, W24
Billy the Kid, W53
Canticle of Freedom, W91
Capriccio, W2
Cat and the Mouse, The, W14
Ceremonial Fanfare, W104
City, The, W56
Concerto for Clarinet and String Orchestra, W79
Concerto for Piano and Orchestra, W31
Connotations, W98
Cortège Macabre, W25
Cummington Story, The, W75
Dance Panels, W95
Dance Symphony, W27
Danse Characteristique, W5
Danzón Cubano, W66
Dirge in Woods, W89
Down a Country Lane, W99
Duo for Flute and Piano, W107
Elegies, W42
Emblems, W100
Episode, W63
Fanfare for the Common Man, W67
Fantasia Mexicana, W47
First Symphony, W35
Five Kings, The, W57
Four Motets, W18

Four Piano Blues, W80
Fragment, for Trio, W13
From Sorcery to Science, W58
Grohg, W28
Happy Anniversary, W105
Hear Ye! Hear Ye! W44
Heiress, The, W83
In Evening Air, W102
In the Beginning, W78
Inaugural Fanfare, W106
Inscape, W103
John Henry, W61
Jubilee Variation, W76
Lament, W10
Larghetto Pomposo, Marcatissimo, W108
Lark, W54
Letter from Home, W74
Lincoln Portrait, W68
Melancholy, W3
Midsummer Nocturne, W81
Miracle at Verdun, W41
Moment Musicale, W4
Music for a Great City, W101
Music for Movies, W69
Music for Radio, W50
Music for the Theatre, W29
Music I Heard, W15
Night, W6
Night Thoughts, W111
Nonet, W96
North Star, W71
Notebook with Original Songs, W7
Of Mice and Men, W59
Old American Songs Set I, W85
Old American Songs Set II, W88
Old Poem, W16
Orchestral Variations, W92
Our Town, W62
Outdoor Overture, An, W55
Passacaglia, W23
Pastorale, W19
Piano Fantasy, W93
Piano Sonata, W64
Piano Variations, W40
Poem, W8
Preamble for a Solemn Occasion, W84
Prelude for Violin and Piano, W11
Prelude (Second) for violin and Piano, W20
Quartet for Piano and Strings, W86
Quiet City, W60
Red Pony, The, W82
Rodeo, W70
Salón México, El, W48
Second Hurricane, The, W51
Sentimental Melody, W32

Sextet, W52
Short Symphony (No.2), W43
Simone, W12
Something Wild, W97
Sonata for Piano, G Major, W21
Sonata for Violin and Piano, W72
Song (E. E. Cummings), W34
Statements, W45
String Quartet (unfinished), W1
Symphonic Ode, W38
Symphony for Organ and Orchestra, W26
Tender Land, The, W90
Third Symphony, W77
Three Latin American Sketches, W109
Three Moods for Piano Solo, W22
Three Sonnets for Piano, W17
Threnody I: Igor Stravinsky in Memoriam, W110
Threnody II: Beatrice Cunningham in Memoriam, W112
Twelve Poems of Emily Dickinson, W87
Two Children's Pieces, W49
Two Compositions for Chorus of Women's Voices, W30
Two Pieces for String Quartet, W36
Two Pieces for Violin and Piano, W33
Vitebsk, W39
Vocalise, W37
Waltz Caprice, W9
What Do We Plant? W46
World of Nick Adams, The, W94

CLASSIFIED LIST
OF COMPOSITIONS

Numbers following each title, e.g. W40, refer to the "Works and Performances" section of this volume.

OPERAS
Second Hurricane, The, W51
Tender Land, The, W90

BALLET MUSIC
Appalachian Spring, W73
Billy the Kid, W53
Dance Panels, W95
Grohg, W28
Hear Ye! Hear Ye! W44
Rodeo, W70

FILM MUSIC
City, The, W56
Cummington Story, The, W75
Heiress, The, W83
North Star, W71
Of Mice and Men, W59
Our Town, W62
Red Pony, The, W82
Something Wild, W97

INCIDENTAL MUSIC FOR STAGE AND TELEVISION
Five Kings, The, W57
From Sorcery to Science, W58
Miracle at Verdun, W41
Quiet City, W60
World of Nick Adams, The, W94

ORCHESTRAL WORKS
Appalachian Spring: Suite, W73
Billy the Kid: Suite, W53
Concerto for Piano and Orchestra, W31
Connotations, W98
Cortège Macabre, W25
Dance Symphony, W27
Danse Characteristique, W5
Danzón Cubano, W66
Down a Country Lane, W99
Fanfare for the Common Man, W67
Fantasia Mexicana, W47
First Symphony, W35
Happy Anniversary, W105
Inscape, W103
John Henry, W61
Jubilee Variation, W76
Letter from Home, W73
Lincoln Portrait, W68
Music for a Great City, W101
Music for Movies, W69
Music for Radio, W50
Music for the Theatre, W29
Orchestral Variations, W92
Our Town, W62
Outdoor Overture, An, W55
Preamble for a Solemn Occasion, W84
Quiet City, W60
Red Pony, The: Suite, W82
Rodeo: Four Dance Episodes, W70
Salón México, El, W48
Short Symphony (No.2), W43
Statements, W45
Symphonic Ode, W38
Symphony for Organ and Orchestra, W26
Tender Land, The: Suite, W90
Third Symphony, W77

STRING ORCHESTRA MUSIC
Concerto for Clarinet and String Orchestra, W79
Rodeo: Hoe-Down, W70
Two Pieces for String Quartet, W36

CHAMBER MUSIC
As It Fell upon a Day, W24
Billy the Kid, W53
Duo for Flute and Piano, W107
Elegies, W42
Fragment, for Trio, W13
Lament, W10
Nonet, W96
Poem, W8
Quartet for Piano and Strings, W86
Sextet, W52
String Quartet (unfinished), W1

Three Latin American Sketches, W109
Threnody I: Igor Stravinsky in Memoriam, W110
Threnody II: Beatrice Cunningham in Memoriam, W112
Two Pieces for String Quartet, W36
Vitebsk, W39

VIOLIN AND PIANO MUSIC
Billy the Kid, W53
Capriccio, W2
Duo for Flute and Piano, W107
Prelude for Violin and Piano, W11
Prelude (Second) for Violin and Piano, W20
Rodeo: Hoe-Down, W70
Sonata for Violin and Piano, W72
Two Pieces for Violin and Piano, W33

KEYBOARD MUSIC (for one piano, two hands, unless otherwise noted)
Billy the Kid (one and two pianos), W53
Cat and the Mouse, The, W14
Concerto for Piano and Orchestra (two pianos), W31
Cortège Macabre (two pianos), W25
Dance Panels, W95
Dance Symphony (two pianos), W27
Danse Characteristique (one piano, four hands), W5
Danzón Cubano (one and two pianos), W66
Down a Country Lane, W99
Episode (organ), W63
Fantasia Mexicana, W47
Four Piano Blues, W80
In Evening Air, W102
Midsummer Nocturne, W81
Moment Musicale, W4
Night Thoughts, W111
Our Town, W62
Passacaglia, W23
Piano Fantasy, W93
Piano Sonata, W64
Piano Variations, W40
Preamble for a Solemn Occasion (organ), W84
Rodeo: Four Dance Episodes (one and two pianos), W70
Salón México, El (one and two pianos), W48
Sentimental Melody, W32
Sonata for Piano, G Major, W21
Symphony for Organ and Orchestra (organ), W26
Three Moods for Piano Solo, W22
Three Sonnets for Piano, W17
Two Children's Pieces, W49
Waltz Caprice, W9

SONGS
As It Fell upon a Day, W24
Dirge in Woods, W89
Melancholy, W3
Music I Heard, W15
Night, W6
Notebook with Original Songs, W7

Old American Songs Set I, W85
Old American Songs Set II, W88
Old Poem, W16
Pastorale, W19
Simone, W12
Song (E. E. Cummings), W34
Tender Land, The, W90
Twelve Poems of Emily Dickinson, W87
Vocalise, W37

CHORAL MUSIC
Agachadas, Las, W65
Canticle of Freedom, W91
Four Motets, W18
In the Beginning, W78
Lark, W54
North Star: Two Choruses, W71
Old American Songs Set I, W85
Old American Songs Set II, W88
Tender, Land, The, W90
Two Compositions for Chorus of Women's Voices, W30
What Do We Plant? W46

BAND MUSIC
Appalachian Spring: Variations on a Shaker Melody, W73
Billy the Kid, W53
Ceremonial Fanfare (brass ensemble), W104
Emblems, W100
Inaugural Fanfare, W106
Lincoln Portrait, W68
Outdoor Overture, An, W55
Preamble for a Solemn Occasion, W84
Salón México, El, W48

INDEX

ABC SEE American Broadcasting
Company.
ASCAP B19, B26, B138, B176, B182,
B309–310, B610, B658, B1124
Aaron Copland p.7, B127–B128, B183,
B200, B204, B240, B299, B485,
B758, B794, B819–B820, B973,
B1006, B1061, B1119
Aaron Copland: a Bibliography of
His Works in Cornell University
Libraries B392
Aaron Copland, a Complete Catalogue
of His Works p.7, B122, B339
Aaron Copland, His Life B885
Aaron Copland, His Life and Times
p.7, B132–B133, B170, B429
Aaron Copland, His Work and Contri-
bution to American Music p.7,
B183, B281, B514, B537, B751,
B930, B1012, B1042, B1044, B1087,
B1180
Aaron Copland School of Music,
Queens College SEE Queens College,
Flushing, New York. Aaron Copland
School of Music.
Aaron's Canon B926
Abel, David W. B151
Abravanel, Maurice D54, D67, D70–
D71, D166, D202, D209, D263, D279,
D291–D292, D304, D314, D316
Academy Award SEE Academy of Motion
Picture Arts and Sciences.
Academy of Motion Picture Arts and
Sciences p.6–7, W83, B312, B652
Academy of Music B892

Academy of St. Cecilia SEE National
Academy of St. Cecilia, Rome.
Academy of St. Martin-in-the-
Fields D254
Acadian Songs and Dances D266
Adagio D365
Adagio and Allegro D6
Adagio for String Orchestra, Op.
11, B Minor D257
Adam, Claus D367
Adams, Nick SEE The World of Nick
Adams.
Adams, Stanley B138
Adams, Val B152
Adams, William W68
Addison, Adele W89, D145, D352,
B808
Adeste Fidelis in an Organ Prelude
D117
Adler, Clarence p.3, B294
After Antwerp SEE Notebook with
Original Songs.
Afternoon of a Faun D300
Las Agachadas W65, D1, B153, B890
Agee, James B470, B1096
Aitken, Webster W15, D214, D216,
D228, D233, D243, D248, B203,
B795
Al Goodman Orchestra D309
Albee, Edward B276
Albert Hall, London B144, B181,
B453, B860, B1031, B1162
Albert Museum SEE Victoria and
Albert Museum.
Albinoni, Tomasco Giovanni B1077

Aldrich, T. B. W7
Alexander, M. B154
Alice Tully Hall SEE Lincoln Center
    for the Performing Arts, New York.
All the Piano Music D74, D111, D134,
    D142, D184, D213, D220, D227,
    D240, D318
Allegro Ball B652
Allen, David B697
Amahl and the Night Visitors D208
Ambassador Auditorium, Los Angeles
    B218
American Academy of Arts and Let-
    ters p.7, B28, B130, B427, B506,
    B563, B704, B934, B1136, B1141,
    B1145
American Academy, Rome B1122
An American Anthology; [Songs &
    Piano Music] D144, D185, D333
American Ballads D242
American Broadcasting Company W74
The American Composer Speaks: a
    Historical Anthology, 1770-1965
    B282
American Composers B902
American Composers: a Biographical
    Dictionary B475
American Composers Alliance p.4,
    B92, B350, B562
American Composers of Our Time B761
American Composers on American
    Music; a Symposium B12, B274
An American in Paris D19-D20, D33,
    D55, D60, D293
American Lyric Theatre B502
American Music for Flute & Piano
    D114
American Music Since 1910 B1108
American Organ Music from Southwark
    Cathedral D117
American Recording Society Orches-
    tra D3, D174
American Society of Composers, Au-
    thors, and Publishers SEE ASCAP.
American-Soviet Music Society B811
American String Quartets, Volume
    II: 1900-1950 D359
American Symphony Orchestra B385,
    B409, B435, B1072
American Symphony Orchestra League
    p.7, B335, B435, B535, B1152
An American Triplych D146
Americana D188
Americana for Solo Winds and String
    Orchestra D259

America's Music, from the Pilgrims
    to the Present B280, B283
Ampico Recording Company W32
Ancient Desert Drone D255
And the Mountains Rising Nowhere
    D116
Anderson, Dale B162
Anderson, Owen B163
Anderson, Ruth B164
Anderson, William B165
Anniversaries D231-D232
Anonymous Suite in D for Trumpet
    and Orchestra D256
Ansermet, Ernest W35
Antheil, George B38, B1037
Antonini, Alfredo W94
Appalachian Spring p.5-7, W73, D2-
    D39, B112, B143, B166-B167,
    B189, B199, B261, B263, B280,
    B283-B285, B306, B310, B332,
    B352, B403, B416, B452, B518,
    B520, B562, B576-B577, B582,
    B629, B690, B694, B705, B757,
    B765, B779, B792, B866, B915-
    B916, B941, B983, B1015, B1030,
    B1032, B1041, B1048, B1111,
    B1176
Aprahamian, Felix B169
Archibald, Bruce B170
Ardoin, John B171
Arensky, Antonii Stepanovich D107,
    B1077
Armando Ghitalia, Trumpet [Vol.2]
    D256
Armenian, Raffi D4
Arlen, Walter B172-B173
Arrow Music Press p.4, B461
Arroyo, Martina B229
The Art of Judging Music B111
As It Fell upon a Day p.3, W24,
    D40, B539, B932, B1041
Ashwell, Keith B177
Aspen School of Music B176, B631
At the River SEE Old American
    Songs, Set II.
Atlanta Symphony Orchestra D34,
    D125, D287, B1172
Au Leukon D331
Austin, William W. B179
Avant de Quitter Ces Lieux D191
Avery Fisher Hall B943

BBC 262, B279
BBC Symphony Orchestra B169, B181

BMI SEE Broadcasting Music Indus-
try.
Babb, Warren B183
Babin, Victor D107
Bach, Johann Sebastian D143, B57,
B184
Bachianas Brasileiras No.5 D101
Backhaus, Wilhelm B700
Bakeless, Katherine Little B185
Baker, Carroll B329
Baker, Doy B186
Ballad, Woodwinds and Horn D40
Ballade que Feit Villon à la Re-
queste de Sa Mere pour Prier
Nostre-Dame D331
The Ballet Box; Favorite American
Ballets D25, D284
Ballet Caravan W53, B502
Ballet for Martha SEE Appalachian
Spring.
Ballet in Seven Movements SEE Dance
Panels.
Ballet in Seven Sections SEE Dance
Panels.
Ballet Russe de Monte Carlo W70,
B773
Ballet Theatre Orchestra D42, D269,
B483
Baltimore Symphony B1115
Balzo, Hugo W80
Le Bananier D237
Band of the Irish Guards D205
Banff B177
Barber, Samuel D3, D11, D86, D117,
D135, D146, D160, D178, D204,
D254, D257, D332, B4, B309-B310,
B412, B491, B568, B768, B887,
B1055
Il Barbiere di Siviglia D191
Barbour, John W91
Barcarolles D226
Barley Wagons SEE Music for Movies;
SEE Of Mice and Men.
Barlow, Howard W50, W62
Barlow, Wayne D259
Barnard, Eunice B188
Barnefield, Richard W24
Barnes, Clive B189
Barnes, Patricia B190
Bartholody, Felix Mendelssohn SEE
Mendelssohn-Bartholdy, Felix.
Bartók, Béla D221, D331, B31, B616,
B640
Barzin, Leon B294
Basie, Count (William James) B822

Bath, John D2
Baton Award SEE Gold Baton Award.
Batuque D101
Bauer, Marion p.4, B192, B474
Baumgarten, P. K. B193
Bavarian State Opera W95, B720
Bazelon, I. A. B194
Be Still D149
Beach, Amy Marcy Cheney D40
Beale, Jane Gutherie B195
Beame, Abraham D. B196
Beardslee, Bethany D332
Beaux Arts Trio B614
Beck, Martin, Theatre SEE Martin
Beck Theatre, New York.
Beethoven, Ludwig van D90, D143,
D373, B1077
Beethoven Hall, Bonn, Germany B197
Behrens, E. B198
Belt, Byron B199
Benjamin, Arthur D107
Bennett, Robert Russell D40
Berezowsky, Nicolai, Mrs. B268
Berfield, David D365
Berg, Alban D331, B110
Berger, Arthur Victor p.7, B49,
B127-B128, B183, B200-B212,
B240, B299, B485, B758, B794,
B819-B820, B973, B1006, B1061,
B1119
Berger, Clarence B459
Berger, Melvin B213
Berges, Ruth B214
Bergsma, William D242
Berkowitz, Freda Pastor B215
Berkshire Music Center at Tangle-
wood, Lenox, Massachusetts p.5,
B101, B113, B145, B176, B216,
B252, B375, B433, B525, B581-
B582, B615, B631, B695, B711,
B918, B938, B942, B977, B993,
B998-B999, B1052, B1082, B1085-
B1086, B1089, B1184
Berkshire Music Festival SEE Berk-
shire Music Center at Tanglewood,
Lenox, Massachusetts,
Berlin Arts Festival B382
Berlin Philharmonic Orchestra B395
Berlin Symphony Orchestra W35
Berlioz, Hector B18, B83, B217
Bernheimer, Martin B218-B219
Bernstein, Leonard W48, W62, W66,
W84, W98, W103, D5, D10-D11,
D13-D14, D19-D20, D25, D41, D46,
D55, D59-D60, D63, D80, D83,

D90–D91, D101–D102, D150, D175–
D177, D229, D231–D232, D268,
D273–D274, D284, D294, D297–
D301, D317, D336, D339, D345,
D347, B4, B77, B157, B160, B171,
B219–B225, B248, B275, B327–
B328, B352, B394, B404, B424,
B456, B462, B464, B483, B501,
B521, B74–B575, B586–B587, B592–
B593, B598–B599, B621, B623,
B625, B631–B632, B689, B719,
B735, B753, B772, B792, B828,
B845, B875, B926, B948, B974,
B980, B991, B996, B1000, B1003,
B1034, B1059, B1121, B1154
Bernstein Conducts for Young Peo-
ple SEE Leonard Bernstein Con-
ducts for Young People.
The Bernstein Years B225
Bessom, Malcolm E. B226
Biancolli, Louis B227
Bible W18, W78, B641, B922
Bicentennial Celebration B177,
B218, B625, B637, B1019
Bielawa, Herbert D115
Biggs, E. Power B290
Billy the Kid p.5, p.7, W53, D41–
D71, B15, B192, B228, B264, B283,
B318, B403, B455, B483, B489,
B502, B559, B561–B562, B573, B763,
B769, B779, B812, B866, B868,
B872, B953, B960, B1015, B1029,
B1041, B1163, B1176
Billy's Death SEE Billy the Kid.
Bing Theater SEE Los Angeles County
Museum of Art. Bing Theater.
Biographical Dictionary of Compos-
ers B1190
Bird, David B229
Blahove, Marcos B1056
Blake, A. B231
Blanks, F. R. B232
Blashfield Institute B28
Blindenklage D331
Blinkerd, Gordon W. D330
Bliss, Arthur D331, B233–B234
Bliss, Robert Woods, Mr. and Mrs.
W96, B398, B1011
Blitzstein, Marc B41, B55, B235,
B582
Bloch, Ernest D84, D135, D196,
D370, B334
Blom, Eric B565
Blood, Frances D144, D185, D333

Blumfeld, Harold B236
Blyth, Alan B237–B238
The Boatman's Dance SEE Old Ameri-
can Songs, Set I.
Boch, Jerry D191
Bolcom, William D137
Bookspan, Martin B244
Boosey & Hawkes Publishing Company
p.7, B119, B148, B245, B746,
B1022, B1123, B1163
Boretz, Benjamin B246, B324, B467
Boston Pops Orchestra W62, W70,
D23, D207, D282, D305, D308
Boston Symphony Chamber Players
D373
Boston Symphony Orchestra p.4, p.6,
W29, W31, W36, W38, W77, W84,
D27–D29, D164–D166, D307, D310–
D311, D342, B96, B246, B249,
B252, B317, B358, B390, B449,
B451, B496, B581, B588, B590,
B615, B695, B701, B703, B725,
B725, B801, B918, B942, B947,
B949, B957, B962, B967, B993,
B1002, B1069, B1084, B1089,
B1183
Boulanger, Nadia p.3–4, W23, W26,
W89, W96, B15–B16, B25, B72–
B73, B113, B138, B212, B263,
B396, B499, B516, B588, B605,
B664, B669, B699, B808, B902,
B927, B964, B1011, B1047, B1064
Boult, Adrian B290
Bowden, Don W47
Bowles, Paul Frederick D204, D332
Boys' High School, Brooklyn, New
York p.3
Brahms, Johannes D373, B259
Brandeis University B450, B459,
B717, B920, B1123
Brant, LeRoy V. B250
Brazilian Dance D101
Bredemann, Dan B251
Bremner, James D117
Briggs, John B252
British Broadcasting Corporation
SEE BBC.
Britten, Benjamin W85, D4, D192,
D265, B10, B234, B287
Broadcasting Music Industry B182
Broadhurst Theatre, New York B441
Brodbin, John B253
Bronx Opera Company B214, B254,
B620, B858, B900

Brook, Donald B255
Brookhart, Charles Edward B256
Brooklyn Academy of Music B358,
    B940
Brooklyn College B305, B1123
Brooklyn Philharmonia Orchestra
    B940
Brown, Alan B256
The Bruce W91
Bryan, Keith D114
Bryant, Celia B258
Buck, Dudley D117
Buckaroo Holiday SEE Rodeo.
Buffalo Philharmonic Orchestra
    D262, B725, B766
Bullock, Bruce Lloyd B259
Bumbry, Grace W88
Bumiller, Elisabeth B260
Burge, David B522
Burgin, Richard B993, B1034
Burns, Mary T. B261
Burnside, Dennis D22, D280
Burton, Eldin D114
Durton, Humphrey B262
Bury Me Not on the Lone Prairie SEE
    Billy the Kid.
Busbey, Fred E. B187, B456, B1080,
    B1175
But Yesterday Is Not Today D332
Butterworth, Neil B263
By Way of Art; Criticisms of Music
    Literature, Painting, Sculpture,
    and the Dance B959

CBS SEE ALSO Columbia Broadcasting
    System.
CBS Playhouse B152, B1051
CBS Radio Network B1034
CBS Television W94, B1018
Cabrillo Festival, Cabrillo, Cali-
    fornia B306-B307
Cage, John B46, B77, B687, B1149
Caine, Milton A. B264
Cairns, David B265
Cakewalk D25, D284
Caldwell, Sarah B893
California Chamber Symphony B531
California Institute of the Arts,
    Valencia B411
California State University, Ful-
    lerton B269
California State University, North-
    ridge. Chamber Singers B890
California State University, North-
    ridge. Symphony Orchestra B890

California State University, North-
    ridge. Wind Orchestra B890
Callas, Maria Meneghini B892
Calta, Louis B266
Cambridge Arts Theatre B448
Cambridge University B295
Cambridge University Opera Group
    B448, B857, B1095
Cammaerts, E. W7
Campos, Ruben M. W48
Camptown Races SEE Lincoln
    Portrait.
Canadian Chamber Orchestra B177
Canby, Edward Tatnall B267
Cancionero Mexicano W48
Candide D19-D20
Canticle of Freedom W91, D72,
    B218, B223, B394, B452, B1025,
    B1172
Capitol SEE United States. Capitol.
Capriccio W2
Capriccio, Piano & Orchestra D165
Caras, Tracy B519
Card Game at Night SEE Billy the
    Kid.
Cardiff Festival Ensemble D250
Cariaga, Daniel B269
Carl Fischer Hall, New York W80
Carlson Festival of the Arts,
    University of Bridgeport B135
Carlyss, Earl D367
Carman, Judith Elaine B270
Carnegie Hall, New York W89, B222,
    B224, B289, B314, B342, B409,
    B462, B609, B618, B690, B801,
    B808, B878, B914, B980, B990-
    B991, B1002, B1019, B1072,
    B1083-B1084, B1126
Carols of Death D146
Carpenter, John Alden D277
Carr, Benjamin D40
Carter, Elliott Cook D144, D185,
    D239, D333, D373, B271, B568,
    B687, B699
Carter, Jimmy B631
Carter, Richard B272
Carter, Rosalynn B631, B800
Casadesus, Jules W16
Cassilly, Richard D340
The Cat and the Mouse p.3-4, W14,
    D73-D77, B258, B339, B596, B830,
    B982, B1048, B1190
Ceculeo D195
Celebration Dance SEE Billy the
    Kid.

Celebration of American Music B676
Centennial Hall, Adelaide, Aus-
   tralia B249
Central Park, New York B178, B685
Century Plaza Hotel, Los Angeles
   B652
Ceremonial Fanfare W104, B635
Certificate of Merit SEE Stereo
   Review Certificate of Merit.
Chamber Concerto for Viola and
   String Nonet D322
Chamber Orchestra of Copenhagen
   D256
Chamber Symphony Society of Cali-
   fornia B652
Chancellor's Medal for Distin-
   guished Achievement, Syracuse
   University B1123
Chanler, Theodore D332, B208, B274
Chapin, Louis B275-B276
Chapman, E. B277-B279
The Chariot SEE Twelve Poems of
   Emily Dickinson.
Charles Eliot Norton Professor of
   Poetry, Harvard University p.6,
   B65, B115, B118, B162, B312,
   B357, B476, B572, B651, B805,
   B834
Chase, Gilbert B280-B283.
Chase, Mary Cole B284
Le Chat et la Souris SEE The Cat
   and the Mouse.
Chatham College, Pittsburgh B285
Chavez, C. B286
Chávez, Carlos W43, W48, W52, D101,
   B12, B59, B378
Chelsea Town Hall, London B238
Cherkassky, Shura B1023
Chicago Opera House W44
Chicago Symphony Orchestra D97
The Children D332
Children of the Night W30
Children's Pieces, Two SEE Two
   Children's Pieces.
Children's Suite SEE The Red Pony.
Childs, Barney B27
Ching-a-Ring Chaw SEE Old American
   Songs, Set II.
Chissell, Joan B290
Chlumberg, Hans W41
Chodack, Walter D212, D253
Chopin, Frederick D143
Choral Art Society D340
Choral Square Dance SEE The Tender
   Land.

Chorale No.1 in G D117
Chorale Prelude on Silent Night
   D117
Christman, A. W52
Christopher Columbus B74
Churchill, Mary Senior W45
Cincinnati Symphony Orchestra W67-
   W68, W76, B227, B244, B746
Circus Polka D107
Citkowitz, Israel D332, B292-
   B293, B474
The City p.5, W56, W69, B910,
   B960
City Center SEE New York City
   Center.
City Opera Company SEE New York
   City Opera Company.
City University Colleges SEE New
   York City University Colleges.
Clarinet Concerto SEE Concerto for
   Clarinet and String Orchestra.
Clements, Joy D340
Cleveland Chamber Music Society
   B614
Cleveland Institute of Music B729
Cleveland Orchestra B614, B725
Cleveland Pops Orchestra
Cliburn, Van B892
Cliburn, Van, Piano Competition
   SEE Van Cliburn International
   Piano Competition, 4th, Septem-
   ber 17-30, 1973, Texas Christian
   University, Fort Worth, Texas.
Cloches à Travers les Feuilles
   D331
Clurman, Harold W25, W28, B50,
   B298-B299, B1102
Cole, Hugh B300-B303
Coleman, Jack B304
College Band Directors National
   Association W100
Collegiate Chorale W54
Colon Opera House, Buenos Aires
   B376
Colorado College B522
Columbia Broadcasting System p.5,
   W50, W61, B667, B1157 SEE ALSO
   CBS.
Columbia Chamber Orchestra D9,
   B983
Columbia String Ensemble D186
Columbia String Orchestra D78-
   D79
Columbia Symphony Orchestra W50,
   W61-W62, D80, D190, D294, D298

Columbia University B64, B697, B726, B1060, B1132
Columbia University Oral History Project B1060
Columbus, Christopher SEE Christopher Columbus.
Commanday, Robert B306-B307
Commander's Cross of the Order of Merit, Federal Republic of Germany p.7, B382
Commission Award for Notable Achievement, Brandeis University B1123
The Complete Music for Solo Piano D73, D110, D131, D141, D168, D182, D210, D217, D223, D234, D354
Composers' Gallery; Biographical Sketches of Contemporary Composers B255
Composers in America; Biographical Sketches of Contemporary Composers with a Record of Their Works B928
Composers of Today B93
Composers' Showcase B566, B617, B877, B932, B1128
Composers Since 1900; a Biographical and Critical Guide B472
Compositions for Chorus of Women's Voices, Two SEE Two Compositions for Chorus of Women's Voices.
Concert Arts Orchestra D5, D30, D257, D270, D286, B210
Concert of American Music D356
Concert Variations on The Star-Spangled Banner, Op.23 D117
Concertgebouw Orchestra B532
Concerto for Clarinet and String Orchestra, with Harp and Piano p.6, W79, D78-D82, B117, B119, B169, B209, B259, B265, B280, B320-B322, B341, B415, B545, B584, B603, B616, B655, B675, B691-B692, B696, B709, B718, B762-B763, B824, B848, B878, B880, B936, B1015, B1069, B1078, B1166
Concerto for Double Bass and Chamber Orchestra B575
Concerto for Piano and Orchestra p.4, W31, D83-D89, B49, B181, B302, B323, B447, B542, B574, B583, B587, B635, B685, B689, B696, B722, B732, B830, B962,

B993, B996, B1030, B1070, B1160
Concerto, Harpsichord, S.974, D Minor D143
Concerto in G Major D231
Concerto, Percussion & Orchestra D163
Concerto, Piano, F Major D87-D88
The Concise Encyclopedia of Music and Musicians B331
Cone, Edward T. B217, B324
Congleton, J. E. B60
Conly, John M. B325
Connotations p.6, W98, D90-D91, B157, B171, B246, B275, B326-B328, B424, B467-B468, B540, B551, B579, B586, B592-B593, B599, B622, B719, B772, B838, B948, B953, B1000, B1016, B1059, B1066, B1094, B1121, B1165
Constitution Hall, Washington, D.C. B721, B800
The Consul D318, D341
Contemporary American Composers: a Biographical Dictionary B164
Contemporary American Music D257
Contemporary American Piano Music D204
Contemporary Composers on Contemporary Music B27
Conversation at the Soda Fountain SEE Our Town.
Conversations D331
Cook, Eugene B329
Coolidge, Elizabeth Sprague W73, B415 SEE ALSO Elizabeth Sprague Coolidge Foundation.
Coolidge, Richard B330
Coolidge Foundation SEE Elizabeth Sprague Coolidge Foundation.
Cooper, Martin B331
Cooper Union B311
Copland, Laurine p.3
Copland [record album] D35, D65, D98, D126, D246, D261, D288, D312, D343, D350, D374
The Copland Album D10, D175, D274, D297
A Copland Celebration B273
Copland Conducts and Plays Copland D89, D108, D140, D203, D290, D366
Copland Conducts Copland D8, D109, D119, D151, D153, D158, D170, D264, B848

Copland on Music p.7, B18, B24,
   B71-B73, B243, B362-B369, B466,
   B659, B717, B796, B821, B884,
   B970, B985, B1067, B1169
Copland Performs and Conducts
   Copland D112, D186, D325
Copland Rehearses Appalachian
   Spring D9
Copland School of Music SEE The
   Aaron Copland School of Music,
   Queens College, Flusing.
Copland-Sessions Concerts p.4, W36,
   B441-B443, B445, B528, B646,
   B650, B784, B851, B877, B938
Copland's Greatest Hits D14, D23,
   D50, D56, D122-D123, D275, D282,
   D301, D305
Copyright Act SEE United States.
   Copyright Act.
Corbett, J. Ralph B1158
Corbett Music Lectures B1158
Corle, Edwin B86
Cornell University Libraries B392
Cornell University Wind Ensemble
   D16, D115
Corral Nocturne SEE Rodeo.
Cortege Macabre W25, B96 SEE ALSO
   Grohg.
Count Basie SEE Basie, Count (Wil-
   liam James).
County Derry D191
Cowell, Henry D40, D254-D255, B12,
   B274, B393-B394, B1037
Cowley, Malcolm B174
Cox, Ainslee B395
The Cradle Will Rock B41, B55
Crane, Hart W73
Crane Chorus SEE New York State
   University College, Potsdam.
   Crane Chorus.
Crane Symphony Orchestra SEE New
   York State University College,
   Potsdam. Crane Symphony Orches-
   tra.
Crankshaw, Geoffrey B396
La Création du Monde D294, D298
The Creative Mind and Method: Ex-
   ploring the Nature of Creative-
   ness in American Arts, Sciences,
   and Professions B80
Creston, Paul D254, D257, D365
Cronkite, Walter B1049
Cross, Christopher B585, B822
Cross, Milton John B397

Cross of the Commander of the
   Order of Merit SEE German Re-
   public Cross of the Commander of
   the Order of Merit.
Crowder, Charles B398
Crowther, Bosley B399
Crusell, Bernard Henrik D82
Cummings, Edward Estlin W34 SEE
   ALSO Song (E. E. Cummings).
The Cummington Story W75, W102
Cunningham, Beatrice B787 SEE ALSO
   Threnody II: Beatrice Cunning-
   ham in Memoriam.

Da Capo Chamber Players B609
Dahl, Ingolf B401-B402
Dallapiccola, Luigi D221, D331
Dallas Symphony Orchestra D58,
   D66, D127, D283, D285, D289,
   D306
Damrosch, Walter p.4, W26
The Dance in the Place Congo D255
Dance Magazine Awards B139, B403
Dance of the Adolescent SEE Dance
   Symphony.
Dance of the Tumblers D107
Dance Panels W95, D92-D93, B301,
   B428, B600, B624, B720, B838,
   B1069
Dance Rhythms D208
Dance Symphony p.5, W27, W38, D94-
   D99, B15, B114, B272, B404-B405,
   B496, B696, B775, B862, B872,
   B890 SEE ALSO Grohg.
Dance to the Piper B946
Danse Characteristique (Unfinished)
   W4
Danse des Moucherons D40
Danza de Jalisco SEE Three Latin
   American Sketches.
Danzón Cubano W66, D100-D108,
   B160, B406-B407, B453, B552,
   B729, B731, B1031, B1073, B1101
Darrell, Robert Donaldson B94,
   B408
Darter, Tom B409
Dartington Summer School B673
Dartmouth University B308
Daugherty, Robert Michael B410
Davies, Dennis Russell D32, B167,
   B576, B916
Davis, Dana B411
Davis, Peter G. B412-B413
The Dawning of Music in Kentucky
   D40

Day, J. B414
Dayton, Daryl B415
de Falla, Manuel SEE Falla, Manuel
  de.
de Gourmont, Remy W12
de Mille, Agnes p.5, W70, B741,
  B946
de Peyer, Gervaise Alan D82
Deane, James G. B416
Dear March, Come In! SEE Twelve
  Poems of Emily Dickinson.
Debussy, Claude D81, D143, D241,
  D300, D331
Declaration of Human Rights W84,
  B402
Del Rosso, Charles Francis B418,
  B603
Del Tredici, David B559, B630
Dello Joio, Norman D113, D237,
  D242, D375, B419
Denby, Edwin p.5, W51, B288, B736,
  B856, B961, B1008, B1088
DePauw University B348
DeRhen, A. B420
Derivations for Clarinet and Band
  D80
Des Marias, Paul B987
Deutsche Kammermusik B35
Deux Pièces pour Violon et Piano
  SEE Two Pieces for Violin and
  Piano.
The Developing Flutist D113, D375
The Dial B962
Diamond, David Leo D257, B582
Diary of One Who Vanished D331
Dickinson, Emily SEE Twelve Poems
  of Emily Dickinson.
Dickinson, Meriel D333
Dickinson, Peter D144, D185, D333,
  B421-B423
The Dictionary of Composers B866
Dictionary of Music and Musicians
  B565
Diether, Jack B424-B426
Dirge in Woods W89, B808
Dirizerskoe Ispolnitle'stvo:
  Praktika, Istorija, Estetika
  B527
Discoveries of a Music Critic B88,
  B958
Dispeker, Thea B428
Divertimento B616
Divertimento for 9 Instruments
  D373
Divertisement, Orchestra, Op.43,
  C Major D154

Dixon, James B455
Dobrin, Arnold p.7, B132-B133,
  B170, B429
The Dodger SEE Old American Songs,
  Set I.
Doerschuk, Bob B409
Donizetti, Gaetano B591
Donn, Jorge B139, B403
Dorati, Antal D21, D53, D58, D104-
  D105, D278, D285, D303, D349,
  B203, B795
Dorian, Frederick B430-B431
Dorian String Quartet D360
Double Exposure B298
Dougherty, Celius D189
Douglas, John R. B432
Douglas, Melvyn D164-D166, B914
Dower, Catherine B433
Down a Country Lane W99, D109-
  D111, B434, B556, B982
Downes, Edward B435
Downes, Irene B446
Downes, Olin D436-B446, B515,
  B750
Dream March and Circus Music SEE
  The Red Pony.
Drew, David B447-B448
Drushler, Paul D81
Duke, John Woods D332
Dumbarton Oaks Research Library
  W96, B398
Dumm, Robert W. B449-B450
Dunham, Harry H. W72
Duo Concertant for Violin and
  Piano D329
Duo for Flute and Piano p.7, W107,
  D112-D114, B420, B629, B726,
  B863, B983 SEE ALSO Duo for Vi-
  olin and Piano.
Duo for Violin and Piano B47 SEE
  ALSO Duo for Flute and Piano.
Durand, Jacques B258
Durgin, Cyrus B451-B452
Dushkin, Samuel W33
Dwight Morrow High School B317

EMI Studio, London B560
East, Leslie B453
Eastman-Rochester Symphony Or-
  chestra D181, D259-D260
Eastman Wind Ensemble D116
Eberle, Bruce B595
Eble, Charles B455
Ebony Concerto D80
Edward MacDowell Association SEE
  MacDowell Association.

Edward MacDowell Colony SEE
    MacDowell Colony.
Edward MacDowell Medal SEE
    MacDowell Medal.
Edyth Totten Theatre, New York W36,
    B443, B445
Eger, Joseph D154
1812 Overture D124
Ein Ger Festival, Israel B554
Eisenhower, Dwight B456
Elegies W42
Elizabeth Sprague Coolidge Founda-
    tion p.6, W73, W86, B416, B715
    SEE ALSO Coolidge, Elizabeth
    Sprague.
Ellsworth, Ray B460
Elwell, Herbert D208
Embittered SEE Three Moods for
    Piano Solo.
Emblems W100, D115–D116, B471,
    B890, B1165, B1174
Emerson, Lake, and Palmer B141
The Emperor Jones D318, D341
Empire Sinfonietta B616, B849
The Encyclopedia of American
    Music B650
Engel, Carl D365
Engel, Lehman W51, B461, B736, B856
Episode W63, D117, B1047
Episodes D84
Epstein, David D86, D99
Erickson, Raymond B462–B464, B608
Ericourt, Daniel W23
Erlendson, William J. D148
Essex House, New York B134
Estribillo SEE Three Latin Ameri-
    can Sketches.
Étrangeté D331
Eugene Onégin D107
Evans, Peter B466–B469
Evans, Walker B470
Everett, Horace W90, B238, B383,
    B470, B477, B511, B525, B678,
    B700, B742, B833, B1082, B1096,
    B1098–B1099, B1130, B1151
Everybody's Music B667
Evett, Robert B471
Ewen, David B98, B397, B472–B475
Eyer, Ronald B475–B477
Exxon Corporation B335

Facsimile D5
Fall River Legend D25, D284
Falla, Manuel de D331
Famous American Composers B872

Famous Musicians of Jewish Origin
    B979
Fancy Free D5, D25, D270, D284,
    D294
Fanfare for the Common Man p.5,
    p.7, W67, D118–D130, B141, B244,
    B478, B627, B632, B636, B638,
    B1164
Fantasia Mexicana W47
Fantasia, String Trio D373
Fantastic Symphony: an Authorita-
    tive Score; Historical Back-
    ground; Analysis; Views and
    Comments B217
Fantasy for Piano SEE Piano Fan-
    tasy.
Farnol, Jeffery W3
Fauré, Gabriel U. D165, B32, B34,
    B37
Federal Overture D40
Federal Symphony Orchestra of New
    York B314
Feld, Eliot B731
Fennimore, Joseph B661
Fenton, John H. B482
Fernández, Oscar Lorenzo D101
Festival Hall, London W101, B150,
    B159, B287, B290, B345, B371,
    B391, B423, B547, B549, B559,
    B561, B732, B867, B976, B1121,
    B1160
Festival of Contemporary American
    Music, Sixth, Columbia Univer-
    sity, McMillan Memorial Theatre,
    May 18, 1950 W87
Festival of Contemporary Music,
    DePauw University B348
Festival of Contemporary Music,
    Tanglewood SEE Berkshire Music
    Center at Tanglewood, Lenox,
    Massachusetts.
Festival of Two Worlds, Spoleto,
    Italy W109, B713
Festivals of Contemporary Ameri-
    can Music at Yaddo, Saratoga
    Springs, New York p.4, B740
Festive Overture D207
Feux d'Artifice D143
Fiddler on the Roof D191
Fiedler, Arthur W70, D23, D207,
    D282, D305, D308, B1034
Fiedler's Favorite Overtures D207
Fierro, Charles D183, D211, D219,
    D238
Fiesta W47

Fifty Voices of the Twentieth Century B672
Fine, Irving Gifford D373, B483-B484
Finkelstein, Sidney B485-B487
Finney, Ross Lee B488, B501
First Symphony p.4, W26, W35, B263, B377, B447, B709, B732, B949, B955, B999 SEE ALSO Symphony for Organ and Orchestra.
First Symphony [by Hilhaud] B8
Fischer, Carl, Hall SEE Carl Fischer Hall, New York.
Fisher, Avery, Hall SEE Avery Fisher Hall.
Fisher, Fred B491
Fitzgerald, Ella B347, B492, B500, B521, B1018
The Five Kings p.6, W57
Five Sea Chanties D189
Five Songs from Chamber Music D332
Fizdale, Robert W70, B945
Flanagan, William B494-B497
Fleisher, Leon D226
Fleming, Shirley B498
Florida International Music Festival, Datona Beach B351
Flute and Piano, Duo SEE Duo for Flute and Piano.
The Flute in American Music D40
A Foggy Day in London Town D144, D185, D333
Foldes, Andor W80, D204, B499
Folk Music and Poetry of Spain and Portugal W65
El Folklore y la Musica Mexicana W48
Fonda, Henry D157-D158, B492, B500, B521, B1018
Fontainebleau School, Salle Gaveau, Paris p.3, W14, W18, W36, W89
For the Gentlemen Suite D40
Ford, Christopher B503-B504
Foss, Lukas D49, D262, B145, B336, B563, B766, B1140, B1143
Foster, Robert E. D191
Foster, Stephen p.5
Four American Landscapes D255
Four Dance Episodes SEE Rodeo.
Four Motets W18, B905
Four Piano Blues p.4, W80, D131-D140, B507, B530, B680, B715, B729, B749, B791, B830, B917, B982, B1101, B1173 SEE ALSO Sentimental Melody.

Four Piano Impromptus B1134
Four Pieces for Violin and Piano, Op.17 D365
Four Sacred Chorales D148
The Fourth of July D20
Fowle, Farnsworth B508
Fox, Charles Warren B509
Fragment, for Trio W13
Frank Glazer Plays American Music D237
Fredericks, Richard D340
Freed, David D368
Freed, Isadore W49
Freedman, Guy B510
Freeman, John W. B511-B512
French, P. B513
French-American Festival B686
Fricker, Peter B1134
Friedberg, Gertrude B514
Fritschel, James D149
From Jewish Life D135
From My Diary D226
From Sorcery to Science p.6, W58
From the Steeples and the Mountains D262
Frost, Robert D144, D185, D333
Frymire, Jack B516
Fuchs, Joseph D329
Fullerton, R. B931
Furie, Kenneth B518

Gagne, Cole B519
Gamarekian, Barbara B521
Gamer, Carlton B522
Gampbel, Lilit B544
Ganz, Rudolf W44
Garfein, Jack B329
Garre, Helmut Schmidt SEE Schmidt-Garre, Helmut.
Garvie, Peter B105, B523-B524
A Gathering of Brooklyn Composers B940
Gauntlett, Helen B525
Gazelle, Marcel D331
Gebert, Armand B526
Genesis SEE Bible.
Geothe-Lieder D331
German Republic Cross of the Commander of the Order of Merit B1050
Gershwin, George D11, D19-D20, D33, D49, D55, D60, D133, D144, D185, D212, D237, D253, D293, D304, D314, D333, D359, B534, B582, B955, B993, B1117

Gershwin, Ira W71
Getke, Richard B1115
Ghitalla, Armando D256
Gibson, Gordon D81
Gieseking, Walter W39
The Gift SEE The Red Pony.
Gilbert, Henry Franklin Belknap
  D255
Ginzburg, Leo B527
Girolo, Nella B595
Gladiolus Rag B680
Glantz, Harry D257, B210
Glazer, Frank D237, B1178
Glenn, Carroll D326, D369, B1112
Gloria D90
Gluck, Christoph Willibald, Ritter
  von B591
Glueck, Grace B529
Going to Heaven SEE Twelve Poems of
  Emily Dickinson.
Gold, Arthur W70, B945
Gold, Don B530
Gold Baton Award p.7, B335, B535,
  B1152
Gold Medal for Music B1136, B1185
Goldberg, Albert B173, B531-B532
Goldberg, Isaac B533-B534
The Golden Willow Tree SEE Old
  American Songs, Set II.
Goldman, Edwin Franko B178
Goldman, Richard Franko B536-B542
Goldman Band W55
Goldmark, Carl D207, B499
Goldmark, Rubin p.3
Goldovsky, Boris B543
Goldsmith, Harris B544
Goldwyn, Samuel W71
Golschmann, Vladimir D257, B210
Goltzer, Albert D257
Goodfriend, James B1116
Goodman, Al D309
Goodman, Benny p.6, W79, D78-D80,
  B209, B321, B415, B545, B692,
  B848, B878, B880, B889, B1015,
  B1166
Goodman Orchestra SEE Al Goodman
  Orchestra.
Goodwin, Noel B546-B551
Goossens, Eugene W67, W76, B244,
  B478
Gordon, Jacques D361-D362
Gorer, Richard B552
Goss, Madeleine Binkley B553
Gottschalk, Louis Moreau D25, D237,
  D284, B1001

Gould, Morton D18, D25, D47, D62,
  D80, D97, D159, D281, D284,
  B352, B1124
Gould, Morton, Orchestra SEE
  Morton Gould Orchestra.
Gounod, Charles François D191
Gourmont, Remy de SEE de Gourmont,
  Remy.
Gradenwitz, Peter B107, B554
Gräter, Manfred B555
Graffman, Gary B1034
Graham, Martha p.5, W73, B112,
  B189 B284-B285, B492, B500,
  B516, B521, B690, B705, B915,
  B1018, B1111
Grainger, Percy Aldridge D191
Grammy Awards SEE National Academy
  of Recording Artists Grammy
  Awards. Trustees Award.
Gramophone Shop Encyclopedia of
  Recorded Music B94
Grand Canyon Suite D292, D308
Grand Concerto, Op.5, F Minor D82
Grand Opera House, Wilmington,
  Delaware B419
Grandfather's Story SEE The Red
  Pony.
Grant Johnson in Recital D241
Grant Park, Chicago B1182
Grant Park Symphony Orchestra
  B1182
Gray, H. W., Company SEE H. W.
  Gray Company.
Great American Ballets D5, D270
Great Modern Composers B1107
Great Music for Violin Lovers D365
Green, Johnny W47
Greenfield, Edward B556-B560
Greenhouse, B. W52
Gregg Smith Singers D146, B759
Gribbs-Smith, Charles Harvard
  B564
Grieg, Edvard Hagerup D124
Griffes, Charles Tomlinson D47
Griffith Music Foundation B184
Griffiths, Paul B562
Grigoriev, L. B563
Grigson, Geoffrey B564
Grimes, Peter SEE Peter Grimes.
Grofé, Ferde D292, D308
Grohg p.3, p.5, W25, W27-W28, B15,
  B374, B404-B405, B915 SEE ALSO
  Cortège Macabre; Dance Symphony.
Gross, Chaim B844
Grossman, Ferdinand D356

Group Theatre Production W60
Grove, George B565
The Grove Dictionary of Music and
    Musicians SEE The New Grove Dic-
    tionary of Music and Musicians.
Grovers Corners SEE Music for
    Movies; Our Town.
Gruen, John B566
Gruenberg, Louis D318, D341
Gualdo da Vandero, Giovanni D40
Guarnieri, Camargo D101
Günther, S. B567
Guggenheim Fellowship p.4, p.7,
    W29, B16, B192, B284, B776
Gun Battle SEE Billy the Kid.

H. W. Gray Company W63
Haberkorn, Michael H. B568
Häusler, Josef B569-B570
Haggin, Bernard H. B571-B574
Haines, Edmund B575
Hakim, Talib Rasul B940
Hall, David B576
Hall, Roger B577
Hambro, Leonid D322, D324, B679
Hamilton, David H. B578-B580
Hammerstein, Oscar, II p.6, W90,
    B120, B389, B881, B977, B1091,
    B1151, B1168, B1192
Hampton Art Center, Quogue, Long
    Island B1056
Hampton Town Hall, London B1134
Handbook of Conducting B93
Haney, Daniel Q. B581
Hanly, Brian D371
Hanson, Howard W25, D116, D181,
    D259-D260, D318, D341, D359, B4,
    B6, B582
Hanson, John Robert B583
Happy Anniversary W105
Happy Birthday W105, B352
Happy Ending SEE The Red Pony.
The Happy Hypocrite D208
Harburg, E. Y. (Yip) B844
Harrington, Richard B585
Harris, Roy p.4, W39, D204, D242,
    D260, D345, D349, D372, B3, B72,
    B222, B256, B456, B637, B699,
    B807, B960, B991, B1037
Harrison, Jay S. B586-B588
Harrison, Max B589
Hartford Opera B1115
Hartford Symphony Orchestra D128,
    D196

Harvard University p.6-7, W78,
    B32, B65, B115, B118, B162,
    B233, B239, B241, B312, B357,
    B381, B476, B482, B541, B571-
    B572, B606, B651, B718, B797,
    B805, B834, B1157
Harvard University Memorial Church
    W78
Harvard University Collegiate
    Chorale W78
Hastings Symphony Orchestra D2
Hautzig, Walter D143
Have Mercy on Us, O My Lord SEE
    Four Motets.
Hawkes, Ralph W60
Hawkins, Erick B139, B403
Haydn, Joseph B1077
Haydn, Michael D256
Hear Ye! Hear Ye! W44
Heart, We Will Forget Him SEE
    Twelve Poems of Emily Dickinson.
Heinrich, Anton Philipp D40
Heinsheimer, H. W. B591
The Heiress p.6, W83, B115, B194,
    B652
Hellinger, Mark, Theater SEE Mark
    Hellinger Theater, New York.
Helm, Everett Burton D276, B592-
    B593
Help Us, O Lord SEE Four Motets.
Helps, Robert D332
Hemingway, Ernest W94
Henahan, Donal B594-B597
Henderson, Robert B598
Hendl, Walter D3, D17, D174, D178
Henry, John SEE John Henry.
Henry Howland Memorial Prize, Yale
    University p.7, B180
Henry Street Settlement Music
    School, New York W46, W51, B188,
    B288, B736, B856, B1008, B1088
Herbage, J. B599
Herbert, Victor D318, D341
Hermann, Bernard B150
Hérodiade D191
Herrmann, Joachim B600
Hershowitz, Alan B601
Heston, Charlton D167
Heylbut, Rose B602
High School of Music and Art, New
    York p.5, W55, D317, B316, B462,
    B1128
Hillsman, Walter D117
Hilton, Lewis B603

Hindemith, Paul p.3, D133, D324,
    D331, B69, B99, B210, B304
Hindsley, Mark H. W48
L'Histoire du Soldat D331, B566,
    B687
History of Music in Sound D331
History's 100 Greatest Composers
    B668
Hitchcock, H. Wiley B604-B605
Hobson, Wilder B606
Hoe-Down SEE Rodeo.
Holbrook, Hal B219
Holidays: Decoration Day D20
Holland, Bernard B608-B609
Hollywood Bowl B696, B722, B936
Homage to Ives SEE Night Thoughts.
Home, Earl of (Alexander Frederick
    Douglas-Home) B482
Honegger, Arthur D156
Hopkins, Gerard Manley W103, B693
Hopkins Center of Music, Drama,
    and Art, Dartmouth University
    B308
Horatio Appleton Lamb Fund, Harvard
    University B381
Horenstein, Jascha B391
Horizons D208
Horst, Louis W73
Horzowski, M. W86
Hosier, John B611
The Housatonic at Stockbridge D255
The House on the Hill SEE Two Com-
    positions for Chorus of Women's
    Voices.
Houston Symphony Orchestra W82
Howard, John Tasker B612-B613
Howard University Cramton Audito-
    rium W96, B1011
Howland, Alice B715, B1132
Howland Memorial Prize SEE Henry
    Howland Memorial Prize, Yale
    University.
Hruby, Frank B614
Hubbard, Charles W16, W19
Hughes, Allen B615-B621
Hume, Paul B622-B638
Humoristic Scherzo SEE The Cat and
    the Mouse.
Hunsberger, Donald D116
Hunter College, New York B254, B620
Hunter College Playhouse, New York
    B214
Hymn and Fuguing Tune D254

I Bought Me a Cat SEE Old Ameri-
    can Songs, Set I.
I Felt a Funeral in My Brain SEE
    Twelve Poems of Emily Dickinson.
I Got Rhythm D49, D144, D185, D333
Igor Stravinsky B86
An Immorality SEE Two Compositions
    for Chorus of Women's Voices.
Improvisation SEE Episode.
Improvisations on Hungarian
    Peasant Songs D331
In Evening Air W102, D141-D144,
    B982
In Medias Res D154
In Memoriam B8
In the Beginning W78, D145-D149,
    B218, B256, B426, B538, B554,
    B641, B759, B890, B922, B1073
Inaugural Concert Committee B187
Inaugural Fanfare W106
The Incredible Flutist D36, D99
Indiana University Beaux Arts
    Trio SEE Beaux Arts Trio.
Indianapolis Arts Chorale B870
Indianapolis Symphony Orchestra
    B870
Inscape p.6, W103, B150, B163,
    B413, B498, B598, B621, B643,
    B693, B724, B838, B861, B863,
    B906, B953, B975-B976, B981,
    B1028, B1046
Inter-American Music Festival,
    2nd, April 25, 1961, Washington,
    D.C. W96, B398, B1011
Interlochen Arts Academy, Inter-
    lochen, Michigan B186
International Composers' Guild B17
International Cyclopedia of Music
    and Musicians B1107
International Music Congress, New
    York and Washington, September
    9-16, 1968 B645
International Society for Contem-
    porary Music B22, B89, B1139
Interplay D25, D284
Introduction and Fugue, 2 Pianos
    D96
Introduction et Tarantelle, Op.43
    D365
Irving, Robert D5, D30, D270, D286
Isacoff, S. B647-B648
L'Isle Joyeuse D241
Isolde B698

I've Heard an Organ Talk Sometimes
   SEE Twelve Poems of Emily Dickin-
   son.
Ives, Charles Edward D11, D17, D20,
   D25, D32, D117, D120, D161, D182-
   D185, D250, D254-D255, D262, D284,
   D328, D330, B11, B82, B127, B286,
   B516, B576, B669, B764, B780,
   B916, B1055, B1116, B1188

Jablonski, Edward B650
Jacksonville University B724
Jacob, Bernard D82, B691
Jacobs, Arthur B651
Jacobs, Jody B652
Jacobs, Paul D137, B917, B1101
Jacobson, Robert B653-B654
Jacques Orchestra B117, B1078
Jamaicalypso D107
James, Henry W83
Janacek, Leos D331
Janssen, Werner D255
Janssen Symphony of Los Angeles
   D255
Japan Philharmonic Symphony Orches-
   tra D95
Jazz Concerto SEE Concerto for
   Piano and Orchestra.
Jazzy SEE Three Moods for Piano
   Solo.
Jennings, Vance Shelby B655
Jirko, Ivan B656
Joachim, Heinrich D370, B417
Johannesen, Grant D241-D242
Johanos, Donald D66, D127, D289
 John F. Kennedy Center SEE Kennedy
   Center for the Performing Arts,
   Washington, D.C.
John Henry W61, D151, B401, B924
Johnson, Grant D241
Johnson, Harriett B657
Johnson, Lyndon B. p.7, B721,
   B1104, B1135
Johnston, Laurie B658
Joio, Norman Dello SEE Dello Joio,
   Norman.
Jones, Charles B659
Jones, Robert B660
Joplin, Scott B680
Josman, Martin B1019
Jubilee Variation W76
Juilliard Concert Hall, New York
   W93, B384, B1127
Juilliard Orchestra B319

Juilliard School of Music p.6,
   W93, B148, B202, B373, B384,
   B400, B538, B619, B939, B972,
   B995, B1004, B1079, B1125
Juilliard String Quartet D251,
   D320-D322, B29, B679

Kalajian, Berge D212, D253
Kapell, William W80, W93, B56,
   B972, B1079
Karman, Charlotte W42
Karman, Ivor W42, D368
Karmel, Alex W97
Karr, Gary B191
Karsh, Yousuf B664
Kastendieck, Miles B665-B666.
Katims, M. W86
Kaufman, Annette D276-D277, D290,
   D364
Kaufman, Louis D276-D277, D290,
   D327, D363-D364, D366
Kaufman, Schima B667
Kaufmann, Helen Loeb B668
Kay, Hershy D25, D284
Kay, Norman B669-B670
Keener, Andrew B671
Kelen, Emery B672
Keller, Hans B673-B675
Keller, Homer D259
Kennan, George F. B704
Kennan, Kent Wheeler D259
Kennedy, John F. B353
Kennedy Center Awards SEE Kennedy
   Center Tonight.
Kennedy Center for the Performing
   Arts, Washington, D.C. B273,
   B492, B521, B622-B623, B626,
   B631, B634, B637, B709, B735,
   B1123
Kennedy Center Honors SEE Kennedy
   Center Tonight.
Kennedy Center Tonight p.7, B168,
   B219, B260, B347, B492, B500,
   B521, B850, B875, B1018, B1147-
   B1148
Kenyon, Nicholas B676-B677
Kerman, Joseph B678-B679
Kern, Fred B680
Kerner, Leighton B681-B682
Kerr, Harrison D372
Keys, Karen D114
Khachaturian, Aram B776-B778
Kincaid, William W107, B420
King, Coretta Scott B1070

King, Martin Luther, Jr. B1070
Kings, Five SEE The Five Kings.
The King's Henchman D318, D341
Kirchner, Leon D226, B47
Kirkpatrick, John W80, B684
Kirstein, Lincoln W53, B502
Kleffens, Eelco H. Van SEE Van
    Kleffens, Eelco H.
Klein, Howard B685-B689
Kleine Dreigroschen Musik D179
Knardahl, Eva D222
Koch, Edward I. B1103
Kodály, Zoltán D365
Kohon Quartet D359
Kohs, Ellis B. D322
Kolodin, Irving B690-B700
Koons, Walter E. B701
Korn, Peter Jona D154
Korsakoff, Nicolai Andreevich
    Rimsky SEE Rimsky-Korsakoff,
    Nicolai Andreevich.
Kostelanetz, Andre W68, W109, B227,
    B244, B490, B544, B746, B882,
    B1049
Kostelanetz, Richard B702
Koussevitzky, Natalie W38, W77,
    B255
Koussevitzky, Serge p.4, W29, W31,
    W36, W38, W77, D27, D29, D164-
    D166, D307, D310-D311, B17, B96,
    B255, B374, B390, B615, B677,
    B703, B711, B744, B957, B967,
    B1089
Koussevitzky Music Foundation W77
Kraft, Victor W48
Kraft, William D163
Krebs, Albin B704-B705
Kremenliev, Boris B706
Kresge Auditorium SEE Massachusetts
    Institute of Technology Kresge
    Auditorium.
Kriegsman, Alan M. B707-B712
Kroeger, Karl B713
Kuppenheim, Hans F. B714
Kurtz, Efrem W82
Kyle, Marguerite Kelly B715-B731

Lade, John B732
Laird, Michael D254
Lake, Mayhew Lester D191
Lamb, Horatio Appleton, Fund SEE
    Horatio Appleton Lamb Fund,
    Harvard University.
Lament W10

Lampert, Vera B733
Lane, Louis D34, D125, D208, D287
Lang, William D258
Lanier, Sidney D40
Lardeo, Jaime D330
Lardner, James B735
Larghetto Pomposo, Marcatissimo
    W108
Lark W54, D152, B256, B890
Latin-American Fiesta D101
Latin American Sketches, Three
    SEE Three Latin American Sketches.
Laurie's Song SEE The Tender Land.
Lawry, W. McNeil B462
League of Composers p.4, p.6-7,
    W39-W40, W42, W45, W66, W80,
    W90, B13, B17, B29, B113, B120,
    B187, B268, B315, B324, B332,
    B349, B360, B379, B389, B435,
    B439, B539, B650, B740, B789,
    B851, B881, B908, B911, B977,
    B1041, B1080, B1091, B1139,
    B1151, B1168, B1192
Lederman, Minna B43
Ledger, Philip D187
Leduc et Cie W37
Leibowitz, René B110
Leinsdorf, Erich B588, B1034
Lenox String Quartet W36
Leonard Bernstein Conducts for
    Young People D300
Let Us Now Praise Famous Men B470,
    B1096
Letelier Llona, Alfonso D195
Letter from Home W74, D153-D155
Letters of Composers; an Anthol-
    ogy, 1603-1945 B49
Levant, Oscar D49, B740
Levine, Joseph D42, D269, B483,
    B741
Levinger, Henry W. B742
Levy, Alan Howard B743
Lewisohn Stadium Series B361,
    B666, B1054, B1071
Lewisohn Stadium Symphony B1071
Library of Congress, Washington,
    D.C. W73, W86, B112, B416, B765,
    B927, B1164-B1165
Liepmann, Klaus W91
The Life and Music of Béla Bartók
    B31
Life Magazine W99
Lilienstein, Saul B1115
Lincoln, Abraham SEE Lincoln Por-
    trait.

Lincoln Center for the Performing Arts, New York p.6, W98, B149, B157, B191, B246, B275, B319, B327-B328, B404, B424, B468, B498, B551, B586, B592-B593, B599, B616, B621, B661, B687, B719, B744, B772, B939, B1000, B1059, B1066, B1070, B1094, B1138
Lincoln Center Summer Festival B575
Lincoln Memorial, Washington, D.C. B875
Lincoln Portrait p.5, p.7, W68, D156-D167, B187, B227, B244, B265, B273, B361, B456, B556, B623, B627, B638, B745-B746, B800, B882, B914, B1048-B1049, B1066, B1069, B1071, B1080, B1175
Lipman, Samuel B747
Lipton, Martha D353
Lisner Auditorium, Washington, D.C. B632
Liszt, Franz B104, B162
Litschauer, Franz D37, D313
The Little Horses SEE Old American Songs, Set II.
Little Orchestra Society D201, D266, B344
Little Theatre, New York B646
The Lives of the Great Composers B1001
Livingston, Herbert B749
Llona, Alfonso Letelier SEE Letelier Llona, Alfonso.
Lobster Quadrille B559, B630
Lockett, David B750
Lockspeiser, Edward B751
Logge, Thomas D332
London Mozart Players D82, B691
London Philharmonic Orchestra B279, B290
London Symphony Orchestra W101, D7-D8, D18, D21, D44-D45, D52-D53, D92-D94, D100, D109, D118-D119, D153, D157-D158, D169-D170, D194, D197-D198, D206, D249, D258, D271-D272, D275, D293, D323, D334-D335, D337, D348, D357, B136, B150, B159, B190, B265, B277-B279, B287, B318, B345-B346, B351, B371, B385, B387, B395, B423, B447, B458, B496, B516, B547, B549, B556, B559-B561, B624, B721, B732, B753-B754, B782, B810, B812, B861-B862, B867, B1028-B1031, B1160, B1181

Long Time Ago SEE Old American Songs, Set I.
Loring, Eugene W53
Los Angeles County Museum of Art. Bing Theater B172
Los Angeles County Music Center B848
Los Angeles Master Chorale B218
Los Angeles Philharmonic Orchestra D19-D20, D163, B936
Los Angeles Sinfonia Orchestra B218
Louisiana Story D266
Louisville Philharmonic Orchestra W92, D195, B714, B860
Love and Money B341
Lowe, Jack D61
Lowry, W. McNeil W529
Luening, Ethel W34, W37, D376
Luening, Otto B412
Lullaby for String Quartet D359
Lustra W30
Luten, C. J. B753-B754
Lynes, Russell B266

M-G-M Chamber Orchestra D171-D173, D180
M-G-M String Orchestra D358
M-G-M Symphony Orchestra D179, D302, B235
M.I.T. SEE Massachusetts Institute of Technology.
Maas, Robert W39
Mabry, Sharon Cody B755
McAdow, Maurice D6
Macauley, Ian T. B756
McBride, Robert Guyn D276-D277
McCandless, William Edgar B757
McCarty, Clifford B758
McCracken, Charles D369, B1112
Macdonald, Calum B759
McDowall, Roddy B298
MacDowell Association B355
MacDowell Colony p.4, W29, W36, B149, B266, B353, B355, B760, B792, B926, B939, B1137-B1138
MacDowell Medal B353
Machlis, Joseph B761
McLane, Ralph W79, B692, B762, B826, B889, B1166
MacLeish, Ada W24
McLellan, Joseph B260, B763-B765
The Macmillan Encyclopedia of Music and Musicians B1177
Maconie, Robin B766

Maddocks, D. Scott SEE Scott-
Maddocks, D.
Mahler, Fritz D128, D196
Mahler, Gustav D90, B30, B34, B62,
B425, B750
Makers of Modern Culture B562
Mann, William S. B767
Man's Right to Knowledge; an Inter-
national Symposium Presented in
Honor of the Two-Hundredth Anni-
versary of Columbia University,
1754-1954 B64
Manziarly, Marcelle D371
Marcus, Leonard B769
Marcus, Omar B770
Marias, Paul Des SEE Des Marias,
Paul.
Mark Hellinger Theater, New York
B189
Marriner, Neville D254
Marrow, Macklin D302
Marsh, Robert C. B771-B772
Marshall, Elise B870
Martin, Frank D149
Martin Beck Theatre, New York W41
Mary-Ann W97
Maskey, Jacqueline B773
Mason, Daniel Gregory D262
Mason, E. B774
Masques D241
Mass for Double Chorus, a Capella
D149
Mass, Op.123, D Major D90
Massachusetts Institute of Tech-
nology Chapel W91, B452
Massachusetts Institute of Tech-
nology Chorus W91
Massachusetts Institute of Tech-
nology Kresge Auditorium W91,
B208, B452
Massachusetts Institute of Tech-
nology Symphony Orchestra W91,
D86, D99
Masselos, William W93, D218, D235,
D245, B373, B384, B400, B648,
B877, B904, B972, B1079, B1127,
B1178
Massenet, Jules Émile Frédéric D191
Masters of Modern Music B213
The Masters Write Jazz D133
Mata, Eduardo D24, D283, D306
Mathers, Edward Powys W19
Matrix: Midland Arts Festival,
Midland, Michigan B526, B815,
B1045

Matthews, David B775
Maury, Lowndes D328
Mayer, William B776-B778
Mayfair Theater, New York W82
Mazurka in C Major, Op.24, No.2
D143
The Meaning in Reading B60
Mear, Sidney D259-D260
Medal of Freedom SEE Presidential
Medal of Freedom for Peacetime
Service.
Meeting at the Summit D80
Mehta, Zubin D19-D20, D163, B943
Melancholy; a Song à la Debussy
(Unfinished) W3
Mellers, Wilfrid B779-B781
Mellquist, Jerome B106
Men and Mountains D262
Mendelssohn-Bartholdy, Felix D96
Mennin, Peter D359
Menotti, Gian Carlo D87-D88, D208,
D318, D341, B1113
Menuhin, Hephzibah W107, B420,
B726
Menuhin, Yehudi D331
Mercury Theatre, Boston W57
Meredith, George W89
Merit Award, Boston Symphony
Orchestra p.6
Merry Mount D318, D341
Mester, Jorge D88
Metropolitan Opera House, New
York W70, B264
Mexican Fantasy SEE Fantasia
Mexicana.
Mexican Pieces, Two SEE Three
Latin American Sketches.
Michigan Opera Theatre B526, B815,
B1045
Midsummer Nocturne W81, D168, B982
Milestone, Lewis W71
Milhaud, Darius W69, D133, D294,
D298, D331, B8, B48, B68-B69,
B74
Mille, Agnes de SEE de Mille,
Agnes.
Miller, F. W86
The Milton Cross New Encyclopedia
of the Great Composers and Their
Music B397
Minneapolis Symphony Orchestra
W45, D104-D105, D278, D303,
D349, B203, B795
Miracle at Verdun W41
Mirage D256

Missa Cantuariensis D331
Mitchell, Donald B782
Mitchell, Howard D39, D69, D130,
  D315
Mitropoulos, Dimitri W45, B435, B690
Mlada D115
Mocsanyi, Edith D370, B417
Modern American Music Series B679
Modern American Piano Music D239
Modern Music-Makers, Contemporary
  American Composers B553
Mödl, Martha B698
Moment Musicale; a Tone Poem W4
Monaco, Richard A. B786
Monson, Karen B787
Montanesa D331
Montgomery, Paul L. B788
Moods for Piano Solo, Three SEE
  Three Moods for Piano Solo.
Moor, Paul B789-B790
Moore, Marianne D144, D185, D333
Morgan, Robert P. B791
Morgenthau, Alma SEE Wertheim,
  Alma Morgenthau.
Moriarty, John D256
Morning on the Ranch SEE The Red
  Pony.
Morris, Alton C. B60
Morris, Bernadine B792
Morton, David B793
Morton, Lawrence B794-B799
Morton Gould Orchestra D62, D281
Moscow Conservatory Grand Hall
  B563
Motel, Michael B526
Motets, Four SEE Four Motets.
Mount Holyoke College B276
Moyers, Bill B848
Mozart, Johann Chrysostom Wolfgang
  Amadeus D191, D373, B9, B259, B294
Muczynski, Robert D113, D375
Munch, Charles W38, B451, B801,
  B1084
Munich Opera Festival B428
Munich Opera House W95
Museum of Modern Art, New York W54,
  B315, B349, B379, B932, B1128
Music and Imagination p.6-7, B27,
  B39, B42, B52, B65, B67, B78,
  B83, B119, B162, B233, B239,
  B241-B242, B474, B476, B541,
  B571-B572, B606, B651, B797,
  B802, B806, B814, B834, B843
Music and People B953

Music and Western Man: the Canadian
  Broadcasting Corporation B105
Music Critics Circle Award B334
Music Featured at the 1973 In-
  augural Symphonic Concert D124
Music for a Great City W97, W101,
  D169, B159, B265, B277, B287,
  B387, B458, B548, B688, B721,
  B753, B786, B809-B810, B838,
  B867, B947
Music for Flute & Piano by Four
  Americans D113, B375
Music for Movies W69, D170-D172,
  B842
Music for Radio p.5, W50, D173,
  B667, B1165
Music for the Baritone Voice and
  Wind Symphony D191
Music for the Theatre p.4, W29,
  D174-D181, B97, B226, B235,
  B280, B344, B530, B538, B605,
  B703, B818, B842, B955, B959,
  B1037, D1046, D1089
Music for Young America D208
Music I Heard W15
Music in Our Time B517
Music in the Nation B574
Music in the United States: a
  Historical Introduction B605
Music Institute B184
Music Library Association W108
The Music Lover's Handbook B53,
  B55, B62, B66, B192, B667
Music Makers of Today B1191
The Music of Israel B107
Music, Right and Left B1110
Musica Viva B481, B662
Musical Exercises for Annaliberia
  D221
Musical Impressions: Selections
  from Paul Rosenfeld's Criticism
  B955
Musical Nationalism: American Com-
  posers' Search for Identity
  B743
The Musicmakers B954
Musique Americaine D212
My Heart Is in the East SEE Note-
  book with Original Songs.

NBC W84
NBS Symphony Orchestra W43, W53,
  W79, B378, B545, B701
The Naked Image B50

National Academy of Recording Art-
   ists Grammy Awards. Trustees
   Award B585, B822, B829
National Academy of St. Cecilia,
   Rome B646, B1185
National Broadcasting Company SEE
   NBC.
National Chorale B1019
National Council of American-Soviet
   Friendship B440
The National Cyclopedia of American
   Biography B332
National Federation of Music Clubs
   B816
National Geographic Society Orches-
   tra D22, D280
National Institute of Arts and
   Letters B28, B113, B174, B336,
   B356, B427, B563, B1141, B1145,
   B1185
National Music Camp, Interlochen,
   Michigan W61, B543
National Orchestral Association
   Alumni Orchestra B294
National Press Club Symposium B768
National Symphony Orchestra D39,
   D69, D130, D315, B272, B385,
   B622-B623, B625, B627-B628, B630-
   B633, B635-B638, B708-B709, B763,
   B768, B875, B888, B937, B1070,
   B1123
National Theater B1111
Natoma D318, D341
Nature, the Gentlest Mother SEE
   Twelve Poems of Emily Dickinson.
Navascues, Pablo Martin Meliton de
   Sarasate y SEE Sarasate y Naras-
   cues, Pablo Martin Meliton de.
Naylor, P. B817
The Neighborhood Playhouse, New York
   W51, B188, B736, B856, B1008
Nelhybel, Vaclar D6
Die Neue Instrumentation B61
The New Book of Modern Composers
   B474
New Concert String Ensemble D267
New Dance, Piano, 4 Hands & Per-
   cussion D154
New England Conservatory Chorus D1,
   D145, D152
New England Countryside SEE The
   City; Music for Movies.
New England Triptych D160
The New Fire B12

The New Grove Dictionary of Music
   and Musicians B179
The New Music Lover's Handbook
   B40, B46, B57, B75, B280
The New Music, 1900-1960 p.7, B15-
   B16, B46, B75-B76, B84, B422,
   B823-B825, B846, B891, B909,
   B1131, B1161
New Philharmonia Orchestra D151,
   D264, D295-D296, D351, B624,
   B1031, B1162
New School for Social Research p.4,
   W34, W37, B108, B354
New York Choral Arts Society B495
New York City Ballet B584, B1015
New York City Center W90, B120,
   B370, B444, B525, B881, B1081,
   B1086, B1168
New York City Center of Music and
   Dance SEE New York City Center.
New York City Center of Opera and
   Drama SEE New York City Center.
New York City Federal Music Project
   B312
New York City Opera Company W90,
   B207, B444, B477, B525, B620,
   B700, B742, B833, B881, B1081,
   B1098, B1151
New York City Symphony B160, B574
New York City University Colleges
   B229
New York Cultural Center B595
New York Flute Club D40
New York Music Critics' Circle
   Award p.6
New York Orchestra B1047
New York Philharmonic Promenade
   Concert W109
New York Philharmonic Symphony
   Orchestra p.6, W45, W73, W98,
   W103, W109, D10-D11, D13-D14,
   D41, D43, D46-D47, D83, D90-
   D91, D101-D102, D150, D159-D160,
   D162, D175-D177, D268, D273-
   D274, D297, D299-D301, D317,
   D339-D340, D345, D347, B157,
   B163, B171, B221, B224, B275,
   B289, B328, B340, B342, B404,
   B413, B424, B462-B463, B490,
   B495, B498, B544, B551, B558,
   B575, B579, B586-B587, B590,
   B592-B593, B598-B599, B618,
   B621, B643, B682, B685-B686,
   B689-B690, B693, B698, B719,

B722, B724-B725, B753, B827-B828,
B861, B906-B907, B943, B948,
B974, B980, B990, B996-B997,
B1000, B1016, B1021, B1046, B1049,
B1083, B1094, B1121, B1126
New York Philharmonic Young Peo-
ple's Concert SEE Young People's
Concert.
New York Quartet W86, D252, B489
New York State University College,
Potsdam. Crane Chorus D72, D193,
B344
New York State University College,
Potsdam. Crane Symphony Orchestra
D72, D129, D155, D193, D338, D344
New York Symphony Orchestra p.4,
W26
New York University B1042
New York Women's City Club B1113
New York World's Fair SEE World's
Fair, New York, 1939.
New Weston Hotel, New York B1113
Newlin, Dika B830
Newman, Bill B831
Newman, William S. B832
Nichols, Lewis B834
Nicklin, Celia D254
Nieuw Amsterdam Trio D370, B417
Night W6
Night Soliloquy, for Flute and
Strings D259
Night Thoughts (Homage to Ives) p.7,
W111, D182-D185, B297, B596,
B728, B982, B1026, B1074
No Country Can My Own Outvie D318,
D341
No for an Answer B55
Noble, J. B835
Nocturne SEE Two Pieces for Violin
and Piano.
Nocturnes, Piano Trio D370
Nonagon Art Gallery B877
Nonet p.6, W96, D186, B313, B339,
B386, B398, B450, B532, B617,
B629, B706, B836-B837, B897,
B927, B983, B987, B1011
Norlin Foundation B1138
Norman, Gertrude B49
North American Ballads D137
North Star W71
North Texas State University Con-
cert Band D6
Northcott, Bayan B838-B840

Norton, Charles Eliot, Professor
of Poetry SEE Charles Eliot
Norton Professor of Poetry,
Harvard University.
Norwood, Ann Bussert B841
Notebook with Original Songs W7
Notes sans Musique B68
Notes Without Music: an Auto-
biography B68
Notturno D76
Novik, Ylda B846
Le Nozze di Figaro D191
La Nueva Musica, Buenos Aires W64
Nun Ich der Riesen Stärksten D331
The Nutcracker D107, D300

Oakes, James Alfred B847
Occidental College B269
O'Connor, John J. B848-B850
Octandre D4
Odets, Clifford W64
Oedipus Rex B100
Of Mice and Men W59, B69, B2,
B1062
Ohio State University B180
Oja, Carol J. B851
Ojai, California Festival W88,
W110, W112, B173, B787
Ojai Festival Orchestra W88, W110,
W112
Old American Songs, Set I p.6, W85,
D187-D193, B161, B209, B344,
B361, B577, B853, B855, B974
Old American Songs, Set II p.6,
W88, D187-D193, B161, B209,
B344, B361, B505, B577, B852-
B855, B923, B974, B1025
The Old Chisholm Trail D208
Old Poem p.3, W16, W19
Olin Downes on Music; a Selection
from His Writings During the
Half-Century 1906 to 1955 B446
Olivier, Laurence W84, B248
On the Beach at Fontana D332
Once a Lady Was Here D332
176 Keys; Music for Two Pianos
D107
Onégin, Eugene SEE Eugene Onégin.
Onnou, Alphonse W39
The Open Prairie SEE Billy the Kid.
Oppenheim, David D322, B679
Oppens, Kurt B858
Oral History Project, Columbia
University SEE Columbia Univer-
sity Oral History Project.

Orchestra of America B878
Orchestral Variations W40, W92,
   D194-D196, B714, B859-B860,
   B975-B976, B1181, B1186
Order of Merit, Cross of the Com-
   mander SEE German Republic Cross
   of the Commander of the Order of
   Merit.
Orga, Ates B861-B863
Organ Symphony SEE Symphony for
   Organ and Orchestra.
Ormandy, Eugene W45, W79, W105, D12,
   D26, D48, D50, D56-D57, D120-D124,
   D161, B692, B762, B889, B1166
Orquésta Sinfónica de México W43,
   W48
Orrego Salas, Juan B864-B865
Osborne, Charles B866-B867
Oscar SEE Academy of Motion Picture
   Arts and Sciences.
Ottaway, Hugh B868-B869
Our American Music; a Comprehensive
   History from 1620 to the Present
   B613
Our Contemporary Composers; Ameri-
   can Music in the Twentieth Cen-
   tury B612
Our New Music; Leading Composers in
   Europe and America p.3, p.5, p.7,
   B34, B55, B66, B76, B84, B422,
   B438, B574, B750, B824-B825, B891
Our Town p.6, W62, W69, D197-D204,
   B872, B918, B974, B1040, B1062-
   B1063, B1068
An Outdoor Overture p.5, W55, D205-
   D209, B160, B178, B314, B316,
   B698, B827, B871, B960, B1083
Overmyer, Grace B872
Overton, H. B873
Overton, James L. B874
Overture Di Ballo D207
Overture to the School for Scandel
   SEE School for Scandel.
Owlett, Carolyn R. B392

PBS SEE Public Broadcasting System.
Padorr, Laila D113, D375
Page, Ruth W44
Paisaje Mexicano SEE Three Latin
   American Sketches.
Palestrina, Giovanni Pierluigi da
   B57
Palmer, C. B876
Paris-American-Gargenville Chorus
   W18

Parmenter, Ross B877-B882
Passacaglia p.4, W23, D210-D216,
   B201, B203, B330, B795, B982,
   B1064, B1173, B1190
Pastorale W16, W19, D40
Pastorale for Oboe, Strings, and
   Harp D259
Patterson, Frank B883
Paul Jacobs Plays Blues, Ballads
   & Rags D137
Paul Rosenfeld, Voyager in the
   Arts B58, B106
Pavlakis, Christopher B884
The Peaceable Kingdom D147
Peare, Catherine Owens B885
Pears, Peter W85, D192
Peck, Gregory D163
Peebles, Anthony D221, B691
Peerce, Jan B886
Pall, Mary Beth D40
Pelléas et Mélisande D165
Penchansky, A. B887
People: a volume of the Good, Bad,
   Great & Eccentric Who Illustrate
   the Admirable Diversity of Man
   B564
Perez, Antonio D191
Persichetti, Vincent B889
Perspectives on American Composers
   B324
Peter Grimes B10
Peterson, Melody B890
Peterson, Melva B891
Petit Portrait SEE Three Moods for
   Piano Solo.
Peyer, Gervaise Alan de SEE de
   Peyer, Gervaise Alan.
Peyser, Joan B51
Phi Mu Alpha Sinfonia B543
Philadelphia Academy of Music W27,
   B1033
Philadelphia Symphony Orchestra
   W27, W79, W107, D12, D26, D48,
   D50, D56-D57, D120-D124, D161,
   B161, B496, B692, B762, B889,
   B1166
Philco Radio Hour W74
Philco Radio Orchestra W74
Philharmonia Orchestra D346
Philharmonic Hall SEE Lincoln
   Center for the Performing Arts,
   New York.
Phillips, Harvey E. B893
Piano Blues, Four SEE Four Piano
   Blues.

Piano Concerto SEE Concerto for
    Piano and Orchestra.
Piano Concerto in A Minor D124
Piano Concerto, Op.38 D86
Piano Fantasy p.6, W93, D217-D221,
    B202, B246, B280, B373, B384,
    B400, B467, B469, B479-B480,
    B491, B589, B661, B691, B706,
    B756, B830, B847, B877, B904,
    B935, B972, B982, B1023, B1073,
    B1079, B1125, B1127, B1167,
    B1178, B1189
Piano Music in America, Vol.2:
    1900-1945 D247
Piano Music of the Twentieth Cen-
    tury D77
Piano Quartet SEE Quartet for
    Piano and Strings.
Piano Rag Music D133
Piano Sonata p.5, W64, B49, B87,
    B203, B245, B522, B568, B684,
    B728, B785, B795, B830, B842,
    B978, B982, D1112, B1125, B1127,
    B1187
Piano Sonata [by Carter] D239
Piano Sonata and Other Works D75
Piano Variations p.5, W40, W92,
    D234-D248, B49, B87, B127, B192,
    B200, B203, B264, B280, B283,
    B338, B605, B795, B868, B915,
    B924, B938, B982, B1125, B1127,
    B1173, B1178, B1187
Picoto, J. C. B895
Pieces D6
Pieces for String Quartet, Two SEE
    Two Pieces for String Quartet.
Pieces for Violin and Piano, Two
    See Two Pieces for Violin and
    Piano.
The Pied Piper B584
Pintavalle, John D370, B417
Pisciotta, Louis Vincent B896
Piston, Walter p.4, D11, D36, D99,
    D113, D114, D204, D359, D373,
    D375, B3-B4, B25, B72, B699,
    B807, B1037
Pittsburgh International Contempor-
    ary Music Festival D156
Pittsburgh Symphony Orchestra D15,
    D31, D38, D51, D64, D68, D156
Plaistow, Stephen B897
Platek, L. B563
The Playhouse SEE The Neighborhood
    Playhouse, New York.

Plaza Hotel, New York B788, B792
Pleasants, Henry B60, B739, B886
Pleshakov, Vladimir D96
Plummer Park, Los Angeles B706
Poem W8
Poems by Edwin Arlington Robinson
    D332
Poems Juifs D196
Poems of Emily Dickinson SEE
    Twelve Poems of Emily Dickinson.
Poet's Song (E. E. Cummings) SEE
    Song (E. E. Cummings).
Pohjola's Daughter D165
Pollikoff, Max B517
Polonaise in A-flat Major, Op.53
    D143
Porgy and Bess D293, D304, D314
Porter, Andrew B898-B901
Portrait of F.B. (Frances Blood)
    D144, D185, D333
Portraits of Greatness B664
Posell, Elsa Z. B902
Posselt, Ruth W72
The Pot of Fat B208
Poulenc, Francis D81, B18
Pound, Ezra W30
Prairie Journal SEE Music for
    Radio.
Prairie Night SEE Billy the Kid.
Preamble for a Solemn Occasion
    W84, D249, B248, B402, B903,
    B924
Prelude D331
Prelude for Violin and Piano W11
Prelude, Fugue, and Riffs D80
Prelude (Second) for Violin and
    Piano W20
Preludes, Piano D212, D253
Première Rhapsodie for Clarinet
    D81
President Theatre, New York B442
Presidential Medal of Freedom for
    Peacetime Service B309, B721,
    B1104, B1135
Previn, André D265, B426, B1030
Princeton University p.7, B175,
    B508, B1185
Pritchard, John D293
Proceedings of the American Acad-
    emy of Arts and Letters and the
    National Institute of Arts and
    Letters B28
Procession of the Nobles D115
Prokofiev, Sergey D154, B374, B1077

Promenade Concert, Albert Hall,
  London B144, B860
The Promise of Living SEE The Ten-
  der Land.
Protée--Symphonic Suite No.2 B8
Public Broadcasting System p.6,
  B273, B848, B875, B1130, B1147
Pulitzer Prize p.6-7, B112, B187,
  B284, B310, B312, B332, B520,
  B788, B902
Pure Contraption: a Composer's
  Essays B952

Quartet, C Minor, Piano and Strings,
  Op.60 D373
Quartet for Clarinet, Violin, Viola,
  and Cello D331
Quartet for Piano and Strings p.6,
  W86, D250-D253, B172, B209, B246,
  B283, B416, B469, B489, B539,
  B676, B715, B765, B799, B894,
  B1041
Quartet in D, Flute and Strings,
  K.285 D373
Quartet in F, Oboe and Strings,
  K.370 D373
Quartet in One Movement, Op.23 D359
Quartet, Strings, Op.11, B Minor
  D135, D254
Quartet, Strings, Op.19, G Minor
  D262
Queens College, Flushing, New York.
  Aaron Copland School of Music
  B229, B608, B912
Quiet City p.5, W60, D254-D263,
  B210, B318, B361, B559, B561,
  B766, B849, B913, B1029

RCA Victor Company p.4, W27, W38,
  B15, B114, B404
RCA Victor Symphony Orchestra D55,
  D59-D60, D63, D336, B483
Rachmaninoff Fund, Inc. B914
Radcliffe, Donnie B260
Radio City Music Hall, New York
  W83, B378
Radio Symphony Orchestra B161
Ragin, John D156
Ragtime D133
Railroad Ballad SEE John Henry.
Ramey, Phillip B915
The Rape of Lucretia B10
Ravel, Maurice D231, B18
Rawsthorne, Alan D331
The Red Pony p.6, W82, D264-D266,

B115, B118, B150, B289, B426,
  B453, B674, B798, B919, B1031,
  B1110
Redes B59
Redlich, Hans F. B921-B924
Reger, Max D331
Reif, Rita B926
Reincarnation, Op.16 D146
Reiner, Fritz W79
Reinthaler, Joan B927
Reis, Claire Raphael B13, B51,
  B908, B928, B1050
Renzi, Dorothy B1128
RePass, R. B929
Respighi, Ottorino D76
The Resting-Place on the Hill SEE
  Our Town.
Revueltas, Silvestre D101, B59
Reyer, C. B931
Reynolds, Gerald W30
Rhein, John Von SEE Von Rhein,
  John.
Rhodes, Phillip D6
Rich, Alan B932-B933
Richter, Alexander W55
Rickman, Michael Lee B935
Riegger, Wallingford D154, D208,
  B878
Riley, Robert B936
Rimsky-Korsakoff, Nicolai Andre-
  evich D107, D115, B162
The Rite of Spring B100, B775
Roach, Hal W59
Robbins, Jerome B584
Roberts, Bernard B589
Robinson, Edwin Arlington W30,
  D332
Roca, Octavio B937
Rochester Philharmonic Orchestra
  W25
Rockwell, John B938-B943
Rodeo p.5, p.7, W70, D267-D291,
  B154, B181, B263, B407, B505,
  B607, B635-B636, B741, B773,
  B861, B944-B946, B974-B976,
  B1015, B1163, B1181
Rodgers, Richard p.6, W90, D25,
  D284, B120, B389, B881, B977,
  B1091, B1151, B1168, B1192
Rodzinski, Artur W73, D159, D162
Rogers, Bernard D25
Rogers, Harold B947-B949
Rome Radio Orchestra D84-D85, D89
Romero, Hector Manuel B951
Rondo Capriccioso D40

The Roosters Lay Eggs in Kansas
D191
Root, Michael B729
Rorem, Ned D226, B352, B952–B953
Rose, Werner D371
Rosenberg, Bernard B954
Rosenberg, Deena B954
Rosenfeld, Paul p.4, B58, B88,
B106, B955–B963
Der Rosenkavalier D107
Rosenteil, L. B964
Rosenwald, H. B965
Rosenwald, Peter J. B966–B967
Rosoff, H. W52
Rossini, Gioacchino Antonio D191,
B259
Rosso, Charles Francis Del SEE Del
Rosso, Charles Francis.
Rostropouich, Mstislav B632–B633
Rother, Arthur D36
Rothstein, Edward B968–B969
Rounds for String Orchestra D257
Roussel, Albert Charles Paul D331
Roxy Theatre, New York W59
Royal Academy of Music B1099
Royal College of Music B817
Royal Festival Hall SEE Festival
Hall, London.
Royal Philharmonic Society B863,
B1121
Rubbra, Edmund D331
Ruggles, Carl D262, B491, B818
A Rumor D254
The Running Sun D332
Ruskin, Abbott D86
Russell, Margaret B970
Rutgers University p.7, B724
Rzewski, Frederic D137

Sabin, Robert B972–B974
Le Sacre du Printemps SEE The Rite
of Spring.
Sadie, Stanley B179, B975–B976
Safford, Laura Tappen B977
Saga of the Prairie SEE Music for
Radio.
Sahr, Hadassah Gallup B978
Saidenberg, Daniel W60
Saidenberg Little Symphony Orches-
tra W60, W69
St. Cecilia Academy SEE National
Academy of St. Cecilia, Rome.
St. Louis Symphony Orchestra D265,
B426

St. Martin-in-the-Fields Academy
SEE Academy of St. Martin-in-
the-Fields.
St. Paul Chamber Orchestra D32,
B167, B576, B916
St. Regis-Sheraton, New York B926
Salas, Juan Orrego SEE Orrego
Salas, Juan.
Saleski, Gdal B979
Salle des Agriculteurs, Paris
W16, W19
El Salón México p.5, W47–W48,
D292–D316, B15, B257, B302,
B340, B342, B354, B447, B450,
B453, B464, B544, B618, B701,
B731–B732, B980, B990, B1031,
B1073, B1126, B1149
Salzman, Eric B981–B987
Saminsky, Lazar W49
Samuel, Gerhard B696
San Francisco Conservatory of
Music B388
San Francisco Symphony Orchestra
B380
San Jose State College A Cappella
Choir D148
Sandburg, Carl D160
Sandler, Myron D328
Sanroma, Jesús María D76–D77
Santa Fe Chamber Music Festival
B676.
Sarasate y Navascues, Pablo
Martin Melitón de D365
Sargeant, Winthrop B988–B991
Satie, Erik D331
Saturday Night Waltz SEE Rodeo.
Schaffer, Aaron W6–W7
Schechner, Richard B50
Schein, Ann D330
Scherchen, Hermann B93
Scherman, Thomas D201, D266
Scherzo for Two Violins, Viola,
and Cello D359
Scherzo Humoristique SEE The Cat
and the Mouse.
Schindler, Kurt W65
Schippers, Thomas W90
Schmidt-Garre, Helmut B992
Schneider, Alexander W86, B543
Schoenberg, Arnold p.3, D115,
D331, B9, B110, B1149
Schoenberg and His School B110
Schola Cantorum W65
Schonberg, Harold C. B993–B1002

School for Scandal D3, D178
Schubart, Mark A. B1003
Schubert, Franz Peter D143, B57
Schuller, Gunther B575
Schuman, William Howard D25, D42,
    D146, D160, D204, D359, B29,
    B412, B637, B960, B1004-B1006,
    B1055
Schumann, Robert Alexander D241,
    B259
Schwantner, Joseph C. D116
Schwartz, Charles B566
Schwartz, Elliott B27, B940
Score of the Month Club SEE Boosey
    Hawkes Publishing Company.
Scott-Maddocks, D. B1007
Scriabine, Alexander B34
Sea-Shell D365
Seattle Symphony B195
The Second Hurricane p.5, W51, D317-
    D318, B188, B192, B225, B288,
    B462, B497, B654, B736, B781,
    B827, B856, B893, B932, B961,
    B1008-B1009, B1081, B1088, B1128
Second Quartet B334
Second Rhapsody D49
Second String Quartet D359
Selig, Robert D256
Sensemayá D101
Sentimental Melody W32, D319 SEE
    ALSO Four Piano Blues.
Serenade D331
Serenade for Clarinet and Strings
    D259
Serenade for Flute, Strings, and
    Harp D259
Serenade for Strings in C, Op.48
    D107
Serenade in D, Flute, Violin, and
    Viola, Op.25 D373
Serenade to Music D90
Seroff, Victor I. B1012
Sessions, Roger p.4, D117, D204,
    D226, D239, D332, D359, B3-B4,
    B6, B445, B807, B851, B877,
    B938, B940, B1037, B1054, B1102
Seventh Symphony B62
A 75th Birthday Celebration D7,
    D44, D92, D118, D157, D197, D271,
    D295
Sextet for String Quartet, Clarinet,
    and Piano W43, W52, D320-D322,
    B431, B509, B609, B679, B1013,
    B1134 SEE ALSO Short Symphony
    (No.2).

Shaffer, Elaine W107, D112, B420,
    B629, B726
The Shakedown Song SEE Las
    Agachadas.
Shakespeare, William W57
Shanes, Estelle M. B1014
Shapero, Harold D237
Shaw, Irwin W60
Shaw, Oliver D40
Shaw, Robert W53, B1172
Shawe-Taylor, Desmond B1015-B1016
Shepard, Richard F. B1017-B1018
Shepherd, Arthur D208
Sherman, Robert B1019
Shields, Roger D247
Shimmy D133
Shneerson, G. B1020
Short Symphony (No.2) p.5, W43,
    W52, D323, B222, B378, B431,
    B496, B509, B775, B921, B991,
    B1021-B1022, B1090 SEE ALSO
    Sextet for String Quartet,
    Clarinet, and Piano.
Shostakovich, Dmitrii Dmitrievich
    D207, D331, B304, B336, B356,
    B563
Shrifte, Miriam Lubell B49
Sibelius, Jean D165, B34, B62,
    B750
Sidlin, Murry B637
Sidorsky, Judith W52
Siebert, F. Mark B1025
Siegmeister, Elie B40, B46, B53,
    B55, B57, B62, B66, B75, B192,
    B280, B667, B940, B1026
Silverman, Robert D75, D138,
    D215, D230, B1027
Simone W12
Simmons, David B1028-B1031
Simple Gifts SEE Old American
    Songs, Set I; Appalachian
    Spring.
Sinding, Christian D222
Sinfonia da Requiem, Op.20 D265
Sinfonia India D101
Sinfonia of London B1032
Sinfonietta, Op.1 D4
Sing Ye Praises to Our King SEE
    Four Motets.
Singer, Joan D74, D111, D134,
    D142, D184, D213, D220, D227,
    D240, D319, D355
Singer, Samuel L. B1033
Six Intermezzi, Op.4 D241
Skladatelé o Hudební Poetice 20
Skoleti: Copland [et al.] B1035

Skovran, D. B1036
Skriabin, Aleksandr Nikolaevich D331
Skyline SEE Music for a Great City.
Slaughter on Tenth Avenue D25, D284
Slee Professor of Music, University
   of Buffalo B337
Sleep Is Supposed to Be SEE Twelve
   Poems of Emily Dickinson.
Slonimsky, Nicolas B49, B1037
A Smattering of Ignorance B740
Smetana, Bedrich B261
Smit, Leo W66, W88, D73, D84-D85,
   D106, D108, D110, D131-D133,
   D140-D141, D168, D182, D199-
   D200, D203, D210, D217, D223,
   D225, D234, D244, D329, D354,
   B311, B542, B574, B596, B648,
   B715, B729, B982, B1038-B1040,
   B1157
Smith, Cecil B1041
Smith, Charles Harvard Gribbs SEE
   Gribbs-Smith, Charles Harvard.
Smith, Gregg, Singers SEE Gregg
   Smith Singers.
Smith, Julia Frances p.7, B183,
   B281, B514, B537, B751, B930,
   B1012, B1042-B1044, B1087, B1180
Smith, Melville W18
Smith, Patricia Beach B1045
Smith, Patrick J. B1046
Smith, Rollin B1047
Smithsonian Institution B1056
Snell, Howard D33
Société Musicale Indépendante,
   Paris W23-W24, W33
Society for Twentieth Century Music
   B1134
Soliloquy for Flute and Strings
   D259
Solomon, Izler D179, D358, B235
Somer, Hilde D224, D326, D369,
   B1112
Something Wild W97, W101, B329,
   B399, B688, B718, B1106, B1165
Sonata, Flute D40
Sonata, Flute and Piano D114
Sonata for Clarinet and Piano D81
Sonata for Flute and Piano D113,
   D375
Sonata for Piano SEE Piano Sonata.
Sonata for Piano, G Major W21
Sonata for Violin and Piano p.6,
   W72, D324-D331, B629, B983, B1112
Sonata in Memory of the Korean War
   Dead D328

Sonata, No.1, in D D237
Sonata No.3 D237
Sonata, Piano D226
Sonata, Piano, No.2 D239
Sonata, Piano, No.14, Op.27, No.2
   C# Minor D143
Sonata, Piano, Op.91, B Minor D222
Sonata, Violin and Piano D330
Sonata, Violin and Piano, No.2
   D328
Sonata, Violin and Piano, No.4
   D330
Sonata, Violin and Piano, Op.11,
   No.2, D Major D324
Sonatina, Flute and Piano D114
Song (E. E. Cummings) W34, D332-
   D333
Song of an Old Woman D332
Song of the Guerrillas SEE North
   Star.
Sonnets for Piano, Three SEE
   Three Sonnets for Piano.
Soria, Dorle J. B1048 B1052
Soundpieces: Interviews with
   American Composers B519
Southwest Radio Orchestra B569-
   B570
Spectrum D115
Spencer, Kenneth D159, D162
Spicknall, Joan Singer B1053
Spiritual and Blues D133
Spirituals for Orchestra D18,
   D97, D159
Spofford, Grace W51
Springfield Mountain SEE Lincoln
   Portrait.
Springtime Overture D207
Spurned Love SEE Notebook with
   Original Songs.
Stadium Concerts SEE Lewisohn
   Stadium Series.
Stadium Symphony SEE Lewisohn
   Stadium Symphony.
Stambler, B. B1055
Starin, Dennis B1056
Starr, Lawrence B501, B1057
Stars and Stripes D25, D284
The State of Music B102
Statements p.5, W45, D334-D336,
   B430, B447, B505, B732, B752-
   B753, B981, B1058
Steinbeck, John W59, W82, B289,
   B798
Steinberg, William W53, D15, D31,
   D38, D51, D64, D68, D156

Steiner, Diana D365
Steinway Hall B528, B784
Stereo Review Certificate of Merit
  B165
Stern, Isaac D325
Stern, Walter H. B1059
Sterne, Michael B1060
Sternfeld, Frederick W. B1061-
  B1063
Stevens, Elizabeth Mruk B1064
Stevens, Halsey D95, B31
Stevenson, Adlai E. D161, B361,
  B1066, B1071
Stevenson, J. B1065
Stewart, Delmar B311
Still, William Grant D276-D277,
  B955
Stilling Mariü mit dem Auf-
  erstandenen D331
Stith, Maurice D16, D115
Stoddard, Hope B1067
Stokowski, Leopold W27, W43, D43,
  D47, B289, B378
Stomp Your Foot SEE The Tender Land.
Story-Lives of American Composers
  B185
Story of Our Town SEE Our Town.
Stratford Ensemble D4
Strauss, Richard D107, D300, D331,
  B34, B750
Strauss, Theodore B1068
Stravinsky, Igor p.3, D80, D107,
  D133, D165, D329, D331, B43, B86,
  B99-B100, B212, B287, B304, B371,
  B394, B582, B639, B775, B787
Stravinsky, Igor, in Memorium SEE
  Threnody I: Igor Stravinsky in
  Memoriam.
Stravinsky in the Theatre B43
Street in a Frontier Town SEE Billy
  the Kid.
Strickland, William W63
String Quartet B379
String Quartet in F Sharp Minor
  D331
String Quartet No.2 D331, D359
String Quartet No.3 D359
String Quartet No.4 B29
String Quartet No.5 D359
String Quartet No.6 D331
String Quartet (Unfinished) W1
String Trio in A Minor D331
The Stronger D353
Strongin, Theodore B1069-B1071
Study on a Jewish Theme SEE Vitebsk.

Subway Jam SEE Music for a Great
  City.
Suite D212
Suite for Violin and Piano, Op.18
  D365
Suite, Op.15, No.2 D107
Suite, Piano D253
Suk, Josef D365
Sullivan, Arthur Seymour D207
A Summer Vacation SEE Notebook
  with Original Songs.
Summerfield, Jack D. B80
Sunday Afternoon Music SEE Two
  Children's Pieces.
Sunday Traffic SEE Music for
  Movies; The City.
Sure on This Shining Night D332
Surette, Thomas Whitney W30
Susskind, Walter D18
Swan, Annalyn B1072
Swan Lake D107
Swearengin, Anita D113, D375
Swickard, Ralph B1073
Swift, Richard B1074
Swingley, Richard D259-D260
Sykes, Gerald W40
Symonette, Randolph D188
Symphonic Ode p.4-5, W38, D337-
  D338, B247, B274, B340, B342,
  B404, B451, B513, B557, B573,
  B618, B801, B862, B957, B990,
  B1084, B1126, B1183
Symphony for Band D6
Symphony for Organ and Orchestra
  p.4, W26, W35, D339, B25, B290,
  B377, B431, B588, B669, B1047
  SEE ALSO First Symphony.
Symphony Hall, Boston W36
Symphony No.1 SEE First Symphony.
Symphony No.1 [by Stevens] D95
Symphony No.2 SEE Short Symphony
  (No.2)
Symphony No.2 [by Ives] D20
Symphony No.3 SEE Third Symphony.
Symphony No.3 [by Harris] D260,
  D345, D349
Symphony No.5 D156
Symphony, No.8, E Flat Major, Pt.1
  D90
Symphony No.13 D254
Symphony of the Air D87-D88, B223
Symphony Orchestra of Radio
  Berlin D36
Symphony Space D352, B941, B1103,
  B1159

Symphony After Plato D339
Symposium on Music Criticism,
   Harvard University W78
Syracuse University B721, B1123
Szell, George B614
Szmolyan, Walter B1076

Taggard, Genvieve W54
Tangents D242
Tanglewood Music Festival SEE
   Berkshire Music Center at Tangle-
   wood, Lenox, Massachusetts.
Tanglewood on Parade B918
Tansman, Alexandre D133
Tarvin, Ronald Dean B1077
Taubman, Howard B1078-B1092
Taylor, Deems D318, D341
Taylor, Desmond Shawe SEE Shawe-
   Taylor, Desmond.
Taylor, M. B1093
Tchaikovsky, Peter Ilich D107, D124
Tcherepnine, Alexandre D371
Tear, Robert D187
Tel Aviv Chamber Choir B554
Temianka, Henri B652
Temple University B716
Ten Fanfares B478
The Tender Land p.6, W90, D340-
   D344, B120, B173, B207, B214,
   B238, B252-B254, B293, B296, B317,
   B370, B375, B389, B444, B448,
   B455, B470, B477, B495, B511,
   B525-B526, B591, B614, B620,
   B654, B678, B686, B700, B742,
   B779, B813, B815, B833, B857-
   B858, B881, B900, B918, B977,
   B989, B1002, B1023-B1024, B1045,
   B1081-B1082, B1086, B1091, B1095-
   B1100, B1115, B1130, B1151,
   B1168, B1187, B1192
Terrance Theater SEE Kennedy Center
   for the Performing Arts, Washing-
   ton, D.C.
Terry, Kenneth B1101
Texas Christian University B1026
Thanksgiving Song SEE The Tender
   Land.
Thatcher, Lorlyn B80
Theatre Guild W41
Theme and Variations, Op.43a D115
There Came a Wind Like a Bugle SEE
   Twelve Poems of Emily Dickinson.
These, My Ophelia D332
They All Laughed D144, D185, D333

Thigpen, Helen B697
Third Symphony p.6, W77, D345-
   D350, B195, B200, B224, B255,
   B334, B336, B338, B383, B390-
   B391, B478, B563, B575, B630,
   B698, B718, B753-B754, B782,
   B795, B827, B936, B943, B991,
   B1030, B1075, B1083, B1160
This Bright Day; an Autobiography
   B461
Thomas, Michael Tilson B787
Thompson, Howard B1106
Thompson, Oscar B1107
Thompson, Randall D147, B6, B256
Thomson, Virgil p.4, D40, D144,
   D185, D204, D266, D333, D359,
   B3-B4, B25, B72, B102, B605,
   B699, B807, B1050, B1108-B1111
Thou, O Jehovah, Abideth Forever
   SEE Four Motets.
3 American Trios D372
3 Dances D25
Three Ghost Rags D137
Three Latin American Sketches
   W109, D351, B490, B544, B558,
   B622, B624, B713, B715, B907
Three Moods for Piano Solo W22
Three Piano Blues SEE Four Piano
   Blues.
Three Places in New England D17,
   D32, D120, D161, D255, B167,
   B576, B916
Three Poems of Robert Frost D144,
   D185, D333
Three Preludes D133, D237
Three Preludes for Unaccompanied
   Flute, Op.18 D113, D375
Three Rag Caprices D133
Three Sonnets for Piano W17
Three Studies, Op.18 D221
Threnody I: Igor Stravinsky in
   Memoriam p.7, W110, B609, B639,
   B787
Threnody II: Beatrice Cunningham
   in Memoriam p.7, W112, B609,
   B728, B787
Threshing Machines SEE Music for
   Movies; Of Mice and Men.
Thurston, Frederick B1078
Tiggs, Harold D276
Till Eulenspiegel's Merry Pranks,
   Op.28 D300
Timbrell, Charles B1115
Tippett, Michael B1116
Tircuit, Heuwell B1117-B1118

Tis the Gift to be Simple SEE
Appalachian Spring; Old American
Songs, Set I.
Tischler, Hans B1119
Toback, James B341
Tomatz, David D371
Toor, Frances W48
Toperczer, Peter D139
Toscanini, Arturo B700
Totten, Edyth, Theatre SEE Edyth
Totten Theatre, New York.
Toward an American Opera, 1911-1954
D318, D341
Toward the Bridge SEE Music for a
Great City.
Town Hall, New York W65-W66, W69,
W72, B344, B842, B1120
Tracey, Edmund B1121
Tredici, David Del SEE Del Tredici,
David.
Trenkner, Evelinde D96
Treigle, Norman D340
Trilogue D371
Trimble, Lester B1125-B1129
Trio à Cordes de Paris D253
Trio for Piano and Strings D250
Trio for Violin, Viola, and Cello
D331
Trio for Violin, Violoncello, and
Piano D372
Trio, Op.34, D Major D371
Trio, Piano and Strings D370
Trio, Piano, No.2 D371
Trio-Sonatas D40
Trois Esquisses pour Piano Seul
SEE Three Moods for Piano Solo.
Trois Pièces Montrées D331
Trois Pièces pour Quatuor à Cordes
D331
Truman, Harry S. B920
Trumpet Air D117
Trumpet Concerto (Sinfonia) in C
Major, P.34 D256
Trustees Award SEE National Academy
of Recording Artists Grammy
Awards. Trustees Award.
Tuck, Lon B1130
Tully, Alice, Hall SEE Lincoln
Center for the Performing Arts,
New York.
Turina, Joaquin D371
Turner, Claramae D340
Turok, Paul B1131

Twelve Poems of Emily Dickinson
p.6, W87, D352-D353, B172, B349,
B393, B410, B484, B497, B697,
B715, B755, B767, B839, B1041,
B1128, B1132-B1133, B1188
Twentieth Century Masterpieces
B359
20th Century Music for Two Pianos
D61
20 Valses D143
Two by Marianne Moore D144, D185,
D333
Two Children's Pieces p.5, W49,
D354-D355, B982
Two Choric Dances, Op.17b D257
Two Compositions for Chorus of
Women's Voices W30, D356
Two Mexican Pieces SEE Three
Latin American Sketches.
Two Nocturnes D242
Two Pieces for String Orchestra
D357-D358 SEE ALSO Two Pieces
for String Quartet.
Two Pieces for String Quartet
W36, D359-D360, B443 SEE ALSO
Two Pieces for String Orchestra.
Two Pieces for Violin and Piano
W33, D361-D366
Two Songs for Alto and Piano B98
The Two Worlds of American Art,
the Private and the Popular
B1146

Ukulele Serenade SEE Two Pieces
for Violin and Piano.
Ulanov, Barry B1146
Das Unaufhorliche B99
Undertow D42
Unfinished Symphony and Other
Stories of Men and Music B215
Unger, Arthur B1147-B1148
Union of Composers, U.S.S.R. B776
United Nations W84, B248, B402,
B427, B882
United States. Capitol B627, B635,
B638
United States. Copyright Act B26
United States. Department of
Justice B440, B1144
United States. Department of State
SEE United States. State
Department.
United States. Embassy B375

United States. House of Represent-
atives. Committee on Un-American
Activities B456
United States. House of Represent-
atives. Judiciary Subcommittee
B26
United States. Information Service
B1003
United States. Inter-American
Relations p.5, B114
United States. Office of War In-
formation. Overseas Unit W75
United States. Senate. Investi-
gations Subcommittee B155
United States. State Department
p.5, B137, B718, B1140
Universal Declaration of Human
Rights B248
University of Bridgeport B135
University of Buffalo B337
University of Chile B720
University of Cincinnati College-
Conservatory of Music B1158
University of Hartford B716
University of Iowa Symphony B455
University of Kansas Symphonic
Band D191
University of Leeds p.7
University of Michigan W103, B163,
B598, B621, B643, B721, B724,
B906
University of New Hampshire
Distinguished Lecture Series B90
University of Oklahoma Trio D372
University of Rhode Island B721
University of Southern California
Hancock Auditorium B1073
University of Southern California
Trojan Band W100
Utah Symphony Orchestra D54, D67,
D70-D71, D167, D202, D209, D263,
D279, D291-D292, D304, D314, D316

Vactor, David Van SEE Van Vactor,
David.
Valencia M., Ernesto B1149
van Beethoven, Ludwig SEE Beethoven,
Ludwig van.
Van Cliburn International Piano
Competition, 4th, September 17-
30, 1973, Texas Christian Univer-
sity, Forth Worth, Texas p.7,
W111, B297, B728, B1026

Van Kleffens, Eelco H. B427
Van Vactor, David D114
Vandero, Giovanni Gualdo da SEE
Gualdo da Vandero, Giovanni.
Vanessa: Intermezzo, Act 4 D160
Vardi, E. W52
Varèse, Edgar D4, B51
Varèse, Louise B51
Varèse: A Looking Glass Diary B51
Varga, Bálint Amdrás B1150
Variations for Piano SEE Piano
Variations.
Variations Brillantes D96
Variations for Orchestra SEE
Orchestral Variations.
Variations on a Kentucky Folk-
song D143
Variations on a Shaker Melody SEE
Appalachian Spring.
Variations on America D20, D25,
D117, D284
Vaughan Williams, Ralph D90, D96
Viardo, Vladimir Vladimirovich
W111, B1026
Victoria and Albert Museum, London
B117, B1015, B1078
Vidal, Paul p.3
Vienna Radio Orchestra D154
Vienna State Academy Chamber
Chorus D356
Vienna State Opera Orchestra D37,
D313
Vienna Symphony Orchestra D17,
D178
Vieux Poème SEE Old Poem.
Villa-Lobos, Heitor D101
Vincent, John B1153
Violin and Piano Prelude SEE
Prelude for Violin and Piano.
Violin Concerto B99
Violin Sonata SEE Sonata for
Violin and Piano.
Vitali, Tomasco Antonio B1077
Vitebsk W39, D367-D374, B192,
B417, B614, B784, B1073, B1112,
B1120, B1164
Vocalise W37, D375-D376, B932
Vojtech, Ivan B1035
Von Rhein, John B1156-B1157
von Webern, Anton SEE Webern,
Anton von.
Voss, Ruth Hemmert B1158
Voyage D144, D185, D333
Vronsky, Vitya D107

Waldorf-Astoria, New York B844
Waley, Arthur W16
Walk to the Bunkhouse SEE The Red
  Pony.
Walker, George D143
Wall-to-Wall Copland/America B1103,
  B1159
Wallenstein, Alfred B685
Walsh, Stephen B1160-B1162
Walter Hautzig Peking Recital D143
Waltz SEE Billy the Kid.
Waltz Caprice W9
Waltz of the Flowers D107
Ward, Robert B1163
Warfield, William D189-D190, B209,
  B361, B1071
Wartburg College Choir D149
Warton, William B887
Washburn, Robert D6
Washington, D.C. National Symphony
  Orchestra SEE National Symphony
  Orchestra.
Washington Square W83
Wasserstrom, William B962
Watanabe, Akeo D95
Waters, Edward N. B1164-B1165
Watt, Douglas B1166
The Wave B59
Webern, Anton von B110
Webster, Beveridge D239
Weill, Kurt D171, D179
Weinberg, Henry B1167
Weiner, William E., Oral History
  Library SEE William E. Weiner
  Oral History Library.
Weisgall, Hugo D353
Weldon, Irene D149
Wellesz, Egon B61
Wells, Orson W51, B736, B856
Werlé, Frederick B1168-B1169
Wertheim, Alma Morgenthau p.4, W31
West Virginia University, Morgantown
  B226
Western Arts Trio D371
What Do We Plant? p.5, W46
What to Listen For in Music p.7,
  B40, B53, B57, B62, B108, B177,
  B408, B465, B611, B710, B816,
  B832, B1155, B1170-B1171
When They Come Back SEE Twelve
  Poems of Emily Dickinson.
Whikehart, Lewis E. D147, B426
Whikehart Chorale D147, B426
White, Chappell B1172
Whiteman, Paul W74

Whitney, Robert W92, D195
Whitney Museum of American Art
  B566, B617
Whittemore, Arthur Austin D61
Whitten, Sammie Gayle B1173
Whitwell, David B1174
Why Do They Shut Me Out of Heaven?
  SEE Twelve Poems of Emily
  Dickinson.
Wiedrich, Bob B1176
Wier, Albert Ernest B1177
Wiese, Lucie B106
Wigmore Hall, London B245
Wilber, Jay D267
Wilbur, Richard B934
Wild, Earl D87-D88
Wilder, Thornton W62, B1068
William E. Weiner Oral History
  Library B844
Williams, Jerome W95
Williams, Ralph Vanghan SEE
  Vaughan Williams, Ralph.
Williams, Tennessee B492, B500,
  B521
Willinger, Edward B1179
Wilson, George C. B543
Wilson, Gladys M. B1180
Wimbush, Roger B1181
Winer, Linda B1182
Winfield, Michael D258
Winograd, Arthur D171-D173, D180
Winter, P. W52
The Winter's Passed D259
Wintle, Justin B562
Wise, Jacob Hooper B60
Wistful SEE Three Moods for Piano
  Solo.
Wittgenstein, Victor p.3
Wolf Trap Farm Park B273, B628,
  B708, B763, B815, B888, B937
Wolffers, Jules B1183
Wolfsohn, Leopold p.3
Wolpe, Stefan B98
Women's University Glee Club W30
Wondrous Love D117
Woodwind Quintet D373
Works for Piano, 1926-1948 D106,
  D136, D229, D244
The World Feels Dusty SEE Twelve
  Poems of Emily Dickinson.
The World of Nick Adams p.6, W94
The World of Twentieth-Century
  Music B473
World War II p.5, B244
World's Fair, New York, 1939 p.6,
  W56, W58

Wren Symphony Orchestra D33
Wright, Elizabeth B409
Wright, Harold D320-D321
Wyatt, Lucius Reynolds B1186

Yaddo Festival SEE Festivals of
    Contemporary American Music at
    Yaddo, Saratoga Springs, New York.
Yale University p.7, B180
Yarmat, Karen B172
Yarustovsky, Boris B1187
York University B726
Young, Douglas B1188-B1189
Young, Percy Marshall B1190-B1191
Young Composer's Guide to the Six-
    Tone Scale D116
Young People's Concert B224, B462,
    B464, B828, B974
The Young Pioneers SEE Two
    Children's Pieces.
The Younger Generation SEE North
    Star.

Zamkochian, Berj B588
Zion's Walls SEE Old American
    Songs, Set II.
Zoff, Otto B1192

About the Author

JOANN SKOWRONSKI is Automated Inventory File Manager for the Library Systems Group at California State University, Northridge. She is the author of two bibliographies, *Women in American Music* and *Black Music in America* and has contributed to *Wheel of Delta Omicron*.

Bio-Bibliographies in Music

Series Advisers: *Donald L. Hixon and Adrienne Fried Block*

Thea Musgrave: a Bio-Bibliography
Donald L. Hixon

Samuel Barber: A Bio-Bibliography
Don A. Hennessee